A COMPLETE GUIDE

Honolulu and O‘ahu Great Destinations Hawai‘i

Life on O'ahu is intimately connected to the sea.

A COMPLETE GUIDE

1ST EDITION

Honolulu and O'ahu Great Destinations Hawai'i

Including Waikīkī

Stacy Pope

The Countryman Press
Woodstock, Vermont

First Edition

ISBN 978-1-58157-041-0

Cover photo © James Randklev

Interior photos by the author unless otherwise specified

Book design by Bodenweber Design

Page composition by Garrett Brown, Opaque Design & Print Production

Maps by Mapping Specialists, Ltd., Madison, WI © The Countryman Press

Published by The Countryman Press, P.O. Box 748, Woodstock, Vermont 05091

Distributed by W. W. Norton & Company, Inc., 500 Fifth Ave., New York, NY 10110

Printed in the United States of America

10 9 8 7 6 5 4 3 2 1

Great Destinations travel guidebook series

Recommended by *National Geographic Traveler* and *Travel + Leisure* magazines.

[A] crisp and critical approach, for travelers who want to live like locals.
— *USA Today*

Great Destinations™ guidebooks are known for their comprehensive, critical coverage of regions of extraordinary cultural interest and natural beauty. The authors in this series are professional travel writers who have lived for many years in the regions they describe. Each title in this series is continuously updated with each printing to ensure accurate and timely information. All the books contain more than one hundred photographs and maps.

Current titles available:

The Adirondack Book
Atlanta
Austin, San Antonio & the Texas Hill Country
The Berkshire Book
Big Sur, Monterey Bay & Gold Coast Wine Country
Cape Canaveral, Cocoa Beach & Florida's Space Coast
The Charleston, Savannah & Coastal Islands Book
The Chesapeake Bay Book
The Coast of Maine Book
Colorado's Classic Mountain Towns: Great Destinations
The Finger Lakes Book
Galveston, South Padre Island & the Texas Gulf Coast
The Hamptons Book
Honolulu & O'ahu: Great Destinations Hawai'i
The Hudson Valley Book
Los Cabos & Baja California Sur: Great Destinations Mexico
The Nantucket Book
The Napa & Sonoma Book
Palm Beach, Miami & the Florida Keys
Phoenix, Scottsdale, Sedona & Central Arizona
Playa del Carmen, Tulum & the Riviera Maya: Great Destinations Mexico
Salt Lake City, Park City, Provo & Utah's High Country Resorts
San Diego & Tijuana
San Juan, Vieques & Culebra: Great Destinations Puerto Rico
The Seattle & Vancouver Book: Includes the Olympic Peninsula, Victoria & More
The Santa Fe & Taos Book
The Sarasota, Sanibel Island & Naples Book
The Shenandoah Valley Book
Touring East Coast Wine Country

If you are traveling to, moving to, residing in, or just interested in any (or all!) of these enchanting regions, a Great Destinations guidebook is a superior companion. Honest and painstakingly critical, full of information only a local can provide, Great Destinations guidebooks give you all the practical knowledge you need to enjoy the best of each region. Why not own them all?

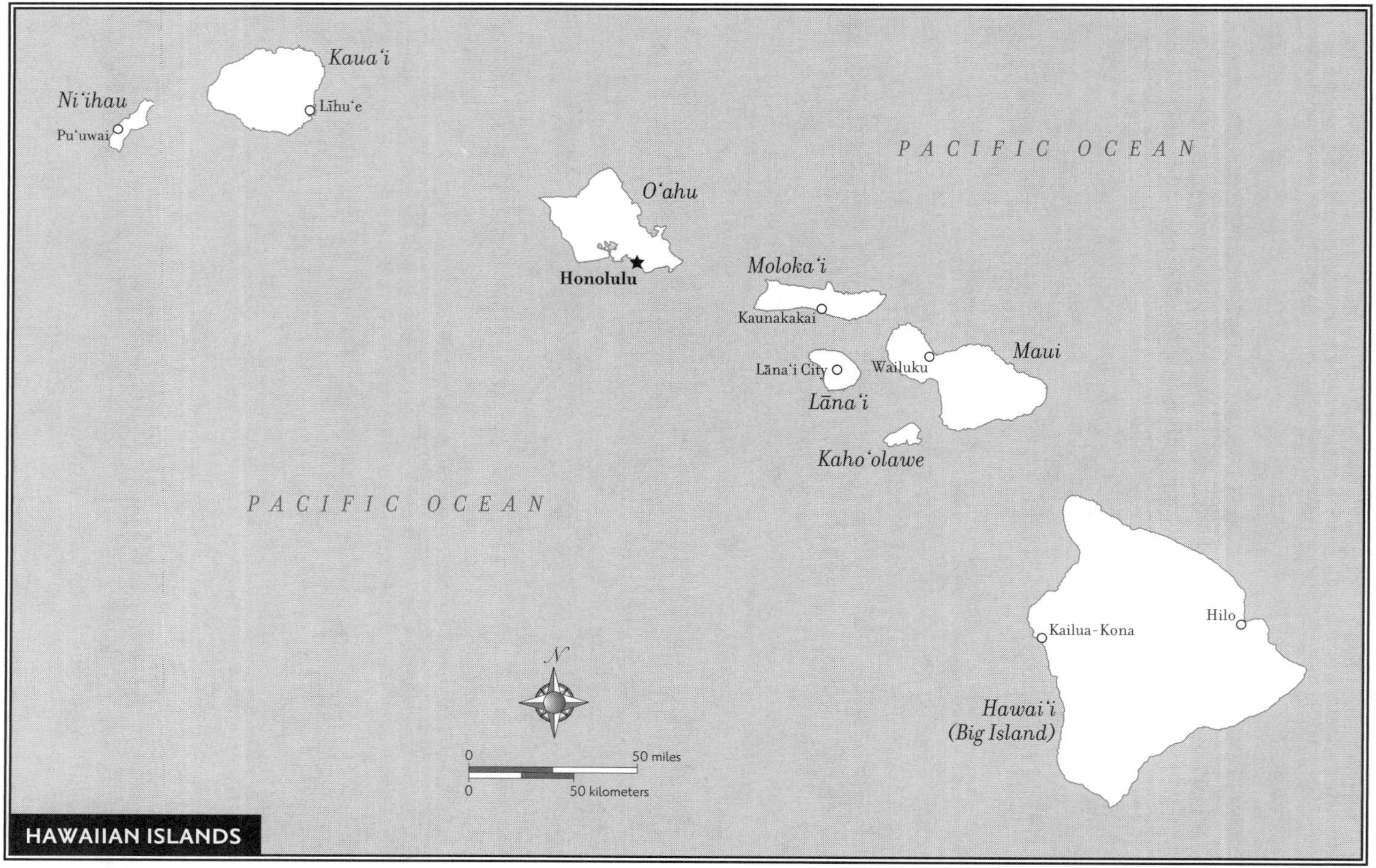

HAWAIIAN ISLANDS
Ni‘ihau
Pu‘uwai
Kaua‘i
Līhu‘e
PACIFIC OCEAN
O‘ahu
Honolulu
Moloka‘i
Kaunakakai
Lāna‘i City
Lāna‘i
Wailuku
Maui
Kaho‘olawe
PACIFIC OCEAN
Kailua-Kona
Hilo
Hawai‘i
(Big Island)
N
0
50 miles
0
50 kilometers

Contents

Acknowledgements 9

Introduction 10

The Way This Book Works 13

1
History
The Hawaiian Islands
15

2
Transportation
Getting to and around O‘ahu
31

3
Lodging
E Komo Mai! Nou Ka Hale
53

4
Culture
Living Local
77

5
Restaurants & Food Purveyors
Mixed Palate, Mixed Plate
133

6
Hawaiians Today
People of the ‘Āina
179

7

Recreation

Everything under the Sun

191

8

Shopping

Taking It to the Limit

235

9

Information

Facts Great and Small

257

General Index 273

Lodging By Price Code 289

Dining By Price Code 291

Dining by Cuisine 293

Maps

- Hawaiian Islands 6
- O‘ahu 35
- Metropolitan Honolulu 40
- Downtown Honolulu 42
- Waikīkī 43
- Windward O‘ahu 44
- Kailua 46
- North Shore 48
- Central O‘ahu 50
- Leeward O‘ahu 51

Acknowledgements

Mahalo to the many individuals and organizations that supported the creation of this Great Destinations first edition book about Honolulu and the island of O'ahu—I hope your expectations will be met.

A special thanks to both my husband and my mom, who joined me in exploring many eateries, sites, and attractions; to my brother, who offered photography tips; and to my dad, who'd be pleased to know how much of his aloha for Hawai'i rubbed off on his daughter.

Stacy Pope
Honolulu, Hawai'i
2007

Introduction

For me its balmy airs are always blowing, its summer seas flashing in the sun; the pulsing of its surfbeat is in my ear; I can see its garlanded crags, its leaping cascades, its plumy palms drowsing by the shore, its remote summits floating like islands above the cloud wrack; I can feel the spirit of its woodland solitudes, I can hear the splash of its brooks; in my nostrils still lives the breath of flowers that perished twenty years ago.

—Mark Twain

How does one "introduce" what are perhaps the most renowned and enchanting isles in the world? For more than two centuries, tales of the distant Hawaiian Islands have stirred our imagination. The call of Hawai'i is so profound that it has almost become encoded in our collective DNA—and millions of people answer each year with pilgrimages across the Pacific toward the promise of paradise.

Surrounded by thousands of miles of sea and sky, Hawai'i did indeed develop as a sort of paradise. When plants and animals found their way to its shores, they were free to reinvent themselves and had little to fear, resulting in a Darwinian landscape filled with unique species and unbridled wilderness.

Eventually, Polynesian voyagers settled these islands in epic migrations that are still only vaguely understood. "Modern Hawai'i" officially begins in 1778, with what must have been an astonishingly surreal first encounter between European voyagers and the Hawaiian people. Within a relatively short time, extensive colonization, a government coup, annexation, two world wars, and statehood turned the isolated Hawaiian Islands into the "crossroads of the Pacific," and one of the most expensive places in the United States to live.

Perhaps the best way to experience Hawai'i's multifaceted history and character is by visiting the island of O'ahu, where both rich cultural diversity and astounding natural beauty are in abundance. Home to the capital city of Honolulu and the majority of the state's population, it's a lively and beguiling destination.

Landmark Diamond Head Crater creates a surreal backdrop for swimming.

Honolulu is a vast city of glass towers, gardens, shopping centers, and suburban homes meandering for miles between steep foothills and sparkling turquoise waves lined with surfers. Life here is original and entertaining in every way, and at the same time passionately traditional—and that's exactly how folks like it. Plantation houses huddle in the shadows of skyscrapers. Floral aloha shirts are popular attire in the financial district. Birthday cake may be eaten with chopsticks. Pink stilettos strut past sandy, bare feet. Hawaiian flower lei shops line Chinatown's streets. And it seems just about everything is served with macaroni salad and two scoops of white rice on the side—even spaghetti.

Waikīkī, Honolulu's most famous neighborhood, has become a virtual brand name for tropical pleasures. Once a thriving

Hawaiian community filled with taro fields, stone temples, and grass dwellings, 20th-century Waikīkī slowly degenerated into a swap meet of wet T-shirt contests, coconut-bra hula reviews, and mai tai hangovers, as well as other easy-to-translate clichés of "life in paradise" that served as a protective barrier between mass tourism and a culturally and environmentally vulnerable land. In the 21st-century, however, Waikīkī is finding its voice both as an upscale district and genuine Hawai'i community—making it a special place to visit and live once more.

Outside the city you'll find that O'ahu is remarkably rural and peaceful, with chickens clucking along the side of the road and kids jumping from bridges into streams. Many travelers don't realize that the island possesses some of the best beaches and surfing in the entire state, as well as some of its most timelessly beautiful scenery. Miss the rest of O'ahu, and you miss much of the heart and soul of Hawai'i.

Best of all, Hawai'i's people radiate a heartfelt warmth that accompanies modesty, quiet passion, and soulful *joie de vivre*. Sure, here and there someone's grumpy, but where else would strangers encourage you to call them "uncle" or "auntie," give you an enthusiastic "shaka-style" hand wave out the car window as thanks for letting them merge in front of you on the freeway, or invite you to join in their family's beach barbecue?

Because O'ahu receives more than five million visitors a year—that's five visitors to each resident—your aloha really makes a difference. Here are a few simple ways you can help preserve the integrity of Hawai'i's unique culture and environment and keep it a wonderful place for everyone.

- Honor local ways of life. Remove shoes before entering a home, avoid using the car horn, wait your turn, and exhibit patience and graciousness when interacting with others.
- Allow natural areas and cultural sites to remain as you found them, including plants, reefs, animal habitats, trails, archaeological or historical elements, and shrines. Resist the temptation to import pets, plants, and foods; and before you arrive in Hawai'i, clean your hiking boots to remove any traces of non-native seeds or insects.
- Consider choosing more personal, low-key, ecologically-friendly activities, such as historic walks or nature club hikes instead of large, "packaged" coach tours and activities.

O'ahu still retains quiet country life and true Hawai'i spirit.

- Respect residents' "personal space," so they can continue to feel at home; this is especially important at very "local" hole-in-the-wall food establishments, surf spots, secluded beaches, campsites, and rural parks outside of Honolulu, where extensive tourism can permanently alter the character of special places.

O'ahu is infinitely more than snorkeling, mai tais, and burgers! In fact, we don't think of ourselves in those terms at all. Definitely go for it with the snorkel gear, but go beyond it, too, and *live* here—at least for the week! We hope this Great Destinations book will help you discover the "real O'ahu" and grow to cherish it as much as we do. We've worked hard to provide an honest, personal, sophisticated, and conscientious guide book that takes you from the very hippest urban bars to earthy family cafés to the most heart-wrenchingly beautiful natural sites—hopefully without sacrificing the integrity of the local community or turning you into a tourist instead of a traveler.

Your guide is an island-born-and-raised author whose family has lived in Honolulu since 1935, and who still thinks O'ahu is *nō ka 'oi*—the best! Whether this is your first visit or your hundred-and-first, we welcome you. Let go and immerse yourself in O'ahu's tropical foliage, pounding surf, local-style grinds, night rains, "slippers rule" attitude, flower lei, trade winds, and eternal and intoxicating spirit of aloha.

—*Stacy Pope*

The Way This Book Works

This Great Destinations book offers a wide variety of information about O'ahu, from local foods to the best beaches to political issues. Use it as a directory for the exact information you need, or read it from beginning to end for a more comprehensive experience.

With but a few exceptions, each chapter of the book introduces a general topic, such as "Recreation," which contains alphabetized subcategories, such as "Beaches." Each subcategory lists alphabetized entries by regions of the island, these being Waikīkī, greater Honolulu, Windward O'ahu, the North Shore, Central O'ahu, and Leeward O'ahu. In some sections of the book, subcategories themselves contain additional subcategories.

Handy, quick-reference sleep-and-eat guides near the back of the book are best used in conjunction with full entries within chapters 3 and 5. The "Lodging Index" lists establishments by region and price, and the "Restaurant Index" displays restaurants listed both by type of food and price.

Every entry in the book includes a contact telephone number and basic street address, if they were available; where helpful, some also include a Web site address and other facts. For brevity, we've omitted telephone area codes except when a number is off-island or toll free. The entire state of Hawai'i uses the area code 808; however, when calling any of the neighboring islands, you must still dial "1-808" before the seven-digit number.

In Chapter 2 you'll find a basic overview of, and directions to, regions of the island from Waikīkī, as well as numerous maps to help you find your way around.

We've attempted to faithfully represent the Hawaiian language, which is written using five vowels (a, e, i, o, u) and seven consonants (h, k, l, m, n, p, w). The letter "w" is sometimes pronounced like a "v,"—and the second-to-last syllables of words are stressed. All foreign words here are italicized, except for place names, foods, and words that have been assimilated into the English language, such as "aloha." Also, foreign words, such as "keiki," are not pluralized with the English "-s" ending; we've followed the same practice with assimilated words, such as "lei," to help preserve their integrity. You'll find use of the *'okina,* or glottal stop ('), which indicates a throat pause in speaking, such as English speakers make in the middle of "uh-oh." The *kahakō,* or macron (¯), indicates a slight lengthening of the vowel it hovers above. These subtle sound differences can change the meaning of a word entirely—for example, *'āina* means "land," *'aina* means "meal," and *aina* means "sexual intercourse!"

No dogged fact checking can keep up with Hawai'i's constant changes—especially after a book has gone to press and hit the shelves. We've done our best to present information on all entries accurately and to confirm details as close to the publication date as possible. Making a quick update call to your destination before heading out will prevent any surprises or disappointments.

Our goal is to help you enjoy O'ahu to the fullest and come away with a deeper appreciation of Hawai'i, as well as with wonderful memories—so we hope this book looks dog-eared, marked up, and worn down by the time you return home. Then it will have done its job.

A banyan tree planted during the monarchy years still stands at 'Iolani Palace.

1

History

The Hawaiian Islands

The Hawaiian Islands are made up of 137 rugged reefs, islands, and shoals stretching nearly 1,500 miles across the Pacific Ocean, more than 2,000 miles from any continental coastline and as far or farther from Tahiti and other southern Pacific high islands. About 1.3 million people live on only the largest seven islands: Maui, Kaua'i, Hawai'i, Moloka'i, Lāna'i, Ni'ihau, and O'ahu, which together comprise about 99 percent of Hawai'i's land.

These are the most remote inhabited islands in the entire world, a reality abundantly clear when en route to their golden shores. After a half-day or longer of flying over the open sea, the sight of Honolulu's glass-tower metropolis and bright green peaks rising from the water seem a preposterous mirage; approach in the evening, and hours of pitch darkness are suddenly broken by fiery rivulets of light winding downhill, like slow-moving streams of lava. Hawai'i's extreme isolation is in fact the cornerstone of its unique and fragile environment and fundamental to its allure.

Hawai'i's cultural history is as emotionally compelling as its breathtaking beauty. An American state for only about 50 years, many residents consider themselves "people of Hawai'i" first and foremost, and take pride in perpetuating traditions distinctly different from Mainland communities. Nowhere else is Hawai'i's storied past more evident than on the island of O'ahu, which is the state's political, economic, and cultural heart and soul.

Natural History

Geography and Climate

Hawai'i is barely visible on the world map, appearing as no more than a sprinkle of dots along the Pacific Ocean's Tropic of Cancer, north of the equator. In actuality, these dots are the above-water peaks of some of the largest mountains on the planet, built up over many millions of years by volcanic eruptions that originate at the very bottom of the ocean. When measured from its undersea base, Mauna Kea on the island of Hawai'i stands 6.2 miles high—taller than Mount Everest. The volcanic process is still underway there, as well as at its little-known southerly neighbor, Lō'ihi Seamount, which is expected to erupt through the waves in about ten thousand years.

The island of O'ahu began to take shape more than 3 million years ago. Once rising at least 10,000 feet above sea level, its two massive shield volcanoes have eroded into 600 square miles of wide plains, steep shorelines, and magnificently rippled mountain ranges less than half of their original heights. Although the ancient volcanoes that created the Wai'anae and Ko'olau Ranges are long extinct, several tuff cones appeared across southeast O'ahu in the last one hundred thousand years or so, some ripping through ancient coral reefs as they violently exploded. These rare formations include Hanauma Bay, Punchbowl Crater and Waikīkī's world-famous landmark, Diamond Head Crater.

The tiny Hawaiian Islands are said to feature as many different climate zones as exist from coastal Alaska to coastal Costa Rica. Kaua'i's Mount Wai'ale'ale is one of the wettest spots on earth, with an annual rainfall exceeding 35 feet; the Island of Hawai'i's Ka'ū Desert is a hot, barren, rocky landscape reminiscent of Mars; and in the distance, the snowdusted, active volcano Mauna Loa rumbles.

Along Windward O'ahu, east of the Ko'olau Range, the climate is significantly rainier and gustier than elsewhere. In some of its mountain areas it can rain more than 200 inches per year. In Leeward O'ahu, or all land west of the Wai'anae Range, the climate is generally dry and hot, with an annual rainfall closer to 20 inches. One of Waikīkī's selling points is its near-perfect mix of sunny weather and gentle, cooling breezes many days of the year—typical for its southeastern coastal location.

Only two true seasons exist in Hawai'i: summer and winter. The summer months of May through September tend to be relatively warm and dry, with refreshing trade breezes blowing 90 percent of the time. On occasion, so-called Kona winds prevail from the south, bringing sluggishly warm weather that can sometimes carry volcanic ash fallout (called "vog") from eruptions. The winter months of October through April bring slightly cooler days, more frequent rain, variable winds, and intermittent storms, although hurricanes and cyclones are rare. Overall, however, Hawai'i's tropical latitude, ocean surroundings, varied topography, and northeasterly trade winds provide consistently balmy, temperate night and day climates between 65 and 90 degrees Fahrenheit and some of the cleanest air in the world.

Under the influence of the North Equatorial Current, Hawai'i receives relatively cool waters with sea surface temperatures ranging between about 72 and 81 degrees Fahrenheit year-round. The spectacular surf for which it's world-famous originates from distant storms in the northern and southern hemispheres. During winter months, northern storms spawn wind-driven waves that travel unimpeded, until hitting Hawai'i's northern shores at heights of up to 25 feet or more. During the summer, north shore waters fall flat and southern storms kick up moderately high surf on the southern shores of the islands. Although tidal range is small, tidal rip currents and waves can be powerful enough to subdue even the strongest swimmers.

Plant and Animal Life

While the Islands have vibrant land habitats, much of their beauty and mystique lie beneath the water's surface. Within and beyond the reefs live 40 different types of corals, more than 500 species of fish and 40 species of sharks, as well as whales, seals, eels, rays, dolphins, turtles, urchins, and other critters, some of which exist only in Hawai'i.

Although the Galapagos Islands are renowned for specialized species, Hawai'i has become an even more important site for evolutionary studies because of its lengthy history of development and isolation. At one time, each island was no more than a rocky basalt and coral landscape. But over the course of 70 million years, plant spores, insects, seeds, and larvae borne on the wind, tucked in the feathers of migrating sea birds, or drifting on bits of wood slowly found their way to each new island and struggled to survive. On average, only one species every seventy thousand years managed to perpetuate its kind.

With few plants and animals to compete with, newly arrived species gradually responded to and flourished in Hawai'i's unusual surroundings, evolving into a remarkable breadth of new creatures found nowhere else on earth. A famed example that rivals Darwin's finches is the Hawaiian honeycreeper, which evolved into more than 50 unique species—each with a distinctive bill adapted for specialized feeding.

Hawai'i once had 1,100 native species and subspecies of flowering plants, of which 89 percent were unique to the Islands. This includes nearly four hundred different types of native ferns, a variety of at least ten thousand insects, nearly one hundred singular bird species, and an array of more than one thousand snails, as well as many other exotic and original plants and animals. Other species live in Hawai'i seasonally, such as the golden plover and humpback whale, both of which travel approximately six thousand miles roundtrip from Alaska every year.

The kōlea, or golden plover, has flown to Hawai'i from Alaska each winter for countless generations.

However, Hawai'i's delicate environment has been taxed to the limit by habitat destruction, human encroachment, pollution, and the continual introduction of alien species—leading to predation on native species, ecosystem damage, competition for resources, and widespread diseases against which native species have little immunity. Each year, more than 20 new alien species are purposefully or accidentally introduced in the Islands, overwhelming native species on both land and sea and presenting new survival challenges.

Nearly every land creature and plant you'll encounter during your stay—from mangoes, pineapples, banyans, and anthuriums to cockroaches, ants, mosquitoes, geckos, sparrows, and myna birds—have been introduced by human beings. It is estimated that more than 4,500 invasive alien species now reside here. Our impact on the environment of these fragile, isolated, volcanic islands cannot be overstated; because of recent human intervention, Hawai'i now suffers the highest rate of species extinction anywhere in the United States and one of the highest in the entire world.

SOCIAL HISTORY

Polynesian Migrations Across the Pacific

The story of the first settlers in the Hawaiian Islands is hotly debated and many historical details have been lost. Several legends exist in Hawaiian folklore as to the origins of its people—the most widely known being that of Hawai'i Loa, one of four intrepid siblings from "the land of the yellow sea of Kāne," who each settled a different region of Polynesia. O'ahu is said to have been the name of one of his sons. Also interesting is the linguistic relationship between the name "Hawai'i" and Polynesian place names, such as Hawaiki, Havai'i, and 'Avaiki, used by New Zealand's Maori and other Pacific cultures (although not Hawaiians) in reference to a legendary ancestral home in the East or an underworld. Samoa's largest island is called Savai'i, another cognate of "Hawai'i." Historical and cultural connections between these names have yet to be fully understood.

Many anthropologists and folklorists believe that original settlers were indeed people from eastern Polynesia and possibly Marquesan, who set sail for the open seas with the intention of discovering new or populating known islands. Radiocarbon dating and study of Hawaiian oral history lead to conflicting information on when initial colonies were established; the most recent findings suggest it was as late as 1,000 years ago, although other data point to at least 1,600 years ago. Whichever timeframe is correct, it's clear that ancient Polynesians were accomplishing epic canoe voyages across the world's largest body of water and settling the remote Hawaiian Islands, and even far-flung Rapa Nui (Easter Island) near Chile, hundreds of years before Columbus stumbled across the American continent.

It's likely that migrations to Hawai'i took place from two distinct island groups during different periods of time: the first from the Marquesas Islands, and the second several hundred years later or more from Tahiti. Overwhelming evidence—right down to place names such as Kealaikahiki, the name of a sea channel between two of Hawai'i's main islands that translates to "the way to Tahiti"—indicates strong cultural and migratory connections between Tahiti and Hawai'i throughout several centuries, which seem to end abruptly by 1200 or perhaps 1300 A.D.

How these separate cultures may have mingled is unclear, but it is probable that the Tahitians subsumed the former. Historical accounts from post-contact Hawaiians also describe a separate race of people they called Menehune, who lived hidden away in deep valleys and forests and reportedly built some of Hawai'i's oldest fishponds and other structures. The Hawaiian word *"menehune"* is no doubt related to the Tahitian word *"manahune,"* or "commoner," although that's where clarity ends. It's possible that these reclusive individuals were remaining members of the old Marquesan race, or they may have been outcasts of Tahitian origin. In 1820, a Kaua'i census yielded more than 60 individuals living in a remote valley who claimed to be Menehune. If any contemporary inhabitants believe themselves to descend from this now-mythical race, they've kept it a secret.

Another legendary race or cultural group, rarely mentioned today but cited in old sources, is the Nāwao, or "wild people," who were said to live in the forests, be of a large and aggressive nature, and rarely associate with other men.

Original settlers in Hawai'i brought at least 35 plants and animals from their homelands, including dogs, small pigs, chickens, taro, potatoes, bananas, and even coconuts, and evidence suggests they were predominantly agrarian. With the arrival of the Tahitians, life in the Hawaiian Islands became heavily governed by the *kapu,* or "taboo" system—a strict code of laws—and a caste system that determined one's role in the community. Large public works such as irrigation systems, terraces, and fishponds dotted the landscape and enabled fruitful living.

Hawaiians resided or spent significant time on Hawai'i's six main islands, as well as the small islands of Kaho'olawe, Ni'ihau, Nihoa, and Mokumanamana. On O'ahu, the lush windward communities now called Kailua, Waimānalo, and Kāne'ohe appear to have been the nuclei of early settlements, and the area now known as Honolulu appears to have been populated at least one thousand years ago. It's estimated that by the 1700s the Hawaiian Islands were home to at least a quarter-million people—and some suggest as many as a million, which would approach the modern population count for the state.

The Arrival of Western Explorers and Settlers

Although it is possible that Hawaiians had encountered a few castaways from other cultures over hundreds of years, it's clear from historical accounts that when the British explorer Captain James Cook and his crew eased their ships into a Kaua'i Bay in 1778, Hawaiians were completely astonished by both the ships and the men. Cook, on his way from Tahiti, to find the Northwest passage, was no doubt surprised to discover land and people where there should only have been water.

Despite his best intentions to protect the Hawaiians during the encounter, the ships left venereal disease in their wakes, and a population lifted of precious belongings and supplies in exchange for novel iron nails and other trinkets. Although Cook had been told that the name of the islands was "Owyhee," in the tradition of Western exploration he officially assigned the Hawaiian Islands the name "Sandwich Isles" after his patron in England.

Cook returned the following winter, eventually pulling the *Discovery* and *Resolution* into Kealakekua Bay, on the Island of Hawai'i. By some accounts, the Hawaiian people had

The fishing village of Kou, now downtown Honolulu, was the subject of numerous depictions by Russian traveler Louis Choris in 1816. Photo courtesy Hawai'i State Archives.

believed he was the returning god Lono, due to a series of unfortunate coincidences. If this was indeed the case, ship records show no indication that captains and crews were aware of the mix-up. Nevertheless, after weeks of tiresome visiting, punctuated by a grand farewell and then a feeble, anticlimactic return of the British with a broken mast shortly thereafter, the relationship between the British and the Hawaiians became strained. Scuffles slowly gave way to incidents and challenges, and finally Cook found himself surrounded by an angry mob that struck him down into the water with clubs and iron knives. Both sides seem to have quickly regretted the destructive and tragic events that led to and followed Cook's death. Before the remaining seamen left Hawai'i, Cook's remains—including several pounds of sliced flesh, charred bone fragments, and hands preserved in salt—were returned to the ships for Western burial rites.

Tales of newly found Pacific islands and an exotic race of men and women still living in the Stone Age soon swirled through the Americas and Europe; and although it was approximately seven years before another European ship was to arrive, Hawaiian culture had been forever changed and Hawaiian priests forsaw its demise.

Kamehameha's Kingdom

Of the many chiefs Captain Cook had met on the island of Hawai'i, one was to later become immortalized as the greatest leader in Hawaiian history: Kamehameha, said to be born under a blazing star. Upon his birth, it was foretold that he would grow to "slay the chiefs" and so was to be killed; instead, he was hidden away and eventually raised as a prince. An enormous man of impossible strength, courage, and determination, by his mid-20s Kamehameha was already in a leading position of power among the nobles of Hawai'i Island.

Several years after Cook's death at Kealakekua Bay, Kamehameha instigated a series of bloody civil wars that waged throughout the islands for more than a decade, all in his desire to unite them as one kingdom. During this time, the Hawaiian Islands were visited by numerous English and American exploration and merchant ships, many of which left men behind on shore and enabled Kamehameha to stockpile Western weapons and vessels. Eventually, the islands of Maui, Lāna'i, Moloka'i, and Hawai'i each fell to Kamehameha.

In 1795 Kamehameha summoned an army of sixteen thousand men to conquer the island of O'ahu. With troops stretched for miles along Waikīkī's shores and beyond, he drove hundreds, perhaps even thousands, of defenders into the mountains and finally off Nu'uanu Pali, a steep precipice 1,000 feet high—marking the final subjugation of the island. In time, Kaua'i and little Ni'ihau conceded their power to Kamehameha without a struggle, and by 1810 the "slayer of chiefs" ruled over all of the Hawaiian Islands.

Once king, Kamehameha proved himself a compassionate, wise, and reasonable leader. Despite many deaths brought by the wars, he grew to be deeply loved by Hawaiians, foreign residents, and visitors, and his rule ushered in an era of peace and stability to the Islands that had long been absent.

But there was no way for Kamehameha to undo or halt the cultural transformations that Western contact had begun. Foreign ships from all over the world continued to arrive in greater numbers, and with them came both desirable and destructive new ways of life. In 1810 he moved his court from distant Waikīkī to the harborfront, marking the beginning of downtown Honolulu's role as the center of Hawai'i's government life. Kamehameha tried to maintain old-school policies while taking advantage of new opportunities, such as selling Hawaiian sandalwood in the East. But by the time of his death in 1819, Hawai'i was a place of unclear identity and uncertain future.

The Impact of the Missionaries

One of the most influential occurrences in the westernization of the Hawaiian Islands was the arrival of missionaries. Inspired by a celebrated, Christianized Hawaiian student then living in New England, as well as accounts of a "heathen" Pacific race, in 1819 the American Board of Commissioners for Foreign Missions gathered up several well educated, newly married men and women and shipped them from Boston Harbor to "save" the people of the Sandwich Islands. This was the first of many missionary companies sent to Hawai'i over four decades, puritan in spirit and committed to the greatest challenge of their young lives. Missionary surnames such as Judd, Baldwin, Dillingham, Alexander, Cooke, Dole, Castle, Rice, Wilcox, and many others still carry both prestige and controversy in Hawai'i today.

What the first missionaries found as the *Thaddeus* entered Honolulu's harbor five months later, was upheaval following the recent death of King Kamehameha. Traditional cornerstones of Hawaiian life, such as religious practices and the *kapu* system, were faltering, creating opportunity for new beliefs and ways of life. When the missionaries introduced the Ten Commandments, Hawaiians welcomed them as a new, more forgiving set of laws.

But conveying the nuances of the Christian religion across linguistic and cultural boundaries proved challenging. Hawaiians remained cheery during sermons that were meant to stir in them the fear of hell; they shuddered at forgoing the well-loved practice of adultery; and they might don a top hat in public, but go without any pants. One devout Hawaiian couple brought their infant to be baptized, requesting the child be given the biblical name "Beelzebub." When they were told this was unacceptable, they compromised by naming the baby "Mikalakeke," or "Mr. Richards," after the baptizing minister. Although it took nearly two decades of effort, by 1840 more than twenty thousand Hawaiians were members of the Christian faith.

While many of the missionaries were instrumental in suppressing essential cultural expressions, such as hula, they can also be credited with caring for the sick and homeless, instituting a census, and introducing new medicines at a time when people were succumbing to Western diseases. Most importantly, they accomplished two historically significant feats: They translated the oral Hawaiian language into written form, assigning 12 letters to represent all the sounds they discerned; and they opened Hawai'i's first formal schools to teach reading and writing in Hawaiian, enrolling more than fifty thousand children and adult students in the first 10 years.

The *palapala,* or "written word," caused quite a stir upon its introduction. King Kamehameha II, after reviewing letters on paper that were said to spell his name, replied, "It looks neither like myself, nor like any other man." From their rustic little frame printing house imported from New England, however, the determined missionaries cranked out millions of pages of hymnals, Bibles, and other literature, and before long the people reveled in reading and writing, trading goods for a few pages of text. Hawai'i soon became known as the most literate society in the world for its day, and by the late 1800s it had an impressive one hundred Hawaiian-language newspapers in circulation.

Despite receiving new medical treatments and divine inspiration from the missionaries, the population of Hawaiian-blooded people had been decreasing at an alarming rate since Captain Cook's first visit in 1778. Introduced diseases, such as measles, influenza, smallpox, and whooping cough killed them, and venereal illnesses led to a decline in births. "Oh, what a dying people this is!" said businessman E. O. Hall of the Hawaiians in 1837. "They drop down on all sides of us, and it seems that the nation must speedily become extinct. . . What we do for people must be done quickly."

By 1831, Hawaiians numbered closer to 130,000 than the 300,000 or more estimated by Cook and modern scholars. By 1853, only 73,000 were left. In 1872, the census counted 52,000. And in 1900, a pathetic 40,000 people of pure- and part-Hawaiian ancestry remained. As their numbers waned, others readily took their place: The 1900 census also counted a total of 110,000 people from America, Europe, Asia, and elsewhere living in Hawai'i. Although in 1853 Native Hawaiians comprised 97 percent of the population, by 1923 they comprised only 16 percent.

The Hawaiian Monarchy

After the death of Kamehameha I, a succession of the Kamehameha bloodline ascended the throne one by one: Liholiho, Kauikeaouli, Alexander Liholiho, and Lot Kapuāiwa. These men were followed by elected rulers from other noble lineages, including William Lunalilo and David Kalākaua. Kalākaua's sister, Lili'uokalani, inherited the throne upon his death and was the last ruler of the kingdom. Kamehameha I's dowager, Queen Ka'ahumanu, remained powerful and instrumental in the rule of the land alongside Kamehameha's two successor sons, Liholiho and Kauikeaouli. In many ways these 75 years of the monarchy grew to resemble life in Hawai'i today more than it did Hawaiian society during Kamehameha I's reign. And because Honolulu was the center of political, cultural, and economic activity for most of the century, much of Hawai'i's modern story is that of ever-changing Honolulu.

Only five years after taking the throne, Liholiho contracted measles during his first visit to England and passed away. Having left no heirs, Liholiho's 10-year-old brother Kauikeaouli was crowned King Kamehameha III and ruled the kingdom aided by Queen Ka'ahumanu and a team of advisors. During his 30-year reign Kauikeaouli faced many of Hawai'i's greatest challenges, including reforming ancient systems into westernized political and social structures; managing international relations; and helping his people cope with new diseases, industries, a growing foreign population, and a derailed sense of purpose. He also weathered a temporary and unauthorized takeover of the Hawaiian kingdom by a British naval captain in 1843 and a brief, also-unauthorized, attack on Honolulu led by a French admiral in 1849.

The sandalwood trade, begun during Kamehameha I's, era temporarily brought unprecedented riches to the kingdom, and royal grass houses overflowed with silks, china, billiard tables, and other Western luxuries. When profits from sandalwood began to trickle out, whaling ships began to arrive. The great hunt stretched from coastal Peru to Japan to the frigid Artic seas, and Hawai'i—as both a mid-Pacific location and whale breeding ground—was the perfect place for crews to restock and repair. In 1846 alone no fewer than 596 enormous whaling ships were docked in the ports of Lahaina and Honolulu. After months of rough ocean life, thousands of rowdy seamen from around the world eagerly filled the grog shops, solicited prostitutes, swaggered through town, and deserted or were dumped by shipmasters. Sea-hardy and curious Hawaiian men also enlisted on whalers in staggering droves, and many never returned home—either dying aboard ship or disappearing into the crowded ports-of-call.

Amid the growing industries of the 1830s and 1840s, small-scale sugar, coffee, and rice plantations also began to quietly take shape. Sugar cane plants had arrived with Polynesian settlers hundreds of years earlier and thrived in Hawai'i's climate; and while coffee and rice sold well and cattle ranches dotted the landscape, the American Civil War dealt a winning hand to sugar production. When the South was unable to provide Americans with sweet satisfaction, Hawai'i's plantations surged into action, exporting millions of pounds of sugar and quickly enjoying the added benefit of tax-free importation to the United States. The sugar boom was to have a much larger historical significance than fueling big business in Hawai'i and bringing wealth to its mostly American businessmen of missionary descent, whose families had been granted large tracts of land; the rapidly growing industry required thousands of workers, and the only solution was to import contract laborers.

During a period of nearly one hundred years, several hundred thousand immigrants from across the globe arrived in Hawai'i to labor on the plantations. The first official group of workers came from southern China in 1852, on five-year contracts and with all essentials to be provided by the plantation—a paternalistic arrangement that continued in various forms through the 1940s. Over the years, nearly fifty thousand Chinese workers arrived, primarily from the Canton region. Beginning in the mid-1880s, more than one hundred thousand Japanese men arrived, many of whom later imported their wives and children, or picture brides, and settled in Hawai'i permanently. At one point, nearly 40 percent of Hawai'i's total population was Japanese. From the Portuguese islands of Madeira and the Azores came nearly twenty thousand laborers in family units; and as Europeans, many of the men elevated in the ranks to become overseers. After the turn of the century, thousands of Koreans began to arrive, followed by about five thousand Puerto Ricans and more than one hundred thousand workers from the Philippines. A small number of workers from Kiribati, Norway, Russia, India, and other countries also contracted with plantations in Hawai'i.

Plantations typically kept ethnic groups separated in worker camps, and each group was treated and paid differently. As contracts expired, some workers left Hawai'i; others moved to Honolulu to start life anew with humble business operations, and many married Hawaiian women or other immigrants. A large percentage of Hawai'i's residents today descend from, or were themselves, plantation workers who arrived during the years of agricultural domination.

Entities known as the "Big Five," which were primarily run by Island-established Caucasian businessmen, began to emerge as the sugar industry grew: American Factors, Theo H. Davies & Co., Alexander & Baldwin, C. Brewer & Co., and Castle & Cooke. Started mainly as factoring agencies, these five powerhouses evolved into corporate fiefdoms that became the core of Hawai'i's business and political world. Executives from the Big Five joined the same clubs, sent their children to the same schools, attended the same churches, married each other's relatives, and amassed constantly expanding wealth and control.

At the urging of several non-Native Hawaiians serving in office, King Kamehameha III approved an infamous "reapportioning" of Hawai'i's land, known as the *mahele,* which resulted in Hawaiian commoners eventually owning a mere 28,000 acres of Hawai'i's 4,158,400 acres of land. Naturalized citizens of Hawai'i who were born in the United States, and soon foreign nationals, were allowed to buy Hawaiian property for the first time—and they scooped it up in multitudes, setting a precedence for offshore ownership and development fervor that continues today.

King Kamehameha IV, Alexander Liholiho, attempted to swing Hawai'i away from the growing presence of American politics and nurtured renewed relations with the British. Aleck, who had succeeded his uncle in 1854 and ruled with the well-loved, royal-born Emma until 1863, hoped to regain footing for the Hawaiian kingdom, proposing "Hawai'i for the Hawaiians." Government representatives with differing agendas, such as one missionary-turned-official who had hoped to sell Hawai'i to an American businessman for $5 million, consistently thwarted his progress.

Alexander died unexpectedly in 1863, and the last of the Kamehameha dynasty, his brother Lot Kamehameha, continued the effort to strengthen the kingdom. But the Caucasian and Hawaiian legislative team became increasingly disenfranchised and rumors of an American coup continued to grow. When Lot passed away in 1872 with no named heir, the first elected king of Hawai'i, Lunalilo, stepped up to the throne; but within a year he contracted pulmonary tuberculosis and joined his many ancestors in the grave.

Although initially the selection of successor David Kalākaua by the American-leaning legislative assembly stirred public outrage, in time he became a favorite of the people. The "Merry Monarch's" controversial and high-profile reign from 1874 until 1891 included relinquishing Pearl Harbor to the U.S. in exchange for tax-free sugar importation, reviving Hawaiian cultural practices such as hula, assessing potential command opportunities over other Pacific nations, building a luxurious, palace in Honolulu, touring the globe, and hosting dignitaries and other public figures in magnificent style. But the most critical incident of his career in office was what became known as the "Bayonet Constitution" of 1887, in which the mostly pro-American legislature, backed by militiamen, forced him to relenquish most of his executive power, under threat of removal from the throne. Included in the new constitution's many amendments were expansive voting reforms that further limited the voting rights of Native Hawaiians, denied voting rights to Hawai'i's numerous Asian citizens, and granted full voting rights to wealthier Europeans and Americans who were not citizens of Hawai'i.

End of a Nation

When Kalākaua died in 1891 while visiting San Francisco, his sister Lili'uokalani became ruler of the Hawaiian kingdom. Her brief reign was fraught with economic downturn as the sugar industry suffered under the new McKinley Act; much more ominous, however, was a brooding knot of Caucasian, pro-American businessmen known as the Annexation Club—many of whom were descendents of the missionaries and in control of finance, land, and labor in Hawai'i—who intended to prevent the queen from ever restoring power stripped by the Bayonet Constitution. In January of 1893, when Lili'uokalani announced her intention to proclaim a new constitution, it was declared an act of treason by the annexationists. Upon witnessing their reaction, she publicly withdrew her statement—but it was too late. Annexationists and armed supporters rallied in the streets, accompanied by sailors and marines from the USS *Boston*, who marched through town. On January 18 the annexationists stormed the government building Ali'iolani Hale in a coup d'état in the name of the United States, and there read a proclamation abrogating the monarchy and declaring their own provisional government. Hoping to avoid bloodshed and believing that the U.S. would not back the overthrow, Lili'uokalani and her party surrendered.

Excerpts from the Queen's Appeal

I, Lili'uokalani of Hawai'i . . . do hereby protest against the ratification of a certain treaty . . . I declare such a treaty to be an act of wrong toward the native and part-native people of Hawai'i, an invasion of the rights of ruling chiefs, in violation of international rights both toward my people and toward friendly nations with whom they have made treaties, the perpetuation of the fraud whereby the constitutional government was overthrown, and, finally, an act of gross injustice to me . . . .

My people constitute four-fifths of the legally qualified voters of Hawai'i . . . my people, about forty thousand in number, have in no way been consulted by those, three thousand in number, who claim the right to destroy the independence of Hawai'i . . . .

Perhaps there is a kind of right, depending on the precedents of all ages, and known as the 'Right of Conquest,' under which robbers and marauders may establish themselves in possession of whatsoever they are strong enough to ravish from their fellows. I will not pretend to decide how far civilization and Christian enlightenment have outlawed it. But we have known for many years that our Island monarchy has relied upon the protection always extended to us by the policy and the assured friendship of the great American republic.

If we have nourished in our bosom those who have sought our ruin, it has been because they were of the people whom we believed to be our dearest friends and allies. If we did not by force resist their final outrage, it was because we could not do so without striking at the military force of the United States . . . .

It is enough that I am able to say, and with absolute authority, that the native people of Hawai'i are entirely faithful to their own chiefs, and are deeply attached to their own customs and mode of government; that they either do not understand, or bitterly oppose, the scheme of annexation.

Hawai'i: An American Asset

The annexationists quickly formed a provisional government in preparation for the long process of annexation to the U.S. The Hawaiian national flag, an amalgam of the American flag and the British Union Jack created in an early stroke of goodwill to both nations, was removed from 'Iolani Palace, and the American flag was raised. Lili'uokalani and her retinue patiently sought an overruling of the coup by the American government, and after a three-month onsite review by President Grover Cleveland's commissioner, Cleveland declared the incident a "lawless occupation of Honolulu under false pretexts by United States forces."

But upon orders from President Cleveland to restore the Hawaiian monarchy, annexationists instead thumbed their noses at Washington D.C. and refused to comply. The American government finally dropped the matter and moved on to more pressing business, and in 1894 (on July 4, no less), the annexationists declared themselves leaders of the so-called Republic of Hawai'i. When a group of Hawaiians was found to be plotting reclamation the following year,

Sanford Dole announces the successful annexation of Hawai'i by the United States, although few Hawaiians were eager to attend the ceremony.

Photo courtesy Hawai'i State Archives.

the deposed queen was implicated without proof and imprisoned in her former palace.

With the arrival of the Spanish-American War in 1898, the U.S. began to fully recognize the value of the small, mid-Pacific islands as a strategic outpost between the East and West, and President McKinley quickly signed a treaty of annexation without the consent or vote of Hawai'i's public—and despite a petition proving that 95 percent of the Hawaiian population was against it. Although the treaty failed in the senate, the annexationists managed to get approval through a joint resolution, which required only a simple majority of both houses of congress—and in 1900 Hawai'i officially became a territory of the U.S. Citizens of Hawai'i became citizens of America, governed by the United States Constitution and represented by one non-voting congressman in Washington D.C. American military defense outposts appeared across the territory, such as at Diamond Head, and all of Hawai'i's governors and judges were appointed by the White House, rather than by Hawai'i's people.

Lili'uokalani's son, Jonah Kūhiō, later landed a seat in the government and earned respect for serving as a Washington delegate for 20 years, during which time he tried to champion Hawai'i and rebuild ethnic pride. His greatest legacy is the Hawaiian Homes Commission Act, intended to redress the Hawaiian people's loss of land for farming.

From American to Americanization

Just after the turn of the century, young Mainlander James Dole arrived in the Islands and opened a one-man pineapple operation that was to eventually have great influence on business, power, and wealth in Hawai'i. Brushed off earlier by the "Big Five" sugar-oriented companies, he soon commanded their interest in a lucrative new industry. By 1922, Dole had purchased the entire island of Lāna'i and controlled vast tracts of land on other islands, including O'ahu, where pineapple fields stretched for miles. But as the Great Depression hit, sales stalled; Castle & Cooke swooped in, eventually making yet another fortune from the acquisition and increasing their empire. Pineapple remained Hawai'i's second biggest industry through the 1940s.

In addition to the explosion of new industries, Hawai'i's social climate was in great flux. World War I had diverted bulk cargo away from the Islands, slowed sugar exportation, and sapped the developing tourism industry. However, when the war ended Hawai'i entered what some describe as a golden age of urban expansion, musical proliferation, sophistication, and romance that masked racial prejudice in schools, workplaces, and society. Once Hawai'i was well established as "America," it became all the rage—and visitors and new residents from the Mainland flooded Honolulu. Movie stars lounged on Waikīkī Beach, the local radio program *Hawai'i Calls* featured Island performers who became known around the world through international broadcasting, and life in the Islands assumed the appearance of American life.

Along with the enthusiasm was a continued increase in many residents' desire for statehood, which had been officially sought by Hawai'i's legislators since 1903. Hawai'i's status as an American territory was seen by some residents as having numerous disadvantages, such as political and economic instability and "second fiddle" respectability. Back in the States, sentiments reflected concern that Hawai'i was too lawless, too racially diverse, too non-Caucasian, and, because of its growing labor unionization, too communistic. Several bills were introduced in congress that would strip Hawai'i of any self-governing capacity at all. One of the key factors in altering Mainland perception of Hawai'i was the bombing of Pearl Harbor during World War II.

The Bombing of Pearl Harbor

"Air raid Pearl Harbor. This is not a drill." Japan's successful December 7, 1941 attack on Honolulu's naval base is an infamous event. That day, Hawai'i was brimming with nearly fifty thousand stationed U.S. military men and women (a number that would jump to a quarter-million by 1945); and at Pearl Harbor, nearly one hundred American battleships, destroyers, submarines, cruisers, minesweepers, and other warships were berthed near countless rows of military aircraft. Although the Pacific arena as a whole was on guard for potential

Shirley Temple strums an 'ukulele on Waikīkī Beach, circa 1930s. Photo courtesy Hawai'i State Archives.

enemy strikes, it came as a complete surprise when more than three hundred Japanese attack planes converged in two waves upon on the island, ripping open U.S. ships and damaging or destroying almost all of its planes. In billows of black smoke, the battleship USS *Arizona* alone took 1,177 men to the harbor's bottom, where it remains to this day.

Miles away near the pineapple fields of O'ahu's central plains, shells dropped from the sky into backyards where children played. Honolulu restaurants and sidewalks blew apart, killing and injuring civilian men, women, and children. Placid beach scenes outside of Honolulu were broken as Japanese midget submarines surfaced. A state of emergency was issued, and by afternoon martial law was enforced. Approximately 2,400 military personnel were dead and 1,200 wounded, and 70 civilians killed, with many more injured. That same day, the United States declared war upon on Japan in response to the attack.

Hawaiian paradise was rapidly transformed by barbed wire, camouflaged building towers, blackened windows, communications censorship, and curfews. Every child had his or her own gas mask and some schools, which had lost nearly a quarter of their teachers and most of their high school seniors, remained closed for months. Thousands of civilians fled to the Mainland, and Hawai'i's 160,000 Japanese residents faced heightened discrimination. In a poignant demonstration of their loyalty to the U.S., hundreds of Japanese Americans from Hawai'i (as well as the Mainland) enlisted in the 442nd Regimental Combat Team and 100th Battalion, both of which became some of the most famous and decorated units of the war. Between 1941 and 1945, approximately 1 million members of the armed forces would become personally acquainted with O'ahu, which served as the headquarters for the Pacific theater of war. The USS *Missouri,* on which Japan officially signed papers of surrender in 1945, can be visited today at Pearl Harbor.

The Fiftieth State

The strongly Democratic landscape of post-war Hawai'i increased as Hawai'i's war veterans furthered their education and entered politics, or fought for their rights through unions and strikes, and the question of pursuing statehood now fell into their hands. Delegates appealed to Washington D.C. to review fundamental economic and population facts about Hawai'i that showed it was ready for statehood, in addition to its extensive sacrifices made during the war, and in 1959 President Eisenhower signed the historic bill.

Jumbo jet service to Honolulu began that same year and the number of visitors to Hawai'i jumped by 42 percent. Throughout the 1960s and 1970s Hawai'i witnessed unprecedented population and urban growth, especially on the island of O'ahu, which had already long been called "the Gathering Isle" for bearing the majority of the state's population and activity. Lowrise cottages and walk-ups quickly gave way to hotel and business towers, quiet valleys filled with large-scale planned communities, and Waikīkī bloated with beach blankets and hula reviews. As tourism overtook defense spending and agricultural production as the state's primary income, "Big Five" corporations transformed themselves into diversified national and international corporations to keep up with the times, closing plantations behind them.

Despite an increase in prosperity after statehood, Native Hawaiians experienced little trickledown, and resentment toward Americanism still smoldered over issues that for many other residents were in the past. Only a handful of ethnic Hawaiians could still speak Hawaiian or authentically reproduce or perpetuate native arts and crafts; Hawaiians held the lowest life expectancy in the state; the Department of Hawaiian Home Lands had failed to properly carry out Prince Kūhiō's plan of distributing land to Hawaiian-blooded individuals for homesteading; and as the American economy continued to strengthen, entrepreneurs, starry-eyed with housing development schemes, served Hawaiian families eviction notices and developers scheduled construction of mega-resorts atop ancient burial sites. These and other indignities stoked the fire for what would come to be called the "Hawaiian Renaissance"—a resounding interest in reclaiming traditional practices and fighting for rightful heritage, encouraged by civil rights movements on the Mainland and abroad.

Land of Struggle and Promise

When the Japanese yen skyrocketed in value in the 1980s, Japan's long infatuation with the Islands played out in the Hawaiian real estate arena. Homes, golf courses, and hotels were scooped up like pebbles on a beach, at double or triple their values, pricing many longtime residents out of the market. At one point, 90 percent of foreign-owned assets in the state belonged to Japanese investors. Designer stores, catering exclusively to Japanese shoppers, alienated many locals who, despite strong historic ties with Japan, felt visitor needs were eclipsing the needs of residents. When the yen crashed in the 1990s, Hawai'i slumped with it, soon falling completely flat as military bases closed (although Hawai'i is still the most militarized state in the country), some of the last plantations closed, California's recession worsened, and travel slowed in response to terrorist attacks. Thousands of Hawai'i residents left the state to find work.

In 2003, Mainland prosperity, low statewide unemployment, and the revitalization of Hawai'i as a destination contributed to a surge in real estate activity and development that has reached new heights. Despite the modest size of homes in Hawai'i, the median price on O'ahu hit $670,000 in 2005, with countless cottages selling for well over $1 million and many for more than $5 million—frequently to nonresidents who already own homes elsewhere. Low-rent units were converted and sold and the homeless population skyrocketed. A significant percentage of Hawai'i's 1.3 million residents took two or more jobs to survive and credit card debt rose to one of the highest in the nation. In 2006, Hawai'i's inflation rate jumped 5.9 percent, more than double the national rate. That year, *Forbes* magazine described Honolulu as one of the most challenging places to live in terms of housing affordability, income, and cost of living.

Honolulu grew from provincial to a Pacific Region powerhouse after statehood in 1959.

The latest economic surge has also brought welcome change to Hawai'i, including one of the lowest unemployment rates in the nation, a revitalization of crumbling lower-income communities, the overhaul of Waikīkī into a place accessible to everyone, and the opportunity for many of Hawai'i's citizens to benefit from higher standards of living than ever before. Residents are banding together across the state to confront questionable new developments and protect the land. And despite the numerous challenges still facing the Native Hawaiian community, an increasing number of well educated and empowered Hawaiians are embracing cultural traditions affecting public opinion, and reshaping the future.

Honolulu landmark Aloha Tower has long been a beacon for travelers to Hawai'i.

2

TRANSPORTATION

Getting to and around O'ahu

Reaching the distant Hawaiian Islands is surprisingly straightforward, since your only options are by plane or ship. No special visas are needed for United States nationals—this is America, folks!

Getting around O'ahu once you're here is another matter. With 85 percent of street and place names written in the Hawaiian language—and almost invariably starting with a "K" and ending with an "A"—you might at one point throw up your hands and resolve to stay put on Waikīkī Beach. Before you give up, though, remember that you're on an island—so even if you get lost, you won't end up in Alaska.

GETTING TO O'AHU

Air Travel from North America

About 95 percent of all travelers to Hawai'i choose the skyways for transportation, and the majority land at Honolulu International Airport (HNL), in the capital city of Honolulu on O'ahu. The largest domestic and international carriers include:

Air Canada: 1-888-247-2262; www.aircanada.com
Air New Zealand: 1-800-262-1234; www.airnewzealand.com
Aloha Airlines: 1-800-367-5250; www.alohaairlines.com
American Airlines: 1-800-433-7300; www.aa.com
Continental Airlines: 1-800-523-3273; www.continental.com
Delta Air Lines: 1-800-221-1212; www.delta.com
Hawaiian Airlines: 1-800-367-5320; www.hawaiianair.com
Japan Airlines: 1-800-525-3663; www.jal.com
Northwest/KLM Airlines: 1-800-225-2525; www.nwa.com
Qantas Airways: 1-800-227-4500; www.qantas.com
United Airlines: 1-800-864-8331; www.united.com

Some excellent air deals can also be found through **Pleasant Holidays** (1-800-742-9244; www.pleasantholidays.com) and **SunTrips** (1-800-248-7471; www.suntrips.com), which operate charter flights and lean toward package presentations. From the U.S. West Coast, expect a direct flight to take at least five hours; from the East Coast, ten hours or more; and from Sydney, Australia, also about ten hours. Ticket prices run the gamut—you might have paid $800 for your coach class seat from San Francisco, but your aisle mate may have paid $350. Shop around, book early, and keep in mind the so-called "high seasons" of mid-December through April and June through August, as well as major holidays, when good deals are harder to find.

Considering bringing "man's best friend" with you on the trip to paradise? Better call a pet sitter instead. Hawai'i's vulnerable ecosystems and absence of rabies mean the state implements a tough-as-nails quarantine for as long as 120 days, should you not obtain extensive lab tests and appropriate paperwork, and pay considerable fees in advance. For more details, contact the **Hawai'i Department of Agriculture (HDA), Animal Quarantine Station** (837-8092; www.hawaiiag.org/hdoa). Guide or service dogs will also require advance paperwork preparation, so be sure to check HDA regulations.

On the flight over, you'll need to complete the "Plant and Animals Declaration Form" to indicate what contraband you have with you, where you're staying, and so forth. And before leaving the Islands at the end of your vacation, your bags will pass through agricultural inspections at the airport. Plants in soil, fresh pulpy fruits and vegetables, fresh gardenias, live insects, and other items will be confiscated, but your flower lei, coconuts, and pineapples shouldn't be a problem. If in doubt when packing, call the **HDA Plant Quarantine office** (832-0566).

Air Travel from Neighboring Hawaiian Islands

If you're already in Hawai'i, you'll find copious interisland flight options both to and from Honolulu.

Aloha Airlines: 1-800-367-5250; on O'ahu: 484-1111; www.alohaairlines.com
go!: 1-888-435-9462; www.iflygo.com
Hawaiian Airlines: 1-800-367-5320; www.hawaiianair.com
Island Air: 1-800-652-6541; www.islandair.com
Mokulele Airlines: 1-866-260-7070; www.mokuleleairlines.com
Pacific Wings: 1-888-575-4546; www.pacificwings.com

All have different prices, schedules, and points of departure to choose from. Aircrafts vary from spacious 717s with snack service to nine-seat props, so be sure to ask what you're getting! Note also that the airlines above are located in two separate terminals adjacent to HNL's main terminal. Interisland flight times range from 17 minutes to about an hour. First and last flights of the day and weekend flights can be the most difficult to book, so call in advance.

For years, the cost of interisland flying was surprisingly high; however, at the time of writing, price wars were so fierce that one of the long-standing airlines actually offered a brief promotion of free tickets to draw passengers back. Depending on the competition when you're in Hawai'i, expect to pay anywhere from $30 to $90 for a one-way seat, plus taxes.

Getting away from the Airport

As one of the busiest airports in the U.S., Honolulu International Airport features most of the amenities and congestion you'd expect. Upon disembarking, you'll quickly be immersed in Hawai'i's balmy climate via the airport's partially open-air design, so be sure to shed your turtleneck before landing. Look for the Wiki Wiki Shuttle that winds along the terminal roadway, and hop aboard for a free lift to the baggage claim if you don't want to walk.

Smoking in the airport is permitted only in a designated center median.

To get away from (or back to) the airport, you can travel via airport shuttle, limousine, taxi, hotel shuttle, the city bus, or rental car. The popular Airport Waikīkī Express coach runs between the airport and Waikīkī hotels every half-hour, 24 hours a day, and charges about $10 per person—or you can call the other listed shuttle services below in advance to arrange a pickup at the airport. If you're staying outside of Waikīkī, make reservations in advance for a special shuttle pickup. Be prepared for significantly higher fares to locations outside of Honolulu.

A taxi to Waikīkī will cost about $35 and can often be faster than a shuttle; dispatchers at the baggage claim area median will coordinate one for you. Limousine and sedan services must also be booked in advance.

Most shuttles and all taxis pick up passengers from the median strip outside the baggage claim. If you book a shuttle airport pickup, be sure to confirm the pickup location.

The city-operated public transportation system, called "TheBus," must be accessed at median strips up on the departure level. Information on luggage restrictions and fares are listed later in this chapter.

All the major car rental agencies have pickup/dropoff locations at the airport and in Waikīkī and can provide directions to get you to your destination.

Shuttles Between the Airport and Waikīkī

Airport Waikīkī Express: 954-8605; www.robertshawaii.com
Hawai'i Super Transit: 841-2928; www.hawaiisupertransit.com
VIP Transportation: 836-0317; www.viptrans.com

Shuttles Between the Airport and Islandwide Destinations

O'ahu Airport Shuttle: 1-866-845-8181; www.oahuairportshuttle.com
Airport-Island Shuttles: 1-800-624-9554; www.shuttleguys.com

Boat Travel From North America

Although less than 5 percent of all visitors to Hawai'i arrived by ship last year, about a quarter million boarded cruise ships once here, to continue on to other international destinations or circle for a week or more within the Islands themselves. All cruise ships dock at Honolulu Harbor, about 4 miles from Waikīkī. Note that the law prevents most ships from allowing passengers to either embark or disembark in American ports other than the main scheduled ports, which can foil your plan to sail here one-way.

Norwegian Cruise Line (1-800-327-7030; www.ncl.com) specializes in luxury cruises to and around the Hawaiian Islands and has several ships and a variety of trips to choose from. Other cruise lines that currently feature Hawai'i itineraries include **Carnival Cruise Lines** (1-888-327-9501; www.carnival.com), **Celebrity Cruises** (1-800-647-2251; www.celebrity cruises.com), **Holland America** (1-800-426-0327; www.hollandamerica.com), **Princess Cruises** (1-800-774-6237; www.princess.com), and **Royal Caribbean International** (1-800-803-5240; www.royalcaribbean.com). All offer a lovely getaway and great overview of Hawai'i, although short port stops allow little opportunity to really get to know each island.

Ferry Travel from Neighboring Hawaiian Islands

Open for business in mid-2007, amid controversy, is the **Hawai'i Superferry** (1-877-HIFERRY; www.superferry.com), the first system in decades to give full interisland ferrying a try with service from downtown Honolulu's Pier 19 to Maui and Kaua'i (to be expanded to the Big Island by 2009). Fares range from approximately $50 to $75 each way for a several-hour journey. At the time of writing, the ferry runs daily to and from Maui, and daily except Saturdays to and from Kaua'i. Although the ferry is designed to transport personal vehicles in addition to passengers, rental car companies do not plan to permit visitors to take rental cars aboard because of liability issues.

The Hawaiian Archipelago

The Hawaiian Islands consist of 137 reefs, shoals, islets, and islands stretching for 1,500 miles across the Tropic of Cancer, north of the equator. Most visitors are familiar only with six of the eight main islands: O'ahu, Kaua'i, Maui, Moloka'i, Lāna'i, and Hawai'i (also called "the Big Island").

Uninhabited Kaho'olawe is the seventh of Hawai'i's eight main islands. A fairly dry, windswept terrain ravaged by goats and extensive military bombing exercises, few people besides teams of archeologists and activists have breached its rocky coastline. Officially transferred back to the State of Hawai'i from the U.S. Navy in 2003, it is now managed by the Kaho'olawe Island Reserve Commission.

Tiny Ni'ihau, the eighth main island, is known as "the Forbidden Isle." Privately purchased from the kingdom of Hawai'i in 1864, it is home to about two hundred Hawaiian-blooded, Hawaiian-speaking individuals. The island is generally off limits to outsiders, for the protection of Ni'ihauans and their way of life.

Beyond Ni'ihau, the numerous Northwestern Hawaiian Islands form the largest protected marine area in the world: the Papahānaumokuākea Marine National Monument. Among them are exotic Nihoa, Mokumanamana, Maro Reef, Laysan Island, and Midway, where the renowned Battle of Midway took place. This unique, 138,000-square-mile natural environment is home to more than 7,000 marine species, a quarter of which exist nowhere else on earth. Cultural remnants include Hawaiian archaeological sites, shipwrecks, and World War II artifacts. The area is closed to the general public.

Most of O'ahu's many offshore islets are sanctuaries for seabirds and native coastal vegetation and are open to the public for very low-impact day visits only, if at all. Although you can wade to several islets at low tide, ocean currents can be surprisingly strong and corals trampled on the way can become weakened or killed. Accessing others via kayak or by swimming can be risky, especially for novices.

Every reef, shoal, and island, excluding Midway, is part of the State of Hawai'i, and the Northwestern Hawaiian Islands are officially part of the City and County of Honolulu.

GETTING AROUND O'AHU

Modes of Transportation

Renting a car is by far the best way to really experience O'ahu's beauty and diversity. However, if you'd like to skip driving, hop onto O'ahu's public bus system, TheBus, or take the Waikīkī Trolley to Honolulu highlights. Guided island tours, even some of the smaller outfits with modest vans, often charge an enormous sum to visit sites you can easily reach on your own—however they have the advantages of ease, keeping you and your belongings secure, and providing interesting histories and facts, which might make them worth your while. Most transportation-oriented guided tour companies in this book are listed in Chapter 7.

We suggest not using a bike or moped as a mode of travel outside Waikīkī, Kailua, or the North Shore, and to definitely pass up hitchhiking (which is illegal on highways). A reasonably

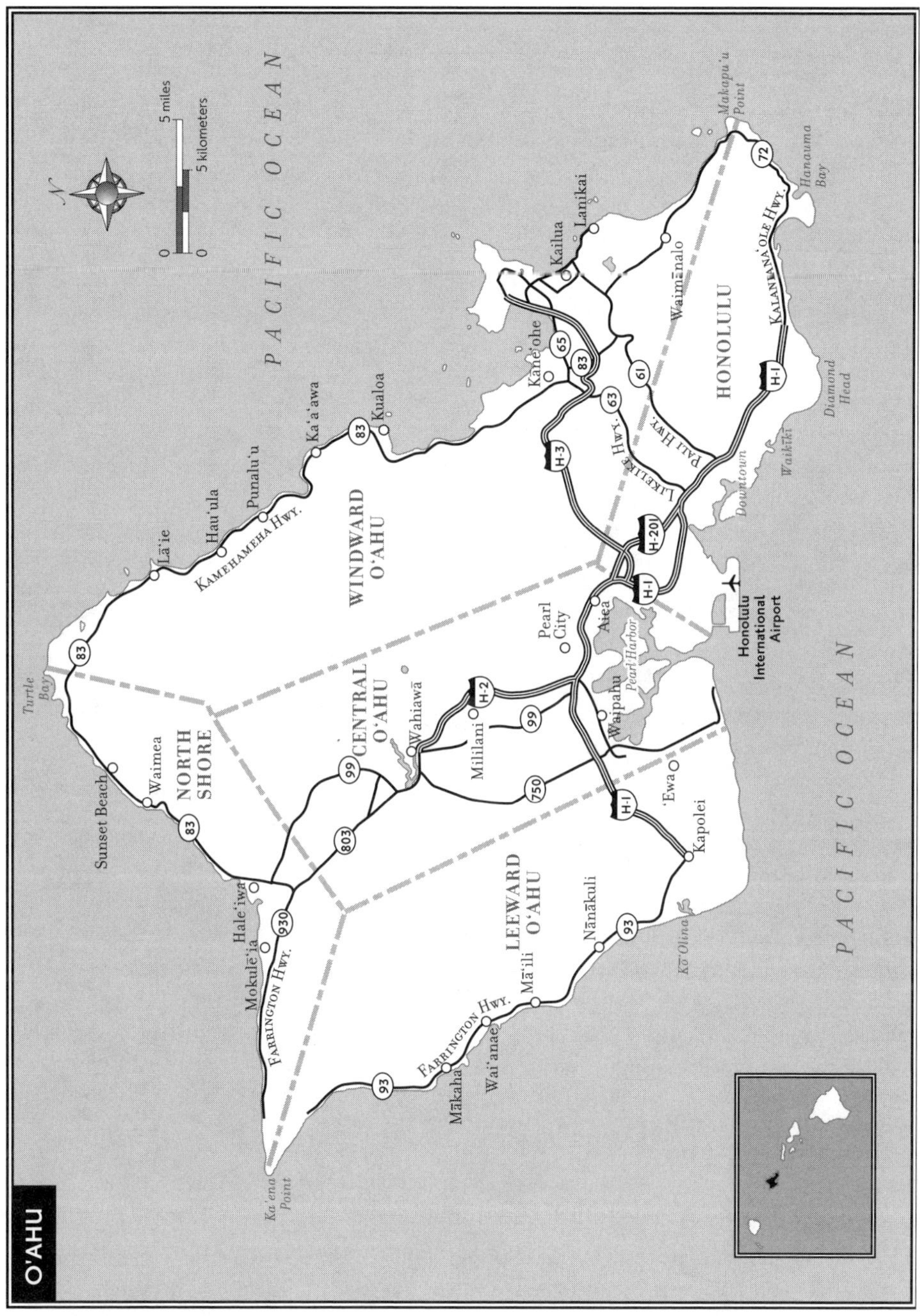

fit person can easily explore the breadth of Waikīkī entirely on foot, but will still need a lift to most other destinations. A note on walking around town: Be sure to press crosswalk buttons to activate walk signals, or you might wait until the end of time to get across the street.

For visitors with physical disabilities who choose not to drive or use the bus system, call **Access Aloha Travel** (1-800-480-1143; 545-1143; www.accessalohatravel.com), a local travel agency that can rent you wheelchair-accessible vans and equipment, such as wheelchairs, and can coordinate special transportation for any activity—as well as book the activities themselves. **Handi-Cabs of the Pacific** (524-3866; www.handicabs.com) can pick you up from the airport or take you anywhere else you need to go, but reservations must be made at least one week in advance.

Deciphering Local Directions

Understanding local-style directions is one of the most challenging aspects for visitors in getting around.

O'ahu has four interstate freeways—known as the H-1, H-2, H-3, and Moanalua Freeway (H-201/78)—all built with federal dollars to connect military bases around the island. Although everyone uses these designations, few residents are familiar with freeway exit numbers, highway numbers, or mile markers; ask someone waiting for the bus along HI 83 where HI 83 is, and they'll probably have no clue. Instead, directions are given using road names, landmarks, and local directional terminology, including the words *mauka*—"toward the mountains" or "on the mountain-side of. . ." and *makai*—"toward the ocean" or "on the ocean-side of . . .". In the Honolulu area in particular, you'll also hear "Diamond Head" and "'Ewa," which point you either in the direction of Diamond Head Crater in the eastern section of the city (even if you end up passing it), or toward the region of 'Ewa, west of the city. Here's an example of how these all work together: "Go Diamond Head on H-1 until it turns into Kalaniana'ole Highway, then keep going to 'Āina Haina; turn *mauka* onto Nenue, just past the stone church, and look for our yard sale sign on the 'Ewa side of the street."

Almost all Hawai'i streets have Hawaiian names—so keep a sharp eye as you whiz past street signs, as many names appear similar. Major highways you'll likely travel include Kalaniana'ole (kah-lah-nee-ah-nah-OH-leh), Kahekili (kah-heh-KEE-lee), Kamehameha (kah-meh-hah-MEH-hah), Likelike (lee-keh-LEE-keh), Pali (PAH-lee), and Farrington (that's an easy one!). In Waikīkī, the three main through roads are called Kalākaua Avenue (kah-lah-KOW-ah), Kūhiō Avenue (koo-HEE-oh), and Ala Wai Boulevard (AH-lah-WHY).

Chinatown street signs feature a fun mix of Chinese, Hawaiian, and English.

Renting a Car

All of the big rental car players have locations in both Waikīkī and at the airport, and shuttles to the airport lots pull up at the median outside the baggage claim. Be sure to compare prices and book before you arrive—prices vary significantly and great deals abound, especially online. All of them can direct you to roadside emergency assistance and set up vehicles for disabled drivers (with advance notice). Disabled drivers or passengers should bring their handicapped parking placards from the Mainland, along with official proof that the placard belongs to them. The placards will be honored anywhere on the island, and may also allow you to park at street meters free of charge for up to two-and-a-half hours at a time.

Alamo: 1-877-603-0615; www.alamo.com
Avis: 1-800-321-3712; www.avis.com
Budget Rent-A-Car: 1-800-527-0700; www.budget.com
Dollar Rent A Car: 1-800-800-4000; www.dollarcar.com
Enterprise Rent-A-Car: 1-800-736-8222; www.enterprise.com
Hertz: 1-800-654-3011; www.hertz.com
National Car Rental: 1-888-868-6207; www.nationalcar.com
Thrifty: 1-800-847-4389; www.thrifty.com

VIP Rentals (922-4605; 234 Beach Walk Ave.; also at 946-7733; 1944 Kalākaua Ave.) is a local company offering some cheap deals on older models, and they seem to please customers well enough for the price. If you dream of renting a Ferrari or other exotic vehicle and cost is no object, call **Paradise Rent-a-Car** (926-7777) or **Luxury Rentals** (222-2277; www.hiluxurycarrentals.com), both in Waikīkī.

In Hawai'i, the best bet is to rent a low-key, moderately sized passenger car with good gas mileage. Hawai'i's gas prices are some of the highest in the nation, and flashy vehicles don't impress outside of town and can even bring you unwanted attention. Frequent rain showers and the searing Hawaiian sun negate some of the fun of convertibles and jeeps; and since most of the people driving them on the island are visitors, they help identify you as a tourist and increase your risk for a break-in.

O'ahu's traffic has crushed many a starry-eyed visitor expecting quaint tropical roads from a vintage postcard. Honolulu is a modern city filled with people going to work, taking the kids to soccer practice, visiting the dentist, shopping, and hitting the beach—all by car. And although it has the same roadway density as other large American cities, the number of cars on the road has recently skyrocketed, and twice as many people are forced to share its limited lane miles. It can be hard to accept the reality of bumper-to-bumper freeway rush hour in a place so profoundly beautiful, but try not to let it ruin your vacation. Residents loathe the traffic too, and we're trying to fix it.

Renting a Motorcycle

For those who prefer the wind in their hair, rent a motorcycle for a country cruise. For moped and bicycle rentals, please see Chapter 7.

Big Kahuna Rentals: 1-888-451-5544; www.bigkahunarentals.com
Harleys® and Sportbikes Hawai'i: 1-888-882-2277; www.harleysandsportsbikeshawaii.com

Local Driving Rules and Tips

Even on the freeway, speed limits are lower than on the Mainland, and drivers moving at 80 miles per hour or more on the freeway face extremely hefty fines and other penalties. Seatbelts are mandatory at all times for front-seat passengers; children under 18 must be belted in back seats. Children ages 4 through 7 must use a safety or booster seat unless they're more than 4 foot, 9 inches tall, or if the vehicle has lap-only seatbelts in the rear seats. Driving with more than .08 blood-alcohol content is illegal.

Although Hawai'i motorists are becoming more aggressive and are glued to cell phones, show your aloha and ease up on the gas pedal; invite them to merge in front of you or pass you; wave "thanks" when offered any courtesy on the road; avoid tailgating; honk only in urgent situations; stop for pedestrians (required by law); resist giving "stink eye" to bad drivers;

and drive especially carefully in the country, where chickens, dogs, kids, coconuts, and deep potholes can be plentiful. Sightseeing down most remote rural roads is often seen as an invasion of privacy and is not recommended. Signs that say *kapu* mean "keep out."

Never leave valuables in your car, especially at beach parks and hiking areas, where theft is common.

"Now That I've Got a Car, Where Do I Put It?"

Parking your car in Honolulu (and especially in Waikīkī) can be an expensive challenge. Most hotels charge between $10 and $25 per day for guests to lodge their vehicles, and public lots in Waikīkī & and downtown can easily run up to $30 per day or more. Many restaurants and shops will validate or even valet park for free if you're patronizing their establishments. Call your destination to find out what they offer before heading out.

Waikīkī's best metered and free street parking is in front of the Honolulu Zoo and along and around the enormous Kapi'olani Park, although they're long walks from central and western Waikīkī. Get there before 10 AM or after 6 PM to more easily score a spot.

In downtown's Capital District area, look for metered street parking on Punchbowl Street; if that fails, the **Kalanimoku "Lot G"** (586-0352; 1151 Punchbowl St., opposite the Capitol) has at least 40 metered stalls for public use, or try the **Makai Garage** (586-0352; 530 Halekauwila St.). In Chinatown, try the **Chinatown Municipal Parking** (864-4688; entrance on the left-hand side of Beretania St., just past Nu'uanu Ave.), which is especially cheap on weekends. If you're headed to Aloha Tower, park at the lots they provide and be sure to get validated at one of its businesses.

In Kailua, a public lot off Aulike Street offers three-hour metered blocks of time. Street meters and other free business lots are also plentiful.

Hopping The Bus

O'ahu's award-winning **TheBus** (848-5555; www.thebus.org) system is a great way to avoid the parking problem, although it "ain't no Swiss train" when it comes to timeliness. Because many roads and communities fringe the shoreline, the plentiful routes of TheBus often pass right by key attractions—including most of its best beaches. Nearly every bus in service is wheelchair-accessible, and all are air-conditioned and equipped with front-load bike racks. Luggage of airline carry-on dimensions are allowed (one per person), but must fit under your seat or in your lap. Although surfboards are not permitted, most bodyboards are welcome.

Busses 19 and 20 run about every half-hour between the airport and Waikīkī, passing through the entire downtown area, Ward Centers, and Ala Moana Center on the way. The 20 also goes on to the *Arizona* Memorial at Pearl Harbor. Other popular visitor busses include the 2, 8, and 13, which all run east-west through Waikīkī. However, only the 2 continues east past the main strip to circle Kapi'olani Park. The 2 and 13 will also take you all the way to downtown Honolulu. Between Waikīkī and Ala Moana Center, you can also take the 8.

Bus Route 22 travels between Waikīkī and Hanauma Bay; Routes 55 and 52, known as the "Circle Island" busses, depart Ala Moana Center for three-hour rides either along the Windward Coast and North Shore, before cutting down the middle of the island back towards the shopping center again, or in the reverse direction.

Printed bus schedules are in stores and kiosks in Waikīkī and elsewhere, or call TheBus seven days a week for route assistance. Exact change in either coins or bills is needed for the $2 adult (senior and disabled adults $1), $1 child (ages 6-17) one-way fare, and must be paid in the machine at the front door upon boarding. Request a two-hour transfer to switch busses. Visitors can also purchase a pass, good for four consecutive days on TheBus, for about $20 at ABC Stores in Waikīkī.

Taking the Waikīkī Trolley

For those of you with limited time, plans to pack a lot into your day, and little care about appearing touristy, you might want to use the open-air visitor trolley system, the **Waikīkī Trolley** (593-2822; www.waikikitrolley.com; DFS Galleria Ticket Counter, 330 Royal Hawaiian Ave., Waikīkī). It's expensive—one ticket for the day will cost about $25 for adults and $12 for children (ages 4–11)—but you can jump on and off of three different lines that stop at major sights throughout the Honolulu area. The four-day pass is a much better value at $45 adults, $18 children.

The Pink Line circles between Ward Centers, Ala Moana Center, and Waikīkī; the Blue Line heads east from Waikīkī, hitting Diamond Head, Kahala Mall, Hanauma Bay, and Sea Life Park; and the Red Line heads west, stopping at the Honolulu Academy of Arts, several key shopping centers, Bishop Museum, and historic downtown sites such as 'Iolani Palace.

Taxis, Sedans, and Limousines

Let someone else worry about the driving! Grab a cab or even hire a luxury sedan or limousine for special occasions. Taxis, however, can be tough to find away from major shopping centers and hotels. Taximeters are set at around $2.80 and charge $2.80 for every mile you travel. For service from the airport, cross to the median outside of baggage claim. Sedans and limousines charge hefty fees for airport transfers, but can be relatively affordable should you wish to be chauffeured around the island. Most charge a flat rate per hour, with a time minimum. Book sedans and limousines in advance.

Taxis

Akamai Cab Company: 944-3400
Charley's Taxi & Tours: 531-1333

Sedan and Limousine Services

Elite Limousine Service: 1-800-776-2098; www.elitelimohawaii.com
Carey Hawai'i Chauffeured Services: 1-888-563-2888; www.hawaiilimo.com
Hawai'i Chauffeur & Limo Services: 522-7950; www.hawaiichauffeur.net

Exploring O'ahu

O'ahu consists of two general states of mind: town and country. "Town" refers to the entire Honolulu metropolitan area, including its outlying suburbs. The rest of O'ahu is pretty well "country," although out-of-town bedroom communities, such as Kailua and Kapolei, don't fall neatly into either category.

Hawai'i's country style is all its own. Forget the Hamptons, Napa Valley, Humboldt County, Nantucket, the Everglades, or Telluride. While we've got every type of resident, from couture models to coconut-frond weavers to developers keen on recreating San Diego living, O'ahu's spirit is far different from J. Crew sunbonnets, dreadlocks, or Teva® sandals. Much of Hawai'i is still old-model Toyotas with surf racks, woven hats with feather hatbands, backyard baby birthday luaus, homegrown chutney mangoes shared with

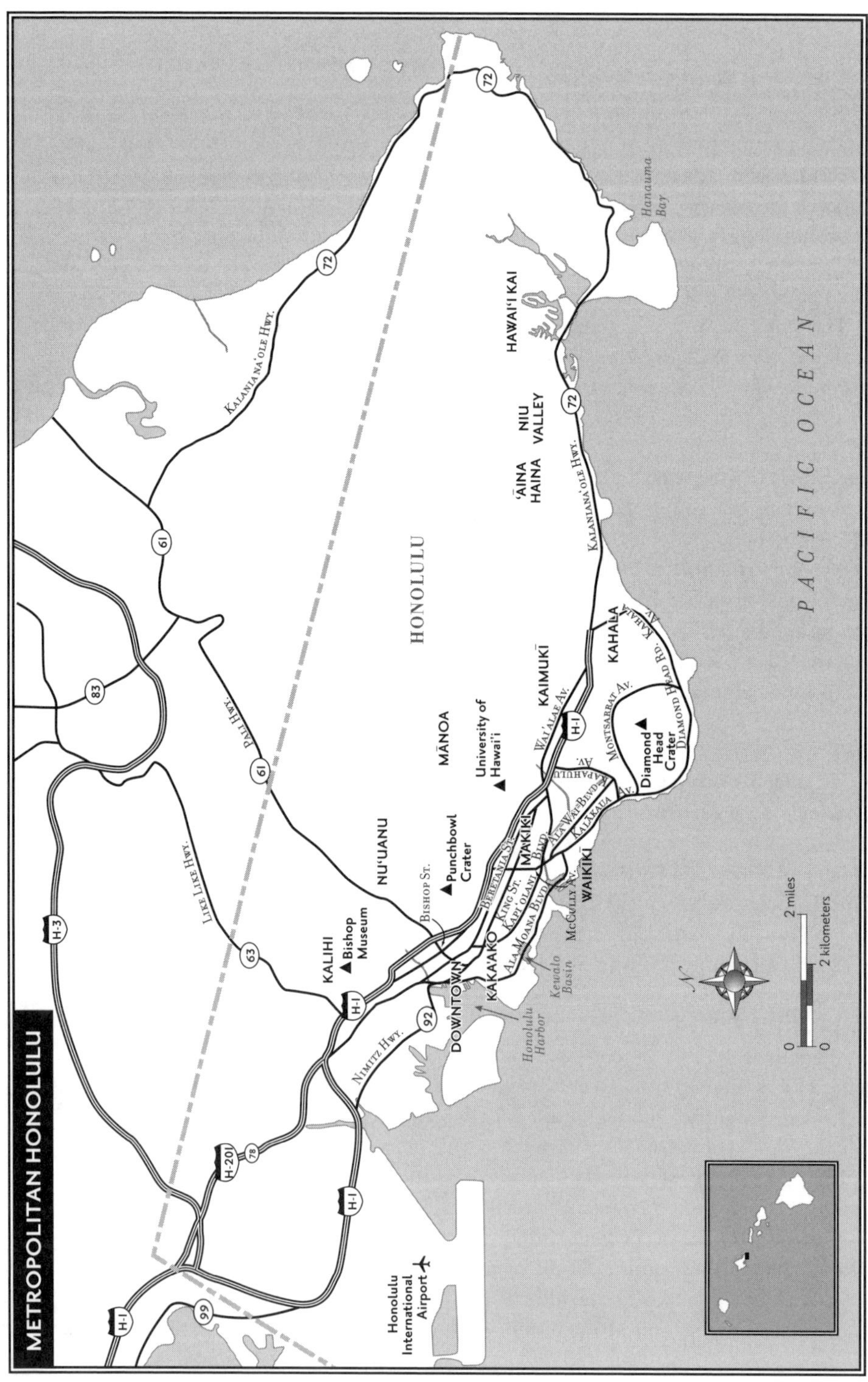

METROPOLITAN HONOLULU
HONOLULU
PACIFIC OCEAN
Honolulu International Airport
KALIHI
Bishop Museum
NU'UANU
Punchbowl Crater
MĀNOA
University of Hawai'i
DOWNTOWN
KAKA'AKO
MAKIKI
WAIKĪKĪ
KAIMUKĪ
KAHALA
Diamond Head Crater
'ĀINA HAINA
NIU VALLEY
HAWAI'I KAI
Hanauma Bay
Honolulu Harbor
Kewalo Basin
Nimitz Hwy.
Likelike Hwy.
Pali Hwy.
Kalaniana'ole Hwy.
Bishop St.
Beretania St.
King St.
Kapi'olani Blvd.
Ala Moana Blvd.
McCully Av.
Ala Wai Blvd.
Kalākaua Av.
Kapahulu Av.
Wai'alae Av.
Montsarrat Av.
Diamond Head Rd.
Kahala Av.
H-1
H-3
H-201
61
63
72
78
83
92
99
0
2 miles
2 kilometers

neighbors, T-shirts advertising local plumbing or plate lunch businesses, dogs and kids in the back of the truck, spearfishing on weekends, and all-day family barbecues in the park. If you keep these images in mind while traveling the island, it might help you to understand the variety of lifestyles you see and better grasp the depth of Hawai'i's soul.

No O'ahu trip is complete without a coastal drive along the southeast corner of the island and back through the mountains, with a stop at the famous Nu'uanu Pali Lookout on the Honolulu side of the tunnels; or the "circle island trip" through Central O'ahu to the North Shore and along the Windward Coast back toward town. More visitors are making it to the Leeward Coast these days as well. All feature breathtaking scenery and unique characteristics that make memorable journeys.

The following are brief descriptions of O'ahu's main regions, plus basic road directions from Waikīkī to get you around.

Honolulu

Although the entire island is officially part of the City and County of Honolulu, the city of Honolulu proper begins around Hālawa Stream, just east of Pearl Harbor, and continues east for about 18 miles to Makapu'u Point, and from the southern coastline to the mountain crests far north of the city. Often referred to on O'ahu simply as "town," Honolulu is the only full urban experience in the entire state and is home to one third of Hawai'i's 1.3 million residents.

Within Honolulu's great expanse live struggling immigrants, movie stars, and everyone else. Its many prized residential suburbs include the venerable and grand neighborhoods of Mānoa and Nu'uanu, as well as glamorous Kahala, Portlock, and Hawai'i Loa Ridge. The downtown area is the heartbeat of the state, and it includes a small business community referred to as downtown, the financial district, or the central business district. It also includes the Merchant Street Historic District, Capital Historic District, Chinatown Historic District, and the historic shipping waterfront.

Then, of course, there's the world-famous Honolulu district of Waikīkī—a tiny, vibrant, shoreline enclave at the foot of Diamond Head Crater, full of history and excitement. Once the center of pre-contact Hawaiian rule and dotted with stone temples, taro paddies, footpaths, and coconut groves, its past can still be felt amid towering hotels and throngs of visitors. Kalākaua Avenue is the main drag, where thousands meander day and night.

There are several basic routes you'll likely take in your explorations. To reach the downtown area from Waikīkī, head west on Ala Wai Boulevard, turn right onto Kalākaua Avenue, and then left onto Kapi'olani Boulevard. Follow the road approximately 2 miles until you see the State Capitol Building on your left.

To visit Diamond Head Crater, head eastbound on Kalākaua Avenue and take the left fork past Kapahulu Avenue and the zoo, called Monsarrat Avenue, to the crater. If you don't take the fork and continue straight between the park and the beach, you'll reach a stop sign where you can turn right for Diamond Head Road and the neighborhood of Kahala. This route will also carry you to the eastern corner of the island.

To get to the University of Hawai'i from Waikīkī, head west on Ala Wai Boulevard and turn right onto McCully Street. Take the next right onto Kapi'olani Boulevard and left onto University Avenue, following it under the freeway to the campus. To visit Mānoa Falls, continue past the university on the same road (it eventually becomes O'ahu Avenue). When it splits, take the Mānoa Road fork, following it to the very end in the back of the valley.

Windward O'ahu

The windward side of the island is also called Windward O'ahu or the Windward Coast. It lies just east of the Ko'olau Range and is rainy, lush, and dramatic. Country-style, low-key, very "local" Waimānalo on its southern end is a cowboy and Hawaiian homesteading town, flanked by a curtain of ridged mountains and an impossibly long, windswept beach. Few amenities or welcome mats for visitors make it best as a scenic drive-by or beach stop only.

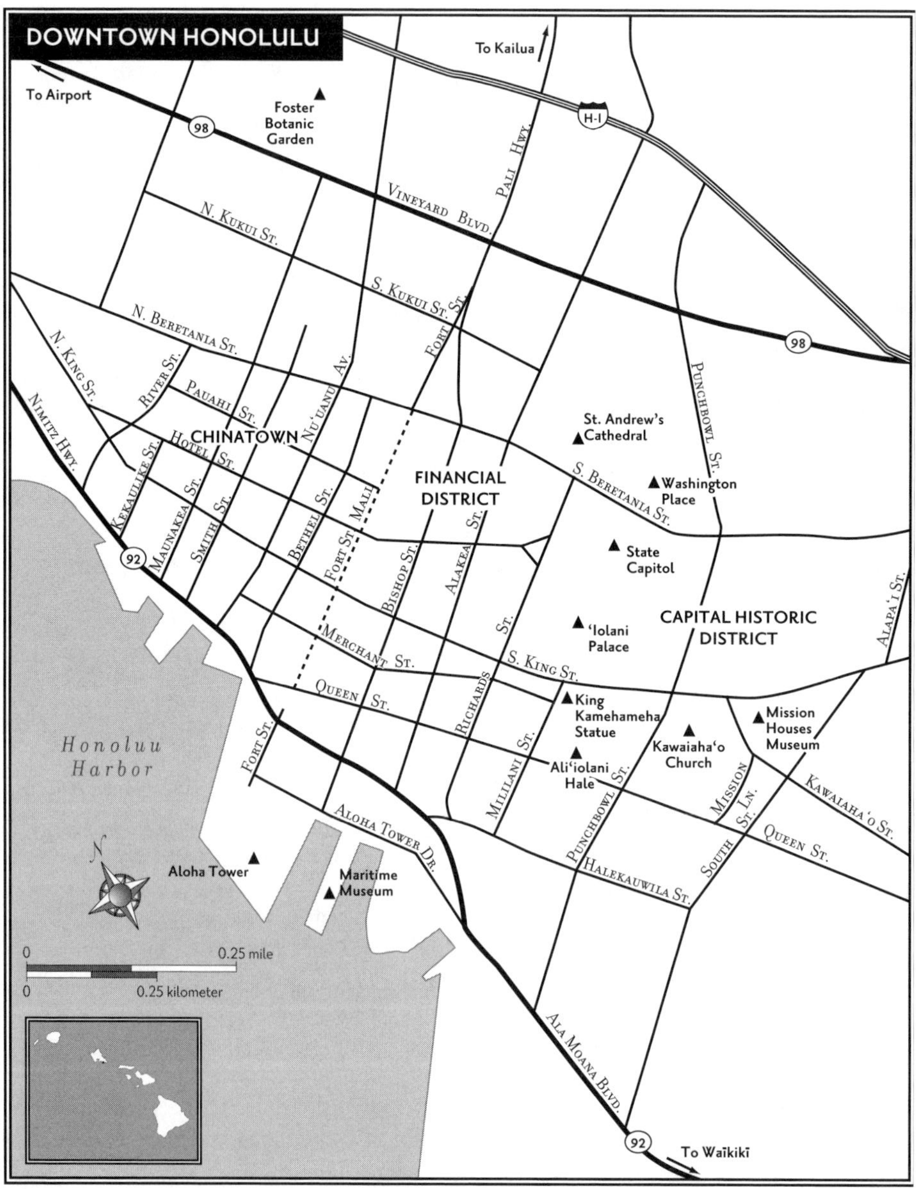

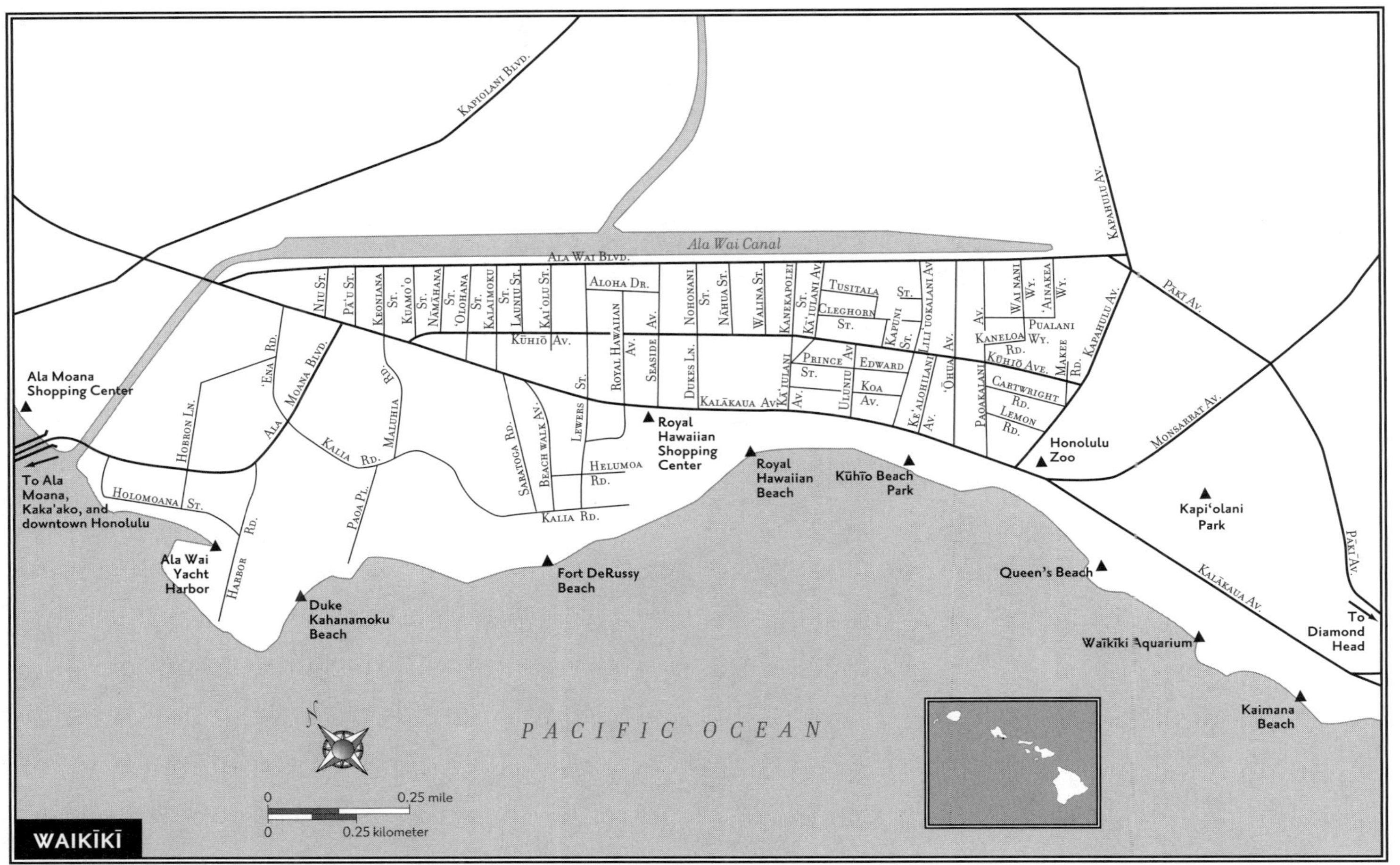
WAIKĪKĪ
Kapiolani Blvd.
Ala Wai Canal
Ala Wai Blvd.
Niu St.
Pā'ū St.
Keoniana St.
Kuamo'o St.
Nāmāhana St.
'Olohana St.
Kalaimoku St.
Launiu St.
Kai'olu St.
Aloha Dr.
Royal Hawaiian Av.
Seaside Av.
Nohonani St.
Nāhua St.
Walina St.
Kanekapolei St.
Ka'iulani Av.
Tusitala St.
Cleghorn St.
Kapuni St.
Lili'uokalani Av.
Wai Nani Wy.
'Ainakea Wy.
Pualani Wy.
Kaneloa Rd.
Kapahulu Av.
Pākī Av.
Kūhīō Av.
'Ena Rd.
Ala Moana Blvd.
Maluhia Rd.
Lewers St.
Dukes Ln.
Ka'iulani Av.
Prince St.
Uluniu Av.
Edward
Koa Av.
Ke'alohilani Av.
'Ōhua Av.
Paoakalani Av.
Kūhīō Ave.
Makee Rd.
Cartwright Rd.
Lemon Rd.
Kalākaua Av.
Ala Moana Shopping Center
Hobron Ln.
Kalia Rd.
Saratoga Rd.
Beach Walk Av.
Helumoa Rd.
Royal Hawaiian Shopping Center
Royal Hawaiian Beach
Kūhīō Beach Park
Honolulu Zoo
Monsarrat Av.
Kapi'olani Park
To Ala Moana, Kaka'ako, and downtown Honolulu
Holomoana St.
Paoa Pl.
Harbor Rd.
Ala Wai Yacht Harbor
Fort DeRussy Beach
Duke Kahanamoku Beach
Queen's Beach
Kalākaua Av.
Pākī Av.
To Diamond Head
Waīkīki Aquarium
Kaimana Beach
PACIFIC OCEAN
0
0.25 mile
0
0.25 kilometer

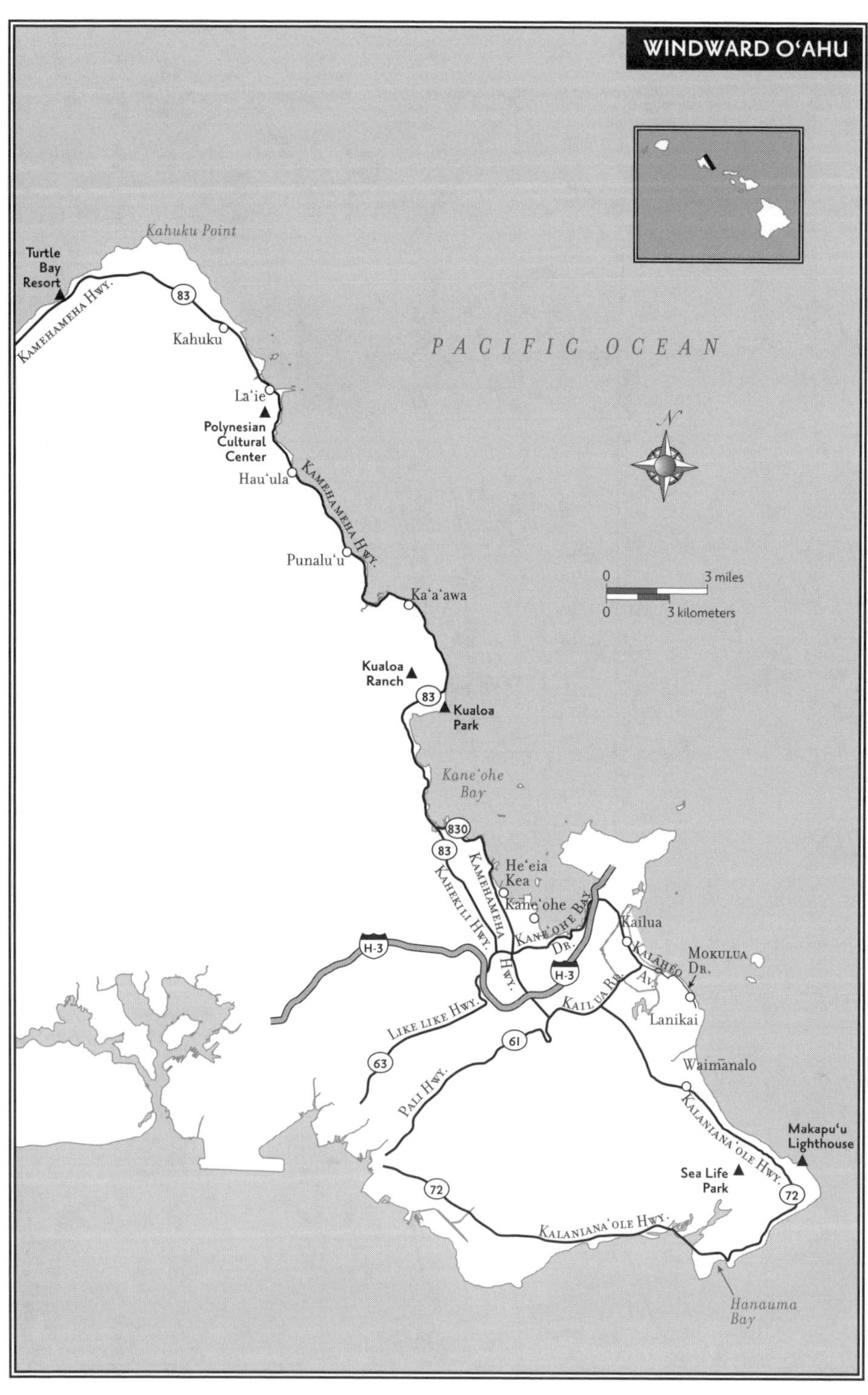
WINDWARD O'AHU
PACIFIC OCEAN
Kahuku Point
Turtle Bay Resort
Kamehameha Hwy.
83
Kahuku
La'ie
Polynesian Cultural Center
Hau'ula
Kamehameha Hwy.
Punalu'u
Ka'a'awa
Kualoa Ranch
Kualoa Park
Kane'ohe Bay
830
He'eia Kea
Kahekili Hwy.
Kamehameha Hwy.
Kane'ohe
Kane'ohe Bay Dr.
Kailua
Kalaheo Av.
Mokulua Dr.
H-3
Kailua Rd.
Like Like Hwy.
63
61
Pali Hwy.
Lanikai
Waimānalo
Kalaniana'ole Hwy.
Makapu'u Lighthouse
Sea Life Park
72
Hanauma Bay
0 3 miles
0 3 kilometers
N

North of Waimānalo you'll find exclusive Lanikai and upper- and middle-class homes in the popular town of Kailua, which features numerous boutiques and small eateries, a laid-back bedroom community feel, and fantastic beaches. Nearby Kāne'ohe is an unfortunate example of hapless suburban planning, but the sculpted mountains surrounding it are miraculous. Beyond it you'll find rustic country life and a stronger Mormon influence in the tiny coastal towns of Ka'a'awa, Punalu'u, Hau'ula, Lā'ie, and Kahuku.

There are three ways to reach Windward O'ahu from Waikīkī. For the southern coastal route, follow Kalākaua Avenue east and turn right onto Diamond Head Road, past the park. Diamond Head Road eventually becomes Kahala Avenue—stay on it past its many mansions until you reach a stop sign, where you can turn left onto Keala'olu Avenue. The road travels several blocks before curving right to merge onto Kalaniana'ole Highway (HI 72) eastbound. This highway travels the coastline along the south and eventually turns up the southern region of the Windward Coast toward Kailua. Assuming no traffic, you should reach Waimānalo within about 30 minutes.

Via the freeway and mountain passes: Take Kalākaua Avenue to Kapahulu Avenue, just before the zoo, and turn left, following the road about 2 miles until it passes under the freeway and curves left to a westbound H-1 freeway entrance. If you're heading to Kailua, take the Pali Highway (HI 61) exit and follow it through the mountains until signs direct you there. If you turn left at the first intersection after descending the mountains, you'll travel along Kamehameha Highway (HI 83) through Kāne'ohe. If you then turn left at Kāne'ohe Bay Drive and right onto the connecting Kahekili Highway (HI 83), you'll keep heading north and pass near sites such as the Byodo-In Temple. If you stay straight on Kamehameha Highway instead of turning onto Kāne'ohe Bay Drive, you'll continue through town (on HI 830) past Windward Mall and eventually through He'eia—a lovely little coastal drive. He'eia State Park is along this route. The road ends at an intersection with a huge banyan tree and the landmark Hygenic Store, where you can turn right to continue on Kamehameha Highway toward the northern windward communities as well as the North Shore. Kahekili also links to the Hygenic Store, where both routes become one. The pretty He'eia "side" route will only delay you by five or ten minutes total.

If you're heading to communities north of Kailua along the coast and want to bypass part of Kāne'ohe, continue on H-1 past the Pali exit and to exit 20A, the Like Like Highway (HI 63) exit, following it through the mountains until signs direct you to Kahekili Highway (HI 83) and Kahalu'u/Lā'ie. Past the Hygenic Store, the road becomes Kamehameha Highway and runs the length of the upper Windward Coast and the North Shore. From Waikīkī, and with no traffic, it takes about 40 minutes to reach Kailua and an hour or more for communities farther north.

The North Shore

Between Turtle Bay Resort in Kahuku and the town of Hale'iwa, you're in "surfer country." The coastal setting of grasslands and hills includes an impressive stretch of breathtaking beaches and powerful waves; in the winter season, though, swimming can be hazardous. Renowned spots, such as Sunset Beach, Waimea, and Banzai Pipeline draw hundreds of thousands of visitors each year, and when the surf's up, traffic along Kamehameha Highway, the North Shore's only thoroughfare, can be backed up for miles as gawkers and water babies drop everything to get to the sand. Amenities are limited mostly to shack-style plate lunch stops until you reach the colorful and funky little town of Hale'iwa, the "surfing capital of the world."

To get there via the Windward Coast, take Kalākaua Avenue to Kapahulu Avenue, just before the zoo, and turn left, following the road about 2 miles until it passes under the freeway and curves left to a westbound H-1 freeway entrance. Once on the freeway, take exit 20A to Like Like Highway (HI 63) and continue through the mountains. Follow signs to Kahekili Highway (HI 83) and Kahalu'u/Lā'ie; Kahekili eventually becomes Kamehameha Highway, a lovely coastal drive. You'll know you're on the North Shore when you reach

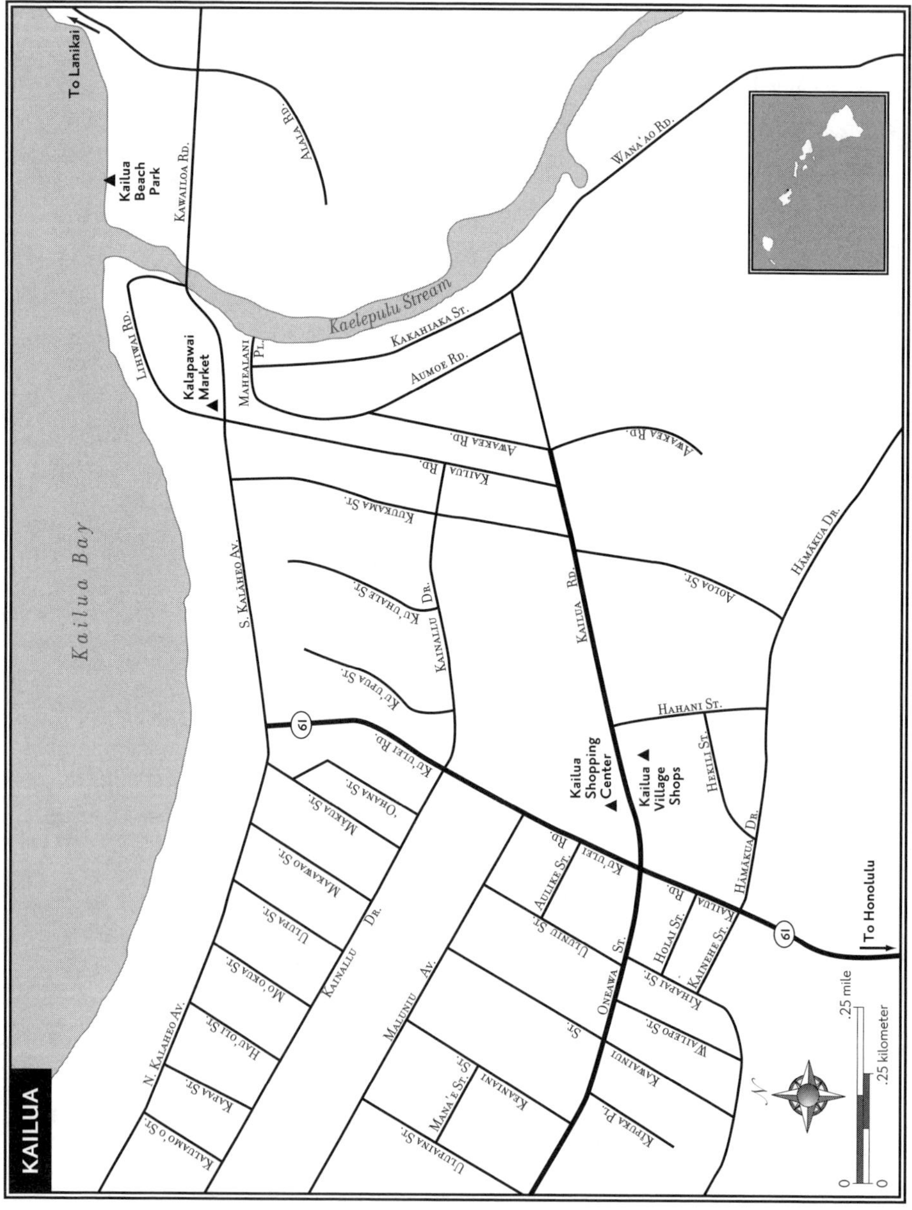

Although Hale'iwa's been gentrifying, it's still got some funky flavor.

Turtle Bay Resort in Kahuku. With no traffic, it'll take you at least 75 minutes to reach Kahuku and 90 minutes before you reach the best of the North Shore.

To reach the North Shore via a Central O'ahu freeway route, take the H-1 westbound past the airport, stadium, and Pearl City to the H-2 freeway. The H-2 will eventually downgrade to the narrow State Route, I 99. You'll travel through the one-horse town of Wahiawā and past Schofield Barracks before hitting a junction; if you're headed for Dillingham Airfield and Mokulēi'a, continue straight toward Waialua on HI 803, which later becomes Farrington Highway (HI 930). For Hale'iwa and most North Shore beaches, take the right turn to continue on HI 99. At the next intersection, turn left; Dole Plantation should be on your right as you head north. Past the pineapple fields, a cutoff for Hale'iwa will appear on your left, taking you into the town on HI 83. If you bypass Hale'iwa, you'll end up along the coast just beyond it, still headed eastbound on HI 83. With no traffic, you should reach Hale'iwa within an hour or so.

Central O'ahu

Stretching between the wide plains of the Wai'anae and Ko'olau Mountains and southward to the sea you'll find the region called Central O'ahu, with lesser known towns such as Wahiawā, Mililani, Pearl City, 'Aiea, and Waipahu. Frankly, the lack of extensive urban mystique, country charm, or extensively lush tropical vegetation puts this region into a

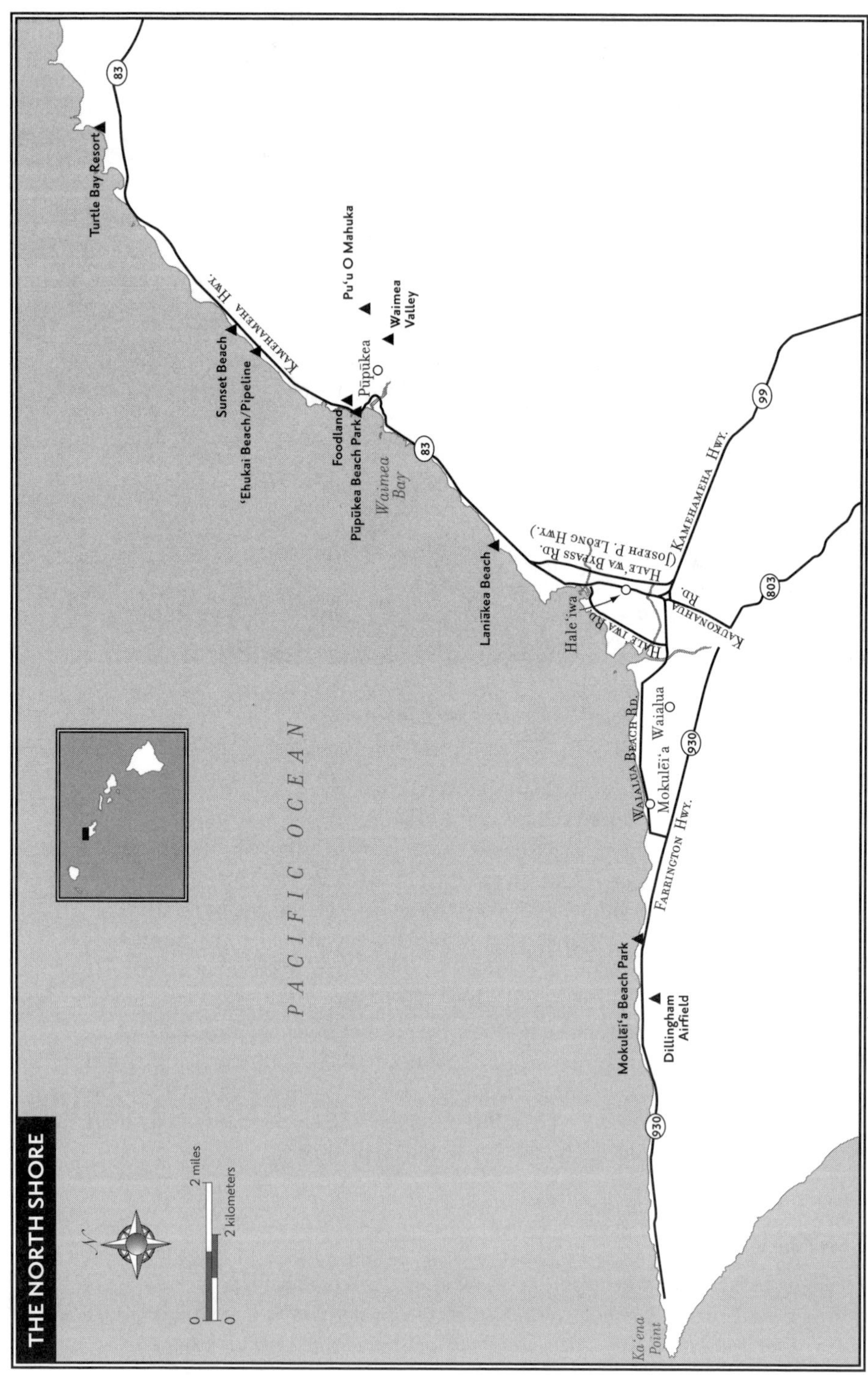
THE NORTH SHORE
2 miles
2 kilometers
0
0
PACIFIC OCEAN
Turtle Bay Resort
83
Kamehameha Hwy.
Sunset Beach
'Ehukai Beach/Pipeline
Pu'u O Mahuka
Waimea Valley
Pūpūkea
Foodland
Pūpūkea Beach Park
Waimea Bay
Laniākea Beach
Hale'iwa Bypass Rd.
(Joseph P. Leong Hwy.)
Kamehameha Hwy.
99
803
Kaukonahua Rd.
Hale'iwa Rd.
Hale'iwa
Waialua Beach Rd.
Waialua
Mokulē'ia
930
Farrington Hwy.
Mokulē'ia Beach Park
Dillingham Airfield
Ka'ena Point

category of agricultural and suburban sprawl that, while set in generally peaceful surroundings, would not feature enough to entice most visitors, were it not for Pearl Harbor. Don't miss visiting its historic sites—including the USS *Arizona* Memorial, USS *Bowfin*, USS *Missouri*, and the Pacific Aviation Museum.

To get there, take Kalākaua Avenue to Kapahulu Avenue, just before the zoo, and turn left, following the road about 2 miles until it passes under the freeway and curves left to a westbound H-1 freeway entrance. Once on the H-1, be careful to stick to it—just a bit beyond downtown the freeway splits, so be sure to follow it toward the airport. Past the airport look for the *Arizona* Memorial/Stadium exit (15A) and follow it to Kamehameha Highway (HI 99), where signs will soon direct you to the *Arizona* Memorial and a parking area that serves all of the above attractions. The drive time from Waikīkī to the *Arizona* Memorial is approximately 30 minutes with no traffic.

To reach the northern corridor of Central O'ahu, follow the H-1 to the H-2 freeway.

The H-3 Freeway connects to the H-1 and H-201/78 near Pearl Harbor and will transport you through the mountains to Kāne'ohe on the windward side. It's a gorgeous route.

LEEWARD O'AHU

For better or worse, Leeward O'ahu is slowly gaining attention as one of the last safe havens from commercialism and crowds. The area begins in 'Ewa in the southwest and continues west to commuter Kapolei, then around the bend northward to Kō 'Olina and the "forgotten" Wai'anae Coast, where you'll find the communities of Nānākuli, Wai'anae, and Mākaha. These areas have a history of unemployment, homelessness, and unfriendliness to outsiders, with a notable lack of appealing amenities and little small-town charm. You'll see people surviving in beach tents, mud-splattered trucks with hunting dogs and conquered boars in the back, and rundown homes. Needless to say, tourists tooling through in red convertibles are not always a welcome sight.

However, a drive to the end of Farrington Highway (HI 93) will reward you with a view of beautiful, deep blue waters and seemingly untouched golden sands, as well as striking mountainous features and wide, open valleys. You may even spot a pod of dolphins offshore. Take extra care to respect the privacy of area residents and, if you choose to stop, stick to well-populated beach parks and discreet, courteous behavior.

To get there, take Kalākaua Avenue to Kapahulu Avenue, just before the zoo, and turn left, following the road several miles until it passes under the freeway and curves left to a westbound H-1 freeway entrance. Stick to the H-1; you'll eventually pass Pearl Harbor, Waikele Premium Outlets, and Kō 'Olina (take this exit if your destination is Kō 'Olina or the J.W. Marriott 'Ihilani). The freeway will eventually become Farrington Highway (HI 93) and travel up the coast. After passing through the last town of Mākaha, the road becomes the 930 and soon degenerates into gravel and then dirt, with no way out other than turning around. The drive time from Waikīkī to Mākaha is approximately 90 minutes with no traffic.

By the way, you may notice that Farrington Highway runs both up the Leeward Coast and along the northwest corner of the North Shore. These roads never connect—although they both strain to meet each other at the impassable Ka'ena Point.

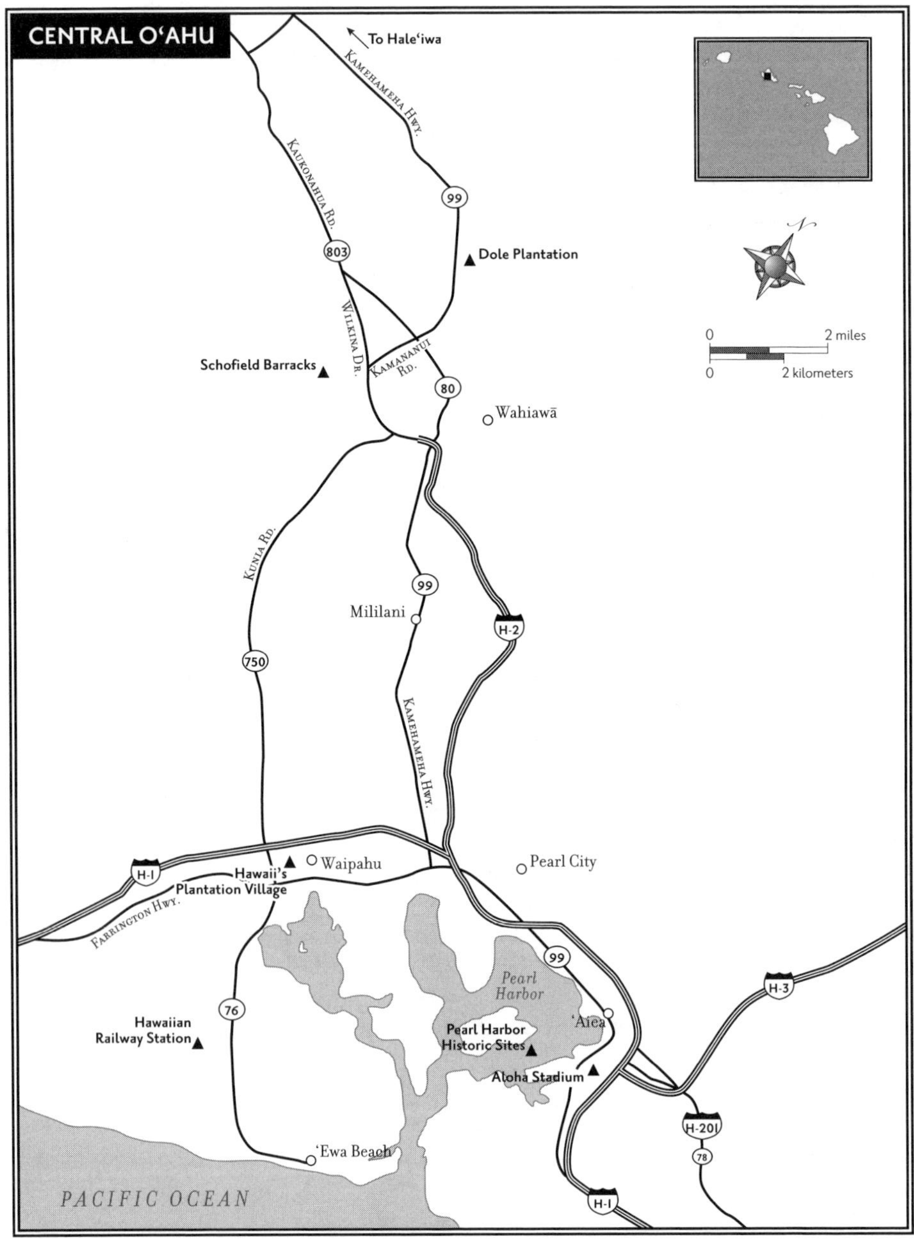

CENTRAL O'AHU
To Hale'iwa
Kamehameha Hwy.
Kaukonahua Rd.
99
803
Dole Plantation
Wilkina Dr.
Kamananui Rd.
Schofield Barracks
80
Wahiawā
0
2 miles
0
2 kilometers
Kunia Rd.
99
Mililani
H-2
750
Kamehameha Hwy.
H-1
Waipahu
Hawaii's Plantation Village
Pearl City
Farrington Hwy.
99
Pearl Harbor
H-3
76
'Aiea
Hawaiian Railway Station
Pearl Harbor Historic Sites
Aloha Stadium
H-201
78
'Ewa Beach
PACIFIC OCEAN
H-1

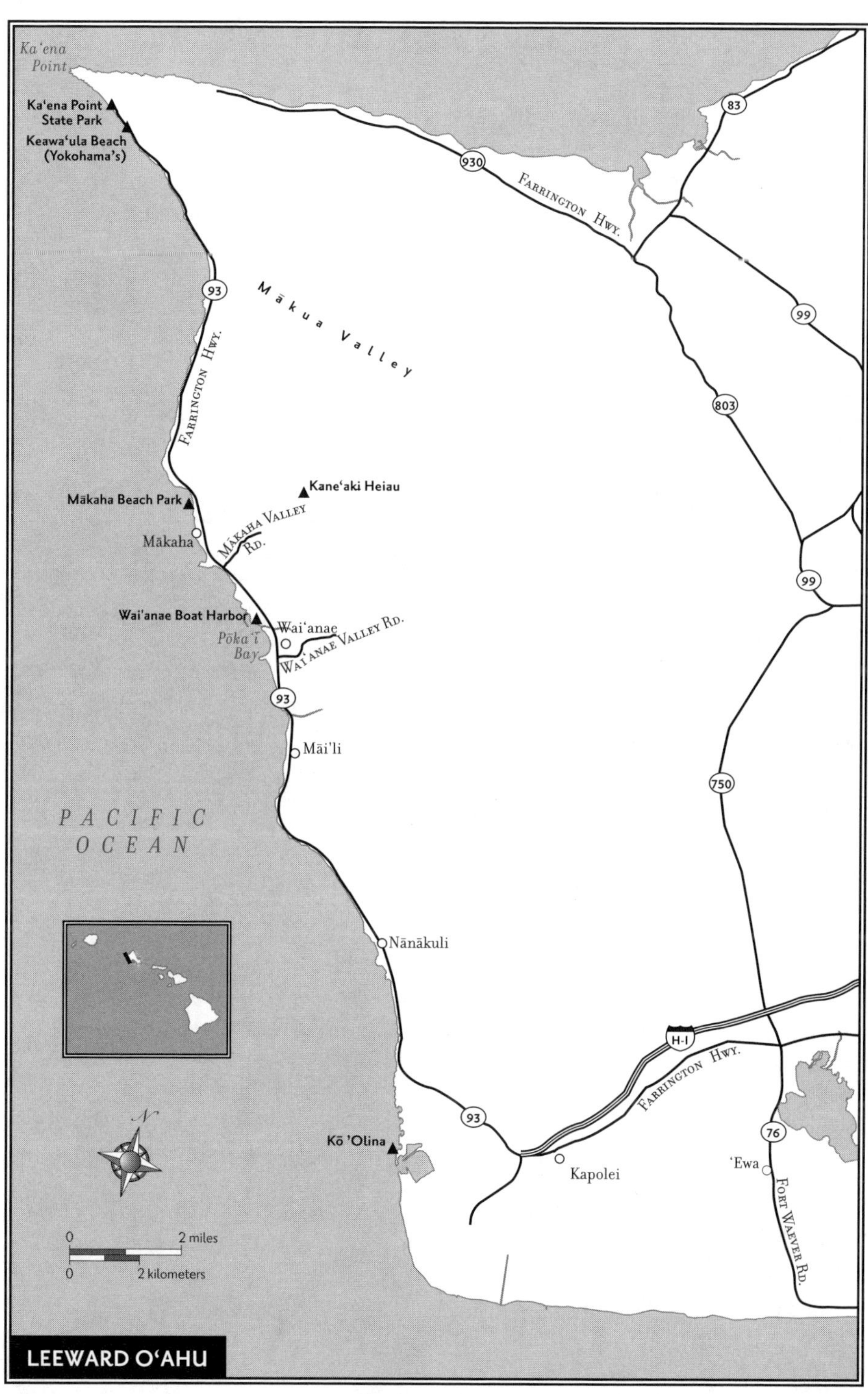
Ka'ena Point
Ka'ena Point State Park
Keawa'ula Beach (Yokohama's)
83
930
Farrington Hwy.
93
Mākua Valley
Farrington Hwy.
99
803
Kane'aki Heiau
Mākaha Beach Park
Mākaha Valley Rd.
Mākaha
99
Wai'anae Boat Harbor
Wai'anae
Wai'anae Valley Rd.
Pōka'ī Bay
93
Māi'li
750
PACIFIC OCEAN
Nānākuli
H-1
Farrington Hwy.
93
Kō 'Olina
76
Kapolei
'Ewa
Fort Waever Rd.
N
0 2 miles
0 2 kilometers
LEEWARD O'AHU

The world-class Halekulani's exclusive Vera Wang Suite is a vision of luxury. Photo courtesy Hotels & Resorts of Halekulani.

3

LODGING

E Komo Mai! Nou Ka Hale

"Welcome! The house is yours." This attitude has always been one of Hawai'i's trademarks, and before its many lodgings were built, both Hawaiian and foreign travelers on the road were welcome—and even expected—to stop and stay with villagers who lived along the way.

More than 5 million people now visit O'ahu every year, and Waikīkī has become one great *hale* filled with visitors. More than 95 percent of O'ahu's accommodations consist of hotel rooms, condo hotels, and timeshare units, and 85 percent are in Waikīkī. Since almost every one of you will choose to stay there, we've focused on reviewing a variety of its hotels, plus recommend a few alternative accommodations around the island. For camping information, see Chapter 7.

Towering Waikīkī is sandwiched between endless ocean and the Ko'olau mountain range.

Waikīkī businesses and hotels are currently undergoing unprecedented changes: new ownership, construction, massive renovation, conversion, gentrification, and anything else you can imagine—much like Las Vegas in the 1990s. By the time you read this, more will already have changed. If you haven't been here for several years, we think you'll be pleasantly surprised at the hip upgrades. Many of the largest hotels now offer services such as wedding planning, vow renewal ceremonies, activity desks, and cultural learning opportunities. Fully nonsmoking facilities, WiFi access, plasma televisions, and seated check-in are becoming standard, and the white rattan furniture so typical of Hawaiian hotel décor is becoming a thing of the past. Brace yourself for some not-so-hip higher room prices these days, however—in 2007, the average room rate hovered around $200, one of the highest in the nation. We don't expect to see it drop, as the Tourism Authority has set their sights on reducing visitor count and increasing per-visitor spending.

For those of you wishing for a country cottage-by-the-sea, a bit of independent Internet research may be necessary—but it's worth it. You can find a vacation condo right in Waikīkī or a vacation home outside of town, which usually rent by the week or the month and can cost much less than a fancy hotel room. Windward O'ahu and the North Shore have countless beach houses for rent, and Kailua in particular is a hotbed of vacation rental activity—a very sore topic for many residents, however, who feel overwhelmed by the increasing influx of vacationers and traffic in their otherwise peaceful and private neighborhoods.

O'ahu has surprisingly few traditional bed and breakfast accommodations, and most are not businesses operating from historic landmark homes, but rather folks periodically renting a room in their house for some extra cash. Also, Hawai'i has strict laws when it comes to food service permits, so the elaborate breakfast fixin's rarely happen. And in some cases, as we've unfortunately found out firsthand, professionalism can be a low priority.

Many of O'ahu's B&Bs and vacation rentals are currently operating without government permits; to a rent room or a house for less than 30 days, owners must have a "nonconforming use" certificate from the city.

Some quick facts you should know before you book any type of accommodation: In Hawai'i, a property claiming to be "beachfront" must be on the water and also have a beach directly in front of it. "Beachside" usually doesn't mean "beachfront." The term "oceanview" can mean "partial ocean view," "full ocean view," or "oceanfront view." Many Waikīkī hotels are now completely nonsmoking, so smokers would be wise to inquire. Almost all offer parking for your rental car, but in space-hungry Waikīkī, it could easily cost you between $10 and $25 per day. Hawai'i's "high season" runs from mid-December to early April, and again from June through August; during this time, as well as holidays, rates often increase significantly. Hawai'i charges a 4.712 percent excise tax and 7.25 percent transient tax on all transient accommodations, and even most unlicensed lodgings will require that you pay it. And no matter what anyone tells you their property offers—there are no private beaches in Hawai'i!

Pricing out Waikīkī hotel rooms these days is about as scientific as guessing which way a feather will blow in the wind. Nevertheless, we applied some high school math and a bit of intuition to basic rack rates to assess the overall average price category of each accommodation we cover—but remember that deep discounts are the travel industry's way of life. Visit hotel Web sites directly for some incredible deals, as well as www.hotels.com, www.expedia.com, and other online businesses. Plus, most hotels offer special AARP and AAA rates, in addition to corporate, military, *kama'āina*, and government rates. O'ahu's hotels do a brisk business, so book as early as you can. Most of the hotels listed here not only have many rooms accessible for handicapped visitors, but some also have rooms specially equipped; be sure to request one advance.

Lodging Price Codes

Inexpensive	Up to $100
Moderate	$100–200
Expensive	$200–300
Very Expensive	More than $300

Credit Cards

AE	American Express
DC	Diners Club
DISC	Discover Card
MC	MasterCard
V	Visa

Hotels and Other Lodging

Waikīkī

Aqua Bamboo & Spa
1-866-406-2782; 922-7777.
2425 Kūhiō Ave.
www.aquaresorts.com.
Price: Moderate.
Credit Cards: AE, DISC, MC, V.

Recent renovations to the boutique Bamboo aimed high, hitting targets such as "trendy" and "refreshingly intimate," but they skimped on quality and there isn't much one can do to fix poor views. The chic décor you'll see online doesn't entirely match the actual product; its teeny rooms feel surprisingly flimsy, the lobby doesn't have the level of sophistication touted, and we hear that the garage is frighteningly tight and that service can be slow. Guests are hip 20-, 30-, and 40-somethings, no doubt attracted by the hotel's online portrayal. On the plus side, it's way cuter than some other hotels in the area, two blocks from the beach, features 32-inch plasma televisions in-room, offers basic spa services, and has an awesome saltwater pool in the back. Staff was friendly enough and it's clean, and you won't see tour bus groups tromping through.

Aqua Coconut Plaza
1-866-406-2782; 923-8828.
450 Lewers St.
www.aquaresorts.com.
Price: Moderate.
Credit Cards: AE, DC, DISC, MC, V.

This brand new boutique addition to the Aqua Resorts family will undergo renovations in late 2007 which may spill into 2008. We expect it to be a good choice once work is complete—the diminutive highrise is already relatively charming and very affordable, just tired. The hotel sits two full blocks from the beach and faces congested Ala Wai Boulevard and the meandering Ala Wai Canal, with pretty city and mountain views and more vista-inhibited Waikīkī views in other directions. All rooms have kitchenettes and most have balconies. The lobby is just the right size and ambience for making new friends at the very basic Continental breakfast or at the Internet-connected computers, and the pool is good for a quick dip.

Aqua Hotel Renew
1-866-406-2782; 687-7700.
129 Paoakalani Ave.
www.hotelrenew.com.
Price: Expensive–Very Expensive.
Credit Cards: AE, DISC, MC, V.

Ultra-hip Hotel Renew features unusual touches and an intimate boutique vibe. Photo courtesy Bud Muth.

Just a half-block from the beach you'll find the totally new and boutique Hotel Renew, where internationally acclaimed San Francisco designer Jiun Ho has managed to meld together a very hip, mod-Asiatic sensibility with sophisticated and luxuriously minimalist statements.

For partial ocean views you'll need to be at the front of the building, above the 5th floor; on the back the city view is very limited and most rooms are a tad small. To compensate for that, the hotel has created some extra-cool rooms. Richly dark woods contrast with graphic lines of cream and hints of red, with black trim adding tailored touches throughout. A 32-inch plasma television hovers above a sleek desk space, decorative trays of trendy, quality products, and chic treats. Shoji screens create blackout window treatments. And with one touch of an iPodesque button by your bedside you can dim the lights—even the one in the bathroom.

Every room not only has free WiFi, but also comes with a wireless computer keyboard so you can sit in bed and surf the Internet. Wireless headphones enable you to let your partner snooze while you watch a movie. And in selected rooms that feel pleasingly Zen-like without a television, press a hidden button and a projector casts an enormous television, movie, and computer screen onto your wall. Very awesome.

Aqua Waikīkī Wave
1-866-406-2782; 922-1262.
2299 Kūhiō Ave.
www.aquaresorts.com.
Price: Moderate.
Credit Cards: AE, DC, DISC, MC, V.

If you judge the Waikīkī Wave by its simple, busy lobby, you won't be impressed. However, head up to any room and you'll find sleek, Asian-inspired, and even artistically vogue, comfortable rooms of decent size with nice modern touches, such as WiFi access. Although the flat-screen television is somewhat small, balconies look out onto modest and even good views, and you're right in the heart of Waikīkī's action and only about a block from the beach. All 247 rooms are nonsmoking and air-conditioned, and there's a small pool. All in all, this hotel is a great value for the price.

Appealing for its central location, the Waikīkī Wave also has a relatively high hip factor.
Photo courtesy Aqua Hotels & Resorts.

Aqua Island Colony
1-866-406-2782; 923-2345.
445 Seaside Ave.
www.aquaresorts.com.
Price: Moderate.
Credit Cards: AE, DC, DISC, MC, V.

This 44-story condo hotel has really improved over the years and gets high marks from many guests. It's a good value, very clean, modern, attractive, and view-friendly, and offers hotel-style rooms, studios with kitchenettes, and one-bedroom suites—plus translucent balcony railings. Although located several blocks from the beach and on a busy roadway, you're removed from the bustle of Waikīkī just enough to feel relief, and within it enough to feel hooked up. Vistas from most rooms run from good to stupendous—sometimes even panoramic. The pool is spacious and very nice, with a wide sunning deck and jet spa. Even for the higher-end rooms, a moderate rate can often be secured.

The Breakers
1-800-426-0494; 923-3181.
250 Beach Walk Ave.
www.breakers-hawaii.com.
Price: Moderate.
Credit Cards: AE, DC, MC, V.

Views aren't always everything! Right in the middle of Waikīkī is a charming, Elvis-era hotel that will appeal to those who love the low key and authentically retro. The Breakers has survived the urban highrise takeover by sheer long-term lease power. This little oasis sits only one short block from Waikīkī Beach.

Of course, the two-story, ranch-style gem is built around a snug little pool. Its wonderfully local staff is easygoing and helpful, and the ambience is peaceful, slow-paced, very clean, and even humble. Most rooms feature atmospheric shoji (sliding Japanese rice-paper doors) and look out onto the central courtyard. Two cute eateries are also on the property. We think this place is fabulous, especially for the price, and many guests return year after year.

The Breakers is a clean and charming hideaway among Waikīkī's mega-hotels.

The Cabana at Waikīkī
1-877-902-2121; 926-5555.
2551 Cartwright St.
www.cabana-waikiki.com.
Price: Moderate.
Credit Cards: AE, DC, DISC, MC, V.

Where do you stay when you're openly gay? The Cabana, of course! Folks flock to this four-story, gay-owned-and-operated hotel around the corner from the beach (including Queen's Surf, a popular gay men's strip) and famous Hula's hangout. Voted in the top 10 North American gay guesthouses by *Out & About,* you'll get a one-bedroom suite with a kitchenette, complimentary Continental breakfast, complimentary drinks during cocktail events, and other goodies. The hotel has no real view or pool, but there's a tiny hot tub next to the check-in counter. We hear it's less of a South Beach-style pickup joint and more of a welcoming, convenient, and moderately festive haven where you can make friends and enjoy Hawai'i. Most of the guests are men. They also organize some really fun trips, including a weekly, clothing-optional catamaran cruise. Note that there's no elevator, so you've got to have strong legs to get to your room.

Diamond Head Beach Hotel
1-800-535-0085; 921-7470.
2947 Kalākaua Ave.
www.marcresorts.com.
Price: Moderate.
Credit Cards: AE, DC, DISC, MC, V.

This moderately priced Marc Resorts hotel is ideally located along the peaceful "Gold Coast" section of Waikīkī: oceanfront, out of the din, and mainly surrounded by parkland. If you'd enjoy a pretty, 10-minute-plus walk into central Waikīkī for activities, meals, and nightlife, and don't have tons of money to spend, then this might be the place for you. Note that service amenities are virtually zero—the place is more condo than hotel, with no real lobby to speak of, no pool, or anything else.

The uniquely shaped Diamond Head Beach Hotel (at left) is a mellow getaway from central Waikīkī's hubbub.

The 1969 building is unusual—long and narrow with a tapering top, only a select few rooms have direct ocean views, while the rest either catch glimpses of Diamond Head Crater, Waikīkī, Kapi'olani Park, or nothing at all. Each unit is privately owned, so the quality of the room décor and upkeep can vary quite a bit. 1-bedroom suites offer full kitchens, eliminating the need to walk far for a meal. All of the units are air-conditioned, and many have balconies. Although it's located right on the water, you'll need to walk about one block to reach a sandy beach.

Doubletree Alana Hotel Waikīkī
1-800-559-4201; 941-7275.
1956 Ala Moana Blvd.
www.doubletreealana.com.
Price: Moderate–Expensive.
Credit Cards: AE, DC, DISC, MC, V.

Overall, this AAA Three Diamond, Hilton-owned property earns good reviews from guests, especially business travelers who appreciate the hotel's less touristy location, 24-hour business center, heated pool, and fitness center. Although located about a 10-minute stroll west from the heart of Waikīkī, you're still only about two blocks from the beach and across from a quiet park. Traffic is heavy along the roadway fronting the hotel.

The lobby is snug and tailored, and more practical than cozy. Service is professional and friendly, and although the hotel doesn't exude country charm, it holds a higher standard than many local boutiques when it comes to cleanliness and updated atmosphere. Rooms have been recently renovated, and all are air-conditioned and feature balconies as well as modest ocean, park, or city views; however, noise levels can be high on the balcony.

'Ewa Hotel
1-800-359-8639; 922-1677.
2555 Cartwright Rd.
www.ewahotel.com.
Price: Moderate.
Credit Cards: AE, DC, DISC, MC, V.

Again, views aren't always everything. The 74-unit 'Ewa Hotel is a perfect choice for many singles and couples, and it hosts numerous middle-aged Canadians who return every year and stay all winter. If the sun's out, you'll see them lining the balconies with legs propped up and novels in hand.

The hotel has one of the tidiest and most elegant micro-lobbies we've seen in Waikīkī, and although rooms start at a remarkably tiny 200 feet, it's relatively cheap to bump up to larger studios and suites, which have balconies and kitchens. (Strangely, microwaves and coffeemakers will cost you extra.) Long-term rates explain the high residency. There's no pool, and views from the lowrise look out onto back alleys and such, but you're right around the corner from the beach. This small and very simple gem is a safe, spotless haven with a warm, caring staff.

Hale Koa Hotel
1-800-367-6027; 955-0555.
2055 Kalia Rd.
www.halekoa.com.
Price: Inexpensive–Moderate.
Credit Cards: AE, DC, DISC, MC, V.

Since 1975, this enormous, 817-room beachfront hotel has served military members and their families—so unless you fall into one of those categories, you can stop reading right here.

Located adjacent to Fort DeRussy, which now consists mostly of a large beach park and the U.S. Army Museum, this hotel has one of the best locations in all of Waikīkī and views to match. It's been renovated and expanded recently, so the entire resort-like complex feels very modern and clean. Its landscaped grounds feature a variety of well-tended, tropical foliage with winding paths leading to the beach and a large swimming pool, and the café and bar surrounding it are popular with younger guests as the night falls. The restaurant Bibas has a great reputation, and all food on the property is relatively inexpensive. Room rates are likewise a bargain and are based on rank and room category.

Halekulani
1-800-367-2343; 923-2311.
2199 Kalia Rd.
www.halekulani.com.
Price: Very Expensive.
Credit Cards: AE, DC, MC, V.

Begun as a beachfront bungalow guesthouse more than one hundred years ago, the Halekulani ("house befitting heaven") has gradually developed into an internationally renowned five-star hotel. Ranked as the 17th best hotel worldwide by *Travel + Leisure* magazine in 2007 and on the "World's Best Places to Stay" list by *Condé Nast Traveller* magazine in 2006, you'll enjoy understated, lap-of-luxury living with excellent service that borders on geisha-like graciousness and professionalism.

Of course, everything you'll need is here, from the intimate spa to the mosaic swimming pool to the Five Diamond French restaurant to the Vera Wang Boutique to the little beach at your doorstep. Rooms are equally upscale, with flat-screen televisions, high-speed wireless service, deep soaking tubs, pure cotton robes, and twice-daily housekeeping—and nearly all have ocean views. The hotel's contemporary, open-air, wood- and golden-cream-trimmed halls, groomed grass courtyard, and sophisticated floral arrangements are unobtrusively elegant. There's no wrong move at the Halekulani. All three of its classic restaurants serve good to outstanding food with memorable views, and the Lewers Lounge bar is thoroughly plush and refined.

Hawai'i Prince Hotel Waikīkī
1-800-321-6248; 956-1111.
100 Holomoana St.
www.princeresortshawaii.com.
Price: Expensive.
Credit Cards: AE, DC, DISC, MC, V.

These are perhaps the most strikingly attractive modern hotel towers you'll ever find. Every single room looks straight onto the harbor and ocean beyond and is large as well as tasteful, contemporary, and sleek—although none have balconies. Glass elevators rise straight up on the outside of each tower, offering city and mountain views, and the grand lobby has an international, albeit slightly impersonal, feel. Situated on the cusp of Waikīkī, you're a five-minute walk from major beaches and Ala Moana Center. The pool overlooks the harbor.

The majority of the hotel's guests seem to be upscale Japanese travelers—perhaps the hotel's leeward-area, Arnold Palmer-designed golf course is the special draw—and residents love to treat themselves to the hotel's elegant Sunday brunch buffet service in the Prince Court restaurant, which we can confirm is indeed gourmet.

Hawaiiana Hotel
1-800-367-5122; 923-3811.
260 Beach Walk Ave.
www.hawaiianahotelatwaikiki.com.
Price: Moderate.
Credit Cards: AE, DC, DISC, MC, V.

This is one of the two quaintest, 1950s-era hotels surviving in Waikīkī, only a brief block from the beach and next to world-class hotels and shops. Once through its tiki-studded gates, you'll be transported to "the way it was" in the Territory days, before jumbo jets and Jamba Juice. Its mostly older "snowbird" guests (who all seem to know each other) come from all over North America and look well kempt, relaxed, and at home. The hotel has 93 clean and simple rooms, all with kitchenettes and some with balconies, that are configured in unpretentious, two- and three-story walkups around two cute swimming pools. The hotel is tasteful, quiet, and full of local-style family aloha—not the kind that implies screaming kids running around with water balloons, but a graciousness that will welcome you back year after year.

Quiet, local-style Hawaiiana Hotel is a modestly priced alternative to the big hotels.

Hilton Hawaiian Village Beach Resort & Spa
1-800-445-8667; 949-4321.
2005 Kalia Rd.
www.hiltonhawaiianvillage.com.
Price: Expensive–Very Expensive.
Credit Cards: AE, DC, DISC, MC, V.

This is Waikīkī's only mega-resort, with nearly 3,000 rooms spread across 22 prime, oceanfront acres of land secured back in the 1950s. The most outrageous place to stay in its day, it hosted many celebrities, such as Elvis, as well as politicians and other wealthy visitors. It still easily makes "top dog" lists such as *Condé Nast Traveller's* Gold List and *Travel + Leisure's* 10 Best Family Friendly Resorts/Hawai'i Hotels, and continues to attract both the famous and nonfamous alike. It consistently receives high satisfaction ratings from guests, although if you're looking for intimate and quaint, you'll be disappointed.

The resort overall isn't about outstanding service; it's about total-package ease. The property is a labyrinth of shops, bars, lobbies, hula shows, penguin and flamingo ponds, swimming pools, and several award-winning restaurants, all on a grand scale—plus there's an onsite chapel, fitness center, full spa, and just about anything else you can think of. The beach fronting the resort is wide and the water placid and shallow, perfect for kids. And whether you stay here or not, catch their

Friday night fireworks show. Note that the construction of a new time-share tower and a lagoon overhaul are underway, so stick to booking in the Ali'i Tower, Diamond Head Tower, or Tapa Tower until work's completed.

Hilton Waikīkī Prince Kūhiō
1-888-557-4422; 922-0811.
2500 Kūhiō Ave.
www.waikikiprincekuhio.hilton.com.
Price: Expensive–Very Expensive.
Credit Cards: AE, DC, DISC, MC, V.

We're inclined to go overboard in complimenting this four-star, brand new addition to the Hilton family. Although it won't fit everyone's budget and it's not oceanfront, you'll get a lot for your money, from a gorgeous interior to views, service, and a great overall location.

In the main lobby area, glamorous wood and marble notes mesh with atmospheric, golden lighting. At its bar/lounge nook, a trendy ambiance in burgundy, soft peach, and pale green prevails. All is spotless, recently renovated, and contemporary. Down the hall you'll find the very mod diner MAC 24/7, which will send food up to your room at any time of the day or night. A complimentary, 24-hour business center is at your beck and call. And of course, all the other requisite amenities are here, including a beautiful heated pool, fitness center, and so on.

All of the rooms are nonsmoking and have been completely redone. Not only are they chic and sleek, but they also feature 42-inch plasma televisions, high-speed Internet access, Hilton Serenity Beds, Crabtree & Evelyn® bathroom toiletries, and a very awesome unit that enables you to use the television screen with your laptop, video camera, MP3 player, and more. Last but not least are the views, which on higher floors give way to spectacular ocean and mountain vistas.

On the outside, the Hilton Waikīkī Prince Kuhio seems nondescript—but the inside is fabulous.
Photo courtesy Lew Harrington.

Hyatt Regency Waikīkī Resort & Spa
1-800-233-1234; 923-1234.
2424 Kalākaua Ave.
www.hyatt.com.
Price: Expensive–Very Expensive.
Credit Cards: AE, DC, DISC, MC, V.

This is probably the most international-looking and impressive hotel on O'ahu. Modern, massive, and architecturally striking with a towering, spaceship-sized, open-air atrium in the middle, it is late 20th-century mega-glamour at its best. In the new millennium, however, it feels like something is missing—maybe heart or charm, and prices for everything from a salad to a suite are marked up for the throngs of upscale Japanese visitors it attracts. Rooms are large, all have balconies, and some have spectacular near-oceanfront Waikīkī Beach and sunset views. The hotel also has a gorgeous swimming pool and Jacuzzi, plus full spa service.

'Ilikai Hotel
1-800-245-4524; 949-3811.
1777 Ala Moana Blvd.
www.ilikaihotel.com.
Price: Moderate–Expensive.
Credit Cards: AE, DC, DISC, MC, V.

The 'Ilikai Hotel has recently changed ownership and extensive renovations are lifting the aging hotel to a respectable status again, making it a solid choice for families or couples. This tri-star-shaped hotel overlooks a lagoon (where restoration is underway by the neighboring Hilton), the Ala Wai Yacht Harbor, and the ocean, and the enormous Ala Moana Center is just a five-minute walk away. It also has the enjoyable notoriety of being in the opening credits of *Hawaii Five-0.*

The hotel features a breezy porte-cochere and a bright, cream-toned, marble-floored lobby that looks out onto the harbor and expansive patio area. The vast building only offers about 350 guest rooms, as residents live in numerous other apartment units or rent them out by the month. All of its restaurants are noteworthy, including Canoe's, Sarento's, and Tanaka of Tokyo West, and the amenities you'd expect from a four-star hotel are all in place. Some rooms also have kitchens, saving you the trouble of leaving your room, and all are surprisingly huge at nearly 600 square feet. Waikīkī Beach is several minutes' walk east, or head about 10 minutes in the other direction to lounge at the more local-style Ala Moana Beach. If you crave the action of Waikīkī street life, however, you might find this hotel a bit too far on the wayside.

'Ilima Hotel
1-800-367-5172; 923-1877.
445 Nohonani St.
www.ilima.com.
Price: Moderate.
Credit Cards: AE, DC, DISC, MC, V.

This 98-room hotel is a good value and great choice, featuring modestly priced, 530-square-foot studios with full kitchens, balconies, air conditioning, and enough room for a family. Definitely shop online with 'Ilima—they offer significant Internet discounts. Little touches such as a free daily newspaper make you feel at home, and a heated dipping pool, fitness room, sauna, and laundry facilities make it hard to leave. Plus, free parking! In addition to studios, you can book larger suites and even penthouse accommodations without a severe price tag. The hotel is located in central Waikīkī along the Ala Wai Canal, about a two-block walk from the beach, with views either toward Diamond Head or downtown. The lobby is very cute and spotless, and the staff is friendly, warm, professional, and helpful.

Moana Surfrider
1-800-782-9488; 921-4640.
2365 Kalākaua Ave.
www.moana-surfrider.com.
Price: Very Expensive.
Credit Cards: AE, DC, DISC, MC, V.

On the National Register of Historic Places, and often called "the First Lady of Waikīkī," the 793-room, beachfront Moana Surfrider has entertained the rich and famous since 1901, with a guest history that includes Frank Sinatra, Lucille Ball, Amelia Earhart, Prince Edward of England, and Joe DiMaggio. It was also once home to the world-famous radio program *Hawai'i Calls,* broadcast to more than 30 countries from 1935 to 1975—somewhat of a "Grand Ole Opry" for Hawaiian music of the day. The hotel is built around a courtyard housing an historic, 150-foot-wide, 75-foot-high banyan, and for the past one hundred years the courtyard was the center of activity for dancing and celebration. It still serves cocktails and hosts Hawaiian musicians, as well as the occasional event. Its veranda is a luscious place to spend an afternoon. The gracious, pillared lobby is a masterpiece of Italianate style, and the entire building has an almost feminine, delicately ornate quality rarely seen anymore.

While the Moana earns rave reviews from most, critics cite small rooms and feel the pool is also somewhat small. The hotel has a plantation charm that suggests peace and quiet, but the lobby is often bustling with browsers, diners, and guests, and service can be spotty. As of 2007, the Moana became a Westin property, and although the hotel underwent a $50-million, award-winning renovation in the 1990s to restore it to its original design, further modifications are pending that could last into 2009.

The beachfront Moana Surfrider exudes bygone-era glamour and a gentile sensibility. Photo courtesy Starwood Hotels & Resorts Hawai'i.

New Otani Kaimana Beach Hotel
1-800-356-8264; 923-1555.
2863 Kalākaua Ave.
www.kaimana.com.
Price: Moderate–Expensive.
Credit Cards: AE, DC, DISC, MC, V.

The 1964 beachfront Kaimana is one of the better boutique choices in Waikīkī. Room décor is muted and tasteful with hints of rattan and florals, and though relatively uninspiring, rooms feature wall-to-wall glass doors leading to private balconies. Some rooms also feature kitchenettes, and all are nonsmoking and air conditioned. Standard parkview rooms run on the moderately expensive side, with partial-to-full oceanview rooms definitely costing some bucks—but if you splurge on the oceanfront deluxe, the vista from your room and balcony are unparalleled and totally romantic. The hotel's Hau Tree Lānai and Miyako Japanese Restaurant are charming, although expensive, dining options with pretty good food. Some guests have complained of indifferent treatment from hotel staff, and while we've received friendly dining service here, we've also noticed an occasional lack of enthusiasm from the front desk.

Undoubtedly the best aspect of the Kaimana is the location. One of just a handful of buildings along the "Gold Coast" section of Waikīkī, you'll be a pleasant 10-minute stroll from the crowds, chaos, and kitsch, and cradled between Diamond Head Crater, enormous Kapi'olani Park, and the sparkling sea. The hotel has no pool, but it sits right on the sands of a swimmable beach.

'Ohana Waikīkī Beachcomber
1-800-462-6262; 922-4646.
2300 Kalākaua Ave.
www.ohanahotels.com.
Price: Moderate–Expensive.
Credit Cards: AE, DC, DISC, MC, V.

A relatively large and modern hotel of 462 air-conditioned rooms, you'll be smack-dab in the center of bustling Waikīkī and just across the street from the beach. Although not by any means a resort, it retains a somewhat old-Vegas-style flavor that it promotes by hosting ritzy, ballroom-sized shows, such as illusionist John Hirokawa's "Magic of Polynesia" (which actually is very entertaining—skip the meal) and an Elvis impersonator show. Until he passed away in 2007, it also was home of the one and only Don Ho Show. All rooms are nonsmoking and several cater to guests with physical challenges.

Outrigger Luana Waikīkī
1-800-688-7444; 955-6000.
2045 Kalākaua Ave.
www.outriggerluanawaikiki.com.
Price: Moderate.
Credit Cards: AE, DC, DISC, MC, V.

A nice surprise: Standing alone along a hotel-less stretch of park a few steps west of the action you'll find the modest and tasteful, clean-as-a-whistle, Three Diamond Luana Waikīkī. Not much from the outside, and in fact fronting traffic-heavy Kalākaua Avenue, the interior is cool, quiet, and spacious, with marble, stone, and wood touches. This mid-priced hotel is highly recommended by many guests and is one of the better values in Waikīkī. Rates can vary widely; some are even a downright steal. Choose from freshly decorated hotel rooms, studios with kitchenettes, and one- or two-bedroom units with complete kitchens, including a dishwasher. A small pool, fitness center, laundry services, and a sufficient business center in the lobby make it a great choice for an easy and affordable long- or short-term stay. All units are nonsmoking and air conditioned, plus feature balconies with pleasurable views onto the 70-acre park, city, or distant ocean. The closest beach access is about a two-block walk through the park.

Outrigger Reef on the Beach
1-800-688-7444; 923-3111.
2169 Kalia Rd.
www.outriggerreef.com.
Price: Moderate–Expensive.
Credit Cards: AE, DC, DISC, MC, V.

At the time of writing, the relatively large Outrigger Reef was undergoing a massive and total $100-million renovation, scheduled to last through 2007 and possibly beyond. The worn-down, cheesy atmosphere should soon be replaced with a more contemporary flair, even a touch of elegance. The lobby will be lovely, with a new design highlighting its one-hundred-year-old Hawaiian koa wood canoe, plus treasures from the esteemed Bishop Museum; among other appealing plans, the hotel intends to bring in a series of Hawaiian cultural masters to share their knowledge with guests. We suspect the price category will rise into the expensive range, but with a beachfront location next to Fort DeRussy Park, nonsmoking rooms with fully modern amenities, and fancy shops and lodgings encircling the hotel, the new Outrigger Reef should be worth every penny.

Note that behind the hotel, construction on Trump Tower may last well into 2008 or beyond, so check on the status and find out where your room is in relation to the construction activity.

Outrigger Waikīkī on the Beach
1-800-688-7444; 923-0711.
2335 Kalākaua Ave.
www.outrigger.com.
Price: Expensive.
Credit Cards: AE, DC, DISC, MC, V.

With more than 500 air-conditioned, nonsmoking rooms—all with complimentary high-speed Internet access, cable television, balconies, and free local calls—plus an oceanfront location between two of O'ahu's most beautiful historic hotels, the Outrigger Waikīkī is a favorite of savvy visitors and garners overall good reviews. The new Waikīkī Plantation Spa in the hotel's penthouse gets high marks from guests and its Zen garden offers sweeping views of the ocean. Just about everyone knows that Duke's on the lobby level is the place for drinks and heavy socializing, as well as views. Don't miss the excellent Hula Grill on the second floor, either, with even better vistas onto Waikīkī Beach. Tastefully tropical rooms range from modest city views to one-bedroom deluxe oceanfront views that will blow you away. A swimming pool and fitness area tie up the package.

The hotel underwent renovation several years ago, and the upstairs lobby is truly beautiful. In the main lobby area, though, the feeling is still a bit 1970s and some of the shops leave much to be desired. Think of the hotel as a good party pad, with a great spa that will squeeze the cocktails from your wilted body the next day.

Park Shore Waikīkī
1-866-372-1732; 923-0411.
2586 Kalākaua Ave.
www.parkshorewaikiki.com.
Price: Moderate.
Credit Cards: AE, DC, DISC, MC, V.

The relatively small Park Shore earns overall high marks from guests, many of whom are repeat customers. The biggest complaint tends to be that the rooms feel small and simple—and they really are—but with very reasonable rates, world-class ocean and Diamond Head vistas, and a perfect location across from the zoo, the beach, and Kapi'olani Park, you may not care. If you don't need a lot of space and don't mind some street noise when on your balcony, this hotel is a good choice.

The lobby is decent, and rooms are tidy, air conditioned, and partly renovated, plus they offer cable television, Internet access, safes, and refrigerators. The smallest room is 300 square feet—too snug for a family. Because the hotel is situated at the end of the strip, east- and south-facing rooms offer gorgeous, unhindered room and/or balcony views from about the fourth floor up, but we suggest you request a room on at least on the ninth floor, or you'll overlook the pool and roof area.

Many rooms at the moderately priced Park Shore Hotel offer awe-inspiring ocean and Diamond Head views.

Queen Kapi'olani Hotel
1-800-367-2317; 922-4671.
150 Kapahulu Ave.
www.queenkapiolani.com.
Price: Moderate.
Credit Cards: AE, DC, DISC, MC. V.

This 19-story, mid-sized hotel seems to have fallen under the radar until lately, but it's a highly economical choice with some ridiculously fabulous views. That said, if you're looking for a hotel that delivers modern, large, sparkling rooms and sharp service, this is not the place for you. The lobby's décor is comprised of dusty, Victorian-style paintings of Hawaiian royalty and tropical touches that resurrect 1970. Don't expect a lot from the rooms; some might even be called rundown and miniscule. All are air conditioned and nonsmoking, and many have balconies. Spring for an ocean view on the east side—you'll be rewarded with one of the best in Waikīkī. Guests are a mix of tour bus groups and independent travelers. Shop online for really great rates.

Queen's Surf/Waikīkī Grand Hotel
1-888-336-4368; 923-1814.
134 Kapahulu Ave.
www.queenssurf.com.
Price: Moderate.
Credit Cards: AE, DISC, MC, V.

We once stayed here and savored our glorious views, but overall this mixed-use rental condo/hotel is fairly shabby and the vaguely indolent atmosphere doesn't help. We've talked to several reasonable-looking folks who feel that, although rooms are mostly tiny and often outmoded, the unbelievable wide-open vistas of Diamond Head and the ocean plus its reasonable price make it well worth it, and we ultimately agree—but only for those that can let go of room expectations. Because they're privately owned, the quality of rooms can really vary. Be sure to insist upon an east-facing room and high floor!

The lobby features a gay-oriented shop, and the state's largest and most famous gay bar on the second level can be a bit noisy for those with balconies just above it. Needless to say, the hotel has a somewhat higher percentage of gay and partying guests, which for some people will be a plus, and for others, like the elderly Midwestern couple we saw drifting in the lobby the other day, an uncomfortable surprise. The small, shady pool in the back is forgettable, but you're right across the street from the beach.

ResortQuest at the Waikīkī Banyan
1-866-774-2924; 922-0555.
201 ʻŌhua Ave.
www.RQWaikikiBanyan.com.
Price: Moderate–Expensive.
Credit Cards: AE, DC, DISC, MC, V.

The Waikīkī Banyan is popular with visitors from the Mainland as well as with residents coming to Oʻahu from neighboring islands, and its many amenities make it a good choice for families in particular. Its classic Hawaiiana lobby is one of the prettiest in Waikīkī, with a totally open-air front, a small waterfall and koi pond meandering through, Balinese-inspired furnishings, stone and dark wood trim elements, tropical plants, and oversized Honolulu landscape paintings and photographs.

All units are one-bedroom suites with about 600 square feet of space, full kitchens, and a sizeable balcony. Upper-story views can be impressive. Because each unit is privately owned, décor can vary, but the hotel is responsible for keeping them clean, which they do. The two guest room towers are linked by a recreation area with an older tennis court, large pool, jet spas, a sauna, putting green, and more. The hotel is on a quieter street about two blocks from the beach, but it's a straight and quick shot. Parking rates are also a good deal, and although rack rates are on the low end of expensive, great online prices are frequently available.

The Waikīkī Banyan offers spacious accommodations and an upscale feel and without the high cost. Photo courtesy ResortQuest Hawaiʻi.

ResortQuest Waikīkī Beach Hotel
1-866-774-2924; 922-2511.
2570 Kalākaua Ave.
www.RQWaikikiBeachHotel.com.
Price: Expensive–Very Expensive.
Credit Cards: AE, DC, DISC, MC, V.

The Waikīkī Beach Hotel is a major player on Kalākaua Avenue, with a recent $60-million renovation and 644 smoke-free, air-conditioned guest rooms—85 percent of which have partial or full views of Waikīkī Beach. The hotel sits directly across the street from the beach and no hotel fronts it, so rooms facing the water have remarkable, panoramic vistas.

The hotel's hip Hawaiiana décor creates a beach-extension atmosphere with peppy neon surfboards, tiki torches, bamboo, and tapa prints, and the well-known Tiki's Grill & Bar restaurant is located next to the pool. Fun amenities include fitness treadmills equipped with individual mini televisions, solar poolside shades that permit indirect tanning, and pack-and-go breakfasts that you can take beachside. A WiFi pool deck and a business area with computer access keep you in touch with the outside world, if you need it.

Rooms are small but intense and original, with dark Indonesian teak furniture, eye-popping bedding, and bamboo-bead closet curtains, plus 32-inch plasma televisions. Many also feature doors that connect two or more rooms together. While prices can be steep, online rates can be pretty good.

ResortQuest Waikīkī Beach Tower
1-866-774-2924; 926-6400.
2470 Kalākaua Ave.
www.RQWaikikiBeachTower.com.
Price: Very Expensive.
Credit Cards: AE, DC, DISC, MC, V.

We're thrilled by this magnificent little property across the street from Waikīkī Beach that keeps itself just under the radar for guest privacy. Yes, it's very expensive, and no online shopping will get you around that fact. However, listen to this: The smallest unit in the Beach Tower is a 1,050-square-foot, two-bedroom, two-bath beauty that can comfortably sleep six. And that's just the beginning—these multi-million-dollar condos and the intimate lobby were completely renovated in 2007 with subtly refined décor and every amenity you can imagine. The units feature elegant, full kitchens with all the extras, including a blender, dishwasher, rice cooker, and china for six; air conditioning; a washer and dryer; bathrobes; a DVD player; a Bose® wave radio; two flat-screen televisions; marble and granite surfaces; weave carpets; and high-speed Internet access. Some have wet bars, and housekeeping service is provided twice daily.

If that's not enough, add to it unobstructed, to-die-for, sweeping beach and ocean views from enormous balconies, plus a hotel pool, Jacuzzi, sauna, complimentary valet parking, and a staff dedicated to providing you with caring, personalized service. An excellent choice.

The ResortQuest Waikīkī Beach Tower is the lap-of-luxury condo living. Photo courtesy ResortQuest Hawai'i.

ResortQuest Waikīkī Circle Hotel
1-866-774-2924; 923-1571.
2464 Kalākaua Ave.
www.RQWaikikiCircle.com.
Price: Moderate–Expensive.
Credit Cards: AE, DISC, MC, V.

When room décor and hotel amenities are way less important than saving a few bucks while still securing an awesome view and location across from the beach, The Circle may be for you. The lobby's more of a desk window, the hotel has no pool, and the rooms are tiny, motel-style simple and a touch tired, but 85 percent of them have partial or full ocean views. Just roll out of bed, drop into the elevator, and step across the street to fall back asleep on the sand. The staff's friendly, and mats, floats, and other beach gear are yours for the borrowing.

ResortQuest Waikīkī Joy
1-866-774-2924; 923-2300.
320 Lewers St.
www.RQWaikikiJoy.com.
Price: Moderate–Expensive.
Credit Cards: AE, DC, DISC, MC, V.

This 93-room hotel on a central side street has long been known as a good standby for visitors. It's gone up in price, but still provides quiet and slightly dated but attractive and clean rooms, plus a bright, floral, open-air lobby that feels very comfortable. All rooms are nonsmoking and air conditioned, and include Jacuzzi tubs, Bose® stereo systems, and complimentary Continental breakfasts. A pool and sauna are on the property. Rack rates are fairly high, but they offer substantial discounts on their Web site.

Royal Hawaiian Hotel
1-800-782-9488; 921-4620.
2259 Kalākaua Ave.
www.royal-hawaiian.com.
Price: Very Expensive.
Credit Cards: AE, DC, DISC, MC, V.

There are few other hotels in Hawai'i that command respect like the Royal Hawaiian. Built in 1927, this historic building hosted the era's most glamorous icons, including Douglas Fairbanks, Shirley Temple, Clark Gable, the Fords, and the Rockefellers. Spanish-Moorish in design and similar to the Beverly Hills Hotel, it also uses pale pink as its trademark color, earning it the name the "Pink Palace of the Pacific."

The beautiful Royal Hawaiian Hotel is on the National Register of Historic Places.
Photo courtesy Starwood Hotels & Resorts Hawai'i.

If you can't find happiness and romance here, it's hard to find it anywhere. One of the three "grand dame" hotels of Waikīkī, it scored a beachfront spread with good swimming and great views of Diamond Head, and it feels spaciously luxurious. The impossibly tall coconut trees that grace the grounds are the last of ten thousand trees surrounding an old temple area called Helumoa, and all are said to be descendents of one palm planted in the 1500s by a Hawaiian chief. The interior of the hotel is perhaps even more beautiful than its exterior. Grand arches that go on forever, richly ornate Oriental-style carpets, natural lighting, and elegant lobby shops make it a pleasure just to walk through.

As of 2007, the hotel will undergo lobby modifications that could last well into 2009.

Sheraton Waikīkī Beach Resort
1-800-325-3535; 922-4422.
2255 Kalākaua Ave.
www.sheraton-waikiki.com.
Price: Expensive–Very Expensive.
Credit Cards: AE, DC, DISC, MC, V.

The centrally located, four-star Sheraton Waikīkī has ramped up over the years from a middling hotel to a powerhouse. This massive beachfront hotel looms over the antique hotels around it, and its unusual tri-star shape means that most of the 1,700 rooms have at least partial views of the ocean—some of which can be tremendous. For the most part, however, we think the hotel forsakes grace and enchantment for production, with a heavy sports bar and conference tone and a crowd management theme. It does have a lovely pool that overlooks the ocean, however, and the Hano Hano Room on the top floor is home to the very chic Cobalt Room lounge and a postcard-perfect view of Waikīkī Beach.

Over the next several years, upgrades will begin in the lobby, shopping venues, and recreation area—including the creation of a fantasy pool—so check in on the progress and ask where the quietest rooms will be.

W Honolulu Diamond Head
1-888-627-7816; 922-1700.
2885 Kalākaua Ave.

www.whotels.com.
Price: Expensive.
Credit Cards: AE, DC, DISC, MC, V.

We don't know what to make of this 49-room Starwood Hotel & Resort-operated W Hotel. The location is fairly dreamy on the ritzy and peaceful end of Waikīkī near the base of Diamond Head, and although not directly on the beach, the hotel sits no more than 100 feet or so away behind a row of condo towers. Attractive and hip things flit in and out of the doorway. Enter the lobby yourself and you'll know you're at a W—trendy and chic Asiatic elements infuse its atmospheric lighting with artsy boutique glamour, and you feel as if something especially enchanting is about to befall you. Unfortunately, we hear from many guests that the service, amenities, and rooms don't live up to expectations. Views don't become notable until you reach the higher floors, there's no pool or flat-screen television, and apparently the über cool attitude normally desirable at a W becomes irritatingly ironic as you dismay at the hefty price you've paid. Whether the W suits you will depend heavily on what you want from a hotel.

The boutique-sized W Hotel's best amenity is its location along the "Gold Coast" of Waikīkī.
Photo courtesy Starwood Hotels & Resorts Hawai'i.

Waikīkī Beach Marriott Resort & Spa
1-800-367-5370; 922-6611.
2552 Kalākaua Ave.
Price: Expensive–Very Expensive.
www.waikikibeachmarriott.com.
Credit Cards: AE, DC, DISC, MC, V.

The Marriott is an impressive hotel, although relatively nondescript, with 1,310 rooms and all the features and amenities you'd expect (including two heated swimming pools, a full spa, and a fitness facility), plus a location right across from Waikīkī Beach. Consisting of two tall towers with some mega views of the ocean and elsewhere, its decentralized design keeps it relatively underwhelming, which is good if you like it quiet and bad if you like to be seen. It's also home to several excellent restaurants, such as the award-winning Sansei, fantastic d.k. Steak House, and Arancino di Mare.

It also has the distinction of capturing one of Hawai'i's greatest songbirds, who gives free performances with family and friends on the Moana Terrace Thursday evenings: Hawaiian legend Auntie Genoa Keawe. Locals actually fly in from neighbor islands to hear this octogenarian sing *hapa-haole* classics in falsetto. This is a truly authentic Hawai'i experience, and one of the very last; we hope it will still be running when you're in town.

Waikīkī Beachside Hostel
1-866-478-3888; 923-9566.
2556 Lemon Rd.
www.waikikibeachsidehostel.com.
Price: Inexpensive.
Credit Cards: AE, DISC, MC, V.

This is the largest hostel you'll find, accommodating up to 170 people of all ages, although the majority is in the 20- to 30-year-old range. If you love the backpacker's life and mixing it up with other travelers, you'll get your fair share here. The staff is a friendly bunch of Hawai'i residents who'll be more than happy to give you travel tips, coordinate tours, or rent you equipment such as a surfboard or snorkel. The traditional dormitory-type rooms fit either four or six people in semi-private nooks, and all have full kitchens, phones for free local calls, bathrooms, and air conditioning. Some have balconies, although no views; there's also no pool. However, you'll be only about 100 paces from Waikīkī Beach.

Waikīkī Parc Hotel
1-800-422-0450; 921-7272.
2233 Helumoa Rd.
www.waikikiparc.com.
Price: Expensive.
Credit Cards: AE, DC, MC, V.

This 297-room, Halekulani-operated hotel tucked around the corner from the action experienced a complete renovation over the past year. Formerly an elegantly staid, Hawaiiana-themed boutique, it has transformed into a trendsetter, perfect for business travelers and the chic set. An exceptional level of personal service is its trademark.

In the immaculate, unfussy lobby, stone flooring and mood lighting contrast with candy-colored mod furnishings and a red Lotus car parked on the area rug. After passing through sleek hallways and into your ocean- or mountain-view room (go above the eighth floor for fabulous vistas), you'll find sharp, traditionalist décor with flat-screen televisions, high-speed Internet access, deliciously comfy beds, and sliding shutters that add just the right touch of charisma.

Waikīkī Parc also has a fitness center, business center, impressive pool, and a location right across from the beach, as well as a 7,500-square-foot glamour restaurant, Nobu Waikīkī, just opened by one of the world's leading Japanese fusion chefs.

The Wyland Waikīkī
1-800-222-8733; 954-4000.
400 Royal Hawaiian Ave.
www.doubletree.hilton.com.
Price: Expensive.
Credit Cards: AE, DC, DISC, MC, V.

The brand new, 405-room Wyland Waikīkī was inspired by the work of world-renowned marine artist Robert Wyland, noted for his leaping dolphin sculptures and mystical, undersea-themed mural paintings. This author doesn't go for such artwork, so we were suspicious—but we marched down there, and it turns out this place is actually pretty cool.

The very contemporary lobby has a touch of 1980s pop, but overall feels stylish and fresh with hip little seating nooks, low-key sculptures, a pillar-shaped aquarium, and several surprisingly beautiful, abstract giclées playing off muted walls. Two gargantuan G5 Macintosh computers await guests free of charge. Teen angst is resolved in the lobby's specialty room, where kids can hang out in beanbag and massage chairs and play XBox on flat-screen televisions, while parents loll nearby at the lovely pool. All guest rooms have balconies, flat-screen televisions, and wood furnishings, although mostly very modest views onto streets. By the time you arrive, the spa should also be complete.

Greater Honolulu

ResortQuest at the Executive Centre Hotel
1-866-774-2924; 539-3000.
1088 Bishop St., Downtown.
www.RQExecutiveCentre.com.
Price: Expensive.
Credit Cards: AE, DC, DISC, MC, V.

Perhaps you're not the Waikīkī type and have no interest in the visitor scene—or, you're a business traveler with a tight schedule. The Executive Centre in downtown's financial district will put you right in the middle of real Honolulu business life. This hotel has an elegant marble-and-glass lobby and sharp rooms with jet spas, and you can even get accommodations with kitchen facilities, a washer and dryer, or a wet bar. Free high-speed Internet access is available, as well as a business center, complimentary breakfast, and a swimming pool.

Note that during the week the hotel and surrounding area are filled with bustle; on weekends, however, downtown becomes a ghost town.

The Kahala Hotel & Resort
1-800-367-2525; 739-8888.
5000 Kahala Ave., Kahala.
www.kahalaresort.com.
Price: Very Expensive.
Credit Cards: AE, DC, DISC, MC, V.

The Hilton-turned-Mandarin-Oriental-turned-The-Kahala is experiencing a rough transition to independent ownership, and in 2007 it lost its Five Diamond AAA status. These days the level of service doesn't always live up to this enclave's hefty price tag, but we aren't sure whether it's a chronic problem or just a passing phase. This 1960s beachfront resort several miles from Waikīkī has always been a gem, with a pedigreed history that rivals the best in the world. Nearly every American president has stayed here since it opened, as well as royalty, rock stars, and other rich and mighty. One of the greatest attractions to high-end visitors is its capability to cloak you in privacy, opulence, and security. No minor bonus are the facts that the building itself is lovely, the food is great, the setting is gorgeous, and the hotel is surrounded by a golf course and wealthy suburbs.

The atmosphere is generally serene, with dolphins lolling in the suite-side lagoon, wind tinkling through a 28,000-piece glass chandelier in the open-air lobby, and the little crescent of sand in front of the hotel melting away in the corners as the tide comes in. On weekdays, stroll farther down the beach away from the property and you might have it all to yourself except for the nearby zillion-dollar mansions owned by international tycoons.

If you don't mind shelling out major money for this ambience and have the patience to tolerate less-than-perfect service for at least the time being, it could still be the setting for a great vacation. Note that the hotel plans a piece-by-piece restoration that may yield impressive results.

The Kahala's lobby reflects a glamour that outshines most Waikīkī hotels. Photo courtesy The Kahala Hotel & Resort.

WINDWARD O'AHU

Schrader's Windward Country Inn
1-800-735-5071; 239-5711.
47-039 Lihikai Dr., Kāne'ohe.
www.schradersinn.com.
Price: Moderate.
Credit Cards: AE, DC, DISC, MC, V.

Schrader's is the type of place you either completely fall for or want to run from. Let's call it a funky, rambling family motel of sorts with a tropical atmosphere, very local touch, and amazing views from verandas. It's located on the side of a rundown country road where several monster trucks are sure to be parked or revving, and you may receive "stink eye" from a neighbor or two, as we did. If you can get past that, you'll find a row of sort of Wild West-style abodes built between plenty of foliage and above an ancient lagoon-like fishpond area with vistas onto dramatic country mountains—and you'll know you're very far indeed from Waikīkī.

They have about 30 rooms and none have any pretense at all—although some have nice views. Choose from studios through three-bedrooms with full kitchens or kitchenettes. The hotel also has a nice little pool and several other modest amenities, plus serves complimentary Continental breakfasts and a free dinner on Wednesdays. Although on the waterfront, there's no beach here, but they'll take you out on their pontoon boat or let you use kayaks and other equipment.

Located in a working-class neighborhood, Shrader's is "real" Hawai'i living with million-dollar views.

NORTH SHORE

Backpacker's Vacation Inn

1-888-628-8882; 638-7838.
59-788 Kamehameha Hwy., Pūpūkea.
www.backpackers-hawaii.com.
Price: Inexpensive–Moderate.
Credit Cards: DISC, MC, V.

This is a hostel that offers both private accommodations and hostel beds. In the crowded season, drive down the North Shore's main highway and you'll suddenly see bunches of mostly young folks tromping around on their way to the beach, having just spilled out of its many doors.

The property includes three lodgings. As its name implies, The Beach House is right on the beach and features studios for up to four people, including private baths and either kitchens or kitchenettes. All have balconies or patios and look right onto the ocean. The Main House is across the street from the beach and has dormitory rooms, plus a kitchen and lounge area. The Plantation Village area down the street offers nine simple, teeny, hippiesque cabins that range from a large ocean view option to dorm style, plus plenty o' chickens running around.

They'll also be able to set up all kinds of activities for you, including biking and whale watching excursions.

Kē Iki Bungalows

1-866-638-8229; 638-8829.
59-579 Kē īki Rd., Sunset Beach.
www.keikibeach.com.
Price: Moderate–Expensive.
Credit Cards: AE, MC, V.

Ten one- and two-bedroom beachside bungalows and one studio bungalow await those who love surfer funk more than sleek or punk. All have been recently renovated and are tropically tasteful, clean, and cozy—and in fact several are downright kickin' with dead-on ocean views. All have full kitchens and the essential beach scene elements such as barbecues, picnic tables, and hammocks.

These little pads get good reviews from travelers, and the owner can even coordinate a wedding ceremony and reception on the beach and property for you. Considering that you can fit up to five or six people in many of the units, the price is great—split it with friends and enjoy a beach house for a few days.

Turtle Bay Resort

1-800-203-3650; 293-6000.
57-091 Kamehameha Hwy., Kahuku.
www.turtlebayresort.com.
Price: Expensive–Very Expensive.
Credit Cards: AE, DC, DISC, MC, V.

There is no real hotel or resort anywhere on peaceful Windward O'ahu or the North Shore—except for Turtle Bay. Built in the 1960s, it has undergone a dramatic upgrade in the last decade and its generously sized oceanview rooms and lobby are truly lovely at last. The property spans 880 oceanfront acres of land and features many hundreds of oceanview hotel rooms, plus cottages, villas, a full spa, two world-class golf courses, tennis, horseback riding, and good restaurants. Laid back and gorgeously situated, except for the moody weather typical of the area, Turtle Bay will make you think you've left O'ahu for a quieter neighbor island.

However, the atmosphere here these days is touchy. Turtle Bay finally intends to make good on their 20-year-old, very controversial plan to build thousands of new time-shares and other luxury highrise hotel units along the pristine coastline. The rural and economically depressed nearby community of Kahuku, as well as long-time North Shore residents, are struggling to decide whether they need service jobs more than their treasured country lifestyle, and some folks are fighting back.

Turtle Bay Condos
1-888-266-3690; 293-2800.
57-091 Kamehameha Hwy., Kahuku.
www.turtlebaycondos.com.
Price: Moderate–Expensive.
Credit Cards: AE, DC, DISC, MC, V.

On the endless property of Turtle Bay Resort you'll find a series of two-story studio, one-, two-, and three-bedroom golf course condos that you can rent for a minimum of two nights. Note that none of them are connected with the resort, although they share land space. Each unit offers a fully equipped kitchen and a washer and dryer; however none have ocean views and each is privately owned, meaning that décor can vary widely. The condo development maintains its own pool and tennis courts. A one-bedroom unit typically features a king or queen bed plus sleeper sofa, and prices are very reasonable for the amount of living space. You'll need to arrange to pick up the unit key yourself from an office in the community of Kahuku, down the road.

Leeward O'ahu

Hawaiian Princess at Mākaha
1-800-776-2541; 696-1234.
84-1021 Lahilahi St., Mākaha.
www.hawaiianprincessmakaha.com.
Price: Moderate.
Credit Cards: AE, DC, DISC, MC, V.

The Hawaiian Princess is by no means a resort—or even really a hotel, for that matter. These are privately owned condo units that are rented to vacationers for a minimum of four nights. Unfortunately, several someones decided a while back that this very rural, economically depressed, and unbroken coastline needed a few highrises to spice it up, and this is one of them. On the other hand, you now have an awesome view of the sandy beach and gorgeous ocean from every otherwise modest one- or two-bedroom unit.

JW Marriott 'Ihilani Resort & Spa at Kō 'Olina
1-800-626-4446; 679-0079.
92-1001 'Ōlani St., Kapolei.
www.ihilani.com.
Price: Very Expensive.
Credit Cards: AE, DC, DISC, MC, V.

Part of the 640-acre Kō 'Olina "empire," the 'Ihilani is a 17-story, 387-room hotel on the ocean and is surrounded by an excellent golf course, villas, and other highrise and lowrise accommodations. Built out of coastal scrubland, it's the only luxurious place to stay on the entire southwestern half of the island and offers pretty much everything you'd need for a restful vacation, including the award-winning restaurant, Roy's. Standard rooms average a whopping 640 square feet and have either mountain or ocean views, although most have at least some view of the water. The hotel also features a renowned 35,000-square-foot spa, plus activities such as catamaran cruising and swimming with stingrays in an enclosure.

The man-made lagoons are picture-perfect and the hotel is moderately grand. However, a few drawbacks to the 'Ihilani are the excruciatingly high prices and your complete isolation on a relatively dry, dusty plain. Frankly, there's nothing to do or see in the neighborhood surrounding the resort, and limited sightseeing on the rugged Leeward Coast, so plan to either drive a long way on the freeway or spend your entire vacation on the hotel property.

The 'Ihilani is an isolated, but beautiful, way to spend a vacation. Photo courtesy John DeMello.

Marriott's Kō 'Olina Beach Club
1-877-229-4484; 679-4700.
92-161 Waipahē Pl., Kapolei.
www.marriottvacationclub.com.
Price: Very Expensive.
Credit Cards: AE, DISC, MC, V.

Another lodging opportunity out at Kō 'Olina is the Beach Club, which consists of waterfront highrise condo units (called "villas") ranging up to three bedroom/three bath in size. Turquoise beach lagoons shape the coastal outline and several swimming pools and Jacuzzis ensure that you'll get your day in the sun—plus guests may use the 18-hole golf course on the property. The villas are lovely, modern, and well stocked with all amenities, including a washer and dryer, wireless Internet access, and a full kitchen.

Again, however, the location is tough if you're planning to sightsee on the island. Also, towers around the property may still be under construction—so be prepared for possible noise. But, if you've got the whole family in tow and have no desire to do much other than loll in the water, you might be very happy here.

Parade pā'ū riders spend hundreds of hours handcrafting their own garlands.

With permission from Aloha Festivals and rider.

4

CULTURE

Living Local

Although much of Hawai'i's claim to fame is year-round warm weather and beautiful beaches, Honolulu has an exciting mix of cultural attractions well worth your missing a few days or more baking in the sun. In fact, visitors to O'ahu need not be interested in nature and outdoor recreation at all to justify the trip. This section of the book will point you toward the best, brightest, and most delightfully "local" cultural activities in Honolulu and around the island that you won't want to miss.

O'ahu has an extensive and unique history with numerous points of interest. One of them happens to be world-famous: Pearl Harbor. The *Arizona* Memorial, USS *Missouri,* USS *Bowfin,* and now the new Pacific Aviation Museum make visiting this National Historic Landmark a fascinating and emotionally powerful experience for anyone.

To explore ethnic Hawaiian history and culture in more depth, be sure to visit the world's premier collection of Oceanic artifacts at Bishop Museum, as well as the lovely 'Iolani Palace, home of Hawai'i's last reigning queen. Guided walking tours of the downtown area are also an excellent way to learn about modern Hawaiian cultural history as well as its period architecture.

The art lover would be amiss in not viewing the eclectic and celebrated collection at the Honolulu Academy of Arts. Serious art enthusiasts may be interested to learn that since 1967, Hawai'i's government has required that at least 1 percent of the costs of every public building be used to purchase or commission art for display in public places. This was the first such legislation in the United States and it has resulted in a tremendous collection, as well as a more attractive Honolulu. Another "artsy" thing you can do is join in the wildly popular First Friday downtown gallery walk and "social hour," held each first Friday of the month from 5 to 9 PM. On the last Friday of the month, many of the same faces appear at the Honolulu Academy of Arts for the themed and stylish "ARTafterDARK," one of the hippest social events in town.

Hawai'i's people have always loved music and performance of every kind. Local symphony, opera, and community theater productions are of high quality and often feature guest stars, and their sophisticated patrons are loyal fans and supporters.

Attending an authentic Hawaiian music concert or hula competition is educational and enjoyable—as well as essential for grasping the soul of Hawai'i's people. Most hula and Polynesian reviews in Waikīkī or at visitor lū'au are tailored for tourists; some are reasonably authentic and others absurdly hokey. We recommend you poke through the local papers and talk to your concierge or lodging hosts for updates on upcoming music and dance concerts geared toward residents. Tickets may be difficult to obtain, even for what may appear to be humble, provincial events, so book as early as possible.

For up-to-the-minute calendar listings of all events around town, do as the residents: Pick up the daily *Honolulu Advertiser* or *Honolulu Star-Bulletin* (the most comprehensive listings are in the *Advertiser's* "TGIF" section, out on Fridays, and the *Star-Bulletin's* "HiLife" section, out on Fridays); the free *MidWeek* (in stands Wednesdays and Fridays), or the more "alternative" and also free *Honolulu Weekly* (in stands Wednesdays). Helpful online calendar resources include the Hawai'i Visitors and Convention Bureau (www.calendar.gohawaii.com), Hawai'i Events Online (www.hawaiieventsonline.com), and Hawai'i Public Radio (www.hawaiipublicradio.org).

The cost of living in Hawai'i is extremely high and salaries are often surprisingly low. Some museums and other activities are forced to charge relatively steep entrance fees to offset costs, but assist residents in affording the exploration of their own hometown by offering *kama'āina* rates—in other words, price breaks. In order to qualify, a Hawai'i identification card must usually be flashed. In addition, active military personnel with ID may qualify for discounts as well. Price ranges listed in this chapter feature standard adult and child rates; if you're a Hawai'i resident, in the military, a senior, or a student, be sure to inquire about reduced rates.

Another great way to save a few bucks is by flipping through the free booklets you'll find in newsstands throughout Waikīkī, which are stuffed with coupons. Steer clear of the "too good to be true" offers peddled on every sidewalk by effervescent salespeople.

Although information in this chapter has been confirmed as close to printing as possible, please always call ahead for the very latest updates.

Beyond the Census: Hawai'i's Rainbow of People

Hawai'i's culture and ethnic diversity are unique and colorful, resulting from centuries of immigration and intermarriage between peoples mostly from Oceania, Asia, and North America. Even today, immigration is at a fever pitch: Nearly 20 percent of its current population was born not only outside of Hawai'i, but also in a country other than the U.S., and almost 30 percent speak a language other than English at home. As you might then imagine, about half of Hawai'i's marriages take place between residents of differing ethnic backgrounds, and more than 20 percent of residents are of "mixed" ethnicity—compared with less than 3 percent nationwide—and we are proud of it. Miss Hawai'i 2006's delightful Hawaiian-Tahitian-Spanish-German-Italian-Filipino-Portuguese heritage, for example, was no doubt admired for its "real local girl" mix.

During your stay, you may encounter terms of identification that have morphed beyond the grasp of a dictionary. None of them are considered by most residents to be derogatory by definition—it just depends on who uses them and how!

You'll probably hear the word *haole*, which, after all is said and done, now simply means "Caucasian." Be aware that a handful of folks—usually *haole*—believe it to be offensive and don't like it. *Kama'āina* is used commercially to identify state residents from visitors, often for the purpose of price breaks, and to indicate born-and-raised residents (often of *haole* background) whose families have a long history in the Islands. *Malihini* refers to newcomer residents, or those who act as if they're "fresh off the boat." All people who live in Hawai'i are called Hawai'i residents; but, only the approximately 20 percent of residents who claim Hawaiian ethnic heritage can also correctly be called Hawaiian, or Native Hawaiian. And although "Native Hawaiian" has found its place in the vernacular, referring to residents as "natives" is never appropriate.

Another subtly confusing term is "local." Most *malihini* refer to themselves as locals, but many longtime residents use "local" to refer only to "real island-style," naturally darker-skinned residents who appear to be ethnically Hawaiian—even if they aren't. The phrase "local resident" is more neutral, encompassing, and standard. "Local" can also be used as an adjective to signify anyone for whom authentic island customs are so ingrained that he or she cannot help but follow them, as well as in complimentary reference to authentic island living and lifestyles (such as the subtitle of this very chapter). It can even jokingly refer to something that has been done or made in a very laid-back, homemade, amateur style instead of "Mainland professional."

Though perhaps not politically correct, in Hawai'i we often use ethnic background and "localness" as a way to describe ourselves or affectionately poke fun at each other. Some of the most beloved island comedians have based their routines on caricaturizing the hilarious and endearing interplay between Hawai'i's various groups of people. A classic skit recording still available in stores is Rap Replinger's *Poi Dog*, and *Pidgin to da Max* is a must-have "dictionary" that implicates every ethnicity in Hawai'i in its comic exploration of local language use and cultural diversity.

ARCHITECTURE

Like its culture, Honolulu's architecture is a summary of many contradictory influences, resulting in what can sometimes amount to architectural mayhem. Even within the design of a single building several fashions often overlap, making stylistic identification negotiable.

While some buildings here have been designed with beauty and environmental harmony in mind, others are clearly "insta-structures," quickly assembled for rapid visitor and resident expansion, especially during the booms of the 1960s, 1970s, and 1980s. Another development frenzy is underway—and as is common, the developers are from outside of Hawai'i. The Trump International Hotel & Tower in Waikīkī set a world record in 2006 by selling all 464 units—a total of $700 million worth of real estate—in only eight hours. A boomtown joke residents like to repeat is that Honolulu's most common bird is the crane.

If you haven't been here before, expect a strong, modern skyline rather than the thematic and feminine lowrise grace for which cities like San Francisco are noted. Honolulu's dramatic tropical setting makes it a beautiful city, and its haphazard mix of pagodas, stately Italianesque mansions, Gothic-style government buildings, futuristic skyscrapers, wooden plantation houses, and everything in between make it an interesting city. Go with the flow and savor the good stuff—there is indeed plenty if you know where to look and understand what you see.

Many of Hawai'i's most notable homes and buildings were either designed or inspired by 20th-century island architects such as Hart Wood, Charles Dickey, Alfred Preis, Oliver Traphagen, and Vladimir Ossipoff. Other internationally famous architects, such as Julia Morgan and I. M. Pei, have also created buildings in Honolulu, including the YWCA and the East-West Center, respectively.

The only authentic (albeit reconstructed) Hawaiian grass hut still in existence on O'ahu is housed in Bishop Museum and was brought from Kaua'i in 1902, with the foresight of preserving the craftsmanship for future generations. The last occupied grass house on the island was an anomaly in Punalu'u, where the respected David Ka'apuawa-okamehameha, his Oregon-born wife, Myrtle, and their children chose to live in traditional style until the late 20th century.

Hawai'i's first frame houses were assembled from kits perhaps as early as 1800 or shortly before. In 1820 the first company of missionaries to the Islands arrived, followed by several frame structures shipped from New England, that were modeled after simple meetinghouses and farmhouses in their homeland. The Mission Houses Museum in the Capital Historic District displays the actual buildings in which these missionaries lived, right where they originally stood. Their design was the first of a series of Honolulu structures that eventually became known as Hawaiian mission or New England-style architecture.

Another excellent example of this type of architecture sits adjacent to the museum and next to a small cemetery filled with the remains of the early settlers themselves. Kawaiaha'o Church was built by hand between 1837 and 1842 using coral blocks chiseled from the reef, and it is one of Hawai'i's most treasured monuments.

Many of Honolulu's highrises feature innovative designs.

European architectural styles, such as Gothic and Renaissance, influenced the development of several of the most important mid- to late-19th century spiritual and governmental buildings in Honolulu. Some of the most noteworthy still standing are St. Andrew's Cathedral, Ali'iolani Hale, and the celebrated 'Iolani Palace.

At the turn of the century, Hawaiian architecture embraced the European Romanesque designs then popular on the Mainland. Although its stern, dark facades were heavy-handed for the Islands, local architects added Hawaiianesque touches, such as dark lava rock, to create a unique look. Several buildings at Bishop Museum exemplify this style.

In the 1920s, Mediterranean design elements such as rounded arch openings, stucco walls, arcades, and tile mosaics and roofs became what is now known as the California mission style. Honolulu Hale (City Hall), the King Kalākaua Building (downtown's post office), the YWCA, and the luxurious Royal Hawaiian Hotel in Waikīkī are several buildings that embraced its carefree tone for a postwar people.

A detail on 'Iolani Palace's exterior is whiskered in the fashion of the day.

Some of the most beautiful craftsman, shingle, colonial plantation, Tudor revival, and bungalow style homes in Hawai'i are in Honolulu's beautiful Mānoa Valley. Once filled with taro paddies, and then rice paddies as Japanese immigrants settled in the back of the valley, Mānoa became a stylish neighborhood for wealthy kama'āina and newcomers in the early 20th century and remains so today. Drive through and delight in its leafy streets and myriad of classic trimmed-lawned, porte-cochered American homes, some of which feature local embellishments such as Japanese gates.

Beaux Arts and art deco design also flourished across the state. Several of Hawai'i's most appealing buildings still stand from this era, including the recently restored Hawai'i Theatre. Architects augmented these styles with Hawaiian motifs and tropical treatments to once again create a unique look and feel more in tune with the Islands.

One of Hawai'i's most influential and pleasant architectural styles dots the landscape in nearly every well-established neighborhood across the state: the Hawaiian plantation-style home. Built mainly during the early- to mid-20th century, these very modest, one-story abodes typically feature wide roofs with deeply bracketed eaves, wooden plank walls, a square box layout, diminutive rooms and nooks, and are often painted in two-toned, contrasting, earthy colors, such as forest green and tan. Sometimes a gracious wraparound or yawning front porch has been added. Classic landscaping often includes mature mango trees, ti plants, and papaya or banana trees.

The plantation-style home seems to convey the laid back, natural, homey qualities many residents cherish; interesting associations, considering most plantation-style houses once did belong to struggling laborers who at the time probably had bigger dreams. In fact, many of today's residents are the descendents of the immigrant plantation workers who lived in these very houses. Perhaps the plantation home's appeal is that it harks back to a humble history and simpler time.

The "between war" years helped set the tone for Hawai'i architecture; the romance of "Hawaiiana" had taken hold and thousands of people were migrating from the Mainland. By the 1950s, minimalism, craftsmanship, and reinvented Asiatic forms became vogue and divisions between rooms dissolved, even between the inside and the outside of the home.

Residents treasure the modesty and history of plantation homes, which are found in older neighborhoods across the state.

The 1960s ushered in a stark transformation not only in Honolulu architecture, but also in highrise construction worldwide. Older hotels and buildings downtown were razed to make way for a new fleet of functional, sealed towers modeled after an American form of Bauhaus architecture, stressing clean lines and dull colors. Island designers offset austerity with interior touches, such as expensive koa wood paneling and soft floral patterns. Built in 1969, the Hawai'i State Capitol Building is a fascinating illustration of how this type of minimalist architecture played out in the tropics. Many of these types of buildings are still erected in Honolulu today, with blue glass exteriors as the latest highrise trend.

Today's more fashionable architectural and interior design tastes echo Hawaiian and Asiatic elements found in quality older homes and public buildings, but add new twists of Pacific fusion. Popular influences include the steep, double-pitched roof reminiscent of grass huts, Hawaiian plantation-style housing, sleek Asiatic (especially Balinese) and Pacific patterns, lines, and décor, the extensive porch or lānai, and plenty of natural breezeways for cooling room temperatures. Textures and shapes augment earthy colors and outdoor living has been reclaimed.

You may hear the word *ho'okipa* used in reference to building architecture and public spaces, meaning "a Hawaiian sense of place." This sense of a structure needing to "belong" in Hawai'i has long been a guiding principle for some of Hawai'i's best architects and designers. A recent resurgence of *ho'okipa* may be partly in response to a growing number of large, air-conditioned, Southern California-style stucco homes being built, especially in wealthier neighborhoods popular with many newcomers. And even today, some homes and other structures are still designed with respect for ancient Hawaiian traditions or superstitions, such as facing doorways and furniture to accommodate the potential passing of night marchers (warrior spirits) through the house. Many new public buildings, office spaces, and private homes often remain unoccupied until they receive a traditional Hawaiian on-site blessing.

Cinema

While O'ahu's movie houses mainly feature large-scale, first run blockbusters, there are a few Honolulu venues that continue to host classics, documentaries, foreign productions, and other "alternative" films. Additionally, the **Louis Vuitton Hawai'i International Film Festival** (528-3456; www.hiff.org) features films from around the world and is considered by some to be one of the best film festivals in the country. The HIFF hosts an annual spring showcase of films and the actual festival in the fall.

One of O'ahu's most popular movie spots over the last several years has been right on the beach at Waikīkī: **Sunset on the Beach** (923-1094). As of 2007, double features were shown only one weekend per month year-round, so be sure to call in advance to check the schedule and selections. If it's happening, head down to the 30-foot screen on the sand across from the Honolulu Zoo and enjoy free live local entertainment and post-sunset movies along with thousands of residents and visitors (get there early for a chair). Movies shown tend to be first runs appropriate for family viewing, but special festival films, and even complete advanced screenings of *Lost* episodes, cast in attendance, are not uncommon. This wonderful event depends on sponsorship, so hopefully it will continue in 2008.

Note that there are no longer any movie theaters in Waikīkī.

Art Houses

Greater Honolulu

The Doris Duke Theatre (532-8768; 900 S. Beretania St., Makiki) is the Honolulu Academy of Arts' pristine theater, named after tobacco heiress Doris Duke. It features a variety of excellent documentaries, foreign films, and alternative productions, in addition to lectures and performances. The homegrown and funky **Movie Museum** (735-8771; 3566 Harding Ave. Suite 4, Kaimukī) is worth the fight for public parking. With a handful of Barcalounger-style seats and a bring-your-own-grub policy, this one man band operated by a true film buff will treat you to vintage and cult classics as well as new goodies.

Commercial Movie Houses

GREATER HONOLULU

The most agreeable locations for big-time movies in town are **Consolidated Theatres Kahala** (593-3000; Kahala Mall, 4211 Wai'alae Ave., Kahala), **Consolidated Theatres Ward Stadium** (593-3000; Ward Centre, 1044 Auahi St., Kaka'ako), and **Signature Theatres Dole Cannery** (526-3456; 735B Iwilei Rd., Iwilei). All feature first run flicks. The Ward theaters have become very popular with visitors and residents, so get set for a lively crowd and severe parking challenges on weekends. **Wallace Theatres Restaurant Row** (526-4171; Restaurant Row, 500 Ala Moana Blvd., Kaka'ako) is great for families or a cheap night out. It features blockbusters a few weeks or months after their debut; therefore, they only charge you about a buck. Expect numerous teens and a lobby in slight disarray.

WINDWARD O'AHU

Signature Theatres Windward Stadium (234-4000; Windward Mall, 46-056 Kamehameha Hwy., Kāne'ohe), **Consolidated Theatres 'Aikahi** (593-3000; 'Aikahi Shopping Center, 25 Kāne'ohe Bay Dr., Kailua), and **Consolidated Theatres Stadium** (593-3000; Temple Valley Shopping Center, 47-260 Hui 'Iwa St., Kāne'ohe) are first run Windward theaters, but the 'Aikahi goes for the edgier titles.

Lā'ie Cinemas (293-7516, Lā'ie Shopping Center, 55-510 Kamehameha Hwy., Lā'ie) is the only movie house serving the entire northern windward side and eastern North Shore areas. It shows family-oriented, G through PG-13 first run movies only and is closed Sundays, in keeping with the town's Mormon lifestyle.

CENTRAL O'AHU

If you're staying in Hale'iwa, you might opt to drive south to **Consolidated Theatres Mililani Stadium** (593-3000; Town Center of Mililani, 95-1249 Mehe'ula Pkwy., Mililani) for a wider selection, Sunday show, or R-rated movie.

LEEWARD O'AHU

Anyone in the leeward area can head to **Consolidated Theatres Kapolei** (593-3000; 890 Kamōkila Blvd., Kapolei) for a blockbuster lineup.

Classes and Lectures

The enormous University of Hawai'i at Mānoa (UHM) hosts all types of free public lectures by resident faculty or visiting experts, such as its **Distinguished Lecture Series** (www.hawaii.edu/uhm/dls).

UHM also offers professional, summer, and noncredit courses through its **Outreach College** (956-5666; www.outreach.hawaii.edu) that can run as short as a day or two, as well as Elderhostel, which enables older adults to participate in interesting community service projects at places like the Honolulu Zoo and USS *Missouri*. They are also considering offering programs for visitors of all ages that combine faculty lectures on Hawai'i history and culture with related community excursions. For information on Elderhostel, or to show your support for or inquire about whether a lecture/community experience has been established, call Tim Slaughter at 956-2036.

In the Kāne'ohe/Kailua area, **Windward Community College's Office of Continuing Education** (235-7400; www.wcc.hawaii.edu) offers noncredit courses lasting a day, a week, or longer, such as Japanese brush painting, the art of bonsai, and writing retreats.

Most of the major museums, such as Bishop Museum and the Honolulu Academy of Arts, also offer lectures and other special learning opportunities, as does the Hawai'i State Library.

Guided Historic Walking Tours

Nothing beats the personal experience of a walking tour, and we highly recommend you do one or more while you're here. If you're staying in Waikīkī, be sure to check with your hotel concierge regarding free Waikīkī history walking tours. With all of the construction at the time of writing, tours had stopped, but we're sure at least one will be resurrected by the time you arrive. Both the historic Moana Surfrider and Royal Hawaiian hotels offer interesting free tours of their properties as well.

For guided culinary tours, see Chapter 5; for other types of cultural and activities-oriented transported tours, see Chapter 7.

GREATER HONOLULU

AIA Architectural Walking Tour (545-4242; www.aiahonolulu.org; 119 Merchant St., Suite 402, Downtown) This wonderful tour is offered by the Honolulu chapter of the American Institute of Architects, so you know it'll be good. Led by well-known architect Frank Haines—who was in charge of restoring the historic Ali'iolani Hale—as well as other local architects, you'll spend about two-and-a-half hours exploring downtown Honolulu's historic and modern buildings and learning about the culture and history. Reserve well in advance; tours take place Saturdays at 9 AM if enough participants sign up. The $10 fee is donated to a fund for scholarships and guest lecturers.

Chinatown Walking Tour (533-3181; www.chinatownhi.com; 42 N. King St., Chinatown) Sponsored by the Chinese Chamber of Commerce, you'll get the inside scoop on the real workings of Chinatown as you spend about two-and-a-half hours poking through its herbal shops, markets, acupuncture shops, and other specialty stores. Reserve in advance; tours take place Mondays at 9:30 AM if enough participants sign up. The fee is $10.

Hawai'i Geographic Society Tours (538-3952; 1-800-538-3950) This local organization is into leading cultural exploration tours both in Hawai'i and overseas. In Honolulu, you can sign up for all kinds of trips, including a visit to Hawaiian petroglyphs and natural sites; a temple tour that includes different religious houses of worship; an architectural and historic downtown walk; and more. At least two people must sign up and the fee is $15 per person.

History Makers Walking Tour of Honolulu's Greater Capital Cultural District (531-0481; www.missionhouses.org; 553 S. King St., Downtown) You'll journey on a two-hour walking tour of the greater cultural district, connecting sites with historical stories of Native Hawaiian and *haole* residents of the 19th and 20th centuries. The tours cost a bit of change, but they have worked hard to dig up extensive and unique information to share with you and all proceeds benefit the nonprofit museum. Call in advance for tour price and schedule, as well as to make reservations.

Historic Buildings and Sites

O'ahu has approximately 120 architectural sites on the National Register of Historic Places, more than 100 of which are right in Honolulu. Several of the sites are actually small historic districts, and three of the best are neatly packaged together in the greater downtown area: the Hawai'i Capital Historic District (as in "capital city," not "capitol building"); Merchant Street Historic District; and Chinatown Historic District.

Once a dusty plain with a small fishing village called Kou, these post-contact downtown districts bloomed around Honolulu's deep harbor. They were the center of urban life from the early days of foreign ships until the end of World War II, when the beaches of Waikīkī became a stronger attraction.

Visit them and you'll still see real life: bank executives relaxing with lattes in the shadow of office towers; down-and-outers trying to make a buck on Hotel Street; senior citizens laden with pink grocery bags waiting for a Chinatown bus; and maybe even the mayor stepping out of a Victorian- or art deco-era government building. One of the charming aspects of Honolulu is that it's so accessible. Government dignitaries and the town's biggest CEOs don't hide within impenetrable office labyrinths; they're more likely sitting at a park bench with friends, eating salad with chopsticks. Seeing these neighborhoods on foot is the best option, although a quick drive-by is possible. Should you choose to walk and want deeper coverage of the area's architecture, consider one of the walking tours listed above.

When visiting the greater downtown area, skip the shorts and resortwear and blend into the grittier, business-oriented urban landscape as you would at home. The highrise area of downtown's financial district, as well as Chinatown, offer scant amusement for children; if you're with kids, stick to the Capital District and Aloha Tower Marketplace areas. Keep sightseeing to daytime hours, when the streets are busy. If you head into Chinatown at night for a meal or performance, be alert and low key.

In Waikīkī, two hotels will really appeal to architectural and historical buffs: the Moana Hotel and the Royal Hawaiian Hotel. These were the first of Waikīkī's luxurious resorts and attracted Hollywood stars and other American royalty since opening day. Amble through on your own, or join in their free history tours.

Parking is a tiresome and expensive challenge both in the downtown area and Waikīkī. TheBus and the Waikīkī Trolley make stops in these neighborhoods and run frequently. Otherwise, see Chapter 9 for suggestions on where to park.

Below you'll find O'ahu's most significant and visited historic structures listed in alphabetical order by region. In addition to the noteworthy sites listed below, be sure to review the "Museums and Galleries" section of this chapter, as most museums on O'ahu are located in beautiful historic buildings as well.

Hawaiian archaeological sites have been specially listed in Chapter 6.

Waikīkī

Moana Surfrider

922-3111.
2365 Kalākaua Ave.
www.moanasurfrider.com.
Historic Status: National Register of Historic Places.

The Moana is the oldest standing hotel in Waikīkī, having opened in 1901, and one of the most beautiful. Many of the golden era's glamorous stars stayed here, and the hotel is full of history—in fact it's officially listed as one of the Historic Hotels of America. In the

1990s it underwent a $50 million renovation that restored it to its former glory and earned it numerous national awards. We recommend you join in their free public tours offered Mondays, Wednesdays, and Fridays at 11 AM and 5 PM. No reservations are needed.

Royal Hawaiian Hotel
949-4321.
2259 Kalākaua Ave.
www.royal-hawaiian.com.
Historic Status. National Register of Historic Places.

The "second" lady of Waikīkī, the Royal is reminiscent of the Spanish/Moorish Beverly Hills Hotel in style, right down to pink walls and palms—and is therefore often called the "Pink Palace of the Pacific." Opened in 1927, it immediately attracted the famous and wealthy from around the world and both its interior and grounds still exude the luxurious and subdued atmosphere of the past. At one time, pineapple juice reportedly flowed from its fountains. A free historical walk is offered to the public every Monday, Wednesday, and Friday at 2 PM, illuminating Hawai'i's past along with interesting stories about the hotel itself.

The Royal Hawaiian has always attracted a fashionable crowd. Photo courtesy Starwood Hotels & Resorts Hawai'i.

GREATER O'AHU

Ali'iolani Hale/King Kamehameha Statue/Judiciary History Center
539-4999.
417 S. King St., Downtown.
www.judiciaryhistorycenter.org.
Open: Monday through Friday 9–4. Closed on state and federal holidays.
Admission: Free.
Historic Status: Building and statue are listed on National Register of Historic Places.

The trilogy of Ali'iolani Hale, the famed King Kamehameha Statue, and the Judiciary History Center are rolled into one tidy location in the Capital Historic District. Read about the Judiciary History Center in the "Museums and Galleries" segment of this chapter.

Designed in the renaissance revival style, Ali'iolani Hale (also known as the Judiciary Building) was originally created to serve as the royal palace for King Kamehameha V, but never fulfilled its destiny; instead, the architectural plans were transformed into the Kingdom of Hawai'i's first and much-needed government building. When it finally opened in 1874 during the reign of King Kalākaua, it housed the legislature, treasury, boards of health and education, and the Supreme Court. It now houses the Hawai'i State Supreme Court, Judiciary Administration, and the Judiciary History Center. On these steps in 1893, annexationists declared their overthrow of the Hawaiian kingdom. A time capsule containing pictures of the royal family, stamps and coins of the kingdom, a newspaper, and other items were buried by Kamehameha V during the construction of the building and still lie beneath its walls.

Fronting Ali'iolani Hale is a statue of Hawai'i's most celebrated and revered king, Kamehameha I, which was commissioned by the Hawaiian monarchy in 1878. Designed by a Boston sculptor, it was bronze cast in Italy and shipped to Hawai'i from Germany—only to be lost at sea when the vessel and its crew sank near the Falkland Islands. The statue you see is a duplicate cast from the same mold, dedicated in 1883 as part of King Kalākaua's coronation ceremony. The first statue was later recovered by fishermen and now rests in the birthplace of the king, on the island of Hawai'i; as predicted by numerous Hawaiians before the original statue had even left Europe, it would never stand anywhere but at Kohala. The 2008 Hawai'i state quarter features this statue.

On June 11, King Kamehameha is celebrated with a series of events and an elaborate parade. One of the highlights of the year is the draping of his statue with 26-foot-long strands of 'ilima and plumeria lei—don't miss it.

Aloha Tower
528-5700.
Pier 9, 1 Aloha Tower Dr., Downtown.
www.alohatower.com.
Open: Daily 9–5.
Admission: Free.
Historic Status: National Historic Landmark, National Register of Historic Places.

An official national landmark on the old harborfront near downtown's Capital Historic District, Aloha Tower rivals Diamond Head and Waikīkī Beach as an internationally recognized Hawai'i icon. Built in a mix of art deco and late Gothic revival styles in 1926, this

10-story tower was the tallest building in the state until nearly 1970. One of the most endearing symbols of Hawai'i's welcome to the world, it is enthusiastically emblazoned with "Aloha" in letters large enough that visitors arriving by ship after a long voyage could see long before they reached the shore. The tower itself is visible from 15 miles out at sea, and in earlier days was a navigational landmark. During World War II, it was painted in camouflage and served as a command and control center.

Take the ancient elevator to the observation lookout at the top for a great view in all directions.

CHINATOWN HISTORIC DISTRICT

Bordered approximately by Nimitz Highway, Nu'uanu Avenue, Vineyard Boulevard, and River Street in the downtown area, Chinatown is still an authentic, working neighborhood—although many of its latest occupants come from Southeast Asia instead of China.

Chinatown is surely one of Hawai'i's most "colorful" districts, built by hundreds of enterprising Chinese immigrants who left the plantations to open their own businesses. In modern times, it has three faces: the trendy, the hardworking, and the derelict. The heartbeat of Chinatown is a bustling population of Asian immigrant families, and mom-and-pop vegetable shops and fish markets overflow with cheery, crochet-vested grandmas armed with pink plastic shopping bags. Over the last ten years, hip boutique shops, galleries, clubs, and restaurants have also established themselves in pockets of the neighborhood.

Long notorious for petty criminal activity, Chinatown also features the most down-and-out prostitutes O'ahu has to offer, and its Hotel Street sidewalks are often laced with troubled individuals seemingly hung-over from harbor grog shops boarded up one hundred years ago. Plenty of "good time" hotspots during World War II are now just sketchy dives—Smith's Union Bar, established in the mid-1930s, is one of several dilapidated remnants of the golden era still operating. These are by no means visitor destinations, but they're interesting when viewed from a historical perspective.

The neighborhood has also had its share of crises. At the turn of the century, Chinatown experienced two consecutive, deadly bubonic plague outbreaks that the Board of Health treated with massive quarantines and destruction of affected areas by fire. The second controlled eradication fire took on a life of its own and by the time it was quelled, 38 blocks were wiped out. And during the 1941 attack on Pearl Harbor, stray anti-aircraft bombs crashed down on Chinatown's northern boundary, killing 12 residents.

The best way to experience Chinatown is simply to wander it by day, or take a walking tour (see "Guided Historic Walking Tours" in this chapter, or "Cooking Classes and Culinary Tours" in Chapter 5). You'll find evidence of the past everywhere, such as at **Lai Fong** (1118 Nu'uanu Ave.), the one-hundred-year-old **O'ahu Market** (corner of King and Kekaulike St.), and **Kuan Yin Temple** (at Foster Gardens, 50 N. Vineyard Blvd.), plus loads of acupuncturists, candy and lei vendors, herbalists, vegetable markets, and noodle shops. Peek into lei shops to watch the flowers being strung by hand. Visit on Saturday morning for the liveliest market atmosphere. Avoid wearing shorts or other "resorty" garb—Chinatown is not a tourist zone.

Honolulu's Chinatown is relatively small, but totally authentic.

Diamond Head Lighthouse

3399 Diamond Head Rd., Diamond Head.
Open: Not open to public.
Historic Status: National Register of Historic Places.

In 1878 a simple lookout was built at a rocky outcropping below Diamond Head crater near Waikīkī, at which Swedish-born "Diamond Head Charlie" was employed to keep an eye out for approaching ships. The first actual lighthouse on the spot was erected near his lookout in 1899 and featured a lens imported from France. When cracks were later found in its base, a new lighthouse was built at the same site in 1918. Diamond Head Lighthouse still houses the original 109-year-old lantern and watch room ironwork. Now fully automated, however, it continues to guide today's vessels as they maneuver off the coast. A keeper's bungalow built in 1921 sits adjacent to the tower. Operated by the U.S. Coast Guard, the lighthouse stands nearly 57 feet high and provides 7,300 candlepower that can be seen from a distance of 18 miles at sea. It's considered one of the best-known lighthouses in the world.

Although there's no place to pull over next to the lighthouse, Diamond Head Road has several lookout points popular for parking. From the lookouts you'll get three sights for the price of one: the lighthouse tower, a famous windsurfing spot offshore, and the spectacular coastline.

Hawai'i Capital Historic District

Bordered approximately by Ala Moana Boulevard, South Street, Vineyard Boulevard, and Richards Street in downtown Honolulu, the Capital Historic District houses many of Hawai'i's most famous historic sites, including 'Iolani Palace, the original mission houses, the statue of King Kamehameha, Ali'iolani Hale, Kawaiaha'o Church, and the State Capitol. Beautiful, wide lawns and mature monkeypod, banyan, and shower trees surround many of the older buildings, making it one of Hawai'i's most lovely and interesting walkabouts—although prepare for excessive vehicular traffic noise. Bustling, renowned Waikīkī may appear to visitors to be the center of Honolulu, but most residents would agree that downtown is still the heart of the city.

Except for a 25-year period during which Lahaina, Maui served as the seat of Hawai'i's government (1820-1845), downtown Honolulu has been the hub of local politics since 1810, when King Kamehameha moved his court from Waikīkī to the ever-busy harbor area. All community life centered on activities at the harbor, which overflowed with ships, commercial transactions, and people of every kind; from palace windows the royal household could at that time observe what was transpiring on the docks.

In the holiday season, the Capital District area is especially attractive, dressed to the nines in city-sponsored Christmas ornamentation as part of the yearly "Honolulu City Lights." The décor-viewing frenzy increases as the big day approaches, culminating in late-night auto gridlock Christmas Eve. By the way, government officials insist that the district name refers to the "capital city," not the "capitol building," and thus the choice of spelling; it's clear, however, that not everyone received, or agrees with, that memo.

Hawai'i State Capitol

586-0178.
415 S. Beretania St., Downtown.
www.capitol.hawaii.gov.
Open: Building courtyard and grounds always open. Tours offered Monday, Wednesday, and Friday at 1:30. Meet outside Room 415, 4th floor. No reservations needed.
Admission: Free.
Historic Status: National Register of Historic Places.

No other capitol building in the United States is reportedly as unusual as Hawai'i's. Opened in 1969—ten years after the Hawaiian Islands became a state—this colossal, open-air masterpiece was purposefully designed to be extremely modern yet pay homage to its unique heritage.

Sometimes buildings look larger than they actually are; but Hawai'i's capitol building is larger than it looks. Nearly 360 feet long and 270 wide at its base, it's flanked by 60-foot-high columns on all four sides and features a towering crown ceiling hovering 100 feet above the ground. In the courtyard below it, the 600,000-piece mosaic "Aquarius" glimmers in the sunlight, 40-foot-long tapestries hang on curved walls, chandeliers made from hundreds of nautilus shells suspend from above, and 15-foot seals weighing 7,500 pounds each mark every entrance.

The capitol's structure itself is a representation of life in Hawai'i. Surrounded by nearly two acres of reflecting pools fed by artesian wells, the building is an island in the Pacific—in fact a volcano, evidenced by a ceiling that opens to the sky and the cone-shaped legislative chambers. The capitol's entirely open-air design signifies a government and people that are open and welcoming.

A statue of Belgium's Father Damien stands at the northern entrance in honor of his dedication to the people of Kalaupapa; the liberty bell near it was a gift of the federal government while Hawai'i was still a territory. At the southern entrance, a humanistic statue of Queen Lili'uokalani, the last royal monarch of the Islands, seems to always be draped with fresh flowers. Also on the property is a memorial to veterans of the Vietnam and Korean wars.

The entire building makes a statement at a glance: strong, united, and unique. Inside, the action begins in late January with the opening of Hawai'i's legislature—a pageantry event worth attending.

Hawai'i Theatre

528-0506.
1130 Bethel St., Downtown.
Open: Guided tours available Tuesday at 11 AM call for reservations.
Admission: $5.
Historic Status: National Register of Historic Places.

Downtown Honolulu's only surviving theater opened in 1922 and featured popular entertainment, theater productions, and films. As the years passed, along with the district's heyday, the need for the theater waned and it closed in 1984. Citizens and local organizations rallied to save the "Pride of the Pacific" from demolition; and in 1996, following an outstanding and national-award-winning renovation of its art deco, Greek, and Roman elements, it reopened to much fanfare.

The exterior design embellishments of the theater are minimal; a docent-guided tour of the art deco interior, however, yields surprising gold-leaf artistry, allegorical murals with antiquated titles such as *Glorification of Diana*, split mohair seating, a mosaic dome, and a wonderful Robert Morgan orchestral theatre pipe organ, brought to the theater in 1936. More than one hundred thousand residents and visitors now crowd into its halls each year for performances ranging from Chinese acrobatics to cultural film presentations.

The delightful art deco Hawai'i Theatre is once again a popular venue for concerts, films, and more.
Photo courtesy David Franzen.

Honolulu Hale
523-4385.
530 S. King St., Downtown.
Open: Monday through Friday 7:45–4:30.
Admission: Free.
Historic Status: National Register of Historic Places.

Honolulu Hale serves as City Hall and houses numerous municipal government offices, the most notable of which is that of the mayor. This 1928 architectural gem reflects the Mediterranean mission style design popular in Hawai'i at the time, with an interior courtyard, stairways, a speaker's balcony, and ceiling details modeled after the Bargello, a 13th-century palace in Florence.

Designed by a team that included renowned island architect Charles Dickey, it was the first government building in Hawai'i to also incorporate Hawaiian motifs. Stonework by Italian sculptor Mario Valdastri and frescos by Einar Peterson complement the beautiful inner courtyard, which has a ceiling that can be opened to the elements. The building also features 1,500-pound bronze front doors and 4,500-pound chandeliers in the courtyard. Like several buildings of its age in Honolulu, restoration is pending.

During the Christmas season, Honolulu Hale is the center of the city's popular "Honolulu City Lights" celebration. Open year-round, its courtyard features work by various island artists, including children.

'Iolani Palace State Monument
522-0832.
364 South King St., Downtown.
www.iolanipalace.org.
Open: Tuesday through Saturday 9–3:45 (upper palace), 9–4:30 (basement). Guided tours 9–11:15, audio tours 11:45–3, self-guided gallery basement tours 9–4:30.
Admission: Guided and audio tours $12–$20, $5 children 5–12; basement tours $6 adults, $3 children 5–12. Children under 5 permitted only in basement.
Historic Status: National Historic Landmark.
Gift shop.

If you choose to visit only one Hawaiian heritage historic site while in Hawai'i, this should be it.

A Victorian palace built for King Kalākaua, 'Iolani Palace follows a long line of powerful and spiritually significant structures that have rested on the same site. Over the years it has served the people of Hawai'i as an official royal residence, republic and territory headquarters, state government capitol, monument, and inspiration.

In ancient times a Hawaiian *heiau,* or sacred stone temple, covered these grounds; all that remains is memory of its existence and its name, Ka'ahaimauli. Homes of several pre- and post-contact Hawaiian chiefs were also located here, as well as the crypts of post-contact royalty. In the mid-1800s, a single-story, coral-block home on the site, belonging to an O'ahu chief, was transformed into the first royal palace; it served during the reign of several kings until the aging structure needed to be torn down.

Today's 'Iolani Palace was completed in 1882 and critics of the time were at a loss in describing its unique mix of mostly Italianate Renaissance architectural styles. Nevertheless, it was a building ahead of its time. With elevators, concrete, full-plumbing bathrooms, telephones, and electric lighting, it was more modern than the American capitol building in Washington D.C., which had neither electric lighting nor extensive plumbing. Crowned heads from around the world came to meet the king and marvel at the palace's magical interior.

Despite its festive opulence, 'Iolani Palace has seen tragedy as much as gaiety. The popular Kalākaua died unexpectedly in 1891 while in San Francisco, and his sister, Lili'uokalani, ascended to the throne as queen. Determined to strengthen the political power of the Hawaiian monarchy to help her people, opposition to her goals mounted, resulting in an overthrow of the kingdom in 1893 by American businessmen and the queen's eventual imprisonment within the palace itself. The monarchy was never restored, despite intentions of President Grover Cleveland to override the act.

Once the monarchy was disbanded, property—including palace furniture and other effects—were considered up for grabs. The Friends of 'Iolani Palace, an organization that today manages the estate, has succeeded in locating approximately four thousand of the estimated ten thousand artifacts dispersed world-wide and has placed them in their original positions within the palace walls.

The lovely grounds of the palace also include the old ʻIolani Barracks, a bandstand dating from 1883, traces of burials, and a banyan tree reportedly planted in the 1880s by Queen Kapiʻolani.

For residents familiar with the history of ʻIolani Palace, its existence is poignant; and Hawaiian rights activists and other groups often use the grassy acreage fronting the palace for protests and important historic commemorations.

Both imposing and charismatic, ʻIolani Palace is Hawaiʻi's most historically significant building.

Kawaiahaʻo Church/Lunalilo Mausoleum/Kawaiahaʻo Cemetery
522-1333.
957 Punchbowl St., Downtown.
Open: Monday through Friday 8–5.
Admission: Free (donations welcome).
Historic Status: The church is a National Historic Landmark and is on the National Register of Historic Places.

The first permanent Christian church to be built in the Islands, Kawaiahaʻo Church is a technological marvel of sorts, as well as one of the most important buildings in the state, where royal coronations were once held and historic events continue to take place. Before it was built, a series of thatched, Hawaiian-style houses served on the same site as places of worship; as the congregation grew, the missionaries were forced to build even larger structures. The final thatched house could hold 4,500 people seated cross-legged on the ground and standing on the sides.

Kawaiaha'o Church was built by hand from thousands of coral stones, each weighing more than a ton.

Completed in the New England style of architecture in 1842, Hawaiian worshippers built the 144-by-78-foot-long Congregational church by hand over the course of five years, using fourteen thousand coral slabs laboriously chiseled from reefs laying 10 to 20 feet underwater. Each block of coral weighed more than one thousand pounds and was ferried to shore by canoe or raft. Some of the wooden beams used in the church's construction were carried by hand over steep mountain passes to Honolulu. The church was eventually named after the nearby spring once frequented by a high chiefess, Ka Wai a Ha'o—"the water of Ha'o." It once wore a wooden steeple, which was damaged in 1885 during a storm and never replaced. The interior of the church is modest, with the most notable characteristic being portraits of the royal family and chiefs lining the upper church walls.

Adjancent to the entrance of the church is a Victorian-gothic mausoleum housing the body of King Lunalilo, Hawai'i's first elected monarch, who passed away in 1874 after only one year on the throne. Rather than be buried at the Royal Mausoleum in Nu'uanu Valley, he reportedly asked to be placed at the church "to be entombed among his people, rather than the kings and chiefs." Entrance is not permitted.

Behind the church is an old cemetery, consecrated in 1823, which contains the remains of the founding missionaries and hundreds of their congregation members, many of whom now rest in unmarked graves or multiple burial sites. For those with tombstones, you'll find names that echo across Hawai'i's oldest buildings, corporations, and trusts. Descendents of the original missionaries are still allowed to be buried here, upon request. You' are welcome to enter and respectfully view the gravesites.

Beyond the church cemetery is the Adobe Schoolhouse, which, at the time of its creation in 1835, was called "the most beautiful room in Honolulu." There the missionaries taught high-status Hawaiian children the "three Rs." Today it serves as a school once again.

MERCHANT STREET HISTORIC DISTRICT

One of the most charming streets on the entire island is the narrow and brief Merchant Street, between Bishop and Nu'uanu Streets in downtown's financial district area. Once the core of Honolulu trading and business, it still is home to law offices and other firms nestled in rows of vintage buildings spanning 150 years of history.

One of its most interesting buildings is the **Kamehameha V Post Office** (46 Merchant St.), built in 1871. When it was in operation, it featured separate service windows for ladies,

Much of Merchant Street looks the same as it did many years ago. This photo was taken in 2007.

foreigners, Hawaiians, Japanese, and Portuguese customers. Murphy's Bar & Grill now occupies the old **Royal Saloon** (2 Merchant St.), opened in 1890—and a bar had existed on the same site for at least 40 years prior. The front sidewalk is made from granite-blocks used to ballast ships en route to the Islands from China. The beautiful **Alexander &**

Baldwin Building (822 Bishop St., on the corner of Merchant) was designed by leading Hawai'i architects Hart Wood and Charles Dickey in 1929 and has long been a powerhouse of big business. Its facade is loaded with symbolic designs, such as the water buffalo, which was used to pull sugar cane carts. From Merchant Street, be sure to also turn up Nu'uanu Avenue, where more historic buildings house tiny galleries and cafés.

Mission Houses Museum
531-0481.
553 S. King St., Downtown.
www.missionhouses.org.
Open: Tuesday through Saturday 10–4. Guided tours at 11 and 2:45 (Thursday at 11 only).
Historic Status: National Historic Landmark.
Gift shop.

The Mission Houses Museum offers tours of the original homes once occupied by Hawai'i's first missionaries.

After months of traveling across the Pacific Ocean, the first missionaries of any kind arrived in Hawai'i from New England, ready to spread the Congregationalist word. The year was 1820; King Kamehameha had just passed away, ending the old Hawaiian system of religious beliefs. Although the Hawaiians were suspicious of their intentions, this small group of young, newly-wed, well-educated men and women were permitted to stay—as long as they settled far enough from the busy and boisterous port. The missionaries were moved into thatched housing along a dusty strip until the arrival of their prefabricated wooden homes, then still at sea.

It was not long before the Hawaiian people began to appreciate the presence of the "long necks," who set about sewing clothing, caring for the sick, translating the oral Hawaiian language into written form, teaching reading and writing, and sharing religious beliefs. Their biggest supporter became Ka'ahumanu, the dowager queen, who would drop by the mission houses to study whenever the passion struck her.

Within these walls several missionary families shared their lives, took in orphaned babies and disabled seamen, taught the people, and produced literally millions of pages of text in both English and Hawaiian with the first printing press in Hawai'i.

The mu'umu'u also originated with the missionaries. In reality a Mother Hubbard dress reshaped to fit voluptuous Hawaiian bodies (Hawaiians viewed obesity as a mark of beauty), it caught on and was all the rage; you'll still see some women wearing them in Honolulu today.

The mission houses in the Capital District are the oldest wood frame buildings still standing in Hawai'i and consist of the Frame House, Chamberlain House, and Printing Office. They sit exactly where they were erected in the 1820s, now among yawning trees and lush grass, and can be explored via guided tour—a great way to understand the depth of the missionaries' influence on the kingdom.

In addition to touring the museum, consider taking its history-professor-led tour of the Capital District. See the "Guided Historic Walking Tours" section in this chapter for more information.

National Memorial Cemetery of the Pacific
532-3720.
2177 Pūowaina Dr., Punchbowl-Tantalus.
Open: Grounds 8–5:30 daily; Information Center Monday through Friday 8–4:30.
Admission: Free.
Historic Status: National Register of Historic Places.

Known to most as Punchbowl Cemetery and a significant site for millions, the National Memorial Cemetery is considered the "Arlington of the Pacific." It is where nearly 47,000 men and women who served in the United States Armed Forces during World War I, World War II, the Korean War, the Vietnam War, and other conflicts are buried.

Punchbowl itself is actually a volcano crater once called Pu'uowaina by Hawaiians, or "hill of sacrifice." Near its base stood as many as four *luakini heiau*, or sacrificial temples, where offenders, such as those who broke the strict taboo system, met their fate, and high chiefs were secretly buried. "Pu'uowaina" has morphed over the years into "Pūowaina," the name of the street that now circles the crater.

The crater's gently sloping, 116-acre interior features manicured lawns; banyan, monkeypod, shower, and plumeria trees; and flat, uniform, marble gravestones in careful rows. Symbols on the stones signify religious beliefs. Because of Punchbowl's semi-lush, mid-valley location, rainbows are often seen arching over the tops of the trees. On the left flank, halfway between the park entrance and its colossal war monument called the Memorial Building, a paved walkway leads to a spectacular lookout at the crest of the crater. At the Memorial Building, a chapel and mosaic gallery outlining the Pacific's role in World War II and the Korean War are well worth viewing. A small visitors center at the entrance is a moving tribute to the individuals interred.

Punchbowl's history, purpose, and natural beauty stir the emotions of many who enter it. Sit under one of the park's many sprawling trees to listen to the wind as it sweeps across the crater.

Our Lady of Peace Cathedral
536-7036.
1183 Fort. St., Downtown.
Open: Monday through Friday 8–6, Saturday 10–12, Sunday 6–1 and 5–7.
Admission: Free.
Historic Status: National Register of Historic Places.

The first Catholic missionaries arrived in Hawai'i from France in 1827 following the Congregationalist missionaries who, having shipped in several years earlier, had the advantage of already gathering the public into its fold. The devout royal family promptly expelled the Catholic missionaries, who were not invited to return until 1839, when the king issued an edict of toleration for other religions. Upon their return, they set about planning the creation of Our Lady of Peace Cathedral.

Reputedly the oldest Catholic church in continuous use in the United States, the charmingly diminutive and simple Romanesque-revival house of worship was built from coral slabs in 1843 and stands in downtown Honolulu on land donated by King Kamehameha III. It has served as the site of significant occasions, such as dignitary funerals, and was where renowned Belgian priest Father Damien was ordained in 1864.

The tower has been rebuilt several times, most recently in 1917, and formerly held two French-made bells hung in 1853. The pipe organ inside the cathedral dates from 1934. The front doors are often locked, but you can enter through side doors.

Queen Emma Summer Palace
595-3167.
2913 Pali Hwy., Nu'uanu.
www.daughtersofhawaii.com/summerpalace.
Hours: Daily 9–4. Closed major holidays.
Admission: $6 adults, $1 youths under 18.
Historic Status: National Register of Historic Places.
Gift shop.

Built in 1848 by part-Hawaiian businessman John Lewis, this beautiful Nu'uanu Valley home was inherited by Queen Emma from her uncle, John Young II, in 1857. Called Hānaiakamalama—"foster child of the moon"— she and King Kamehameha IV, along with their adored young son Prince Albert, retreated to this home frequently from glamorous 'Iolani Palace for more "personal living."

Although bestowed with extreme grace, intelligence, education, and power, the royal couple was destined to encounter a series of tragedies overcome only by the enduring determination and faith of Queen Emma. Their story is told in this house and visible in the cherished possessions, lovingly restored to their original state by the nonprofit Daughters of Hawai'i organization.

Docents from the organization will walk you through the home's several rooms, sharing information about the palace's history and artifacts. If you know how to play the piano, you may be invited to do so on one of two that once belonged to the queen. The tour groups tend to be very small, which makes visiting an especially delightful, intimate, and educational experience. The gift shop has a charming selection of handcrafted items and books.

Shangri La
1-866-385-3853; 532-3853.
900 S. Beretania St. (Honolulu Academy of Arts meeting point), Makiki.
Open: Wednesday through Saturday 8:30–1:30 (tour hours, not museum hours).
Admission: $25. Children under 12 are not permitted. Advance reservations required.

The exotic Shangri La houses valuable Islamic artifacts collected by heiress Doris Duke. Photo courtesy Doris Duke Charitable Foundation Archives, Duke Farms, Hillsborough, NJ.

Shangri La, the former estate of American tobacco heiress Doris Duke, opened to the public in 2002, nearly 10 years after her death. During an around-the-world honeymoon tour in 1935, this unique woman developed a deep love of Islamic art and artifacts, which she collected over her lifetime. Duke's home is a breathtaking and unique testament to her interest: Not only is it filled with authentic treasures, but the home itself has been designed to replicate elements of Moroccan, Turkish, Spanish, Syrian, Egyptian, and Indian architecture; rooms glisten with thousands of mosaic tiles, and fountains trickle amidst a stunning, tropical oceanfront setting.

Tours of the estate are offered only through the Honolulu Academy of Arts, which coordinates your roundtrip transportation between the museum and the site. Docents take you through public rooms in the main house and through portions of its 5-acre grounds. Your Shangri La ticket also permits you to tour the Academy, so be sure to plan for both on the same day. Book in advance—tickets can be difficult to get. Paid parking for the museum is available nearby at the Academy Art Center at Linekona, on Beretania and Victoria Streets.

St. Andrew's Cathedral
524-2822.
Queen Emma Square, Downtown.
Open: Monday through Friday 7–6, Sunday 7–4.
Admission: Free.
Historic Status: National Register of Historic Places.

During a visit with Queen Victoria in 1861, King Kamehameha IV and Queen Emma were greatly impressed by the Church of England; upon their return to Hawai'i, they began commissioning for an Anglican church to be built in Honolulu. At their request, in 1862 Bishop Thomas Staley and two priests arrived in Honolulu from London to help develop the Episcopal Church in Hawai'i, then known locally as the Hawaiian Reformed Catholic Church. When the king passed away in 1863 on Saint Andrew's Day, his brother and successor chose to name the church after that day. By 1867, the cornerstone for the dramatic, Gothic-revival St. Andrew's Cathedral was laid on land bestowed to the Episcopalians in downtown Honolulu. The cathedral was assembled piece by piece throughout the years; the last of it set in place in 1958, nearly one hundred years after it was begun. The cathedral is the centerpiece of St. Andrew's Priory, a private girls' school founded in 1867 along with the church.

Washington Place
586-0248.
320 South Beretania St., Downtown.
Open: Monday through Friday, by appointment only.
Admission: Free.
Historic Status: National Register of Historic Places.

In 1842, wealthy American sea captain John Dominis constructed what was to be one of the grandest residences in the entire Hawaiian Kingdom—an impressive colonial Greek revival home built from coral block. On the long journey to China to purchase furnishings for his family's new home, however, Dominis was lost at sea.

The captain's son eventually married a young Hawaiian noblewoman, who in 1891 ascended to the throne as Hawai'i's Queen Lili'uokalani and left Washington Place for

'Iolani Palace, located right across the street. Deposed only two years later during a coup coordinated by American businessmen, she was eventually arrested and imprisoned within the palace. After her release, she lived out her years at Washington Place.

Upon her death in 1917, Washington Place became the residence of all governors of the territory—and later the state—until 1999. The current governor now resides in a new mansion just behind the property, so that the public may view the historic home's exquisite interior year-round. In December, Washington Place is beautifully decorated and opened to the public for one subtly glamorous evening that recaptures the glory of its past.

YWCA of O'ahu, Laniākea
538-7061.
1040 Richards St., Downtown.
Open: Monday through Thursday 6–9, Friday 6–7, Saturday and Sunday 7:30–4:30.
Admission: Free.
Historic Status: National Register of Historic Places.

"Laniākea" means "open skies" or "wide horizons"—accurate descriptions of this vintage, open-air building created for the betterment of women and girls in Hawai'i. World-renowned Julia Morgan, architect of the famed Hearst Castle, designed the building in 1925 and later claimed that, of the more than seven hundred buildings she worked on throughout her career, this was one of her favorites. The graceful Mediterranean-style building is lined with archways, sculpted column heads, and ornate balconies that reflect her fondness for classicism. Step in during business hours for a glimpse of her work.

WINDWARD O'AHU

Byodo-In Temple
239-9844.
47-200 Kahekili Hwy., Kāne'ohe.
Open: Daily 7–6.
Admission: $2.
Historic Status: National Register of Historic Places.
Gift shop.

Hidden at the back of a peaceful windward valley is the beautiful Byodo-In Temple, a scaled replica of Japan's 11th-century temple at Uji, itself is a World Heritage site. Byodo-In was built in 1968 to commemorate the centennial of the first Japanese immigrants' arrival in Hawai'i. Constructed without the use of any nails, its architectural design is meant to characterize the mythical phoenix. Inside the main hall an 8-foot, gold-leaf lotus Buddha, carved by famed Japanese sculptor Masuzo Inui, sits laced in aromatic incense; remove your shoes before entering. Peacocks meander across the temple's lush, shady gardens and several benches sit near the 2-acre pond filled with thousands of koi (carp), making it a perfect spot to relax with a book—if you're wearing mosquito repellent, that is. Be sure to ring the enormous brass bell to experience its calming resonance.

Byodo-In is a house of worship for all denominations. Reach it via the Valley of the Temples Memorial Park, an expansive Shinto, Christian, Buddhist, and pet cemetery in the windward town of Kāne'ohe.

Steep, luxuriant cliffs provide a dramatic backdrop for the peaceful Byodo-In Temple in Kāne'ohe.

CENTRAL O'AHU

Pearl Harbor

Pearl Harbor was known to Hawaiians as Wai Momi, or "water of the pearl." The United States began secretly scouting the site in the mid-1800s after reports indicated it could serve as an excellent harbor and defense area, and in 1887 the Hawaiian kingdom granted the lagoon to the U.S. through a controversial reciprocal arrangement. Over the years, it has served as a naval fleet support system for sheltering, repairing, and arming submarines and aircraft. Pearl Harbor itself is a National Historic Landmark.

Whether or not you're interested in Hawai'i's past, the military, or world history, visiting the sites at Pearl Harbor is still a one-of-a-kind experience. You should be able to see the USS *Arizona* Memorial, battleship USS *Missouri*, submarine USS *Bowfin*, and new Pacific Aviation Museum in one trip if you head out by mid-morning. Many outfits offer packaged tours that take you to Pearl Harbor, but you can easily get there yourself. See driving directions in Chapter 2. TheBus stops at the USS *Arizona* Memorial, and several Waikīkī hotels even offer direct shuttle service to Pearl Harbor.

Prepare for exasperatingly long waits at the *Arizona* Memorial, even early in the morning. Also, renovations to restore the Memorial platform will soon be underway, although most work will take place at night. Do not bring purses or other belongings to any of the sites; you'll be required to check them in for security measures. Best bet is to leave all that doesn't fit in your pockets either at your hotel or, if not valuable, in your vehicle.

Tickets to the *Arizona* Memorial cannot be obtained in advance, but you can reserve tickets to the USS *Missouri* and USS *Bowfin* in advance. The **USS *Missouri* Memorial Association** (973-2494; www.ussmissouri.com) offers a package program called "Navy Day Pearl Harbor," which includes entrance to both ships, a guided tour of the *Missouri*, a photo onboard, an audio tour of the *Bowfin* and nearby museum, a ride on a flight simulator, a simple lunch served on the *Missouri*, and more.

Be sure to also read about Pearl Harbor's new Pacific Aviation Museum in the "Museums and Galleries" section of this chapter; although the museum itself is not a historic site, it's located on historic Ford Island and is an integral complement to the sights listed below.

Battleship Missouri Memorial

423-2263 or 1-877-MIGHTYMO (644-4896).
63 Cowpens St., Ford Island, Pearl Harbor.
www.usmissouri.com.
Open: 9–5 daily (ticket window closes at 4) except Thanksgiving Day, Dec. 25, and Jan. 1.
Admission: Self-guided or audio tour \$16 adults, \$8 children under 12. Guided tours \$22–\$45 adults, \$14–\$20 children under 12. Reservations can be booked online or by phone.
Historic Status: National Register of Historic Places.
Gift shop.

The 887-foot-long "Mighty Mo" is a famed battleship that served both in World War II and the Persian Gulf War, and it housed as many as 2,400 men at one time. The Japanese officially surrendered their position in World War II by signing an agreement while on its very decks. Sign up for a guided tour of the USS *Missouri* to get the most out of your visit. A lift can bring mobility-impaired individuals up to the main and upper deck.

USS Arizona Memorial
422-0561.
1 Arizona Memorial Pl., Pearl Harbor.
www.nps.gov/usar.
Open: 7:30–5 daily except Thanksgiving Day, Dec. 25, and Jan. 1.
Admission: Free; tickets offered on first-come, first-served basis.
Historic Status: National Historic Landmark.
Gift shop.

Upon your arrival at the USS *Arizona* Memorial, head to the Visitor Center, which is the hub of activity and where you receive your tickets. While you wait for your tour to begin, visit the interesting museum on the premises that covers events of World War II and presents personal accounts and other artifacts, bringing you closer to the attack on Hawai'i.

The tour itself begins with a brief and powerful documentary on Pearl Harbor's attack and culminates in a somewhat surreal boat ride across the harbor, which delivers you to a platform built above the sunken remnants of the USS *Arizona*—a battleship that, when attacked by Japanese fighters during World War II, went down in several minutes with more than eleven hundred men aboard. The Memorial is actually a national park, and therefore operates under the National Park Service. One of the best things about visiting is that on most days, one or more survivors of the attack—both civilians who lived here during the war as well as veterans—are at the Visitor Center sharing stories about the experience with anyone who wants to listen.

USS Bowfin Submarine Museum & Park
423-1341.
11 Arizona Memorial Dr., Pearl Harbor.
www.bowfin.org.
Open: 8–5 daily except Thanksgiving Day, Dec. 25, and Jan. 1. Last tour is at 4:30.
Admission: $4–$10 audio tour and museum. Children under 4 may not board the vessel.
Historic status: National Historic Landmark.
Gift shop.

This World War II submarine is one of only about 15 still in existence, making a visit quite unique. The 312-foot USS *Bowfin* housed nearly one hundred volunteer men within its confines and sank 44 enemy ships during the war. Visitors who are uncomfortable in tight quarters or unable to easily duck and climb may want to poke around the top deck of the submarine only. In addition to exploring this fascinating craft, visit the 10,000-square-foot museum exhibiting submarine-related artifacts such, as a Poseidon C-3 missile (the only one on display anywhere).

Libraries

Whether you need obscure reference materials on Hawaiian nose flute designs or a reading break from sun and surf, you'll find several excellent libraries in Honolulu.

Greater Honolulu

A great place to poke around is the **Hawai'i State Library** (586-3400; 553 S. King St., Downtown). Built in 1913, this Carnegie-funded Greco-Roman library is the main branch

The famous battleship USS Missouri *can be toured inside and out at Pearl Harbor.*
Photo courtesy USS *Missouri* Memorial Association, Inc.

of the only statewide library system in the U.S. Visitors may purchase temporary library cards, borrow Hawaiian music CDs, browse hundreds of volumes on Hawai'i and other Pacific islands, or surf the Internet from one of its public computers (reserve in advance). The library is on the National Register of Historic Places. For a public library closer to the beach, head to the smaller **Waikīkī-Kapahulu** branch (733-8488; 400 Kapahulu Ave., Kapahulu).

Bishop Museum's Library and Archives (848-4148 library; 848-4182 archives; 1525 Bernice St., Kalihi) holds vast amounts of books, periodicals, newspapers, music, art, and more relating to Hawai'i and the Pacific. **The Hawaiian Historical Society** (537-6271; 560 Kawaiaha'o St., Downtown) on the grounds of the Mission Houses Museum features more than twenty-five thousand books, newspapers, photos and other items, with an especially strong collection of material on early voyages and travels. **The Hawaiian Mission Children's Society Library** (531-0481; 553 S. King St., Downtown), also located at the Mission Houses Museum, is likewise a treasure trove of more than twelve thousand books and other materials relating to Hawaiian and mission history.

At the **Hawai'i State Archives** (586-0329; Kekauluohi Bldg., 'Iolani Palace Grounds, 364 S. King St., Downtown), a massive collection of state government historic records, genealogical indexes, photographs, and other fascinating volumes are available for viewing. **The Honolulu Academy of Arts' Robert Allerton Art Research Library** (532-8755; 900 S. Beretania St., Makiki) houses a non-circulating collection of art related materials that you can browse. In 2004, storms caused the **University of Hawai'i's Hamilton Library** (956-7204; University of Hawai'i at Mānoa, 2550 McCarthy Mall, Mānoa) to sustain heavy flooding damage, and the toll was great. However, it still is the largest collection of reading materials in the state, with approximately 3.5 million volumes, periodicals, and documents.

What is "Local" Culture?

Ask longtime residents to define local culture, and we'll probably become noticeably excited. People from Hawai'i take great pride in being "local"—and in being different from folks on the Mainland. Sure, we drive SUVs, shop at Costco, and discuss *Desperate Housewives* or *Lost* as frequently as you. But with our rich diversity of historical influences that range from British to Filipino, unique mix of ethnicities, and location within the Polynesian Triangle, a distinctive lifestyle has developed here that is both original and deeply treasured.

One of our favorites is the wearing of split-toe "slippers." Known on the Mainland as flip-flops or go-aheads, it's virtually mandatory for all Hawai'i residents to own several pairs or more, and especially at least one pair of inexpensive "rubbah slippahs" for "junk use."

Slippers can be worn with pants or dresses, to outdoor weddings or school, and everything in between, unless a more formal dress code is stated or the setting has a more elegant feel, such as a fancy restaurant or symphony concert. Fit them to your feet "local style" by choosing a pair small enough that your toes and heel touch each edge. Always remove slippers before entering someone's home, an old Japanese custom. If you see mountains of slippers in front of a doorway, you can guess a good party's taking place inside!

In addition to our fondness for slippers, many of us speak varying degrees of Hawai'i's unique "pidgin" language, or at least pepper our speech with vocabulary from Hawaiian and Asian languages; eat white rice with every meal; dance hula or create traditional Hawaiian craftwork; wear tucked-in aloha shirts to the office; eat Spam® musubi or "loco moco" for breakfast; surf, race outrigger canoes, spearfish, or hunt wild boar; regularly use the terms "auntie," "uncle," or "tūtū" for people outside our blood kinship; live with three or even four generations of our family; and, yes, we really do give flower lei to each other in celebration of birthdays, graduations, or other special events.

The list could go on and on. Most residents, though, will often sum up life and local culture in Hawai'i in a single sentence about living "with aloha"—in other words, living each day with respect, love, and gratitude for the world around us.

Museums

Many museums on O'ahu are housed in historic structures, providing a double dose of visiting pleasure. The most famous are arguably Bishop Museum and the Honolulu Academy of Arts; both are must-sees for their magnificent collections and architectural beauty.

Galleries listed here present art in an educational context, emphasizing "art for art's sake." See Chapter 8 for a list of primarily retail-focused galleries and craft shops.

Greater Honolulu

Bishop Museum

847-3511.
1525 Bernice St., Kalihi.
www.bishopmuseum.org.
Open: Daily 9–5, except Dec. 25.
Admission: $15.95 adults, $12.95 children under 13, free for children under 4.
Historic status: Selected buildings are on the National Register of Historic Places.
Gift shop.

Hawai'i's largest museum contains one of the most expansive natural history and specimen collections anywhere in the world. Its collection of Hawaiian and Pacific cultural artifacts (about 2.5 million) is indeed the biggest in the world, earning this nearly 120-year-old institution recognition for unique research and discovery.

The center of the campus is indisputably the beautiful, Victorian-era Hawaiian Hall, which is undergoing a significant structural renovation scheduled to be complete in the spring of 2008. Upon the reopening of this anthropological treasure, visitors will find an entire first floor dedicated to the world of pre-contact Hawai'i, a second level focused on Hawaiian daily life and cultural traditions, and a third exploring the enduring resilience of the Hawaiian people. In addition to its authentic grass house, reconstructed stone temple, koa wood outrigger canoe, and suspended sperm whale skeleton that have been the museum's trademark icons, other priceless and rare historical objects will be reassembled to convey accurate historical portrayal and meaning.

As well as the restoration of Hawaiian Hall, the Picture Gallery will be upgraded to feature extraordinary oil paintings and rare books on a rotating basis. Another must-see region of the museum is Polynesian Hall, a gallery of two floors representing Pacific Island cultures from Polynesia, Melanesia, and Micronesia; and the Kāhili Room, featuring royal portraits and traditional court effects.

The newest building in the museum is the Science Adventure Center—an absolutely state-of-the-art and artful presentation of island geology, geography, oceanography, and biodiversity, interactively oriented toward children. The highlight is a 26-foot-high re-imagining of a Hawaiian volcano vent that belches steam and bubbles with simulated lava.

Other great aspects of the museum include a planetarium, the Hawai'i Sports Hall of Fame, natural history artifacts such as a fascinating seashell display, and nationally rotating exhibits.

The collection of books available in the gift shop is excellent; a modest and inexpensive café is on the premises as well, enabling you to take your time and enjoy the collections. In summer, several concerts by some of Hawai'i's best Hawaiian music performers take place under the stars on the Great Lawn. The museum offers free parking.

The Contemporary Museum

526-0232.
2411 Makiki Heights Drive, Tantalus.
www.tcmhi.org.
Open: Tuesday through Saturday 10–4, Sunday 12–4. Closed Monday and major holidays.

Admission: $5, free for children under 13.
Historic Status: National Register of Historic Places.
Gift shop.

This exquisite 3.5-acre, 1925 estate designed by renowned local architect Hart Wood for the Cookes—one of Hawai'i's most prestigious families—was converted to a museum in 1988. Its gorgeously expansive and hilly gardens offer a moderate view of Honolulu and Diamond Head, and the grounds house a fantastic café and gift shop, making it destination enough. But happily, the museum's rotating, 2,500-strong permanent collection and temporary exhibits also tend to be inspiring, controversial, and fresh for those who appreciate modern art. The collection covers all media, spanning from 1940 to the present time.

The Contemporary Museum (TCM) offers gallery talks, workshops, and other educational and fun opportunities to visitors of all ages. The Museum is also planning to expand onto historic properties nearby, which will certainly mean more excellent presentations in the future. Free parking is available.

The Contemporary Museum at First Hawaiian Center (999 Bishop St., Downtown) is an extension of TCM with a rotating, free exhibit on view in the building's lobby.

Hawai'i Maritime Center
536-6373.
Pier 7, Honolulu Harbor, Downtown.
www.bishopmuseum.org/exhibits/hmc/hmc.html.
Open: Daily 8:30–5, except Dec. 25.
Admission: $7.50 adults, $4.50 children 4–12, free for children under 3.
Historic Status: The *Falls of Clyde* is a National Historic Landmark.
Gift shop.

A hidden gem just next door to Aloha Tower, the Hawai'i Maritime Center is operated by the world-renowned Bishop Museum and features interesting and thoughtfully presented accounts of Hawai'i's rich relationships with the sea.

Built on a pier once occupied by King Kalākaua's boathouse, which harbored more late-night royal poker games than boats, its most noticeable piece is a National Historic Landmark floating just outside the museum's door: the *Falls of Clyde*. Built in 1878 in Scotland, this ship is the last fully rigged, four-masted sailing vessel in the world and the first to fly Hawai'i's flag.

If not on a sea voyage or at an educational engagement, bobbing nearby on the swells is the even more historically significant *Hōkūle'a*—a beautiful, authentic reproduction of an ancient Hawaiian double-hulled canoe. The *Hōkūle'a* made world news in 1976 when its local crew set sail for distant Tahiti guided only by natural elements, proving that Hawaiian ancestors could have made such a trip.

The interior of the Maritime Museum is extremely well organized, clean as a whistle, and attractive, featuring a glass elevator and a complete humpback whale skeleton dangling from the ceiling. From life on a whaling ship to life on luxury liners transporting visitors in the 1950s, the collected artifacts leave a strong impression. Adults who appreciate detail may benefit from the displays more than children. Take advantage of the self-guided audio tour, which walks you through most of the museum within about an hour. Paid parking is available in lots adjacent to the museum.

The Falls of Clyde *sailing vessel at the Hawai'i Maritime Museum dates from 1878.*

Hawai'i State Art Museum
586-0900.
250 South Hotel St., 2nd Floor, Downtown.
www.state.hi.us/sfca.
Open: Tuesday through Saturday 10–4, except state and federal holidays.
Admission: Free. Guided tours at 11 and 2, or by special arrangement.
Historic Status: National Register of Historic Places.
Gift shop planned for late 2007.

One of Hawai'i's newer museums has long been in the making. Although opened in 2002, its history can be traced to 1965, when the State Foundation on Culture and the Arts was founded by the Hawai'i State Legislature to promote, perpetuate, preserve, and encourage the arts as a fundamental aspect of Hawai'i's quality of life. In 1967, Hawai'i was the first state in the U.S. to pass a law requiring one percent of the cost of every state building to be used for the acquiring or commissioning of visual art to beautify the environment. Since that time, the state has amassed approximately 5,000 works of art by 1,400 island artists, and the museum houses selected works from this collection of unique sculptures, paintings, photography, and other pieces. Audio guides are not available, as the artwork rotates frequently.

The museum's starkly beautiful Spanish-mission style building features Italianate scrollwork and other architectural details inspired by Florence's Davanzatti Palace. Constructed in 1928 by the Armed Services YMCA, it rests on the site of King Kamehameha V's original and distinguished Royal Hawaiian Hotel, erected in 1872, which reportedly also served as a template for the newer building.

Some of Hawai'i's best Hawaiian music performers play for free at the Hawai'i State Art Museum on the first Friday evening of the month.

On the first Friday of each month, the museum joins in downtown's First Friday festivities by staying open late and offering free concerts featuring Hawaiian music legends, as well as other events. Its café opened in 2007 and is run by one of Honolulu's hottest young chefs. The museum does not offer parking.

Honolulu Academy of Arts
532-8700.
900 S. Beretania St., Makiki.
www.honoluluacademy.org.
Open: Tueday through Saturday 10–4:30, Sunday 1–5 (every third Sunday 11–5). Closed major holidays.
Admission: Audio tour: $12. Self-guided: $7 adults, free for children under 12. Free first Wednesday and third Sunday of the month.
Historic Status: National Registry of Historic Places.
Gift shop.

Even if you only visit the Honolulu Academy of Arts museum for its outstanding gift shop and fabulous café, you'll have the benefits of passing through this poetic building and glimpsing its displays on the way. However, if you appreciate beautiful traditional and contemporary fine arts and crafts or quiver when you hear names such as Picasso, do not miss the chance to visit the galleries by purchasing a ticket.

Founded by the Cooke family in 1927, who donated the land of their former home—as well as countless pieces of their private art collection—for the construction of this superb little museum, it now holds nearly forty thousand items ranging from Southeast Asian headdresses to oil portraits of Hawaiian royalty to an ancient Egyptian falcon mummy case to French impressionist master works.

Rotating exhibits are generally impressive and extremely educational, and as the Academy is the hub of Hawai'i's fine arts scene, openings are big events packed with residents. Galleries are open for self-guided walks, audio tours, or docent-led tours. On Sundays and Tuesdays, the museum offers its "Afternoon Tour & Tea" program—topic-oriented docent tours accompanied by tea and socializing. On the last Friday of the month, the "ARTafterDARK" event in the museum courtyards is a decadently hip destination.

The Doris Duke Theatre on the premises features documentaries, independent films, and foreign films, as well as exotic music and dance concerts and educational lectures. Also worth the extra money is a tour organized by the museum that takes visitors to Shangri La, tobacco-heiress Doris Duke's extravagant, Turkish-style mosaic palace on a 5-acre beachfront estate near Diamond Head.

Paid parking is available kitty-corner to the museum at the Academy Art Center at Linekona, on Beretania and Victoria Streets.

CENTRAL O'AHU

Hawai'i's Plantation Village
677-0110.
94-695 Waipahu St., Waipahu.
www.hawaiiplantationvillage.org.
Open: Monday through Saturday for guided tours only, offered on the hour 10–2.
Admission: $13 adults, $5 children 4–11, free for children under 2.

Historic Status: Selected buildings are on the National Register of Historic Places.
Gift shop.

Several hundred thousand people from China, Japan, Portugal, Puerto Rico, Okinawa, Korea, the Philippines, and other nations arrived in Hawai'i between about 1850 and 1940 to work on its sugar plantations. They lived in "camps" near the fields and performed backbreaking work for low pay. Many people living in Hawai'i today descend from these immigrant laborers or were plantation laborers themselves.

This unusual outdoor museum tells their story. Both original and precisely recreated plantation camp buildings, such as the community bath, plantation store, and houses, as well as numerous artifacts, a film, and other memorabilia, unfold the workers' lives in detail.

Also moving are the stories of picture brides from Japan, Okinawa, and Korea, who arrived at the Honolulu docks to be married to laboring men they'd never met. If you've never seen the 1994 film *Picture Brides* by Hawai'i-born director Kayo Hatta, rent it before your visit for a good introduction to sugar plantation life.

The museum is located in the old sugar mill town of Waipahu, further authenticating your experience.

Pacific Aviation Museum
441-1000.
www.pacificaviationmuseum.org.
Hangar 37, Ford Island, 319 Lexington Blvd., Pearl Harbor.
Open: Daily 9–5, except major holidays.
Admission: $12 adults, $7 children 4–12; purchase tickets at USS *Bowfin.*
Gift shop.

The $90-million Pacific Aviation Museum at Pearl Harbor is the nation's first aviation battlefield museum. The first phase opened in 2006, on the 65th anniversary of the Japanese attack on Pearl Harbor. The museum is situated in the middle of the famous harbor on the 433-acre Ford Island, a National Historic Landmark that still looks much like it did during the heat of World War II.

The museum is a significant and complementary addition to the trilogy of fascinating sites already at Pearl Harbor and is earning accolades for its historical accuracy and striking presentations, such as aircraft backdrops painted by Hawai'i's opera technical director.

Three hangars will comprise the museum upon its final phases of completion: Hangar 37, nearest the old control tower, features a film on the war and displays seven World War II aircrafts and other artifacts, plus a flight simulator; Hanger 79, which enables visitors to listen to first-hand accounts of the experience and view evidence of the actual attack on Ford Island; and Hangar 54, devoted to the Korean and Vietnam wars and current naval operations in the Pacific.

Other Interesting Museums and Galleries

Most of the little museums and galleries listed below are free or charge a nominal fee. If you plan to visit those at the University of Hawai'i at Mānoa, we strongly suggest you go on Sunday, when the public is permitted to park right on campus.

Waikīkī

US Army Museum of Hawai'i

(955-9552; Battery Randolph, Kalia Rd.) What happens when you try to knock a 1911 military battery down with a wrecker ball, but it won't budge? You turn it into a museum, that's what. And thus began this free museum right on prime beach property in Waikīkī. From tanks to traditional Hawaiian weapons lined with shark teeth, it's a great break from the sun. Open Tuesday through Sunday 10–4:15. Gift shop open daily.

Greater Honolulu

East-West Center Gallery

(944-7177; University of Hawai'i at Mānoa, John A. Burns Hall, 1601 East-West Rd., Mānoa) Located on the University of Hawai'i at Mānoa campus, the internationally renowned East-West Center was established by the U.S. Congress to promote good relations between the U.S. and the Asia/Pacific region. Its educational gallery presents several exhibitions per year on traditional and contemporary arts of the Pacific, such as "Toys Across Asia," "Japanese Temple Architecture in Hawai'i," and "Quiet Splendor: Yupik Eskimo Culture." While there, be sure to step into the nearby Japanese Garden, donated by Japanese businessmen, and see the Thai Pavilion, a gift from the king of Thailand. Open Monday through Friday 8–5, Sunday 12–4.

Honolulu Police Department Law Enforcement Museum

(529-3351; Main Police Station, 801 South Beretania St., Makiki) Remember how cool *Hawai'i Five-0's* cops were? Then check out the Honolulu Police Department's free museum; it's a labor of love for Officer Eddie Croom, who has spent 20 years collecting local artifacts that range from exotic weapons to cockfighting equipment. Learn about the Honolulu Police Department's royal beginnings and the story behind the legendary fictional character Charlie Chan, who was based on real-life Honolulu tough guy Charlie Apana. Open Monday through Friday 9–3:30.

Japanese Cultural Center of Hawai'i

(945-7633; 2454 S. Beretania St., Mō'ili'ili) Japanese cultural influence in Hawai'i cannot be overstated. Immigration from Japan during plantation years was enormous—at one time nearly 40 percent of the entire state's population was Japanese. Today, many thousands of their descendents still live here, and a high visitor count from Japan ensures that the Islands always look to the East. At the Japanese Cultural Center, learn more about the deep relationship between Japan and Hawai'i and the contributions and sacrifices Japanese-Americans have made here through its historical gallery. Also enjoy rotating presentations on Japanese-oriented subjects in the community gallery. Open Tuesday through Saturday 10–3.

John Young Museum of Art

(956-3634; University of Hawai'i at Mānoa, Krauss Hall, 2500 Dole St., Mānoa) Local painter John Young (1909-1997) spent a lifetime creating and collecting eclectic pieces of art in hopes that one day the University would establish its first museum for the betterment of students and the general public. Shortly after his death, that vision was realized.

The growing collection presented here emphasizes Asia and the Pacific in particular, with many noteworthy items originating in ancient China. Early Buddhist figurines from Korea and Khmer ceramics are among the free museum's highlights. The building itself dates from 1931. Open Monday through Friday 11–2, Sunday 1–4.

Judiciary History Center
(539-4999; Ali'iolani Hale, 417 S. King St., Downtown) Inside Ali'iolani Hale you'll find a charming and free little museum worth your while: the King Kamehameha V Judiciary History Center. It includes several brief movies on land use rights and water privatization, an antique courtroom, and galleries filled with information on the evolution of the Hawaiian legal system, martial law in Hawai'i, and the trial of Queen Lili'uokalani. Also interesting is a detailed model of Honolulu in the 1850s. Open Monday through Friday 9–4.

Ramsay Museum
(537-2787; 1128 Smith St., Chinatown) This small museum is more like a gallery showcasing the fascinatingly detailed pen-and-ink architectural works of Ramsay Goldstein, recognized as a "Living Treasure of Hawai'i for Outstanding Achievement" by the city of Honolulu. Ramsay has also been instrumental in promoting Hawai'i artists, hosting nearly 200 solo shows over the last 26 years. Open Monday through Friday 10–5, Saturday 10–4.

Tennent Art Foundation Gallery
(531-1987; 203 Prospect St., Nu'uanu) This gallery is devoted to displaying the works of well-known painter Madge Tennent. Born in London, raised in Cape Town, and artistically trained in Paris, she lived in Hawai'i for the last 50 years of her life and became known for her voluptuous portraiture of Hawaiian women. Her son Arthur and his wife now oversee the gallery. Call for hours and directions.

University of Hawai'i Art Gallery
(956-6888; www.hawaii.edu/artgallery; University of Hawai'i at Mānoa, Art Bldg., 2444 Dole St., Mānoa) "Greek and Russian Icons," "International Shoebox Sculpture Exhibition," and "The Art of Asian Costume" are several interesting shows recently presented at this visual arts forum. Its smaller Commons Gallery showcases student work as well as that of visiting artists. Open Monday through Friday 10:30–4, Sunday 12–4:30. Closed in summers and between shows. Check the Web site above or call to confirm that a show is on.

WINDWARD O'AHU

Gallery 'Iolani
(236-9155; 45-720 Kea'ahala Rd., Kāne'ohe) The sharp-looking, 1,800-square-foot space at Windward Community College's Palanakila Humanities Building features a variety of quality works and interesting themes, ranging from vintage European posters to abstract paintings to nude drawings from students and other artists. Open Tuesday through Saturday 1–5.

NORTH SHORE

North Shore Surf and Cultural Museum
(637-8888; North Shore Marketplace, 66-250 Kamehameha Hwy., Hale'iwa) Take a break from the beach and stop by this very funky and free little handmade museum for a unique history of surfing and surf culture. Situated in the surfing capital of the world, this is the real deal. Glass Japanese fishing net floaters, old surfboards once belonging to the pros, and other curios convey the true North Shore lifestyle. Open Wednesday through Sunday 11–5:30 or 11–6.

CENTRAL O'AHU

Tropic Lightning Museum
(655-0438; Schofield Barracks, Building 361, Wai'anae Ave., Wahiawā) Learn more about the U.S. Army's famed 25th Infantry Division, the first infantry activated upon the bombing of Honolulu. It sits on historic Schofield Barracks, featured in films such as *Pearl Harbor* and *From Here to Eternity*. This interesting little museum houses displays of uniforms, artillery guns, equipment, and military vehicles. Open Tuesday through Saturday 10–4.

LEEWARD O'AHU

Hawaiian Railway Society
(681-5461; 91-1001 Renton Rd., 'Ewa) That's right, there used to be a railroad here—in fact, the railroad was key in the development of the sugar industry across the state, and in addition to public carrier lines and military routes, 47 plantations had their own systems. Nearly 7 miles of O'ahu tracks from 'Ewa to Nānākuli have been restored and listed on the National Register of Historic Places. The 90-minute trip is fully narrated and a nice complement to Hawai'i's Plantation Village, located in the same area of the island.

Nightlife

There are hundreds of spots on the island in which you may imbibe festively or with panache, ranging from cocktail clubs to surf and turf stops to Korean hostess bars to jazz taverns to catamaran cruises. Honolulu is home to the island's most stylish bars and nightclubs, so you might want to drive into town if you're staying elsewhere. Those listed below are a few of the best.

While many have no dress codes, slippers and shorts—or at least shorts—anywhere but a casual bar are generally a "no-no." Note, however, that most places wishing to exude a more sophisticated atmosphere will expect your fashion participation in full. Call ahead to check dress codes as well as music selection and cover charges, all of which can vary according to the night of the week.

Many nightspots serve edibles ranging from light pūpū (appetizers) to a full menu. If you plan on spending the evening chained to the bar, consider doubling it as a dining table as well. The drinking age in Hawai'i is 21, and driving with a .08 percent or greater blood alcohol level is illegal. Also, since 2006, smoking is not allowed inside, or within 20 feet of entryways, of bars and nightclubs.

Care for a casual evening in Waikīkī? Relax at the lesser-known DFS Galleria Starbucks, a garden patio oasis open until 11 nightly. People-watch from a window of the Moana Hotel's streetfront Honolulu Coffee Company. Browse books until 9:30 PM at Borders Express. Grab fabulous ice cream at the Hilton Hawaiian Village location of Lappert's Ice Cream, open until 11 PM, and take it to the beachfront walkway near the shop. Browse for clothing, jewelry, and knick-knacks until late at night (many stores in Waikīkī are open until 11 PM). Meander down Kalākaua Avenue, along with thousands of visitors and residents and enjoy the aimless bustle. Or, take a stroll down Waikīkī Beach itself—much romantic nestling takes place behind the canoes pulled up on the sand, and night swimming in front of the hotels is generally safe, exhilarating, and memorable.

"Blue Hawai'i" Cocktail Hour

Get in the mood with the ultimate Hawai'i experience: cocktails, sunsets, and Hawaiian music. Below are several of the best spots—perfect for everyone.

Waikīkī

The historic Moana hotel's **Beach Bar** (922-3111; Moana Surfrider, 2365 Kalākaua Ave.) is a must for anyone, although its service and drinks are not the top draw. Located in a romantic, oceanfront courtyard beneath an ancient banyan, this was the center of Waikīkī's nightlife for much of the last century and home of the famously nostalgic *Hawai'i Calls* radio program that once broadcast Hawai'i's music worldwide. Live performances of dreamy Hawaiian songs will help transport you back in time.

Famed hotel Halekulani's **House Without A Key** (923-2311; Halekulani, 2199 Kalia Rd.) is a superb experience; both residents and visitors have frequented this spot since the 1930s. With a picture-perfect oceanfront view that includes the amazing Diamond Head, and wistful, classic Hawaiian music—accompanied most evenings by gentle hula by former Miss Hawai'i Kanoe Miller—your cocktail hour will likely be fabulously soothing. Time your visit with the sunset and stay for the light dinner fare if you can't tear yourself away.

Of the two "Mai Tai Bars" in Honolulu, the lovely and historic Royal Hawaiian Hotel's **Mai Tai Bar** (923-7311; Royal Hawaiian Hotel, 2259 Kalākaua Ave.) is reputedly where the mai tai drink came of age. While folks debate whether the Royal's mai tais are the best, none take issue with the elegant beachfront setting and well-known Hawaiian music performers.

Greater Honolulu

Did you say "authentic tiki bar?" Then get thee to the 50-year-old, harborfront **La Mariana Sailing Club** (848-2800; 50 Sand Island Access Rd., Sand Island) and drink up some salty brew amongst netted glass balls, tiki columns, balloon fish lanterns, and perhaps a sea captain or two. It's awesome. They stop serving around 9 PM. Call to request exact directions.

"Gay" Sera, Sera

You're here, so you might as well be out...on the town. These spots are plenty of fun.

Waikīkī

Angles Waikīkī (926-9766; 2256 Kūhiō Ave. 2nd Floor) is an easygoing gay hangout with pool tables, dancing, games, and even high-speed Internet access. Hip young gay things party at **Fusion Waikīkī** (924-2422; 2260 Kūhiō Ave.)—and if dancing and drinks until 4 AM don't draw you in, the drag queens and male strippers probably will. **Hula's Bar & Lei Stand** (923-0669; www.hulas.com; Waikīkī Grand Hotel, 134 Kapahulu Ave., 2nd Floor) is one of the longest-running clubs of any kind in Honolulu, and an institution in the gay scene worldwide. Day or evening, you can drink, dance, Web-surf, play pool, make new friends, or just enjoy the remarkable ocean view.

Rockin' Hangouts

Dudes and dudettes, you don't have to flip up your polo collars to have a good time! Loosen up at any one of the following establishments and meet local folks and fellow travelers.

Waikīkī

Brew Moon Restaurant & Microbrewery (955-9045; Local Motion, 1958 Kalākaua Ave., 2nd Floor; also at Ward Centre, 593-0088; 1200 Ala Moana Blvd., 2nd Floor, in Kaka'ako) is a lively setting with good grub and award-winning beers. Both locations feature open-air patios and live entertainment; the Waikīkī site is convenient, but the Ward Centre site stays open later.

A heavily decorated ode to the "father of modern surfing," **Duke's Canoe Club** (922-2268; Outrigger Waikīkī Hotel, 2335 Kalākaua Ave.) is one of the most festive food and drink scenes in Waikīkī and appeals to several fun-loving generations. Purposefully over-the-top in grass-thatch and surf décor, it's a good hotspot jammed mostly with tourists. Head over in time for sunset and work it for a table on the lānai, built right on the sand.

The Hideaway (682-2731; 1913 Dudoit Ln.) behind 7-Eleven is a mellow, non-touristy, cool bar with little artistic flair but plenty of mixed-group camaraderie and hangout appeal for the hardier bar set. Your new drinking buddy could be a Harley biker, journalist, junkie, punk, student, or shrimp farmer. The low-key and enjoyably unhip **Harbor Pub** (941-0985; 1765 Ala Moana Blvd.) below the Chart House welcomes you. Get to know the local boat owners, fishermen, retirees, surfers, and everyone else; drink specials are so reasonably priced you can buy everyone a round.

Greater Honolulu

Off-the-grid, rock- and blues-minded kickback classic **Anna Bannanas** (946-5190; 2440 S. Beretania St., Mō'ili'ili) has been open since 1969 and features live bands on weekends. Ala Moana Center's **Mai Tai Bar** (Ala Moana Center, 1450 Ala Moana Blvd., Ala Moana) is popular with younger residents as a casual place to meet up, drink, and "talk story," and an easy stop after a tough day of shopping; but you might want to split after sunset or so, when the crowd lets loose with a bit of rowdiness and heavy cruising.

In a well-known, 150-year-old saloon spot once frequented by waterfront merchants, ship captains, and even Hawaiian royalty, **Murphy's Bar & Grill** (531-0422; 2 Merchant St., Chinatown) continues the storied tradition. Get your fish n' chips, Guinness, and shuffleboard fixes here.

Erykah Badu, Everclear, Led Zepplica, and Los Lobos are some of the many mid-sized concerts held in recent years at the **Pipeline Cafe & Sports Bar** (589-1999; Pohukaina St., Kaka'ako). Purple-felt pool tables, darts, a sports bar, and a dance floor make this younger and more casual scene always popular. **The Kona Brewing Co. & Brew Pub** (394-5662; Koko Marina Center, 7192 Kalaniana'ole Hwy., Hawai'i Kai) looks out onto a marina and is justifiably packed on weekends for its beer and live entertainment.

Windward O'ahu

Live music and bar food share the evening's menu along with plenty o' beer at the popular, surf-themed **Boardrider's Bar & Grill** in Kailua (261-4600; 201 Hāmākua Dr., Kailua). Longtime crusty kickback favorite **Buzz's Original Steak House** (261-4661; 413 Kawailoa Rd., Kailua) features a cash-only, full bar scene graced with more than a touch of the tropics.

North Shore

Kainoa's Sports Bar (637-7787; 66-197 Kamehameha Hwy., Hale'iwa) has a grungy local hangout feel at night, with live bands and karaoke. **Jameson's by the Sea** (637-6272; 62-540 Kamehameha Hwy., Hale'iwa) has been popular for years, and now attracts mostly older tourists. A moderate view of Hale'iwa's harbor area and full bar make it a pleasant sunset stop.

Wine Bars

A wine bar is the perfect place for good drinks, a sophisticated atmosphere, and tasty food—and O'ahu has several that are well worth your time.

Waikīkī

Rustic and Italian-owned little **Pane e Vino** (923-8466; 408 Lewers St., 2nd Floor) is both a charming wine bar and café, and it stays open until 2 AM, except on Sundays.

Greater Honolulu

Another destination is **Brasserie Du Vin** (545-1115; 1115 Bethel St., Downtown), which draws crowds at night. The hip **Formaggio Wine Bar** (739-7719; Market City Shopping Center, 2919 Kapi'olani Blvd., Kaimukī) carries a wonderful selection of wines as well as premium vodkas, gins, liqueurs, bourbons, and more. Serious wine lovers should definitely visit **Vino Italian Tapas & Wine Bar** (524-8466; Restaurant Row, 500 Ala Moana Blvd., Kaka'ako), which features one of the best wine selections in the state, presided over by master sommelier Chuck Furuya. It was recently named one of "America's 50 Most Amazing Wine Experiences" by *Food & Wine* magazine. All three establishments also offer a menu of delicious dishes to complement the wines.

Ultralounges and Ultraclubs

Kitten purrs, gold lamé shifts, sharp-collared shirts, and martini olives all say ultra groove. Anyone over 21 can enjoy an ultralounge when the outfit and attitude are right. Those ready to take it to the next level should patronize the ultraclub.

Waikīkī

Thirty floors up at Sheraton Waikīkī's Hanohano Room you'll find the **Cobalt Lounge** (922-4422; Sheraton Waikīkī, 2255 Kalākaua Ave.), a soothing and über-sleek minimalist setting with a surreal vibe. Savor caviar and champagne along with the view and very toned-down groove music. On the first and third Saturdays of the month, the space transforms into **Skyline**, one of Honolulu's glitziest, sexiest dance club scenes for younger visitors and residents.

The Halekulani's luxuriant and design-award-winning **Lewers Lounge** (923-2311;

Halekulani, 2199 Kalia Rd.) comes in first place for cocktails and hosts Rat-Pack-style live music that attracts a more mature crowd. Add the final touch of class to a mellow evening with caviar or chocolate fondue.

A new club called **Waikīkī Nei** (Royal Hawaiian Shopping Center, 2201 Kalākaua Ave., 4th Flr.) is scheduled to open in early 2008 and will reportedly be reminiscent of clubs like Studio 54 in Las Vegas, with acrobatics, a high-tech video and sound room, and space for one thousand gyrating bodies. The W's decadent Friday and Saturday night **Wonder Lounge** (922-1700; W Honolulu, 2885 Kalākaua Ave.) is the hottest, hippest nightclub in Waikīkī—cat-eyed go-go dancers in fur boots get the groove going for this veteran night crowd. Don't bother showing up before 11 PM.

A bit of New York in Honolulu: the Halekulani's swanky little Lewers Lounge.
Photo courtesy Hotels & Resorts of Halekulani.

Greater Honolulu

Downtown at the atmospheric Indigo's very stylish **Green Room/Opium Den & Champagne Bar** (521-2900; Indigo, 1121 Nu'uanu Ave., Chinatown), the young professional set savor sake martinis and Mandarin cosmos mixed with jazz, reggae, dancehall, hip-hop, electro, punk-disco, and drum and bass.

Pearl Ultralounge (944-8000; Ala Moana Center, 1450 Ala Moana Blvd., Ala Moana) is more upscale nightclub than lounge and attracts Generation X, Generation Y, and Boomers. The appetizer selection is notable. **The Veranda** (739-8888; Kahala Hotel & Resort, 5000 Kahala Ave., Kahala) is casual swanky and draws a slightly older, mellower, seated crowd with its alluring setting and jazzy classics.

Performing Arts

Dance, theater, and live music performances are plentiful enough on O'ahu. From legends like Jerry Lee Lewis and U2 to off-Broadway sensations such as *Stomp*, Honolulu gets its fair share of star performances.

Local performances are often world-class, or close to it. The Hawai'i Opera Theater features international operatic stars that sing to full houses and the Honolulu Symphony is likewise an excellent bet; tickets for most performances are usually in great demand. Look for the award-winning **Hawai'i International Jazz Festival** (941-9974; www.hawaiijazz.com), which is currently regrouping for spring events, and check out community theater productions for homegrown fun. The University of Hawai'i's Outreach College also sponsors the **Chamber Music Series** (956-8246; www.outreach.hawaii.edu).

Your visit to Hawai'i may be greatly enriched by experiencing an authentic Hawaiian music or dance event. Hula and the 'ukulele may be some of the most misrepresented cultural treasures in the world, so you might be surprised by what you find. Hawaiian performances are often inexpensive or free, yet are highly coveted by residents. In fact, choose the right show and you may be one of the only out-of-towners in the house, giving you the opportunity to see hula, slack-key guitar, 'ukulele, and falsetto singing in a different light. Be aware that the term "Hawaiian music" is used loosely for a variety of very different styles, including *hapa-haole*, traditional, chant, "Jawaiian," contemporary, slack-key guitar, 'ukulele, and so on, and may or may not include singing in the Hawaiian language. If in doubt as to what you'll be getting, ask a few questions first.

Many Hawaiian musicians of local and even international fame play frequently around town in restaurants, Waikīkī's hotel bars, or at events and fundraisers, making it fairly easy to catch a show. Cross your fingers that you'll be able to catch concerts by music legends the Mākaha Sons or octogenarian Auntie Genoa Keawe. Some of today's hottest performers also include Maunalua, Amy Hānaiali'i Gilliom, Nā Palapalai, Jake Shimabukuro, and Raiatea Helm—but there are many other talented, well-known, and popular Hawaiian musicians of past and current fame performing in town, so check the papers for listings.

The Royal Hawaiian Band has been playing since 1836 and is the only full-time municipal band in the U.S. One of its most famous bandmasters, a Prussian who shipped to the Islands in 1872, so popularized European music in Honolulu that it was said Hawaiians whistled grand opera airs while pounding poi. Catch a free performance every Friday at noon at 'Iolani Palace and selected Sundays at 2 at Waikīkī's Kapi'olani Park Bandstand.

In the summer months, observe a *bon* dance at one of the many *hongwanji* around the island. A centuries-old Buddhist tradition in the season of *obon,* which honors the ancestral dead, residents of Japanese and Okinawan descent show up in *happi* coats to dance to the beat of taiko drums and other traditional instruments. A handful of other folks in the wings soak up the colorful and hypnotic atmosphere and good local food. Hawai'i's *bon* dances are a step back in time to traditions that have since faded in Japan, and although their atmosphere is modestly lively, their spiritual significance is still taken very seriously. Check local papers for listings.

For a rundown of big concerts and events, contact the **Neal S. Blaisdell Center/Waikīkī Shell** (591-2211; www.blaisdellcenter.com; 777 Ward Ave., Kaka'ako); or **Ticketmaster** (1-877-750-4400; www.ticketmaster.com). Note that super-sized concert and sport events, such as the Pro Bowl, often take place at Aloha Stadium; tickets are generally sold through Ticketmaster.

For smaller performances ranging from sitar masters to barbershop quartets, contact downtown's beautifully restored, art-deco **Hawai'i Theatre** (528-0506; www.hawaiitheatre.com; 1130 Bethel St., Downtown); the Academy of Arts' **Doris Duke Theatre** (532-8700; www.honoluluacademy.org; 900 S. Beretania St., Makiki); **Imin Center-Jefferson Hall** (944-7111; www.eastwestcenter.org; University of Hawai'i, 1601 East-West Rd., Mānoa) at the East-West Center; or the **Honolulu Box Office** (550-8457; www.honoluluboxoffice.com).

Greater Honolulu

Army Community Theatre

438-4480.
Richardson Theatre, Fort Shafter, Building 500.
www.squareone.org/ACT.
Season: September through May.
Tickets: $8-$17.

This theater company, known most simply as ACT, has been a notable presence in Hawai'i since 1942, just when Hawai'i became fully engrossed in World War II. The theater itself is called the Richardson Theatre and is located on the Fort Shafter military base; however, performances are open to the general public. Recent productions include *Cats, Miss Saigon,* and *The Secret Garden,* and they schedule a season of four musicals and four plays per year.

Ballet Hawai'i

1-877-750-4400.
www.ballethawaii.org.
Season: Fall.
Tickets: $25-$75.

Ballet Hawai'i partners with the Honolulu Symphony for several traditional performances per year, including *The Nutcracker,* in which additional guest artists from other top ballet companies also participate. Founded more than 30 years ago, the organization runs the state's premier ballet training program, as well as coordinates performances by other dance companies such as the Mark Morris Dance Group.

Diamond Head Theatre

733–0274.
520 Makapu'u Ave., Kaimukī.
www.diamondheadtheatre.com.
Season: September through July.
Tickets: $12–$42.

The third oldest continually operating theater company in the U.S., Diamond Head Theatre has been in operation since 1915, when it was founded as The Footlights by some of Honolulu's most prominent women, who also starred in early productions. During World War II, they entertained thousands of troops throughout the Pacific. Popular, innovative, fun, and cozily stylish, productions usually feature guest stars in the main roles. Book in advance, as seats fill quickly. Recent shows include *La Cage aux Folles* and *The Full Monty.*

Hawai'i Opera Theatre
Neal S. Blaisdell Concert Hall, 777 Ward Ave., Makiki.
596–7858.
www.hawaiiopera.org.
Season: January through March, and July.
Tickets: $29-$120.

Hawaiian Opera Theatre, or HOT, productions are highly anticipated and often feature international operatic stars in lead roles. A sophisticated, well-dressed crowd attends three operas in the spring and one operetta each summer; if you can get tickets to the opening production, you'll experience the entire audience rising before the curtain opens to sing Hawai'i's former national anthem—now the state anthem—"Hawai'i Pono'i". The 2007 season included *Samson & Delila, Don Giovanni,* and *Madama Butterfly*. Sets and costumes are always magnificent, especially considering the moderate stage size at the Blaisdell Concert Hall. The Opera Ball held each autumn is one of Hawai'i's most glamorous events and HOT's biggest fundraiser.

Honolulu Symphony
792-2000.
Neal S. Blaisdell Concert Hall, 777 Ward Ave., Makiki.
Season: September through May.
Tickets: $12–$78.

Performing since 1900, the Honolulu Symphony is the oldest American orchestra west of the Rocky Mountains. A masterworks season, with themes such as "American in Paris," and a pops season with stars such as The Temptations, means a wide range of excellent performances are almost always taking place. The Honolulu Symphony Chorus is also wonderful and has performed at Carnegie Hall. All performances are held at the Blaisdell Concert Hall. The exquisite, black-tie Symphony Ball fundraiser is held every spring.

Honolulu Theatre for Youth
Tenney Theatre, 229 Queen Emma Square, Downtown.
839-9885.
www.htyweb.org.
Season: August through May.
Tickets: $8–$20.

Founded in 1955, this exceptional nonprofit theater group presents professional one-hour weekend productions for the young, such as *Tales of Old Hawai'i,* at Tenney Theatre at downtown's historic St. Andrew's Cathedral. *Christmas Talk Story,* a local-style production performed each year, is especially popular. Other lovely productions have included *Snow White* and *A Thousand Cranes.*

Iona Contemporary Dance Theatre
262-0110.
www.iona360.com.
Season: Year-round.
Tickets: $15–$45.

This small performance company favorite blends art and life with surreal, adventurous, meditative, and beautiful modern dance productions. Recent show titles include *Destiny, The Mythology of Angels,* and *Worshipping Sun.* Costumes are avant-garde masterpieces. Shows are limited throughout the year, although the dancers make brief appearances at various events. Venues change with the production.

Kennedy Theatre

956-7655.
University of Hawai'i, 1770 East-West Rd., Mānoa.
www.hawaii.edu/kennedy.
Season: September through April.
Tickets: $11–$16.

The University of Hawai'i at Mānoa's Kennedy Theatre presents a wide range of productions, such as *As You Like It* and the more unique *Kyôgen,* a program of four traditional plays featuring this medieval Japanese farcical form. Shows are student performed and held on the campus, giving you a chance for insight into the daily workings of the local university.

Kumu Kahua Theatre

536-4441.
46 Merchant St., Downtown.
www.kumukahua.org.
Season: October through April.
Tickets: $10-$16.

As this University of Hawai'i at Mānoa-affiliated, 100-seat theater moves closer to its 40th birthday, is as strong as ever. Featuring well-written, locally created productions, such as *Folks You Meet at Longs, Aging Is Not for Sissies,* and *Who the Fil-Am I?,* this is a special opportunity for a glimpse at authentic island life. Be prepared for liberal language choices in some performances, ranging from curses to thick "pidgin."

Mānoa Valley Theatre

988-6131.
2833 East Mānoa Rd., Mānoa.
www.manoavalleytheatre.com.
Season: September through August.
Tickets: $15–$30.

Mānoa Valley Theatre (MVT) has had an enthusiastic following since opening in 1969. Located in the verdant and cozy neighborhood of Mānoa, the theater is on the site of a 19th-century chapel and surrounded by an old Hawaiian graveyard. Saunter up to the bar before the show for wine, biscotti, and other refreshments. Recent productions include *The Graduate*, David Sedaris's *Santaland Diaries*, and the controversial and celebrated *M. Butterfly.*

WINDWARD O'AHU

Palikū Theatre
235-7310.
Windward Community College, 45-720 Kea'ahala Rd., Kāne'ohe.
www.windward.hawaii.edu/paliku.
Season: Spring and fall.
Tickets: $18–$26.

Folks staying on the windward side of O'ahu should take note that Windward Community College has recently opened a beautiful 300-seat theater, eliminating the need to drive into town at night. Productions include concerts, dramas, musicals, dance programs, film festivals, lectures, and Hawaiian music sessions; recent performances have included *James and the Giant Peach* and the Aspen Santa Fe Ballet.

Seasonal Events Islandwide

Honolulu is a festive city, entertaining nearly 1 million residents and more than 5 million visitors each year—so the list of events is endless. Below is a great "starter's kit" for goings-on across the island, organized alphabetically by event name. Be sure to check local papers to be fully clued in on the week's activities.

Aloha Festivals Waikīkī: Ho'olaule'a and Floral Parade
(589-1771; Waikīkī) Hawai'i's largest block party is not to be missed—and hard to avoid, since it's held in the middle of Kalākaua Avenue in Waikīkī. The parade erupts with floral lei, pageantry, and *pā'ū* riders in true Hawaiian-style. These back-to-back events take place in September.

Annual Easter Sunrise Service
(532-3720; National Memorial Cemetery of the Pacific, Punchbowl-Tantalus) For nearly 110 years, people of many faiths have gathered at Punchbowl for an Easter morning sunrise service. Services usually begin at about 6 AM.

Bayfest Hawai'i
(254-7679; Marine Corps Base Hawai'i, Kāne'ohe) This June extravaganza is O'ahu's biggest summer carnival and draws thousands, with major fireworks exhibitions, carnival rides, and more.

Hawai'i All-Collectors Show
(941-9754; Blaisdell Center, Makiki) This July event is the largest collectibles/antiques show in Hawai'i. You'll find vintage Hawaiiana, as well as treasures such as estate jewelry, old postcards, coins, ivory, and baseball cards. A grand Parisian flea market it is not, but it might yield a unique souvenir or two. A small admission fee is charged.

Hawaiian Slack Key Guitar Festival
(971-2510; Kapi'olani Park, Waikīkī) Local folks love the guitar—especially slack-key style, which originated in Hawai'i nei. Roll out the beach blanket and listen to slack-key masters perform magic all day at this August festival.

Hawai'i International Film Festival

(528-4433; throughout Honolulu) Considered one of the best film festivals in the U.S., it features films from around the world, with a special emphasis on selections from Asia, the Pacific, and North America. It's presented by Louis Vuitton in October. Admission fees.

Announcing the pā'ū queen in September's Aloha Festivals Floral Parade is an honor many people would wish to have. With permission from Aloha Festivals and rider.

Honolulu City Lights

(523-4385; Downtown Honolulu) This old-fashioned event has become an island tradition. The celebration kicks off on the first weekend in December, with a parade through downtown and the official lighting of City Hall's Christmas tree. Throughout the month and into the first week of January, thousands of residents bring their families into the Capital District at night to admire the extensive decorations. Brief tours of the lights via trolley, antique fire truck, or horse-drawn carriage make it even more fun.

Honolulu Festival & Parade

(926-2424; Hawai'i Convention Center, Ala Moana Center, and Waikīkī Beach Walk) This major March event promotes cultural exchange and harmony between Hawai'i and Asian-Pacific nations through weeklong events, such as a hula competition, craft fair, performances, and more. It culminates in a colorful ethnic heritage parade through Waikīkī.

Honolulu Marathon

(734-7200; throughout Honolulu) Nearly 30,000 entrants, from Ethiopia to Shanghai, ran in December's 2006 marathon—and almost 14,000 were first timers. Will you be next? Sign up in advance for this scenic 26-mile course running along the coast and into Waikīkī.

King Kamehameha Floral Parade

(586-0333; Downtown Honolulu to Waikīkī) More than 90 years old, this June parade is one of Honolulu's golden events. Although fewer floral floats appear each year due to budget shortages, the beautiful horseback *pā'ū* riders, royal court, and multitude of flowers are still its signature. Be sure to attend the King Kamehameha statue decoration ceremony in the Capital Historic District (usually held the day before the parade), when 26-foot flower strands are laced around the statue's arms and neck.

King Kamehameha Hula Competition

(536-6540; Blaisdell Arena, Makiki) If you really want to say you've seen hula, purchase tickets for this multi-day event in June and leave well educated. This event is very popular with residents and is in its 35th year.

Korean Festival

(792-9321; Kapi'olani Park, Waikīkī) Reportedly drawing more than one hundred thousand people at its 2006 event, this two-day August celebration is filled with food, dance, and more in honor of Hawai'i's thousands of Korean and Korean-American residents.

Lei Day Celebration

(692-5118; Kapi'olani Park, Waikīkī) The cherished local ritual of wearing fresh flower lei on May Day (May 1) began back in 1928. This Waikīkī celebration continues the unique tradition with a full Hawaiian royal court and some of Hawai'i's best entertainers.

Local Motion Surf into Summer

(523-7873; Sandy Beach, Hawai'i Kai) Memorial Day at hardcore Sandy Beach is crazy-packed when Hawai'i's largest amateur surf contest, presented by O'Neill, blazes into action.

Memorial Day Ceremonies at Punchbowl
(532-3720; National Memorial Cemetery of the Pacific, Punchbowl-Tantalus) This solemn Memorial Day commemoration at Punchbowl includes decorating more than thirty-five thousand graves with flower lei, government dignitary presentations, squadron jet formations overhead, and a 21-gun rifle salute.

Men's Moloka'i to O'ahu Canoe Race
(218-2047, Kahanamoku Beach, Waikīkī) This October race is an island tradition in which residents take special pride. Local, national, and international teams of men race against each other in Hawaiian-style outrigger canoes across the rough ocean channel between the islands of Moloka'i and O'ahu—a distance of about 41 miles. Cheer their arrival at Waikīkī's Kahanamoku Beach.

Messiah at Central Union Church
(941-0957; Central Union Church, Punahou) Each November, the one hundred-voice Oratorio Choir and Handel Festival Orchestra perform Handel's Messiah in this beautiful Congregationalist church built in 1924.

Mission Houses Museum Holiday Craft Fair
(531-0481; Mission Houses Museum, 553 S. King St., Downtown) Perhaps the most charming and tasteful holiday fair on the island is held at the Mission Houses Museum in late November. Handmade wooden bowls, glass ornaments, Hawaiian feather lei hatbands, jams, and much more are sold by the artists themselves.

NFL Pro Bowl
(1-877-750-4400; Aloha Stadium, 'Aiea) The American Football League's best players challenge the National Football Conference's in this greatly anticipated yearly all-star football game. The game is held in February, and there is an admission fee.

OceanFest
(545-4880, Waikīkī) Celebrate the birthday of ultimate surfer boy and ocean enthusiast, Duke Kahanamoku. This weeklong series of events in August includes a paddleboard championship, canoe race, longboard surf contest, tandem surfing championship, ocean swim, block party, and more.

Okinawan Festival
(676-5400; Kapi'olani Park, Waikīkī) This enormous, two-day September event kicks off with a parade through Waikīkī and ends with a festival featuring stage performances, food booths, and *bon* dancing.

Pacific Handcrafters Christmas Fair
(254-6788; Thomas Square, Makiki) High-end, handcrafted treasures are sold by the artists themselves at this special Handcrafters Guild December fair. Thomas Square itself is a historic site with beautiful banyan trees and is located across from the Honolulu Academy of Arts museum.

Pan Pacific Hula Festival Matsuri Parade
(926-8177; Ala Moana Center and Kalākaua Ave., Waikīkī) The Pan Pacific Hula Festival forges new relationships by showcasing hula troupes from Japan and Hawai'i. The *ho'olaulea* (block party) blowout in Waikīkī includes international entertainers, street performers, and great food, but the highlight is the parade that travels right down Kalākaua Avenue in Waikīkī.

In late November, the Mission Houses Museum hosts one of O'ahu's most authentic holiday season craft fairs.

Prince Lot Hula Festival
(839-5334; Moanalua Gardens, Moanalua) Spend the day immersed in traditional Hawaiian crafts, hula dancing, games, and more. This 60-plus-year-old event held in July is a great getaway from Waikīkī and an authentic experience with high resident turnout. Donations are requested.

Quiksilver Big Wave Invitational in Memory of Eddie Aikau
(637-2299; Waimea Bay, North Shore)
As big as its title, this event is held in winter—that is, if the waves on the North Shore stabilize at a minimum of 20 feet. If you hear the surf's up, keep tabs on the newspaper for an announcement that the contest is on. Good luck parking, and be aware that surf conditions of this nature are hazardous, even for viewers onshore, so observe all cautionary regulations to the letter. This is not a family picnic event.

Sony Open in Hawai'i
(523-7888; Wai'alae Country Club, Kahala) Each January some of the biggest stars in golf play this week-long, $5 million-purse PGA tour event to raise money for local nonprofit organizations. An admission fee is charged most days.

'Ukulele Festival
(732-3739; Kapi'olani Park, Waikīkī) Approaching its 30th year, this August concert features some of the best 'ukulele players in the world along with Hawai'i's favorite entertainers. Come see why we love this little instrument and how it can shine.

Vans Triple Crown of Surfing
(637-2299; Hale'iwa Beach, Sunset Beach, and 'Ehukai Beach, North Shore) The North Shore is so crowded during the Vans Hawaiian Pro, O'Neill World Cup, and Rip Curl Pro Pipeline Masters that you may never find parking. But if you truly love surfing or are a fan of the 1980s cult classic film, *North Shore,* go anyway and wear your hottest-looking bikini or board shorts. Be sure to call ahead—events get postponed all the time according to the quality of the waves. Runs November and December.

World Invitational Hula Festival

(591-2211; Waikīkī Shell, Waikīkī) Here's your last big chance of the year to really get schooled in the art of hula. Troupes from around the world perform both ancient and modern styles at this annual November event.

Hawai'i-style shave ice from Aoki's adds the final touch to a perfect North Shore day.

5

RESTAURANTS & FOOD PURVEYORS

Mixed Palate, Mixed Plate

Hawai'i's cuisine is unique, and although many people love to poke fun at our Spam® consumption, the luncheon meat doesn't begin to describe local cooking any more than trail mix characterizes Californian gastronomy. Our cuisine is as diverse and colorful as the people that have lived together on these isolated shores for the last two hundred years, and is truly a story of sharing well-loved food traditions.

In fact, our very humble, classic "plate lunch"—typically barbecued teriyaki beef or something similar served with two scoops of "sticky" rice and macaroni salad on a paper plate—originates in the yesteryear practice of Hawai'i's multiethnic plantation workers sharing their lunches with each other during break time.

Plate lunch is a true local-style meal.

Our culturally mixed schools and offices are not much different, and sampling each other's food is virtually *de rigueur.* Although we grow up chowing down on American-style Italian pizzas, we also snack on Chinese crack seed, fill up on Hawaiian poi and kalua pork at baby lū'au, trade Korean kim chee recipes, savor Hawaiian raw fish poke in shoyu, say "thanks" with Portuguese malasadas or Japanese mochi, and crave late-night Japanese saimin noodles with fish cake. Breakfast in a local restaurant might include fish, soba noodles, hamburger patty, eggs, Portuguese sausage, fried rice, and taro bread, and it may be eaten with chopsticks.

Many of these are "local" foods at their most basic and hearty. But Hawai'i also has gourmet cuisine born from these elements and raised by classically trained Hawai'i chefs. The Hawai'i Regional Cuisine movement emphasizes fresh local ingredients and a creative, healthful, upscale approach to preparing eclectic Island comfort dishes. Chefs such as Sam Choy, George Mavrothalassitis, Peter Merriman, Philippe Padovani, Alan Wong, Roy Yamaguchi, Russell Siu, Hiroshi Fukui, Bev Gannon, Wayne Hirabayashi, and D. K. Kodama have reached local, national, and in some cases international fame, and still preside over many of Hawai'i's best kitchens. Their work has influenced the development of the culinary industry in California and far beyond. You'll find the pleasures of Hawai'i Regional Cuisine, plus the now internationally popular Pacific Rim fusion, mom-and-pop-style local dishes, and regional takes on American classics everywhere you go on O'ahu.

Let's not forget true Hawaiian food. Most residents don't eat ethnic Hawaiian food on a day-to-day basis, but enjoy it for special occasions. Look for the sidebar in this chapter to learn more about traditional Hawaiian dishes—and we encourage you to taste them whenever the opportunity arises.

Because we're on a remote island, foods you take for granted at home may have had to be super-jetted in for your consumption. Restaurants must pay top dollar for everything from boxed cereal to escargot and will pass the cost along to you. Eating in Waikīkī in particular can be very expensive.

Cigarette smoking is no longer permitted in Hawai'i restaurants and bars; should you need to light up, the law requires you to step outside and about 20 feet away from the door to do so. Dress codes are generally minimal, and "aloha attire"—essentially meaning "relaxed nice" or "resortwear"—is common. At night, bump things up a notch; you probably won't get kicked out of most elegant restaurants for arriving in clean shorts, slippers, and a T-shirt, but they won't be excited to see you, either. (Men: Tuck in your aloha shirts for a more formal look, and wear covered shoes.) Residents dress similar to Mainlanders when it comes to a finer night out, although suits are unusual. An excise tax of 4.712 percent will appear on your bill, as well as on any other grocery purchase, food and otherwise. Tipping practices are standard American, with 15 percent or more the going rate for good service.

O'ahu has hundreds of eateries, from dim sum cafés to a Five Diamond French restaurant. Writing this chapter was very difficult, as we have room for only a handful of the best in our efforts to provide you with a wide selection of flavors, prices, ambiances, and locations. Before you trundle off to eat, however, call ahead to get the latest scoop—the restaurant you have your heart set on might have closed for renovations or may already be booked for the evening.

All entries below are organized by region, then alphabetized. Traditional, sit-down/table service restaurants are listed first, followed by food purveyors and take-out-style establishments, such as sandwich shops, coffee stops, bakeries, ice cream stores, and the like, as well as a list of the best afternoon teas, interesting markets, wine bars, and culinary opportunities. A brief index at the back of this book allows you to search for restaurants by price or cuisine type, instead of alphabetically, and a glossary below will help you wade through food terminology.

The price codes below are general cost estimates for an average person's restaurant meal, including appetizer, entrée, and dessert, but not including drinks of any kind, tax, or tip. Since lunch is often less expensive than dinner, places that serve both are assigned an overall averaged price rating—meaning you may might pay a little less at lunch and a little more at dinner. Where helpful and applicable, we've listed two categories (for example, "moderate-expensive") to indicate when costs may be on the higher end of moderate, or lower end of expensive.

Please note that specific menu items featured below may have changed since the time of writing. Although any restaurant can have a bad day or not be to your personal taste, the following entries have good reputations for fairly consistent quality and are some of the local favorites. We hope they'll be at their best upon your visit.

DINING PRICE CODES

Inexpensive	Up to $15
Moderate	$15–30
Expensive	$30–65
Very Expensive	$65 or more

Credit Cards

AE	American Express
DC	Diners Club
DISC	Discover Card
MC	MasterCard
V	Visa

Other Codes

B	Breakfast
L	Lunch
D	Dinner
SB	Sunday Brunch
SSB	Saturday and Sunday Brunch

BASIC FOOD GLOSSARY

The pronunciation guides below approximate the way words are most frequently pronounced by residents and are followed with everyday meanings.

adobo (ah-DOH-boh)—both a dish and marinating and stewing technique
'ahi (AH-hee)—Hawaiian tuna, including albacore, bigeye and yellowfin
aku (AH-koo)—skipjack or bonito fish
apple-banana—small, sweet, firm variety of banana
a'ukū (ah-OO-koo)—swordfish
azuki (ah-ZOO-kee)—sweetened black or red bean (whole or paste)
bento (BEN-toe)—takeout, boxed meal
butterfish—black cod
crack seed—dried fruit (such as plum), seasoned sweet and/or sour
furikake (fur-ee-KAH-keh)—roasted seaweed, salt, and sesame seed flavoring

haupia—(haoo-PEE-ah) coconut pudding
huli huli chicken (HOO-lee)—barbecued chicken turned repeatedly while cooking
imu (EE-moo)—traditional Hawaiian underground oven
kālua pig/pork (kah-LOO-ah)—salty pork dish baked in an underground oven
kampachi (kahm-PAH-chee)—amberjack fish
kau kau (KAOO-kaoo)—pidgin word meaning "food"
kiawe (kee-AH-veh)—mesquite-related wood used in barbecuing
kūlolo (koo-LOH-loh)—taro root and coconut cream pudding
laulau (LAOO-laoo)—taro leaf and meat (often pork) packet baked underground
li hing (lee-HING)—blend of sugar, salt, and five-spice often used to flavor snacks
liliko'i (lee-lee-KO-ee)—yellow passion fruit
limu (LEE-moo)—commonly used to refer to seaweed
loco moco (LOH-koh-MOH-koh)—fried egg/hamburger patty/white rice/gravy dish
lomilomi salmon (LOH-mee)—salsa-like salted salmon, onion, and tomato dish
lumpia (LOOM-pee-ah)—spring-roll-like wrap with vegetables and bits of meat inside
lū'au (LOO-aoo)—now used to refer to a "traditional" Hawaiian feast and celebration
mahimahi (mah-hee-MAH-hee)—dolphin fish (not the mammal!)
malasada or *malassada* (mah-lah-SAH-dah)—ball-shaped donut rolled in sugar
manapua (mah-nah-POO-ah)—steamed, moist bun usually filled with pork
mochi (MOH-chee)—steamed rice flour cake
moi (MOH-ee)—threadfin fish
musubi (MOO-soo-bee)—rice block often topped with Spam® (Spam *musubi*)
'ōhelo berry (oh-HEH-loh)—a native berry related to the cranberry
'ō'io (oh-EE-oh)—bonefish
okazuya (oh-kah-ZOO-yah)—traditional Japanese take-out shop
onaga (oh-NAH-gah)—red snapper
ono (OH-noh)—large mackerel-type fish
'ono (OH-noh)—Hawaiian word meaning "delicious"
opah (OH-pah)—moonfish
'ōpakapaka (oh-pah-kah-PAH-kah)—blue snapper
phô (FUH)—beef and noodle soup
plate lunch—meat entrée, two scoops of white rice, and macaroni salad
pohā berry (POH-hah)—similar to cape gooseberry
poi (POH-ee)—starchy, pudding-like side dish made from taro root
poke (POH-keh)—marinated dish, usually of raw and diced tuna or octopus
Portuguese sausage—garlic-heavy pork sausage, usually served for breakfast
pūpū (POO-poo)—Hawaiian word now meaning "appetizer"
saimin (sye-MIN)—ramen-style noodles in dashi-flavored broth
sashimi (sah-SHEE-mee)—thinly sliced raw fish, usually tuna
shave ice—local version of snow cone (no "d" on "shave")
shoyu (SHOY-yoo)—soy sauce
soba (SOH-bah)—narrow buckwheat noodles
tako (TAH-koh)—octopus
taro or *kalo* (TAH-roh or KAH-loh)—tuber plant primarily used to make poi
teriyaki beef (teh-ree-YAH-kee)—teriyaki-marinated broiled or grilled beef
tī or *kī leaf* (TEE or KEE)—leaf of the tī plant, used to wrap foods and for other purposes
ulua (oo-LOO-ah)—selected species of crevalle, jack, or pompano fish

Restaurants

Waikīkī

Aqua Café
922-6888.
Waikīkī Shopping Plaza, 2250 Kalākaua Ave., Ground Floor.
Open: Year-round.
Price: Moderate.
Cuisine: Regional American.
Serving: B, L, D.
Credit Cards: AE, MC, V.
Handicapped Accessible: Yes.
Reservations: Not accepted.

Animated without attitude and Island style without sacrificing vaguely trendy urban influences, you'll get some very decent-to-good food at the Aqua as well as friendly service. Breakfast selections include loco moco, haupia-stuffed sweetbread French toast, and buttermilk pancakes. Lunch and dinner flirt with local touches too, such as barbecued kalua pork quesadilla and Mr. Mau's oxtail soup, and also do up old favorites, such as the veggie burger, spinach salad, and clam chowder. Expect a strange onslaught of three different music selections playing at once from various quarters of the mall, but these distractions fade quickly.

Arancino
923-5557.
255 Beach Walk Ave.
www.arancino.net.
Open: Year-round.
Price: Moderate.
Cuisine: Italian.
Serving: L, D.
Credit Cards: AE, DC, DISC, MC, V.
Handicapped Accessible: Yes.
Reservations: Not accepted—but call ahead to put your name on the wait list.

Tucked into a cozy space on Beach Walk Avenue is the adorable Arancino—tidily rustic and easy-going, yet stylish, busy, and professional enough to make a visit special. If there's a wait, write your name on the list posted at the door; once inside, your food will likely come quickly and without a fuss. Napoli-style thin-crust pizzas are excellent, with selections such as asparagus, fresh tomato, and gorgonzola cheese; or try mussels, clams, calamari, and shrimp in tomato sauce. We expected personal sized pizzas and were pleased to find they can feed two average appetites. Other dishes include minestrone soup, beef carpaccio, and risotto.

The Japanese-visitor-oriented menu has a high markup on wines by the glass and on some of its bottles, although they offer several good selections. Arancino's newer sister restaurant closer to Diamond Head, **Arancino di Mare** (931-6273; Waikīkī Beach Marriott Resort & Spa, 2552 Kalākaua Ave.), is equally as good.

Bali by the Sea
941-2254.
Hilton Hawaiian Village, 2005 Kalia Rd.
www.hiltonhawaiianvillage.com.
Closed: Sundays.
Price: Expensive–Very Expensive.
Cuisine: Pacific Rim/Continental.
Serving: D.
Credit Cards: AE, DC, DISC, MC, V.
Handicapped Accessible: Yes.
Reservations: Strongly recommended.
Special Features: Open-air, oceanfront dining.

Delicious Waikīkī beachfront views await you at this very elegant hotel restaurant, as well as exceptional food and an award-winning wine selection recognized by *Wine Spectator* magazine. Bali By the Sea is recognized among the Distinguished Restaurants of North America and earned the AAA Four Diamond Award. Chef Adam Hightower is highly skilled in all areas of preparation and has represented the United States in the 2000 World Championship Culinary Olympics in Europe.

Experience its many alluring dishes,

including sugar cane crusted scallops, Kahuku sweet corn and Maui onion soup, chilled sashimi plate, roasted island beets and goat cheese salad, sautéed ʻōpakapaka with macadamia nuts and cilantro, and oven roasted Colorado rack of lamb. Desserts, such as liliko'i cheesecake and guava sorbet, are the final touches on a perfectly crafted menu. Pair your meal with a glass or bottle from the restaurant's championship collection of fine French and California wines and cap it off with rich port, dessert wine, or pure mamaki tea.

Canoes at the ʻIlikai
951-6861.
ʻIlikai Hotel, 1777 Ala Moana Blvd.
www.ilikaihotel.com.
Open: Year-round.
Price: Moderate–Expensive.
Cuisine: Hawaiʻi Regional.
Serving: B, L, D.
Credit Cards: AE, DC, DISC, MC, V.
Handicapped Accessible: Yes.
Reservations: Strongly recommended.
Special Features: Patio dining and moderate harborfront views.

A Waikīkī tradition for many, this ʻIlikai signature restaurant has an understatedly upscale café feel. Sit inside its glass walls to cool off, or choose the large patio area with harbor views—you'll see residents enjoying business lunches and visitors kicking back before or after a day on the golf course or beach.

The food is overall good, and its pasta, salads, and beef have all won local awards. The menu emphasizes Island produce and seafood, and includes egg white vegetable frittata, buttermilk pancakes, loco moco, double onion steak sandwich, Thai lettuce wraps, seared ʻahi salad, ginger crusted Pacific snapper, blue crab crusted mahimahi, and chocolate créme brulee bread pudding.

California Pizza Kitchen
924-2000.
Center of Waikīkī, 2284 Kalākaua Ave.
www.cpk.com.
Closed: Thanksgiving Day and December 25.
Price: Moderate.
Cuisine: Californian/Eclectic.
Serving: L, D.
Credit Cards: AE, DC, DISC, MC, V.
Handicapped Accessible: Yes.
Reservations: Not accepted.
Special Features: Open-air patio dining.

Yes—this is a good family choice for high-priced, high-end Waikīkī. If you've never eaten at this outrageously popular chain, expect creatively delicious pizzas, such as mango tandoori chicken, tasty salads (the Waldorf's really good), and a wide mix of other dishes that will address every need. The kids' menu includes basic salads and Hawaiian pizzas. The best part: it's located right in the middle of Waikīkī on the main drag, making it an easy choice for dining without heavy fuss.

Cha Cha Cha Waikīkī
923-7797.
342 Seaside Ave.
Closed: Thanksgiving Day and December 25.
Price: Inexpensive–Moderate.
Cuisine: Caribbean-Mexican.
Serving: L, D.
Credit Cards: MC, V.
Handicapped Accessible: Yes.
Reservations: Not accepted.

Tucked away in the middle of Waikīkī, this perky little Carib/Tex-Mex spot has both a colorful personality and pretty tasty food for the price. You'll find a creatively casual menu with Jamaican jerk chicken burritos, mahimahi quesadillas, garlic soup served with tortilla strips, blackened fish Caesar salads, and more—plus happy hour from 4–6 PM and again from 9–11 PM. May we call that double happiness? A kids menu with "itty bitty" burritos and other goodies, super friendly local-style service, a shorts-and-slippers attitude, and a streetfront outdoor patio make it a great place for an unpretentious and enjoyable evening with the gang, or to hang out with your sweetie.

Cheesecake Factory
924-5001.
Royal Hawaiian Shopping Center, 2301 Kalākaua Ave.
www.thecheesecakefactory.com.
Closed: Thanksgiving Day.
Price: Moderate.
Cuisine: American.
Serving: B (from 11 AM), L, D, SB.
Credit Cards: AE, DC, DISC, MC, V.
Handicapped Accessible: Yes.
Reservations: Not accepted.
Special Features: Sidewalk patio dining.

Simply put, Waikīkī has few middle-income places to eat. So when this chain opened several years ago, visitors and residents went nuts. Someone put on their thinking cap before swinging a hammer, and the hard-to-find sidewalk café appeared along with innovative and appealing design elements throughout. Of all the Cheesecake Factories in the U.S., this operation is by far the biggest grossing, and at one point waits were longer than an hour and a half to get in the door for its heaping plates of good food. Dig into fire-roasted fresh artichoke, pesto chicken pizza, beef burgers, miso salmon, fresh fish tacos, a "lū'au" salad, and massive desserts of all kinds. On Sundays they offer a brunch menu from 10-2.

Diamond Head Grill
922-3734.
W Honolulu, 2885 Kalākaua Ave.
www.w-dhg.com.
Open: Year-round.
Price: Expensive–Very Expensive.
Cuisine: Regional Italian.
Serving: B, L (hotel guests only), D.
Credit Cards: AE, MC, V.
Handicapped Accessible: Yes.
Reservations: Recommended.
Special Features: Views of Diamond Head.

The W does everything with hip flair, so expect no less of its resident restaurant, Diamond Head Grill. The menu blends regional Italian with European and Californian influences, featuring savory dishes that complement the sleek, contemporary, natural tones and ambiance of the restaurant, and play off the understatedly dramatic view of Diamond Head and Kapi'olani Park. House-cured duck prosciutto, char-grilled local octopus, spinach and ricotta dumplings, Hawaiian yellowfin tuna belly, Muscovy duck breast, and braised lacinato kale are but a few of the creative dishes awaiting you. Reviews of the restaurant tend to be mixed, however, regarding both the quality of the food and service for the price.

See and be seen at the W Hotel's cosmopolitan Diamond Head Grill. Photo courtesy Starwood Hotels & Resorts Hawai'i.

Duke's Canoe Club
922-2268.
Outrigger Waikīkī, 2335 Kalākaua Ave.
www.dukeswaikiki.com.
Closed: One day per year in December (the date changes each year).
Price: Moderate–Expensive.
Cuisine: Regional American.
Serving: B, L, D.
Credit Cards: AE, DC, DISC, MC, V.
Handicapped Accessible: Yes.
Reservations: Recommended for lunch and dinner.
Special Features: Patio dining and beachfront views.

This auspicious, Jimmy-Buffet-style, ten-year Waikīkī veteran has become almost as iconic as its namesake, famed swimmer and surfer Duke Kahanamoku. The breakfast crowd is a trickle of locals mixed with visitors from every walk of life, all of whom have arrived for two reasons: the all-you-can-eat buffet and the picture-perfect, open-air views directly onto Waikīkī Beach's busiest stretch. Most of the food is only pretty good—but that's not the point. Lunch is popular, but as cocktail hour approaches, the sand-level deck opens and the place explodes with energy and crowds that don't ease up until long past the dinner hour.

The menu goes a fairly standard route with crab and macadamia nut won tons, mango barbecue ribs, tuna melts, prime teriyaki sirloin, and shrimp scampi. Many of its entertainers are top local performers, however, and the vintage Hollywood-Hawaiiana décor infused with memorabilia of "The Duke" and other beachboys is festive and unpretentious.

Eggs 'n Things
949-0820.
1911-B Kalākaua Ave.
www.eggsnthings.com.
Closed: December 25.
Price: Inexpensive.
Cuisine: American.
Serving: B.
Credit Cards: MC, V.
Handicapped Accessible: No.
Reservations: Not accepted.

While it's true that Eggs 'n Things only serves breakfast, don't go thinking that they're closed in the evenings. After all, some people need their pancakes well before dawn. Therefore, they open at 11 PM and serve until 2 PM the next day. Crowds rotate from off-duty strippers, cops, partiers, and hotel desk workers to Japanese tourists, retirees, and late sleepers.

The décor is virtually nonexistent, and somehow that works. This friendly institution has been open since 1974 and really doesn't need to upgrade its look; it already has a painful wait on any given morning, and you'll be certain that tour busses arrived just before you did. Worth it? Perhaps. Fun items include banana pancakes, sour cream crepes, and pineapple waffles, plus delicious, fresh fish caught by the owner pops up alongside omelets and other unsuspecting dishes.

Hau Tree Lānai
921-7066.
New Otani Kaimana Beach Hotel, 2863 Kalākaua Ave.
www.kaimana.com.
Open: Year-round.
Price: Expensive.
Cuisine: Pacific Rim.
Serving: B, L, D.
Credit Cards: AE, DC, DISC, MC, V.
Handicapped Accessible: Yes.
Reservations: Recommended.
Special Features: All patio oceanfront dining.

In Waikīkī, you pay a premium for perfect settings. The Hau Tree Lānai sits right on the sands of spectacular Kaimana Beach, framed by an old railing once belonging to the graceful estate that sat here, and shaded by the same gnarled hau tree that Robert

Louis Stevenson reputedly enjoyed sitting under while he wrote. Charming day and night, this is a magical, romantic, and moderately festive nook.

Traditional cuisine is infused with Pacific influences, such as fresh poi pancakes, seafood omelets, sweetbread French toast with coco-macadamia nuts, Portuguese bean soup, papaya chicken salad, Gemini lobster tail, Cajun 'ahi sashimi, and charbroiled filet mignon beef. Note that the food of late doesn't always match the high tabs. Few dishes are true standouts, which can downgrade an otherwise idyllic Hawaiian experience. Still yet, mealtimes draw many local folks who look as if they could have afforded to eat elsewhere if they wanted to.

Holokai Grill
924-7245.
Waikīkī Beach Walk, 226 Lewers St.
www.holokaigrill.com.
Open: Year-round.
Price: Moderate.
Cuisine: Pacific Rim.
Serving: B, L, D.
Credit Cards: AE, DC, DISC, MC, V.
Handicapped Accessible: Yes.
Reservations: Recommended.

Newly opened in 2007, Holokai Grill is the second successful restaurant emerging from the team that created the popular Tiki's Grill & Bar, on the other end of Waikīkī. Pacific Rim foods are balanced with American comfort classics in a cozily casual, Polynesian voyaging canoe-themed environment. Fresh, locally grown ingredients from both land and sea, late serving hours, and a location along Waikīkī's newest strip make it a tasty experience.

The new Holokai Grill creates savory Pacific Rim dishes in a fun atmosphere. Photo courtesy Holokai Grill.

House Without a Key
923-2311.
Halekulani, 2199 Kalia Rd.
www.halekulani.com.
Open: Year-round.
Price: Moderate–Expensive.
Cuisine: Regional American.
Serving: B, L, D.
Credit Cards: AE, DC, MC, V.
Handicapped Accessible: Yes.
Reservations: Not accepted.
Special Features: Open-air patio oceanfront dining with Diamond Head views.

We can't say enough about the setting of this world-class hotel's patio restaurant. Immortalized in 1925 in a Charlie Chan novel, House Without a Key is quintessential Hawai'i glamour—and its many decades of delighting residents and visitors attests to its perfect atmosphere. The setting is spacious and mellow, with views onto the ocean and Diamond Head in the distance; and from the late afternoon until early evening, soothing vintage Hawaiian performances will transport you back in time.

The food is good to very good, although it's not the main draw. They serve a moderately expensive buffet for breakfast, but the fairly priced lunch and dinner are more popular, with items such as a watercress salad, grilled lemongrass chicken sandwich, saimin, sautéed fresh mahimahi, and seared New York steak.

House Without a Key should be on your menu at some point during your stay, even if just for sunset drinks and appetizers.

Hula Grill Waikīkī
923-4852.
Outrigger Waikīkī Hotel, 2335 Kalākaua Ave., 2nd Floor.
www.hulagrillwaikiki.com.
Closed: December 24, December 25, and January 1.
Price: Moderate.
Cuisine: Hawai'i Regional.
Serving: B, D.
Credit Cards: AE, DISC, MC, V.
Handicapped Accessible: Yes.
Reservations: Recommended.
Special Features: Open-air, oceanfront dining and Diamond Head views.

This may be the best place in Waikīkī to eat breakfast, although with the outrageously popular Duke's just below it, many haven't noticed. A Maui-born restaurant with contemporary, soft, native ohia-wood plantation décor and a restful atmosphere, the remarkably, unhindered view includes Waikīkī Beach all the way to Diamond Head.

While Duke's serves a chaotic party buffet in the mornings, you'll relax with warm tableside service, really good coffee, and creative, overall tasty à la carte dishes, such as traditional buttermilk pancakes with bananas and macadamia nuts, or crab cake eggs benedict. Prices for breakfast are amazingly reasonable—especially considering the prime location. Dinner is on the high end of moderately priced, with Pacific-oriented fare like macadamia nut crusted mahimahi, shrimp kung pao stir fry, baby back barbecue ribs, and coconut créme brulee. Validated parking is offered at the hotel.

Hy's Steak House
922-5555.
Waikīkī Park Heights, 2440 Kūhiō Ave.
www.hyshawaii.com.
Open: Year-round.
Price: Expensive.
Cuisine: Continental with Euro/Pacific/American influences.
Serving: D.
Credit Cards: AE, DC, DISC, MC, V.
Handicapped Accessible: Yes.
Reservations: Recommended.

For many residents and visitors, Hy's is the ultimate splurge. It has been recognized by *Zagat Survey* as a top Hawaiian steak house and is the recipient of numerous local awards for food and dining ambiance, including being voted the island's best steak house by *Honolulu Magazine*. It would be hard to not deeply satisfy your every red meat fantasy at this long-standing restaurant.

Forget coconut cocktails and pineapple burgers for a moment and transport yourself instead to a moody, plush, Victorianesque men's club where your whims are taken seriously by congenial, tuxedoed waiters. Menu highlights include filet mignon tartar, Beluga caviar, beef tenderloin with black truffle sauce, roast rack of lamb, kiawe-broiled steak, Chateaubriand, oriental-style Hawaiian snapper, and strawberry flambé. Their prime beef cuts are dry-aged and trimmed right on the premises, and children have their own menu options. Add an extensive and award-winning wine list recognized by *Wine Spectator* magazine that focuses on savory California reds, after-dinner drinks such as Remy Martin Louis XIII, and legendary Hawai'i performers, and you'll experience an evening to remember. Valet and self-parking are available and collared shirts are required for men.

Keo's in Waikīkī
951-9355.
2028 Kūhiō Ave.
www.keosthaicuisine.com.
Open: Year-round.
Price: Moderate.
Cuisine: Thai/Hawai'i Regional.
Serving: B, L, D.
Credit Cards: AE, DC, DISC, MC, V.
Handicapped Accessible: Yes.
Reservations: Recommended for dinner.

Nearly three decades in business, Keo's grew from a small Thai eatery to one of Hawai'i's most well-known restaurants. Its foyer walls are thick with autographed photos of international celebrity diners, drawn to its succulent preparations and lush décor. *Newsweek* magazine has called it "one of the choicest dining spots in Honolulu," *Gourmet* bestowed it with the Top Table Award, and *Bon Appétit* named it "America's Best Thai Restaurant."

The restaurant's mood is deeply exotic and borders on gaudily luxuriant, with dim illumination enhanced by open-air sunlight, fanciful sprays of orchids, and bronzed sculptures that seem to fuse into a dreamscape. Restaurateur Keo Sananikone is so insistent on fresh herbs and spices that he grows them himself on his North Shore farms. Breakfast is not their best meal, although the specials are really a great deal. Lunch and dinner are what you really want—Thai ginger soup, string beans with ginger and chili, cashew nuts with chicken, Panang curry, shiitake mushrooms with snow peas, grilled country game hen, Bangkok duck, apple-banana in coconut milk. The portions are medium in size and meant to serve two. Free valet parking is available. The only ding we give Keo's is for the recent addition of an electronic message board touting the restaurant.

La Mer
923-2311.
Halekulani, 2199 Kalia Rd.
www.halekulani.com.
Open: Year-round.
Price: Very Expensive.
Cuisine: Neoclassical French.
Serving: D.
Credit Cards: AE, DC, MC, V.
Handicapped Accessible: Yes.
Reservations: Strongly recommended.
Special Features: Open-air, oceanfront dining and Diamond Head views.

How does one describe a perfect dining experience? As the world-renowned Halekulani hotel's signature restaurant, La Mer is the only AAA Five Diamond restaurant in the entire state of Hawai'i.

It may be the professionalism and warmth you feel from its staff; or perhaps the open-air window views onto Diamond Head and the blue ocean. Or, it could be the stellar, carefully crafted dishes that appear before you, such as langoustine rosemary skewer, golden imperial Osetra caviar, tournedos of roasted venison, bouillabaisse in puff pastry, and Grand Marnier soufflé. Maybe it's the award-winning wine list. For this author, it's the dreamlike atmosphere and décor—glowing warm tones from polished golden woods, Japanese teahouse touches, such as sliding rice paper and bamboo doors, and an ambience that is both subdued and charged with almost spiritual energy.

We've heard several complaints over the years that the restaurant didn't meet expectations or was too expensive, and it's certainly possible that La Mer doesn't always deliver. If you can afford to dine here, however, we recommend it. The hotel offers free valet parking. A jacket is not required for men, but strongly suggested; a collared shirt is required.

MAC 24/7
921-5564.
Hilton Waikīkī Prince Kūhiō,
2500 Kūhiō Ave.
www.mac247waikiki.com.
Open: Year-round.
Price: Moderate.
Cuisine: Contemporary American/Diner.
Serving: B, L, D.
Credit Cards: AE, DC, DISC, MC, V.
Handicapped Accessible: Yes.
Reservations: Optional.
Special Features: 24-hour service.

MAC 24/7 stands for "modern American cooking" and full service around the clock—a bonus not lost on Waikīkī crowds that often keep nonconformist hours. Chomp on enormous portions of comfort foods like "Elvis" chunky peanut butter pancakes swirled with crispy bacon, pecan praline French toast, Fox's egg cream, Rueben corned beef sandwiches, sirloin meatloaf, and cupcakes—and savor its hip, streamlined, coffee-shop look. You can order anything off the menu at any time. Local-boy chef Pedro Rivera Rosa has worked as Steven Spielberg's private chef. Free validated parking, eye candy décor that contrasts pleasingly with the lush garden view, and a full bar with a flat-screen TV seal the deal.

All night and all day, every day of the year, MAC 24/7 serves up home-style food with a twist.
Photo courtesy Lew Harrington.

Michel's
923-6552.
Colony Surf, 2895 Kalākaua Ave.
www.michelshawaii.com.
Closed: December 25.
Price: Expensive–Very Expensive.
Cuisine: Neoclassic French Continental.
Serving: D, SB.
Credit Cards: AE, DC, DISC, MC, V.
Handicapped Accessible: Yes.
Reservations: Strongly recommended for dinner; recommended for Sunday Brunch.
Special Features: Open-air, oceanfront dining.

Another of Honolulu's many treasured restaurants is Michel's, which opened in 1962 and was an instant star. Eventually it sold to a series of owners who couldn't keep up the magic; in recent years it has come to rest once again in the care of a master restaurateur and it's better than ever. You'll be transported into the lap of luxury when you enter this romantic, open-air, oceanfront retreat, where you'll feel right at home. Arrive shortly before sunset to breathe in the outstanding panoramic view of shimmering waves, tiki torches, and endless horizon—then settle in for an evening of five-star service and cuisine. Although the waiters wear tuxedos, you don't have to; upscale resort attire is very welcome (collared shirts for men are a must), as are hearty laughter and large groups.

Please your senses with Parisian abalone, Burgundy escargot, ʻahi carpaccio, steak tartare, lobster bisque, crisp island ʻōpakapaka, seared scallops, filet mignon Madagascar, Chateaubriand for two, baked Camembert, and cherries jubilee, among other tantalizing selections. An extensive wine list offers plenty to pair with, and subdued entertainment includes a Grammy® Award-winning slack-key guitarist and a harpist. Valet parking is available at the entrance.

The ą la carte Sunday brunch at Michel's is an institution and a lovely affair.

Miyako Japanese Restaurant
921-7077.
New Otani Kaimana Beach Hotel, 2863 Kalākaua Ave.
Open: Year-round.
Price: Moderate–Expensive.
Cuisine: Traditional Japanese.
Serving: D.
Credit Cards: AE, DC, DISC, MC, V.
Handicapped Accessible: Yes.

Reservations: Recommended.
Special Features: Open-air, oceanfront dining.

Choose your level of comfort: a simple, Western-style dining room that de-emphasizes décor and instead lets pure ocean views speak; a table on the open-air balcony high above the beach; or seating in a traditional tatami room. Kimono-clad servers will bring you made-to-order selections wherever you are. Choose from a variety of dishes, such as fresh island tuna with Japanese yam, oyster platter with butter herb sauce, lobster tempura, beef tataki with ponzu sauce, red soybean soup, and sushi rolls. You can also go prix fixes with appetizer, soup, entrée, and dessert.

Orchids
923-2311
Halekulani, 2199 Kalia Rd.
www.halekulani.com.
Open: Year-round.
Price: Expensive.
Cuisine: Pacific Rim/Seafood.
Serving: B, L, D, SB.
Credit Cards: AE, DC, MC, V.
Handicapped Accessible: Yes.
Reservations: Recommended.
Special Features: Open-air oceanfront patio dining with Diamond Head views.

Yet another Honolulu winner is the Halekulani hotel's Orchids, set right on the oceanfront. The décor has a light and airy casual elegance with orchid sprays enveloping patrons in delicate colors. Best known for its breakfasts—and especially its award-winning Sunday brunch—you'll pay out but get great returns. Flute and harp accompaniments add an extra layer of richness to Sunday mornings. (For those of you who suddenly decided this is the perfect place to take Mom for Mother's Day Sunday brunch [and it is], call immediately—they take reservations for the occasion up to a year in advance.) à la carte brunch dishes include haupia French toast sandwich with caramelized fresh island pineapples and eggs benedict with Alaskan king crab cake. Be sure to order their signature popovers.

Lunch and dinner are also excellent, with delicious dishes, such as tofu and corn cakes, cinnamon-spiced kabocha soup, charbroiled red salmon, seared jumbo scallops, Kona-raised Maine lobster, and signature island-raised moi. Free valet parking is available.

Roy's Restaurant
923-7697.
Waikīkī Beach Walk, 226 Lewers St.
www.roysrestaurant.com.
Open: Year-round.
Price: Expensive.
Cuisine: Hawai'i Fusion.
Serving: L, D.
Credit Cards: AE, DC, DISC, MC, V.
Handicapped Accessible: Yes.
Reservations: Strongly recommended.
Special Features: Open-air patio dining.

Roy's is one of Hawai'i's top restaurants and hip founder Roy Yamaguchi is known internationally as a culinary pioneer. When he opened the first of his international locations in Honolulu in 1988, *Food & Wine* magazine called it the "crown jewel of Honolulu's East-West eateries" and *Condé Nast Traveller* named it in their "Top 50." *Gourmet* magazine has called Yamaguchi "the father of modern East-West cooking."

This is the newest of O'ahu's several locations—open as of mid-2007—and the only one in Waikīkī. Outstanding dishes include items such as Szechuan baby back ribs, island 'ahi poke, Hawaiian style misoyaki butterfish, and melting hot chocolate soufflé. All dishes emphasize high-quality, fresh local ingredients. The award-winning and impeccable wine list will add to an already perfect evening.

Sansei Seafood Restaurant & Sushi Bar
931-6286.
Waikīkī Beach Marriott Resort & Spa,

2552 Kalākaua Ave., 3rd Floor.
www.sanseihawaii.com.
Open: Year-round.
Price: Moderate–Expensive.
Cuisine: Contemporary Japanese/Sushi/Pacific Rim.
Serving: D.
Credit Cards: AE, DISC, MC, V.
Handicapped Accessible: Yes.
Reservations: Recommended.

A Hale 'Āina Award-winning restaurant founded by local celebrity chef Dave (D. K.) Kodama, expect a fusion of exciting and delicious dishes and sushi-like Asian shrimp cake, Japanese calamari salad, panko-crusted fresh 'ahi sashimi sushi roll, lobster and blue crab ravioli, mild chili-porcini mushroom-crusted filet of beef tenderloin, and macadamia nut tempura fried ice cream. The seafood and sushi in particular are constantly raved about—and to prevent burning a tiny hole in your pocket, take advantage of the restaurant's special pricing during early bird hours and late night dining (they stay open until 2 AM Fridays and Saturdays!).

One of the best aspects of this festive dining experience is the wine list. Hawai'i has only two master sommeliers, and one of them, Chuck Furuya, presides over Sansei's wine selection. Needless to say, *Wine Spectator* has given it an award of excellence.

Shanghai Bistro
955-8668.
Discovery Bay Center, 1778 Ala Moana Blvd.
Open: Year-round.
Price: Moderate–Expensive.
Cuisine: Contemporary Chinese/Asian Fusion.
Serving: L, D, SSB.
Credit Cards: AE, DC, DISC, MC, V.
Handicapped Accessible: Yes.
Reservations: Recommended.

This beautiful and contemporary restaurant on the edge of Waikīkī suffers for its location, but the innovative preparations are good and the atmosphere chic. Some critics suggest that the food pairings can be too eclectic. At lunchtime, choose from set menus, ą la carte items, or a range of Hong Kong, Shanghai, and Northern style dim sum selections such as braised prawns, pan fried turnip cake, unagi tofu roll, or pork siu mai; dinner entrées include mid-priced dishes, such as sweet and sour crispy sea bass, bistro pork chops, and spicy eggplant with seafood. However, should you care to ramp it up, you'll find items rarely featured at the average Chinese restaurant, including abalone and shark fin steak and Maine lobster. Be forewarned that should you order these specialties, your bill will most definitely skyrocket into the "expensive–very expensive" price category.

Singha Thai Cuisine
941-2898.
1910 Ala Moana Blvd.
www.singhathai.com.
Closed: Thanksgiving Day.
Price: Moderate–Expensive.
Cuisine: Contemporary Thai/Pacific Rim.
Serving: D.
Credit Cards: AE, DC, DISC, MC, V.
Handicapped Accessible: Yes.
Reservations: Recommended.

Another star restaurant for both residents and visitors in Waikīkī is Singha, beautifully decorated in rich woods, orchid bouquets, and bronze and wood Buddha sculptures. Opened by famed Thai chef Chai Chaowasaree in 1988, it has earned numerous accolades both locally and overseas, and is the only Thai restaurant in Hawai'i to be certified by the Royal Thai Government. This is not "your grandmother's" Thai—although she'll love it too.

Graze through as many dishes as you dare to order—Thai curry puffs, fresh 'ahi katsu, Thai yellow curry with pineapple and potato, wok-seared jumbo black tiger prawns with Thai chili ginger sauce, fresh mahimahi, and spicy Siamese fighting fish are just a few of the savory selections to share at the table. Follow them up with mochi ice cream with fresh berries or fried caramelized banana cream cheese puffs with Grand Marnier sauce. Singha also offers prix fixes dinners crafted for two to five people and a large selection of wines, tropical drinks, sake, and micro beers. One of the most colorful aspects of the restaurant is its live Thai dancers. Free validated parking is available in the building.

Tanaka of Tokyo Central
922-4702.
Waikīkī Shopping Plaza, 2250 Kalākaua Ave., 4th Flr.
www.tanakaoftokyo.com.
Open: Year-round.
Price: Moderate–Expensive.
Cuisine: Japanese Teppanyaki Steak/Seafood.
Serving: D.
Credit Cards: AE, DC, DISC, MC, V.
Handicapped Accessible: Yes.
Reservations: Recommended.

In addition to the above Tanaka of Tokyo location, there are two others in Waikīkī: **Tanaka of Tokyo West** (945-3443; 'Ilikai Hotel, 1777 Ala Moana Blvd.) and **Tanaka of Tokyo East** (922-4233; King's Village, 131 Ka'iulani Ave.); and although all are great and offer the same delicious food, the Waikīkī Shopping Plaza location is the most popular with visitors, many of whom come from Japan.

Tanaka's has been in Hawai'i for decades and has received numerous local and national accolades, such as "best Japanese restaurant in Hawai'i" by *Honolulu Magazine* and "best teppan room anywhere" by *Zagat Survey*. If you've been to a Benihana restaurant, you know the teppanyaki drill: Place eight chairs in a semi-circle around a giant tabletop grill, then activate a chef who can not only cook well, but can entertain. Tanaka's chefs can indeed do both—we've seen fried rice sent flying through the air only to land neatly in a tiny bowl, and cutting knives juggled while steam and sizzle roar from the grill. Needless to say, this is a fun place for families and groups.

Fortunately, the food is really good, although perhaps a touch salty here and there. The menu centers around certified Black Angus sirloin steaks, imported lobster tails, shrimp, scallops, and melt-in-your-mouth filet mignon. Your entrée selection automatically comes with a series of other dishes, such as tossed salad, miso soup, rice, and dessert, which makes the overall cost per person very reasonable.

Tiki's Grill & Bar
923-8454.
ResortQuest Waikīkī Beach Hotel, 2570 Kalākaua Ave., 2nd Flr.
www.tikisgrill.com.
Open: Year-round.
Price: Moderate–Expensive.
Cuisine: Regional American/Pacific Rim.
Serving: L, D.
Credit Cards: AE, DC, DISC, MC, V.
Handicapped Accessible: Yes.
Reservations: Recommended.
Special Features: Open-air, oceanview patio dining.

Tiki's has been popular with residents and visitors since the day it opened, and is perfect for families and groups of 20- or 30-somethings wanting to have a great time. Its open-air design features sweeping views across Kalākaua Avenue and Waikīkī Beach, and a festive interior exudes hip, South Pacific retro design elements built around the classic icon of tiki carvings. They've won several local and national awards, including "best new restaurant," "most spirited staff," and "good neighbor"—the last relating to its commitment to community development.

We would not call Tiki's "gourmet," but the Island-casual food is good: coconut shrimp, garlic shoyu edamame, beef tenderloin skewers, horseradish crusted prime rib, Mongolian pork chops, pan-seared 'ahi, and guava cheesecake are just a sampling. Add local entertainment, a few drinks, and free validated parking, and you're set for the evening.

Todai
947-1000.
1910 Ala Moana Blvd.
www.todai.com.
Open: Year-round.
Price: Moderate.
Cuisine: Japanese/American.
Serving: L, D.
Credit Cards: AE, DC, DISC, MC, V.
Handicapped Accessible: Yes.
Reservations: Taken up to one day in advance for early dining only.

This international chain features an all-you-can-eat sushi and seafood spread that rivals Las Vegas buffets in size: a whopping 160 feet long. Their specialty is 40 different kinds of sushi, plus they offer snow crab legs, prime rib, and an endless array of other hot entrées, salads, and desserts. Go ahead and stuff yourself—they expect it. Add on wine, imported beer, and Japanese sake to wash it all down.

Atmosphere is not Todai's main draw, so don't expect much except quite a bit of bustle and noise. Lunch costs less than dinner, and during the week both are a little bit less expensive than on weekends. They offer special pricing for kids under 12, according to height (this must have something to do with the quantity one can consume). There may be a crowd outside when you arrive, but the large interior ensures a reasonable wait. Validated parking is available in the building.

Wailana Coffee House
955-1764.
1860 Ala Moana Blvd.
Open: Year-round.
Price: Inexpensive.
Cuisine: Regional American.
Serving: B, L, D.
Credit Cards: AE, DC, DISC, MC, V.
Handicapped Accessible: Yes.
Reservations: For groups of eight or more only.
Special Features: 24-hour dining.

Like a cozy old sweater, Wailana becomes a good friend. A classic coffee shop with more than decent, not-too-greasy food, appropriate pricing, and friendly *wahine* servers, you'll think you're back in small-town America—until you see Spam® and papaya on the menu. Other standard local diner fare includes omelets, paniolo burgers, mahimahi sandwiches, fried saimin, and hot fudge ice cream cake. Service is fast and the atmosphere is easy-going; locals line the bar reading their morning papers and in the booths brightly-clad visitors discuss the day. The best part: This is a 24-hour diner with validated parking in the building.

GREATER HONOLULU

12th Avenue Grill
732-9469.
1145C 12th Ave., Kaimukī.
www.12thavegrill.com.
Closed: Sunday.
Price: Moderate.
Cuisine: Contemporary American.
Serving: D.
Credit Cards: MC, V.
Handicapped Accessible: Yes.
Reservations: Recommended.

A casually upscale, cosmopolitan, award-winning retro-American bistro in the snug neighborhood of Kaimukī, 12th Avenue Grill may be just what you're looking for. This little place doesn't cater to tourists—it caters to resident foodies. Leave beachwear behind and bring an appetite for seasonal dishes and specials, such as pan-fried trout with truffle butter, kim chee steak with sweet-sour cabbage and rice cake, signature pork chops, short ribs, and maple créme brulee, plus a great wine selection. Most produce is locally grown and organic whenever possible.

Service is warm and efficient, and the atmosphere is lively and somewhat loud due to poor acoustics. Parking might be a challenge—you'll need to mill about the nearby public metered lots (the Grill is happy to make change for you) or cruise side streets, but it's worth it. This is a popular place, so expect crowds.

Alan Wong's Restaurant
949-2526.
1857 S. King St., 3rd Floor., Makiki.
www.alanwongs.com.
Closed: Thanksgiving Day and December 25.
Price: Expensive.
Cuisine: Hawai'i Regional.
Serving: D.
Credit Cards: AE, DC, MC, V.
Handicapped Accessible: Yes.
Reservations: Strongly recommended.

If you have a deep appreciation for top-of-the-line cuisine and want a truly authentic Honolulu dining experience, make reservations for Alan Wong's immediately. Let's look at a few of the facts: Named by *Gourmet* magazine as one of the Top 50 Restaurants in the U.S. for 2006 (Wong's came in eighth); selected by *Food & Wine* magazine as one of the 376 hottest restaurants in the world; and voted locally as Hawai'i's best restaurant numerous years in a row.

Alan Wong himself was one of the pioneers of Hawai'i Regional Cuisine and has a world-class reputation as a chef and restaurateur. He is one of only a handful in Hawai'i to earn the highest culinary accolade, a James Beard Award. Wong is always combing for the freshest ingredients and new presentations, so the menu changes all the time. Some star dishes he's showcased include fork-tender oil-poached lamb rib-eye with three sauces; beet and tomato salad with shiso buds and li hing mui-ume vinaigrette, ginger crusted onaga, macadamia nut-coconut crusted lamb chops with Asian ratatouille, and Hawaiian vanilla mascarpone cheesecake. They also offer five- and seven-course menu tastings, paired with or without wines.

Alan Wong's is so prestigious that you might expect to feel intimidated. On the contrary—this is a local, almost even casual, dining environment where you can have a great time. Valet parking is available.

Cassis by Chef Mavro
545-8100.
Harbor Court, 66 Queen St., Downtown.
www.cassishonolulu.com.
Closed: Sundays and Thanksgiving Day.
Price: Expensive.
Cuisine: French bistro classics with Hawai'i Regional influence.
Serving: L (except Sat.), D.
Credit Cards: AE, DC, DISC, MC, V.
Handicapped Accessible: Yes.
Reservations: Recommended.

Opened in mid-2007 by culinary genius and Provence native George "Chef Mavro" Mavrothalassitis, Cassis celebrates the comforts of neighborhood French bistro dining. Inspired by the cuisine and atmosphere of the French Mediterranean port town of Cassis (ka-SEES), as well as elements of Paris, the Alsace, and Honolulu, its unique dishes add high-end local twists on classics such as flounder grenobloise, cassoulet, and lamb tajin.

This is the second Honolulu restaurant he owns—the flagship Chef Mavro on King Street has earned international acclaim for its exlusive French fare and Chef Mavro was awarded the extremely prestigious James Beard Award. Cassis offers a more casually elegant experience, one that should earn many regular customers. Parking is available in the building.

Chai's Island Bistro
585-0011.
Aloha Tower Marketplace,
1 Aloha Tower Dr., Downtown.
www.chaisislandbistro.com.
Closed: July 4 and December 25.
Price: Expensive.
Cuisine: Hawai'i Regional/Pacific Rim.
Serving: L (Tuesday through Friday), D.
Credit Cards: AE, DC, MC, V.
Handicapped Accessible: Yes.
Reservations: Recommended.

Winner of *Gourmet* magazine's America's Top Table Award and voted into O'ahu's top 10 restaurants year after year, you can bet that Chai's will offer something special. Thai chef Chai Chaowasaree also owns the excellent Singha in Waikīkī, but this restaurant is his masterpiece. Kataifi and macadamia nut encrusted jumbo black tiger prawns, fresh 'ahi katsu, lobster ravioli, grilled salmon linguini, crispy whole snapper, seafood risotto with fresh Big Island heart of palm, grilled Mongolian lamb chops with brandy demiglace, and white chocolate amore truffle should soothe you into the comfort zone. Classic Hawaiian entertainment by Hawai'i's biggest names is a huge draw. When coastal Thailand was hit by the 2004 tsunami, Chai orchestrated a massive fundraiser in just three days to help out with relief—and every single cent was donated. Go to Chai's Web site to print an exceptional coupon, saving you at least $25 on selected nights. Free valet parking is available.

The Contemporary Café
523-3362.
The Contemporary Museum, 2411 Makiki Heights Dr., Tantalus.
www.tcmhi.org.
Closed: Mondays and major holidays.
Price: Moderate.
Cuisine: Contemporary Mediterrean/Regional American.
Serving: L.
Credit Cards: AE, DISC, MC, V.
Handicapped Accessible: Yes.
Reservations: Recommended.
Special Features: Outdoor patio seating.

Most people have wised up to the fact that museums tend to have excellent cafés and gift shops. True for the petite Contemporary Museum as well, which is perched in a historic home on a verdant bluff. This hidden spot is a semi-secret favorite of many residents and a peaceful and artistic retreat for anyone. The current menu features fresh and inventive Americanesque classics such as gazpacho salad, hummus and pita plate, curried chicken salad wrap with pineapple chutney, shrimp and crostini tower, and lentil burger, as well as hot entrée specials and freshly squeezed lemonade.

Grand Café & Bakery
531-0001.
31 N. Pauahi St., Chinatown.
www.grandcafeandbakery.com.
Closed: Mondays, Thanksgiving Day, and January 1.
Price: Moderate.
Cuisine: Regional American.
Serving: B, L, D (Fridays only), SSB.
Credit Cards: MC, V.
Handicapped Accessible: Yes.
Reservations: Recommended for three people or more weekdays, two or more weekends and Friday nights.
Special Features: Outdoor patio dining.

Who would have thought this charming café would appear in one of Chinatown's ancient buildings? You might think you're in Santa Barbara, not Honolulu, when you dine indoors or al fresco on its little courtyard patio. And although relatively new, its history in the area harks back to 1923, when Executive Chef Anthony Vierra's great grandfather ran the original Grand Café & Bakery. Many of the recipes are the same—and they're delicious. You'll likely meet one or more of the family during your meal, and service is always warm, courteous, professional, and even stylish, while at the same time humbly gracious.

Chef Vierra is especially fond of eggs benedict, so be sure to try any variation he offers at breakfast. Another breakfast winner is the bananas foster French toast. At lunchtime, house favorites include traditional meatloaf, quiche, and chicken pot pie. All the pastries in the cupboard are homemade and tasty, so don't hold back. Get to Saturday and Sunday brunch by 9 AM for a little peace and quiet, or later to be part of the crowd.

Grand Café & Bakery offers delightful courtyard patio dining as well as delicious, quality dishes.

E & O Trading Co.
591-9555.
Ward Centre, 1200 Ala Moana Blvd., 2nd Floor., Kaka'ako.
www.eotrading.com.
Closed: July 4, December 25, and January 1.
Price: Moderate–Expensive.
Cuisine: Southeast Asian Fusion.
Serving: L, D.
Credit Cards: AE, DC, DISC, MC, V.
Handicapped Accessible: Yes.
Reservations: Recommended.
Special Features: Open-air patio dining, view of ocean from semi-private rooms.

Although E & O Trading Co also has locations in California, it was started by a couple of Honolulu boys. Their menu draws from Asian countries such as Indonesia, Vietnam, Thailand, Malaysia, and India, and the owners work hard to keep the heart and soul in each recipe.

Not everyone agrees that E & O's food is fabulous, but most feel upgraded by its trendy and truly beautiful British-Asiatic interior design and subtly sexy ambiance, especially the younger crowd. Dishes include Indonesian corn fritters, seared 'ahi and soba noodles, firecracker chicken, claypot mussels, and lemongrass skewered duck breast, plus they offer 20 wines by the glass and unusual cocktails, such as Broken Down Rickshaw, with amaretto and a dash of lime. Thursdays are popular, with live jazz and a special menu served on its open-air patio.

Hale Vietnam
735-7581.
1140 12th Ave., Kaimukī.
Closed: Thanksgiving Day.
Price: Moderate.
Cuisine: Vietnamese.
Serving: L, D.
Credit Cards: AE, DISC, MC, V.
Handicapped Accessible: Yes.
Reservations: Not accepted.

Many of Honolulu's best neighborhood restaurants are now found in the homey community of Kaimukī, which is gradually turning upper-middle-class boutique. Here you'll find Hale Vietnam—probably the city's favorite Vietnamese restaurant—although it is perhaps not quite as authentic as it once was. Some rave about Hale Vietnam, and some find it very overrated. On weekend nights in particular, it's packed with folks from all walks of life, and although more of a trendy spot than family diner, kids and parents should do well here.

Dishes are served family-style and are meant to be shared.

Classic Vietnamese menu items such as green papaya salad, phô, and summer rolls are consistently decent to good, and the eggplant dishes are delicious. Regarding parking, you'll have to fight it out for metered or street spots in the vicinity.

Hōkū's
739-8888.
Kahala Hotel & Resort, 5000 Kahala Ave., Kahala.
www.kahalaresort.com.
Open: Year-round.
Price: Expensive–Very Expensive.
Cuisine: Pacific Rim.
Serving: D.
Credit Cards: AE, DC, DISC, MC, V.
Handicapped Accessible: Yes.
Reservations: Recommended.
Special Features: Enclosed oceanfront dining.

This is yet another award-winning hotel restaurant, located in what was, until recently, the Kahala Mandarin Oriental. Executive Chef Wayne Hirabayashi blends the freshest Pacific ingredients into perfect harmony, making Hōkū's extremely popular with residents as well as visitors-in-the-know, and we've had excellent experiences here. You'll sweep into its gracious, warm-wood-tone, contemporary dining room and, if you arrive before sunset, will look out onto the tranquil ocean and leaning coconut trees.

The already-breathtaking interior has recently been upgraded with Christofle silver, Italian bone china, new wood flooring, and other touches, and the menu wholly freshened, lightened, and expanded. Everything is delicious, with selections that vary from Chinese-style whole fish to pancetta-crusted onaga, pan-seared island moi, salt-crusted rack of Wisconsin lamb, and mango tart tatin. Its incredibly stellar wine list was also bumped way up in price, but brush it off if at all possible—a night at Hōkū's is about feasting and celebrating life, not adding up the dollars. Despite its natural opulence, the ambience is congenial and festive, and dress is casual upscale.

Rumors have it, unfortunately, that with the recent management changes at the hotel service is slipping everywhere—including at its restaurants. We hope that Hōkū's maintains its fine tradition.

Arrive at Hōkū's before dusk to savor its romantic oceanfront views. Photo courtesy The Kahala Hotel & Resort.

Hong Kong Harbour View Seafood Restaurant
566-9989.
Aloha Tower Marketplace,
1 Aloha Tower Dr., Downtown.
www.shanghaibistrohawaii.com.
Open: Year-round.
Price: Inexpensive–Moderate.
Cuisine: Chinese.
Serving: L (from 10 AM), D.
Credit Cards: AE, DC, DISC, MC, V.
Handicapped Accessible: Yes.
Reservations: Recommended for dinner.
Special Features: Enclosed harborfront views.

Spacious and contemporary with dark wood and ornate carpeting, Harbour View draws visitors who stumble upon it at touristy Aloha Tower Marketplace, and residents who know that the restaurant has great seafood, dim sum, and service.

You can order dim sum from mid-morning to mid-afternoon and choose from heaps of well-priced, well-made items, such as steamed pork dumpling, stuffed green pepper with black bean sauce, leaf-wrapped mochi rice with chicken, and fried bean-curd shrimp rolls. Sit here for half the day, if you like, gazing out the window and grazing from the menu.

India Café
737-4600.
Kilohana Square, 1016 Kapahulu Ave., Kapahulu.
www.indiacafehawaii.com.
Open: Year-round.
Price: Inexpensive–Moderate.
Cuisine: Indian.
Serving: L (Friday through Sunday), D.
Credit Cards: AE, DC, DISC, MC, V.
Handicapped Accessible: Yes.
Reservations: Recommended for dinner.

Many residents agree that India Café serves the most savory Indian food on the island. In a state that has few Indian restaurants, it may or may not be the best Indian food you've ever had anywhere—but it should more than satisfy. A family café with dishes based on grandma's recipes, tastes are Southern Indian/Malaysian and the setting earthy and easy-going. The pleasantly extensive menu includes samosas, several types of chutneys and dosai, lamb masala, fish curry, cauliflower kari, and coconut cabbage. They specialize in curries, breads, and dosai, so be sure to include one or more in your order.

Indigo Eurasian Cuisine
521-2900.
1121 Nu'uanu Ave., Chinatown.
www.indigo-hawaii.com.
Closed: Sundays, Mondays, and major holidays.
Price: Moderate–Expensive.
Cuisine: Eurasian.
Serving: L, D.
Credit Cards: DC, DISC, MC, V.
Handicapped Accessible: Yes.
Reservations: Recommended.
Special Features: Open-air patio dining.

Since opening in 1994, Indigo has garnered numerous local awards and recognition from national publications such as *Bon Appétit, Gourmet*, and *Condé Nast Traveller*. Its atmospheric indoor-outdoor décor recalls an exotic Hong Kong hideaway or old New Orleans jazz bar; hip and moody, it manages to attract the gentler folk for pre-Hawai'i Theatre dining, as well as the clubby set, who ease into the restaurant's Green Room/Opium Den & Champagne Bar later in the evening. Drop your car off in front with the dinner valet service, and enter Indigo's for sassy goat cheese won tons, thousand-loved crab cakes, roasted tomato garlic crab soup, black mustard and black pepper crusted 'ahi steak, liliko'i glazed sweet and sour baby back ribs, or ocean raised moi roasted in banana leaf. A large wine selection offers more than 30 wines by the glass. Lunch is served both ą la carte and all-you-can-eat buffet.

The atmospheric Indigo Eurasian Cuisine is a cornerstone of Chinatown's thriving new scene.
Photo courtesy Chris Barron.

Le Bistro
373-7990.
5730 Kalaniana'ole Hwy., Niu Valley Shopping Center, Niu Valley.
Closed: Tuesdays, December 25, and January 1.
Price: Expensive.
Cuisine: French.
Serving: D.
Credit Cards: AE, MC, V.
Handicapped Accessible: Yes.
Reservations: Recommended.

It takes something extra these days to convince this author's mother that good food is worth paying good money for—especially if it's French—but Le Bistro hit the note. This restaurant, located in a no-man's land shopping strip, surprises you with a buttery dining room, charming lighting, flowers, and a festive, subtly elegant attitude that will envelop you before you even taste the delicious dishes and wines to come. Everything's fantastic—the escargot de Bourgogne, foie gras with red currants and quince, New Orleans scallops, filet mignon, and incredible desserts, as well as the service. The restaurant offers nightly specials and a selection of "petite" entrées as well. Parking is joyously plentiful.

Little Village Noodle House
545-3008.
1113 Smith St., Chinatown.
www.littlevillagehawaii.com.
Open: Year-round.
Price: Inexpensive–Moderate.
Cuisine: Chinese.
Serving: L, D.
Credit Cards: AE, DISC, MC, V.
Handicapped Accessible: Yes.
Reservations: For parties of five or more only.

This strangely wonderful Chinese restaurant in the depths of Chinatown has grown into a favorite for local Chinese families, visitors, and everyone else. The owners grew up in Hong Kong and know food—and Little Village has picked up big local awards to prove it. Family-sized dishes are simple, fresh, savory, and non-greasy. This author's friend labeled the pecan spinach salad "the best salad ever," and the dried green beans, orange chicken, garlic spinach, and pan-fried beef with chili and garlic are standouts. The extensive, non-MSG menu features all of the classics, plus specials on the board. Décor is tasteful and even fanciful, and the restaurant is tidy and well lit. On weekends, expect a wait. Customer parking is located in a lot just past the restaurant.

Mariposa
951-3420.
Neiman Marcus, Ala Moana Center, 1450 Ala Moana Blvd., Ala Moana.
www.neimanmarcus.com.
Closed: Easter Sunday, Thanksgiving Day, December, 25 and January 1.
Price: Expensive.
Cuisine: Pacific Rim.
Serving: L, D.
Credit Cards: AE, MC, V (plus Neiman Marcus and Bergdorf Goodman cards).
Handicapped Accessible: Yes.
Reservations: Recommended.
Special Features: Open-air patio and ocean-view dining.

The food at Neiman Marcus's signature restaurant ranges from pretty good to quite good (and it has won several local awards), although service can be spotty and prices will remind you you're in a high-end department store. Never mind all that—go anyway.

This is local glamour at its best, and by high noon Mariposa is packed with business luncheons, upscale couples, and bridal showers. Their fresh popovers are legendary—encourage them to indulge you with as many as possible. An adorably teensy weensy cup of consommé follows popover delivery. Good menu choices include the applewood-roasted salmon salad, seared breast of chicken, seared 'ahi, and laksa seafood curry, and the desserts are positively sinful. Most days you'll see models working the floor dressed in the latest fashions. If you don't mind traffic noise, request to sit on the open-air patio for views of Ala Moana Beach Park, rows of coconut trees, and the wide, blue ocean. They also offer afternoon tea service on Sundays.

Mediterraneo
593-1466.
1279 S. King St.
www.mediterraneohawaii.com.
Closed: Sunday, December 25, and January 1.
Price: Moderate.
Cuisine: Italian.
Serving: D (Monday through Saturday).
Credit Cards: AE, DISC, MC, V.
Handicapped Accessible: Yes.
Reservations: Recommended.

There are several really wonderful and popular Italian trattorias in Honolulu, but in our opinion Mediterraneo has the most charming ambience. Opened 15 years ago by Fabrizio Favale, who grew up in Rome, the eatery features home-style cooking with fresh ingredients; housemade sauces, pastas and ravioli; and flavorful dishes like insalata di mare, veal piccata, carbonara, and tiramisu. The interior glows as if a fireplace is roaring, and colorful ceramic and tile artifacts nestled around the walls are cozy and attractive. This is a small, quiet restaurant with a neighborhood feel, and it's surprisingly romantic. Service is very subdued. The only downside is it's desolate mid-town location. A tiny parking area in the back is available for guests.

Panya Bistro & Bar
946-6388.
Ala Moana Center, 1450 Ala Moana Blvd., Ala Moana.
www.panyabakery.com.
Closed: Thanksgiving Day and December 25.
Price: Inexpensive–Moderate.
Cuisine: Eurasian.
Serving: B, L, D.
Credit Cards: AE, DC, DISC, MC, V.
Handicapped Accessible: Yes.
Reservations: Not accepted for lunch; suggested for dinner.

We keep returning to Ala Moana Center's Panya ("the bread house" in Japanese), despite the fact that several of its youthful servers seem slightly indifferent to our presence. It never stops us from enjoying this unique, fun, simple, and tasty dining spot started by a couple of gals from Hong Kong.

An extensive predominantly Asian fusion menu features laksa noodles, Russian borscht, shrimp scampi, and Hokkaido bread pudding. Its atmosphere of vaguely clubby music, mirrored walls complete with dangling strands of silver disks, and a blue-tinted bar area serving lychee martinis belies the fact that patrons are mostly area professionals and mall shoppers, not Japanese pop musicians. The front area of the restaurant features a small Japanese-Euro bakery, and its Hokkaido-style cakes and buns are very popular. Breakfast has room to improve.

The Pavilion Café
532-8734.
900 S. Beretania St., Makiki.
www.honoluluacademy.org.
Closed: Sundays, Mondays, and major holidays.
Price: Inexpensive–Moderate.
Cuisine: Regional American with Mediterranean influences.
Serving: L.
Credit Cards: AE, DISC, MC, V.
Handicapped Accessible: Yes.
Reservations: Strongly recommended.
Special Features: All open-air patio dining.

At the Honolulu Academy of Art's Pavilion Café, you'll be nestled in understated, natural elegance. The peaceful setting features arts and crafts/Balinese style teak furniture, ceramic Japanese sculptures along a waterfall, and a mature monkeypod tree shading a terrace. Fresh local ingredients and simple, yet elevated, dishes leave you feeling nourished.

We recommend the niçoise salad with seared coriander crusted ʻahi and roasted shallot vinaigrette, the beef tenderloin sandwich, and of course the chocolate pot de créme. Try their housemade ginger lemonade. The crowd is predominantly casually-chic residents enjoying artsy business lunches or discussing their next exotic vacation. Call for reservations in advance—they often book up.

Don't skip the opportunity to buy an entrance ticket to the excellent museum itself and browse its memorable grounds, collections, and gift shop. Paid parking is available kitty-corner to the museum at the Academy Art Center at Linekona, on Beretania and Victoria Streets.

The Pavilion Café at the Honolulu Academy of Arts is a must for an earthy-chic lunch.
Photo courtesy Honolulu Academy of Arts.

Phuket Thai
942-8194.
McCully Shopping Center, 1960 Kapiʻolani Blvd., McCully.
Closed: December 25 and January 1.
Price: Inexpensive–Moderate.
Cuisine: Classic Thai.
Serving: L, D.
Credit Cards: AE, MC, V.
Handicapped Accessible: Yes.
Reservations: Recommended for dinner.

If you've never been to Thailand, you might not know that this regional name is pronounced approximately "poo-KET." That issue aside, this is a delicious, tasteful, contemporary destination just across the border from Waikīkī. Over the years it's grown in popularity as a reliable neighborhood spot and has started to attract a number of outside visitors as well. It serves standard family-sized Thai dishes, with a popular following for its mee krob, shrimp rolls, tom yum gai, and paht Thai. Curries can be ordered mild on up. They also serve nice little desserts, such as Thai sticky rice with coconut milk and ice cream. Park in the shopping center lot.

The Pineapple Room by Alan Wong
945-6573.
Macy's, Ala Moana Center,
1450 Ala Moana Blvd., Ala Moana.
www.alanwongs.com.
Closed: Thanksgiving Day, December 25, and January 1.
Price: Moderate–Expensive.
Cuisine: Hawaiʻi Regional.
Serving: B (Saturday and Sunday), L (daily), D (Monday through Saturday).
Credit Cards: AE, DC, DISC, MC, V.
Handicapped Accessible: Yes.
Reservations: Recommended.

The Pineapple Room is not even remotely about beach blankets and tropical cocktails. And don't be discouraged when you hear it's located in Macy's and has no view. This is a first-class bistro owned by international culinary genius and father of Hawaiʻi Regional Cuisine, Alan Wong, and it exhibits all the style and flavor you'd expect and hope for.

The tone is set by an extremely spacious, contemporary, and warm interior illuminated with sleek woods and diffused light, plus casually elegant furnishings and professional service. A lava-clad, wood-burning oven in its exhibition kitchen is of special note. Taste the creations of a master: seared 'ahi and furikake crusted tofu salad, kiawe-grilled kalbi short ribs, housemade North Shore Cattle Company meatloaf, Singapore-inspired chili clams, fresh Big Island whole moi, and warm bread pudding.

Plumeria Beach House
739-8760.
Kahala Hotel & Resort, 5000 Kahala Ave., Kahala.
www.kahalaresort.com.
Open: Year-round.
Price: Expensive.
Cuisine: Contemporary American/International.
Serving: B, L, D, SB.
Credit Cards: AE, DC, DISC, MC, V.
Handicapped Accessible: Yes.
Reservations: Recommended.
Special Features: Oceanfront patio dining.

Although not an award-winning restaurant like its upstairs sister, Hoku's, Plumeria Beach Café serves pretty good food nevertheless—sometimes very good food, with the extremely awesome bonus of a dreamy, elegant, grassy beachfront setting. Removed from the clutter of Waikīkī Beach, this restaurant is truly a peaceful retreat. Sit outside beneath its umbrella-covered tables for full enjoyment. Dinner buffets Thursday through Saturday rotate between Italian, seafood, and Asian dishes. The Sunday buffet brunch at this gorgeous location is memorable and popular with residents as well as visitors. Service may or may not be up to par these days, but the setting always is.

Sam Choy's Diamond Head
732-8645.
449 Kapahulu Ave., 2nd Floor., Kapahulu.
www.samchoys.com.
Closed: Monday after Thanksgiving Day.
Price: Expensive.
Cuisine: Hawai'i Regional.
Serving: D, SB.
Credit Cards: AE, DC, DISC, MC, V.
Handicapped Accessible: Yes.
Reservations: Recommended.

Twelve years and running, Sam Choy's Diamond Head is yet another local gem created by culinary idol Sam Choy. Aloha business attire and aloha attitude rule, and the spacious dining room brims with festive bustle as residents and friends gather to celebrate.

One of Choy's best menu offers is poke (pronounced approximately "POH-keh"), a traditional Hawaiian dish made of marinated, diced raw fish. If you love sashimi, you'll probably love poke! And you won't find it in many other restaurants. Other delectables include Hau'ula tomato salad, red wine braised short ribs, kalbi marinated butterfish, seafood laulau, and a lychee float with mango tapioca and liliko'i sorbet. Plus, head down Sunday morning for the Sam Choy's Celebration Sunday Brunch Buffet and chow on a variety of cold foods, poke selections, hot entrées, waffles, omelets, and desserts.

Soul de Cuba
545-2822.
1121 Bethel St., Downtown.
www.souldecuba.com.
Closed: Sundays and selected holidays.
Price: Inexpensive–Moderate.
Cuisine: Cuban.
Serving: L (Tuesday through Saturday), D (Tuesday through Saturday), SB.
Credit Cards: AE, DISC, MC, V.
Handicapped Accessible: Yes.
Reservations: Recommended.

Small, busy, hip, and downtown may not be right for a family meal, but the rest of you will probably dig it. This is the second restaurant for Jesus Porto, the first being in

New Haven, and its casual, folksy, home-style Cuban sabor and smart interior hit it big in Honolulu from day one—without even advertising. The walls are lined with the owner's old family portraits, images of Cuban life, and colorful prints, and the food is affordable and absolutely delicious. Try the black bean soup, camarones, ropa vieja, and lechon asado.

Town
735-5900.
3435 Wai'alae Ave., Kaimukī.
www.townkaimuki.com.
Closed: Sunday, Thanksgiving Day, December 25, and January 1.
Price: Moderate.
Cuisine: Mediterranean-inspired American.
Serving: B (Continental), L, D.
Credit Cards: AE, DC, DISC, MC, V.
Handicapped Accessible: Yes.
Reservations: Recommended, especially on weekends.

Chef Ed Kenney had already built a reputation in Honolulu for culinary excellence—and then he opened Town, which instantly became one of Kaimukī's hottest and most eclectic restaurants. The mellow, modern, minimalist interior of dark woods against soft green and oranges is comforting and unpretentious. When the bistro fills with people, especially the dinner crowd, you'll feel it and hear it.

Kenney's philosophy is simple and appealing: local first, organic whenever possible. The kitchen is always working on new dishes and the menu changes daily, focusing on Mediterranean flavors, slow-roasted meats, fresh herbs, and quality. Dishes served in the past include tomato-ginger soup, tomato tart, salt cod brandade fritters, crispy fried green beans with remoulade, braised lamb, and almond olive oil cake. Service is sometimes spotty, but that hasn't curbed its popularity.

Wai'oli Tea Room
988-5800.
2950 Mānoa Rd., Mānoa.
www.thewaiolitearoom.net.
Closed: Thanksgiving Day, December 25, and January 1.
Price: Inexpensive–Moderate.
Cuisine: Regional American.
Serving: B (Saturday through Sunday), L.
Credit Cards: AE, DC, MC, V.
Handicapped Accessible: Yes.
Reservations: Recommended.
Special Features: Open-air patio dining.

We'd be amiss in not sharing this historic spot with you, even though the food ranks only at "pretty good" most of the time. There are few dining experiences like this in the state and on O'ahu anymore.
Opened by the Salvation Army in 1922 to teach girls the art of cooking and "gracious living," it has served the public as a bakery and restaurant for decades, consistently attracting residents who cherish its old-time, peaceful setting and atmosphere. Nestled in a plantation-style cottage on 8 acres of tropical jungle, and with an antique car parked in the garage, this is authentic Hawai'i. The menu (which is also in Braille) offers items such as guava and berry French toast, roast beef sandwich, corned beef sandwich, and home-made soup, and on weekends a Hawaiian guitarist often performs. Housemade teas add extra charm, and afternoon tea service is a pleasure. The building is on the National Register of Historic Places.

The charming Wai'oli Tea Room is one of Honolulu's few remaining vintage cafés.

The Willows
952-9200.
901 Hausten St., Mōʻiliʻili.
www.willowshawaii.com.
Open: Year-round.
Price: Moderate.
Cuisine: Hawaiian/Regional American.
Serving: L, D, SB.
Credit Cards: AE, DC, DISC, MC, V.
Handicapped Accessible: Yes.
Reservations: Recommended.
Special Features: Open-air patio dining.

Yet another classic dining room on Oʻahu is The Willows, which opened in 1944. Although tucked into a nondescript neighborhood near Waikīkī, enter through its gates for a surprisingly contemporary oasis of tropical foliage, trickling water, and floating terraces. Both The Willows and Waiʻoli Tea Room make older residents misty eyed, although this restaurant's extensive renovations in the 1990s swept away the antique charm. It sits on an ancient spring where royalty once picnicked and swam, and later became an estate home and gardens that the family opened to the public for light lunches and Hawaiian entertainment.

The pretty-good food still draws local families for celebrations. Instead of attending a lūʻau, you might sample traditional Hawaiian foods here instead, as they serve a mixed cuisine, all-you-can-eat lunch and dinner buffet. Sunday brunch attracts many residents and is a nice way to spend a lazy morning.

Yanagi Sushi
597-1525.
762 Kapiʻolani Blvd.
Open: Year-round.
Price: Moderate–Expensive.
Cuisine: Japanese.
Serving: L, D.
Credit Cards: AE, DC, DISC, MC, V.
Handicapped Accessible: Yes.
Reservations: Strongly recommended.

Open since 1978, this Japanese restaurant is a local institution with nearly every type and style of Japanese food, including one-pot stewed nabe dishes, teishoku, and shabu shabu. Cozy nooks throughout feature comfortable furnishings and the hours run impressively late, so understandably this is an excellent and merry hangout. Their sushi is legendary, and two sushi bars work full time to deliver to the crowds. Complete dinners are a fabulous splurge and private tatami rooms are available for those who want the full experience.

Windward Oʻahu

Baci Bistro
262-7555.
30 Aulike St., Kailua.
www.bacibistro.com.
Closed: Superbowl Sunday and Thanksgiving Day.
Price: Moderate.
Cuisine: Italian.
Serving: L (Monday through Friday), D.
Credit Cards: AE, MC, V.
Handicapped Accessible: Yes.
Reservations: Recommended.
Special Features: Open-air patio dining.

An adorable little neighborhood place with old-world as well as Hawaiʻi charm, local customers make Baci Bistro a second home for its savory Italian dishes. Fresh food is its trademark and every dish is made to order. An extensive wine list emphasizes Italian wines, but also includes many from California and Australia. Choose seating either on the open-air patio or in the enclosed atrium.

Rustic dishes include fresh island moi, homemade ravioli, gnocchi con pesto, bruschetta, prosciutto e melone, and tutti mari. Desserts receive special nods from patrons, and their tiramisu earns extra applause. Service could use a professional touch-up here and there, but overall the folks are friendly and helpful.

Kailua's Baci Bistro is perfect for a touch of romantic dining.

Boots & Kimo's Homestyle Kitchen
263-7929.
119 Hekili St., Kailua.
Closed: Monday, December 25, and January 1.
Price: Inexpensive.
Cuisine: Regional American.
Serving: B, L.
Credit Cards: Not Accepted.
Handicapped Accessible: Yes.
Reservations: Not Accepted.

There's at least one reason to get up early and hover around on a sidewalk in front of the unpretentious Boots & Kimo's restaurant: pancakes with a special macadamia nut sauce on top. If you don't like pancakes, perhaps you'll want to sleep in. If you do want them, set your alarm now. This is a very family oriented, kickback, local-style eatery, which means it's very popular. Other good dishes include the grilled short ribs and crab omelet.

Brent's Restaurant & Deli
262-8588.
629A Kailua Rd., Kailua.
Closed: Major holidays.
Price: Inexpensive–Moderate.
Cuisine: American.
Serving: B, L.
Credit Cards: MC, V.
Handicapped Accessible: Yes.
Reservations: Not accepted.
Special Features: Open-air patio dining.

The same Brent Brody who started Los Angeles' famed deli opened this little Kailua spot, and it gets raves from locals and visitors. For breakfast, select from more than 30 egg dishes, plus lox, smoked fish, bagels, and more. Lunch selections are super tasty as well, with Reuben sandwiches, Philly cheesesteaks, chopped liver, pastrami, and everything else you'd expect from a good deli.

The feasting's good at Brent's in Kailua.

Buzz's Original Steak House
261-4661.
www.buzzssteakhouse.com.
413 Kawailoa Rd., Kailua.
Closed: Thanksgiving Day and December 25.
Price: Moderate–Expensive.
Cuisine: Regional American.
Serving: L, D.
Credit Cards: Not accepted.
Handicapped Accessible: Yes.
Reservations: Suggested.
Special Features: Open-air patio dining.

A Windward O'ahu tradition for more than 45 years, family-run Buzz's is a landmark that fits like your favorite pair of slippers. Food's pretty good, but the best part is that it sits nearly on the sand across from the otherwise café-deprived Kailua Beach Park—needless to say, it's no secret. Even President Clinton chowed at Buzz's on one of his visits.

The building is vintage Hawai'i, with a long, steep roof and wraparound porch area. Inside, very dark wood, a vague beachcomber atmosphere, and plenty of tourists hint at the standard, Island themed cuisine to come. A crusty sea captain or two may be lingering at its full bar, and the waitresses know their way around. Specialties include Chinese-style fish, kiawe-broiled steaks, and big salads.

California Pizza Kitchen
263-2480.
Kainalu Plaza, 609 Kailua Rd., Kailua.
www.cpk.com.
Closed: Thanksgiving Day and December 25.
Price: Moderate.
Cuisine: Californian/Eclectic.
Serving: L, D.
Credit Cards: AE, DC, DISC, MC, V.
Handicapped Accessible: Yes.
Reservations: Not accepted.
Special Features: Open-air patio dining.

For comfortably priced eats that ring a familiar bell, try CPK in Kailua. Actually a "CPK/ASAP" category eatery, meaning that the menu's abbreviated for speed, it's still a sit-down event where you'll find their beloved signature pizzas, salads, hot panini sandwiches, soups, and more.

Cinnamon's Restaurant
261-8724.
Kailua Square, 315 Uluniu St., Kailua.
www.cinnamonsrestaurant.com.
Closed: December 25 and January 1.
Price: Inexpensive–Moderate.
Cuisine: Regional American.
Serving: B, L, D (Thursday through Saturday).
Credit Cards: DC, DISC, MC, V.
Handicapped Accessible: Yes.
Reservations: For parties of five or more only.
Special Features: Open-air patio dining.

A Windward O'ahu favorite for breakfast since 1985, family owned Cinnamon's was locally voted one of Hawai'i's best restaurants three years in a row. It's a bit pricey considering the food can be very hit-or-miss and service details may be overlooked, but its neighborhood appeal gets high marks.

Cinnamon's serves mostly traditional diner fare. It has an old-style coffee shop atmosphere inside and airy courtyard seating outside, which is tented and packed on weekends. With homey touches, like great coffee and a newspaper while you wait to be seated, plus a very friendly staff, they make it easy to settle into the comfort zone and order up a pile of buttermilk pancakes or a loco moco omelet. Arrive early on weekends to avoid long waits.

Formaggio Grill
263-2633.
305 Hahani St., Kailua.
www.formaggio808.com.
Closed: Major holidays.
Price: Moderate–Expensive.
Cuisine: Mediterranean/Steak/Seafood.
Serving: L (except Monday), D, SSB.
Credit Cards: AE, MC, V.
Handicapped Accessible: Yes.
Reservations: For parties of seven or more for seating prior to 6 PM only.

Kailua's Formaggio opens in late 2007 and will be as hot a destination for food and good wine as its Honolulu location. This rustic, Tuscan-atmosphere venue straddles the wine bar and restaurant worlds by offering 50 wines by the glass from around the world and a Mediterranean-infused menu.

Formaggio restaurateurs Wes Zane and Almar Arcano each spent more than two decades at the prestigious Hy's Steak House in Waikīkī, so Formaggio's steaks are sure to be delicious. Flavorful and robust dishes include grilled vegetable Napoleon, beef Bourguignon, lobster bisque, lollipop shortribs, and paella Valenciana. Sign up for their "Desperate Housewives" Cooking Class, held on the second Monday of each month, to learn culinary tricks from the chef.

Hale'iwa Joe's Seafood Grill
247-6671.
46-336 Ha'ikū Rd., Kāne'ohe.
www.haleiwajoes.com.
Closed: Thanksgiving Day and December 25.
Price: Moderate–Expensive.
Cuisine: Regional American/Pacific Rim.
Serving: D, SB.
Credit Cards: MC, V.
Handicapped Accessible: Yes.
Reservations: Not accepted.
Special Features: Open-air garden view dining.

What's the next best thing to dining while overlooking the ocean? Dining that looks out onto a lush botanical garden. This picture-perfect setting over the 6-acre Ha'ikū Gardens includes a lily pond, exotic flowers, and a tiny gazebo on the water, all of which are open and free to the public for browsing. Once seated in the low-slung, open-air restaurant, choose from island-influenced dishes like tempura crab roll, Hawaiian premium sashimi, crunchy coconut shrimp, beef satay, filet mignon, and fresh baked fish. We've found the service friendly, but the food only moderately tasty. The Sunday brunch is a relaxing way to begin your day.

Hale'iwa Joe's looks out onto a lush botanical garden and pond.

Koa Pancake House
235-5772.
46-126 Kahuhipa St., Kāne'ohe.
Open: Year-round.
Price: Inexpensive.
Cuisine: Regional American.
Serving: B, L.
Credit Cards: MC, V.
Handicapped Accessible: Yes.
Reservations: Not accepted.

The Chung family knows how to do diner food right—and they charge real diner prices. Quick and local-style friendly service complements un-yuppified, island-style breakfast fare and particularly hefty, tasty pancakes. You might wait, along with residents and a handful of visitors, to get in—even on weekdays—but it's worth it for a totally unpretentious meal. The simple interior hints at a cross between a Swiss chalet and tropical hut and is strangely comforting. Limited parking is available in front of the restaurant's very nondescript building.

Lucy's Grill & Bar
230-8188.
33 Aulike St., Kailua.
www.lucysgrillnbar.com.
Closed: July 4, Thanksgiving Day, and December 25.
Price: Expensive.
Cuisine: Pacific Rim.
Serving: D.
Credit Cards: MC, V.
Handicapped Accessible: Yes.

Reservations: Strongly recommended.
Special Features: Open-air patio dining.

This is considered one of the Kailua area's star restaurants; and although not always entirely up to par, it's a good choice for an evening of relatively upscale Windward Side dining. Walls are artfully lined with surfboards, aquariums, and Hawaiian stone poi pounder displays. The atmosphere is bustling—and sometimes downright loud—with residents who know that the portions will more than satisfy. Sit on the tiki-torch-lit patio and take in the experience. The ʻahi tower, kalua pig tacos, chicken satay with Thai peanut/lilikoʻi sauce, macadamia nut crusted lamb shank, and chocolate soufflé cake are just a few of Lucy's many delicious dishes. On Wednesdays, the restaurant offers most of its bottles of wine at half price if you purchase an entrée.

Shiso-Zen
262-5661.
20 Kainehe St., Kailua.
Closed: Major holidays.
Price: Moderate.
Cuisine: Japanese.
Serving: L (Tuesday through Saturday), D.
Credit Cards: MC, V.
Handicapped Accessible: Yes.
Reservations: Recommended on weekends.

Simple, well made, Hawaiian-style Japanese dishes and sushi are the order at this tidy little contemporary space in Kailua. Paper lanterns, bamboo screens, and other Zen-mod touches meld with reggae and warm woods for an inviting and unintimidating ambience, and the menu includes an array of choices that are enough to constitute an evening or midday distraction. Oyster shooters, sautéed shiitake mushrooms, tonkatsu, udon, shrimp tempura, steamed crab legs, and rainbow sushi roll are just a few classic options for its variety of clientele. A small parking lot is available in front.

North Shore

21 Degrees North
293-6000.
Turtle Bay Resort, 57-091 Kamehameha Hwy., Kahuku.
www.turtlebayresort.com.
Closed: Sunday and Monday.
Price: Expensive.
Cuisine: Contemporary Regional with French accents.
Serving: D.
Credit Cards: AE, DC, DISC, MC, V.
Handicapped Accessible: Yes.
Reservations: Strongly recommended.
Special Features: Oceanfront views.

This is the North Shore's most elegant restaurant, located at the oceanfront Turtle Bay Resort. The hotel-atmosphere hexagonal dining room is simple, with framed, full-glass window views onto both the resort's pool deck and ocean—so arrive before sunset if you can.

The menu is formal and elegant, with dishes such as oysters, blackened ʻahi, organic greens with macadamia nut crusted goat cheese, filet mignon, roasted Peking duck, braised Kona lobster, and ʻōpakapaka filet with tiger shrimp. Homemade ice creams are not to be missed—flavors such as orange truffle with chocolate are fantastic and original.

Banzai Sushi Bar
637-4404.
66-246 Kamehameha Hwy., Haleʻiwa.
Closed: Major holidays.
Price: Moderate.
Cuisine: Japanese.
Serving: L (Tuesday through Sunday), D.
Credit Cards: MC, V.
Handicapped Accessible: Yes.
Reservations: For parties of six or more only.
Special Features: Open-air patio dining.

Not your typical sushi bar, this popular and casually hip pad is Brazilian-owned, and it shows on the menu via ceviche and other Latin dishes as well as Japanese sushi standards. Inside, cool music and surf videos play, photos plaster the interior, and décor hints at Rastafarian pleasures. Out on the patio, folks are seated at small tables or on Asiatic pillows around low tables, and the atmosphere is totally cruiser chic. Live musicians perform on selected evenings.

Café Hale'iwa
637-5516.
66-460 Kamehameha Hwy., Hale'iwa.
www.web.mac.com/cafehaleiwahawaii.
Closed: Thanksgiving Day and December 25.
Price: Inexpensive–Moderate.
Cuisine: Regional American with Mexican influences.
Serving: B, L.
Credit Cards: AE, MC, V.
Handicapped Accessible: Yes.
Reservations: Not accepted.

All walks of authentic North Shore life celebrate the breakfast hour at this 25-year-old, very casual café. Bite into thick French toast slabs, their famously tasty omelets, or perhaps something with a little more Mexican or regional flair. Also hearty are its local-style plate lunches. The colorful interior is surf/fiesta-like and covered with psychedelic paintings. Just kick back and enjoy affordable food.

Hale'iwa Joe's Seafood Grill
637-8005.
66-011 Kamehameha Hwy., Hale'iwa.
www.haleiwajoes.com.
Closed: Thanksgiving Day and December 25.
Price: Moderate.
Cuisine: Regional American/Pacific Rim.
Serving: L, D.
Credit Cards: MC, V.
Handicapped Accessible: Yes.
Reservations: Not accepted.
Special Features: Open-air harborfront views and patio dining.

Mellow tourist eatery by day, popular local restaurant by night, Hale'iwa Joe's seems to appeal to most everyone, although we find the food only pretty good. The décor is somewhat generic, but views are fairly tasty—request seating on the open-air patio to gaze onto nearby Hale'iwa Harbor. Most folks find that Joe's is one of the best area picks for sit-down dining, and without much else to do at night on the North Shore, making an evening out of your meal is a good idea. Pick up a fork and tuck into Sumatran beef salad, crunchy coconut shrimp, grilled salmon, signature whole moi, or mini plates such as fire shrimp, tempura crab roll, or seared 'ahi. For dessert, try their evil "love" cake, filled with hot cream cheese and chocolate and smothered in raspberry sauce. Joe's also has a bar off to the side.

Jameson's by the Sea
637-6272.
62-540 Kamehameha Hwy., Hale'iwa.
Open: Year-round.
Price: Expensive.
Cuisine: Regional American/Seafood.
Serving: L, D, SSB.
Credit Cards: AE, DC, DISC, MC, V.
Handicapped Accessible: Yes.
Reservations: Recommended.
Special Features: Open-air patio dining and harbor views.

Jameson's has been around forever, and it used to be such a quality island restaurant that this author's parents would drive all the way from town to eat there. It's still not bad, although it feels very touristy these days and even a touch rundown. Known for its fresh fish dishes and harbor views (from across the road), at cocktail hour the patio is lined with visitors timing the last drop of liquor with the sunset, which paints the sky brilliantly over this vast ocean vista. Some of its best menu items are the 'ōpakapaka poached in white wine and mahimahi. If you visited Jameson's for dinner in the past, you might remember the upstairs dining room, which was quite nice. That's closed—all dining takes place on the streetfront patio and first floor these days.

Lei Lei's
293-2662.
Turtle Bay Resort, 57-049 Kuilima Dr., Kahuku.
www.turtlebayresort.com.
Open: Year-round.
Price: Moderate–Expensive.
Cuisine: Regional American/Continental.
Serving: B, L, D.
Credit Cards: AE, MC, V.
Handicapped Accessible: Yes.
Reservations: Strongly recommended for dinner.

Lei Lei's is a casual golf course restaurant and one of the best places to eat on the entire North Shore, with a surprisingly top-rack selection of savory dishes. Although located on Turtle Bay Resort property, it's independently and locally owned and exhibits true aloha for customers as well as for its loyal staff and the community. Residents drive from as far as Mililani to spend the evening with their families at low-key Lei Lei's, as do many of the North Shore's heart-and-soul residents.

For breakfast, try the Hawaiian sweet bread French toast and plantation iced tea; lunch offers a step up in selection and price, with fresh grilled Hawaiian fish plate, seared ʻahi sashimi Caesar salad, and shrimp cocktail; and dinner ramps it up further with escargot, oyster shots, crab stuffed salmon, prime rib, and double cut pork loin chop. During the day and twilight hours the view onto the golf course is very pleasant.

Ola
293-0801.
Turtle Bay Resort, 57-091 Kamehameha Hwy., Kahuku.
www.olaislife.com.
Closed: Major holidays (the dates vary each year).
Price: Expensive.
Cuisine: Hawaiʻi Regional.
Serving: L, D.
Credit Cards: AE, DC, DISC, MC, V.
Handicapped Accessible: Yes.
Reservations: Recommended.
Special Features: Open-air, oceanfront patio dining.

Well-known island chef Fred DeAngelo opened Ola in 2005 and presides over its excellent and award-winning kitchen. Although located at Turtle Bay Resort, the restaurant is independent and the menu more playful, trendy, and regional than the resort's lauded restaurant, 21 Degrees. It's also slightly less expensive. Ola sits right on the beach and its open-air, wood beam design creates a patio dining experience (which can at times be a touch windy).

Ola's romantic setting is coupled with savory, award-winning dishes. Photo courtesy Debbie Friedrich Photography.

Lunch prices are surprisingly moderate, with delectable items like traditional ʻahi poke, bruschetta salad, and fresh island fish sandwich. Be sure to order Kahuku corn whenever it's listed—it's grown right in the area and is sweet and very good. At dinnertime, you'll find dishes such as endive salad, crab cakes, miso butterfish, grilled ʻahi,

Hāmākua mushroom risotto, and kiawe-smoked beef tenderloin. Fresh local ingredients, characteristic of the cuisine, are paramount in Ola's preparations.

CENTRAL O'AHU

Helemano Plantation
622-3929.
64-1510 Kamehameha Hwy., Wahiawā.
www.helemano.org.
Closed: December 25 and January 1.
Price: Inexpensive.
Cuisine: Chinese/American.
Serving: B, L, SB.
Credit Cards: MC, V.
Handicapped Accessible: Yes.
Reservations: Strongly recommended.

Here's a great way to stuff yourself and feel good about it: Eat at Helemano Plantation. This unpretentious, entirely local enterprise is a unique, 45-acre community that provides developmentally disabled adults the chance to learn skills and work for a living. We think you'll be pleasantly surprised by the caring, joyful atmosphere at the Country Inn Restaurant, where the team offers an incredibly affordable, all-you-can-eat Chinese lunch buffet—complete with dessert items. They also serve breakfast, sandwiches, salads, and baked goodies in the Bake Shop, and their on-site vegetable garden is farmed for fresh ingredients. On Sundays, the restaurant opens for brunch.

Reservations in advance are a must, as they often reach capacity with tour group visits. Helemano is right next door to Dole Plantation, on the Hale'iwa side.

LEEWARD O'AHU

ROY'S RESTAURANT
676-7697.
Kō 'Olina Resort & Marina,
92-1220 Ali'inui Dr., Kapolei.
www.roysrestaurant.com.
Open: Year-round.
Price: Expensive.
Cuisine: Hawaiian Fusion.
Serving: L, D.
Credit Cards: AE, DC, DISC, MC, V.
Handicapped Accessible: Lower restaurant level is accessible.
Reservations: Strongly recommended.

Roy's is hands-down one of Hawai'i's top restaurants, and hip founder Roy Yamaguchi is known internationally as a culinary pioneer. Even if the Leeward Coast weren't restaurant-poor, Roy's would still be an obvious choice for a special night of fine dining. Signature dishes include crisped seafood potstickers, yellowfin 'ahi poketini, roasted macadamia nut mahimahi, and hibachi-style grilled salmon. They also feature an outstanding wine list, so be sure to prepare your palate.

Other Eats and Treats

Below you'll find inexpensive eateries where walk-ins are welcome and table service is

Isn't That Hawaiian Food?

Many visitors naturally assume that food served in Hawai'i is Hawaiian food. Or, at least, that the food served with a pineapple wedge on the side or glazed with teriyaki sauce is Hawaiian food. While our "local" food draws from many different cultures and eras, authentic and traditional Hawaiian food draws from pre-1778 Hawai'i. Modern Hawaiian food often includes several introduced ingredients and preparations that mostly compliment, rather than dominate, originally eaten dishes.

One traditional item you'll never see on the menu is dog meat, once a delicacy for Hawaiians (we knew that would wake you up!). However, most other Hawaiian staples can still be tasted today and are prepared using original and contemporary methods. Two of these delicious dishes are kalua pork and laulau, both cooked in a heated earthen pit called an *imu*. Chicken and fish were also eaten in abundance, as well as crayfish, crab, freshwater shrimp, breadfruit, sweet potato, yam, coconut, banana, and sugar cane—but the most important was the taro, or kalo, plant.

Kalo is so central and sacred to Hawaiian culture that the University of Hawai'i's genetic explorations with local varieties have been met with profound controversy. In Hawaiian mythology, the kalo plant grows from the grave of the first child ever born to the ancient gods. The second-born child is the ancestor of the Hawaiian people. From the kalo root comes the Hawaiian staple starch, poi. Nutritious, easy to digest, hypoallergenic, and tasty—especially when eaten with salty fish or pork—this mellow side dish was once enjoyed with every meal.

Since the 1800s, the word "lū'au" has been used to describe Hawaiian-style celebratory feasts. The modern visitor lū'au typically features cocktails, all-you-can-eat traditional and nontraditional buffet dishes, and a glitzy Polynesian dance revue. If a lū'au is part of your plan, we suggest the pricey but beautifully situated Royal Hawaiian Hotel's **Royal Hawaiian Lū'au** (931-8383; www.royal-hawaiian.com) in Waikiki, the Polynesian Cultural Center's **Ali'i Lū'au** (293-3333; www.polynesia.com) near the North Shore, or **Germaine's Lū'au** (949-6626; www.germainesluau.com).

basic, or where you can grab-n-go. Plus, we've included sweets stops, natural food stores, afternoon teas, culinary tours, and other miscellaneous food-related tidbits, big and small. Be sure to call to check hours of operation first, then dig in and try it all!

Afternoon Tea

Enjoying afternoon tea—which usually includes finger sandwiches, scones with cream, a variety of teas, and other tiny treats—is deep luxury and a fantastic way to unwind and connect with Hawai'i's historical British influences. Reservations are recommended.

Waikīkī

Afternoon tea at the Moana Surfrider's **Banyan Veranda** (921-4600; Moana Surfrider, 2365 Kalākaua Ave.) is a longstanding tradition and is considered by many to be the best. Expect old world glamour and ease at this daily seaside event. Dress the part. "Keiki Tea" for children is also available.

Greater Honolulu

The **Wai'oli Tea Room** (988-5800; 2950 Mānoa Rd., Mānoa) offers afternoon tea in a tropical, beautiful Hawaiian plantation setting Tuesday through Sunday. Reservations must be made at least a day in advance. At the Kahala Hotel & Resort's gorgeous **Veranda** (739-8760; Kahala Hotel & Resort, 5000 Kahala Ave., Kahala), even if you don't see a celebrity, you'll at least feel like one. This is an elegant spot for tea.

Afternoon tea at the Wai'oli Tea Room is easy and soothing.

Bakeries, Sweets, and Other Treats

Unfortunately vacations usually don't quell that certain craving for something sweet or salty—so here's where you can find both local- and American-style standbys. Give local goodies a try!

Waikīkī

Beard Papa's Cream Puffs (926-8247; Waikīkī Beach Walk, 227 Lewers St.) features a popular cream puff from Japan, which is baked and filled with whipped-cream custard. **Cold Stone Creamery** (923-1656; 2570 Kalākaua Ave.) makes its own ice cream, stirring in gobs of goodies at your command. **Godiva Chocolatier's** (922-2430; 2270 Kalākaua Ave.) luxurious, individually made chocolates are expensive, but delicious. Kaua'i-founded **Lappert's Gourmet Ice Creams and Coffees** (943-0256; Hilton Hawaiian Village, 2005 Kalia Rd.) serves incredible, chunky, creamy ice cream in flavors such as Kaua'i Pie and white chocolate macadamia nut. **Mondo Gelato** (926-6961; Waikīkī Beach Walk, 226 Lewers St.) sells good Italian ice cream, although they charge premium prices for it. **Saint-Germain Bakery** (924-4305; 2301 Kūhiō Ave.) is popular with residents and sells all kinds of baked goods, including muffins, breads, desserts, and sandwiches. **Teuscher** (922-5454; Hyatt Regency Shops, 2424 Kalākaua Ave.) chocolates are some of the finest in the world and are flown in fresh each week from Switzerland for your enjoyment.

Greater Honolulu

Plenty of sweets reside at Ala Moana Center (1450 Ala Moana Blvd., Ala Moana): **The Crack Seed Center** (949-7200) offers Chinese-origin snacks that are as local as it gets—try these dehydrated and sweet- or sour-seasoned fruit treats. **The Epicure Department at Neiman Marcus** (951-8887) sells luxury European chocolates by the piece and box. **The Patisserie La Palme D'Or** (941-6161) features beautifully made upscale cakes and sweets. And **Shirokiya** (973-9111) is a quintessential Japanese department store (originating in Edo, Japan 350 years ago!) with an amazing array of ethnic snacks and mini meals on its top floor.

At Ward Centre (1200 Ala Moana Blvd., Kaka'ako) and Ward Warehouse (1050 Ala Moana Blvd., Kaka'ako): Stop at Ben & Jerry's (593-7090; Ward Centre) for Chunky Monkey and the rest of the famous ice cream makers' best. The Honolulu Chocolate Company (591-2997; Ward Centre) offers rows of incredible, elegant, locally made chocolates. The Honolulu Cookie Company (597-8182; Ward Warehouse) sells tasty, local-style shortbread cookies that are perfect gifts to bring back home. Satura Cakes (537-1206; Ward Centre) features organic Japanese cakes and more, developed by a chef who baked for three Japanese prime ministers.

In the downtown area, visit at the very unassuming **Char Hung Sut** (538-3335; 64 North Pauahi St., Chinatown), which is one of the best places on the island to try manapua, a classic local treat resembling the Chinese steamed pork bun. **Padovani's Chocolates** (536-4567; 841 Bishop St., Downtown) sells velvety, European-style chocolates handmade in Hawai'i by some of the state's top chefs. **Shung Chong Yuein** (531-1983; 1027 Maunakea St., Chinatown) will give you an authentic Chinese bakery experience with zero pretension. Try its lotus seed cakes.

Saturday mornings mean food shopping in Chinatown, and the popular Shung Chong Yuein bakery overflows with customers.

In the Kapahulu/Mō'ili'ili/Mānoa areas of town, visit **Bubbies Homemade Ice Cream & Desserts** (949-8984; 1010 University Ave., Mō'ili'ili) for delectable mochi ice cream and naughty flavors such as "Multiple Orgasm." Bubbies made it onto Oprah's *O Magazine* "O List." No other bakery treat better represents Hawai'i than the malasada, and for more than 50 years, **Leonard's Bakery** (737-5591; 933 Kapahulu Ave., Kapahulu) has sold the best. Also be on the lookout around the island for its signature red-and-white-striped wagons, which serve 'em up hot. The 65-year-old **Waiola Bakery & Shave Ice** (735-8886; 525 Kapahulu Ave., Kapahulu) is the best place in town to try shave ice—they offer around 40 flavors, including some very unique selections.

Further east, visit **Café Laufer** (735-7717; 3565 Wai'alae Ave., Kaimukī) for specialty cakes and pastries, in addition to Germanic dishes. **The Patisserie** (735-4402; Kahala Mall Shopping Center, 4211 Wai'alae Ave., Kahala) is a 40-year-old institution that offers up wonderful pastries (and also serves great Germanic meals at night).

Near Hanauma Bay, you can stop for yet another scoop of **Bubbies Homemade Ice Cream & Desserts** (396-8722; Koko Marina Shopping Center, 7192 Kalaniana'ole Hwy., Hawai'i Kai).

WINDWARD O'AHU

Have a light breakfast at **Agnes' Portuguese Bake Shop** (262-5367; 46 Ho'ola'i St., Kailua), which specializes in malasadas, but serves many other good pastry items as well.

Elvin's Bakery & Café (Kailua Shopping Center, 600 Kailua Rd., Kailua) sells yummy island-style pastries, plus tea, coffee, sandwiches, and salads. Island Snow (263-6339; 130 Kailua Rd., Kailua) will address your post-beach shave ice (as well as surf clothing) needs; be sure to request that they add ice cream in the cone. Nene Goose Bakery (262-1080; 1090 Keolu Dr., Kailua) features well-made French bread, mochi anpan, sweet potato tart, and other pastries.

NORTH SHORE

Aoki's Shave Ice (637-7017; 66-117 Kamehameha Hwy., Hale'iwa) is the Aoki family's 20-plus-year-old store, but they've been selling shave ice since the 1930s. Although not as publicized as Matsumoto's next door, it's equally as tasty. **Matsumoto Shave Ice** (637-4827; 66-087 Kamehameha Hwy., Hale'iwa) serves more than 1,200 shave ices each day and is swamped with tour busses, but it's still a goody. **Ted's Bakery** (638-5974; 59-024 Kamehameha Hwy., Sunset Beach) only requires that you enter and speak the magic words: chocolate-haupia cream pie.

Cafés and on-the-Go Eats

Most of these spots don't offer table service—or if they do, it's minimal. They're also all affordable choices where you can return again and again for a quick bite.

WAIKĪKĪ

Le Jardin (921-2236; Hyatt Regency, 2424 Kalākaua Ave.) creates very fresh smoothies, juices, sandwiches and crepes—a touch pricey, but a lovely and convenient location. Japanese visitors crowd the unpretentious little **Kiwani Ramen** (924-6744; Waikīkī Shopping Plaza, 2250 Kalākaua Ave., Ground Floor.) for authentic ramen noodles, and so should you. They also favor the simple Tokyo bar setting of **Ramen Nakamura** (922-7960; 2141 Kalākaua Ave.), which is open all day and until late in the evening for ramen and fried rice. **Teddy's Bigger Burgers** (926-3444; Waikīkī Grand Hotel, 134 Kapahulu Ave.) forks over fresh, juicy, quality burgers, and extras—even peanut butter shakes. It's a local favorite. For gourmet on-the-go, head to **Wolfgang Puck Express** (931-6226; ResortQuest Waikīkī Beach Hotel, 2570 Kalākaua Ave.) for really fantastic thin-crust pizzas, rosemary rotisserie chicken with garlic mashed potatoes, and much more.

GREATER HONOLULU

In the Kapahulu/Diamond Head area, you'll find **Bogart's Café** (739-0999; 3045 Monsarrat Ave., Diamond Head) for quick breakfasts and lunches that residents love. We can't emphasize enough how incredibly tasty the deli selections are at **Diamond Head Market & Grill** (732-0077; 3158 Monsarrat Ave., Diamond Head)—the gourmet prices are worth every penny. **The Grill** next to the Market offers quality, high-end, and affordable plate lunches. Classic mom-and-pop **Ono Hawaiian Foods** (737-2275; 726 Kapahulu Ave., Kapahulu) is just short of becoming a tour-bus stop instead of a local treasure. You don't want that, and neither do residents. It has some of the best traditional Hawaiian food in the state, so do visit—but help preserve its rustic, local atmosphere by taking your food to go (we take ours to the beach!). **Rainbow Drive-In** (737-0177; 3308 Kana'ina Ave., Kapahulu) is a full-on local stop offering up a hardcore plate lunch—the teri beef plate and beef stew plate are the best. Again, take food to go; even most residents do, since the seating area is unsavory.

Genki Sushi (942-9102; Ala Moana Center, 1450 Ala Moana Blvd., Ala Moana) is a lot of fun, if you don't mind crowds—it's a sit-down experience with sushi floating by on a conveyor belt, but you can be done in 15 minutes in the off hours, when bar seats are available.

At Ward Centre (1200 Ala Moana Blvd., Kaka'ako), check out **Kaka'ako Kitchen** (596-7488) for quality plate lunches (as well as breakfasts and dinners) overseen by one of Hawai'i's cutting-edge chefs; we're not always impressed, but residents swear by it and the prices are right. Next door is the burger shop everyone loves, local-style **Kua 'Āina** (591-9133).

If you're downtown and don't have long for breakfast or lunch, try **Honolulu Café** (533-1555; 741 Bishop St.) for upscale, healthy fare and a gorgeous, vintage architectural arcade setting.

In east Honolulu, enjoy dinner or a weekend lunch at the delicious and bustling Greek/Mediterranean **Olive Tree Café** (737-0303; 4614 Kilauea Ave., Kahala). Buy a bottle of wine next door and enjoy it on the café's open-air patio. Near Hanauma Bay, the perfect stop for lunch is **The Shack** (396-1919; Hawai'i Kai Shopping Center, 377 Keahole St., Hawai'i Kai) for scrumptious burgers right on the canalfront.

The casual and quick Honolulu Café in downtown Honolulu gets a brisk lunchtime crowd from the financial district set.

WINDWARD O'AHU

Aloha Salad (262-2016; Kailua Shopping Center, 600 Kailua Rd., Kailua) offers endless, and even unexpected, goodies for self-designed salads. Health-conscious, Middle Eastern **Paprika** (262-3777; 35 Kainehe St., Kailua) was recently opened by a former University of Hawai'i Hebrew instructor, and is a charming spot for lunch and dinner dining. The landmark, 1932-founded **Kalapawai Market** (262-4359; 306 S. Kalāheo Ave., Kailua) has a little sandwich shop inside that's perfect for beach picnic fixings; the owners recently opened the amazing little breakfast/lunch/dinner locale, **Kalapawai Café & Deli** (262-3354; 750 Kailua Rd., Kailua), which features wonderful upscale deli dishes and more. **Teddy's Burgers** (262-0820; Kailua Village Shops, 539 Kailua Rd., Kailua) is a local favorite with quality, mega-juicy burgers made to order.

Teddy's in Kailua is always busy flipping mega-juicy burgers.

Past Kailua and on your way north, you'll find **Ono Loa Hawaiian Foods** (239-2863; 48-140 Kamehameha Hwy., Waiāhole). This homespun to-go stop operates out of a vintage poi factory, and owner Maxine farms some of the food herself in the valley. Ono Loa keeps limited hours; if it's open, you'll be treated to delicious and authentic Hawaiian food, as well as a story or two.

Between Punalu'u and Kahuku (and even beyond), you'll see that a shrimp truck war is on, with new peel-and-eat shrimp shacks opening on the roadside seemingly every day. They all serve similar plates and are all pretty good—despite the fact that **Giovanni's Shrimp Truck** (one of the originals, next to the old sugar mill) has become a tour-bus stop. We like **Romy's** (56-781 Kamehameha Hwy., Kahuku), because it harvests its shrimp daily from the aquaculture pond next door (despite public belief that the shrimp trucks serve esteemed Kahuku shrimp, most don't), offers views onto the pond and marsh birds, and has a convenient sink for customers to wash up in—a must after hand-peeling garlicky, buttery shrimp.

Roadside fruit stands dot the landscape in the area also, and any of them can crack open a coconut for you, slice pineapple with a machete, or sell you apple-bananas. These are fun snack stops.

North Shore

Cholo's Homestyle Mexican (637-3059; 66-250 Kamehameha Hwy., Hale'iwa) is festive all day and evening long, although the food's average. Also very popular with visitors and residents is the **Grass Skirt Grill** (637-4852; 66-214 Kamehameha Hwy., Hale'iwa) for shrimp, salads, fish plates, and more. **Kua 'Āina** (637-6067; 66-160 Kamehameha Hwy., Hale'iwa) is a classic favorite for super tasty burgers and earthier sandwich selections. The psychedelically painted **Paradise Found Café** (637-4540; 66-483 Kamehameha Hwy., Hale'iwa) is a tiny gem tucked in the back of Celestial Foods, a health food store. It conveys the true free spirit and warmth of the North Shore, and makes some of the most delicious and healthiest food around, using ingredients from local organic farmers.

Central O'ahu

Molly's Smokehouse (621-4858; 23 S. Kamehameha Hwy., Wahiawā) has earned accolades for serving up an insane barbecue with all the extras you'd expect. **The Poke Stop** (676-8100; 94-050 Farrington Hwy., Waipahu) is famous for its very Hawaiian-style poke dishes prepared by a well-known island chef, but they also offer delicious gourmet sandwiches and plate lunches sure to please everyone.

Leeward O'ahu

Hapa Grill (674-8400; The Marketplace at Kapolei, 590 Farrington Hwy., Kapolei) has built a huge following for its thoughtfully and tastefully prepared creations, and its signature teriyaki beef is outstanding. Weekend breakfasts are also popular.

All the other little healthful food stops along the Leeward Coast have closed down, and we're dismayed to announce that it seems fast food continues to triumph there. We have to toss up our hands and suggest you pick up a plate lunch from **L & L Barbecue** (696-7989; 85-080 Wai'anae Valley Rd., Wai'anae), on Farrington Highway—a local chain we think is mediocre but has a big following.

Coffee Houses and Tea Cafés

The brooding writer huddled up with black coffee and a laptop is not very Hawai'i-style and the coffee house culture is still fledgling here, but you'll find a few cozy spots for a morning brew.

Waikīkī

The Coffee Bean & Tea Leaf (926-4951; Waikīkī Beach Walk, 227 Lewers St.) is a local gourmet tea and coffee shop with more than 30 varieties of full leaf teas and 32 varieties of Arabica coffees. The charmingly diminutive **Euro Market Café** (922-3876; 2310 Kūhiō Ave.) serves fabulous coffee and other specialty goodies. At the locally owned **Honolulu Coffee Co.** (533-1500; Moana Surfrider, 2365 Kalākaua Ave.) you'll find excellent coffee bar items and a window onto the world. Of its endless locations on O'ahu, the **DFS Starbucks** (926-4863; DFS Galleria, 330 Royal Hawaiian Ave.) is one of the best—it's a hidden, garden-like oasis right in the middle of Waikīkī. Or, to watch the waves while you sip, try the location on the corner of Kalākaua and Kapahulu Avenues. **MaHaLo Hawai'i Deep Sea Water Showroom** (926-5696; Waikīkī Shopping Plaza, 2250 Kalākaua Ave.) is quite unique: This sleek, Japanese-mod bar serves two-thousand-year-old, desalinized water from Hawai'i's deep Pacific, along with teas and coffees made from the same.

Greater Honolulu

At Ala Moana Center (1450 Ala Moana Blvd., Ala Moana), the locally owned **Honolulu Coffee Co.** (949-1500) offers high quality coffees, treats, and a cool space to hang out. There's perhaps no better place to enjoy tea on the island than **The Pacific Place Tea Garden** (944-2004), which serves fine teas—many made from real fruit nectars, native herbs, and flowers from Hawai'i—in an open-air setting.

On weekdays in the downtown area, stop by the **Honolulu Coffee Co.** (521-4400; 1001 Bishop St., Downtown) to see the best of financial district business folks, or **rRed Elephant** (545-2468; 1144 Bethel St., Downtown)—no, that's not a typo—seven days a week for a hipper climate and some live performances.

Windward O'ahu

The Coffee Bean & Tea Leaf (262-7220; Kailua Marketplace, 108 Hekili St., Kailua) is a local gourmet tea and coffee shop with more than 30 varieties of full leaf teas and 32 varieties of Arabica coffees. **Morning Brew** (262-7770; Kailua Shopping Center, 600 Kailua Rd., Kailua) attracts local folks for its outstanding coffee. **Starbucks** (263-9548; Kailua Village Shops, 539 Kailua Rd., Kailua) occupies a good people-watching corner.

North Shore

The adorable **Coffee Gallery** (637-5355; 66-250 Kamehameha Hwy., Hale'iwa) boasts endless roasts and is the place to go.

Leeward O'ahu

Starbucks (563 Farrington Hwy., Kapolei) found a Leeward Coast niche in the commuter town of Kapolei, near Kō 'Olina.

Cooking Classes and Culinary Tours

Join food scientist and Southeast Asian cultural expert Walter Rhee on **A Cook's Tour of Chinatown** (391-1550). Weave through a myriad of colorful Chinatown markets for insights into authentic preparations of its meats, seafood, produce, herbs, and spices; or, enjoy his **Chinatown Eateries Tour**. Well-known local food writer Anthony Chang leads the **Culinary Walking Tour of Chinatown** (533-3181), stopping at noodle shops, dim-sum parlors, food courts, bakeries, tea stands, and other downtown venues. **Gourmet Cooking Hawai'i** (735-7788; www.gourmetcookinghawaii.com) offers hands-on as well as demonstration cooking classes with Hawai'i's most celebrated chefs, right in their restaurants. Choose your own chef, menu, and date, or join scheduled classes offered on Saturdays year-round. Matthew Gray's **Hawai'i Food Tours** (1-800-715-2468; 926-3663; www.hawaiifoodtours.com) offers three outstanding guided restaurant tours: the **Hole-In-The Wall Tour**, the **Hawaiian Feast in Paradise Tour**, and the **Gourmet Trilogy Tour for Food & Wine Lovers,** all in and around Honolulu. Gray is a former professional chef and considered one of Hawai'i's top food experts.

Farmers' Markets, Juice Bars, Gourmet Shops, and Health Food Stops

Although O'ahu isn't known as a New Age or organic destination, we have a few folks on the right track and more behind them.

WAIKĪKĪ

Marie's Health Foods/Organic Café (926-3900; Kalākaua Business Center, 2155 Kalākaua Ave., Suite 110) makes pretty good sandwiches and smoothies, plus stocks a few health product basics. **Jamba Juice** (926-6260; Waikīkī Trade Center, 2255 Kūhiō Ave.) is a good standby for fresh juice drinks. The tiny **Ruffage Natural Foods** (922-2042; 2443 Kūhiō Ave.) has a long history of serving wonderful, very homemade (in a good way!) sandwiches, creative smoothie drinks, and more for breakfast, lunch, and dinner. On Tuesdays and Fridays from 7–1 you'll find the little **Waikīkī Farmers' Market** (923-1802; Waikīkī Community Center, 310 Paoakalani Ave.), where you can pick up island-style foods and produce.

GREATER HONOLULU

Down To Earth (947-7678; 2525 S. King St., Mō'ili'ili) is O'ahu's best-known and most popular organic grocery and deli, along with the excellent natural foods cooperative **Kōkua Market** (941-1922; 2563 S. King St., Mō'ili'ili), which offers organic and/or locally-grown produce, meat, and other products, including sandwiches.

At Ala Moana Center (1450 Ala Moana Blvd., Ala Moana), stop by **Vim 'N Vigor** (955-3600)—it's been there for years and covers all the basics, plus it has a lunchtime food bar.

O'ahu's first **Whole Foods Markets,** which will carry many organic items, are set to open in 2008 at Ward Centers and Kahala Mall.

Jamba Juice (585-8359; 130 Merchant St., Downtown) is nearby your historic sites walk; stop in and freshen up. **R. Field Wine Co.** (596-9463; inside Foodland Super Market, 1460 S. Beretania St., Makiki) offers an outstanding (although tiny) selection of gourmet produce, wine, meat, chocolate, and miscellaneous food items.

The **Saturday Farmers' Market** (391-3804; Kapi'olani Community College, 4303 Diamond Head Rd., Kaimukī) is the choicest farmers' market on the island—get there early (it opens at 7:30) and eat your way through. **'Umeke Market and Deli** (739-2990; 4400 Kalaniana'ole Hwy., Kahala) is a family owned natural foods and products store that also features a fabulous gourmet deli.

WINDWARD O'AHU

Down To Earth (262-3838; 201 Hāmākua Dr., Kailua) is a staple organic grocer and deli that has been in business for many years. For a fresh pick-me-up, stop at **Jamba Juice** (263-0975; Kailua Village Shops, 539 Kailua Rd., Kailua) after hitting the beach. The **Kailua Farmers' Market** (391-3804; Kailua Town Center Parking Garage, 609 Kailua Rd., Kailua) is short but sweet, Thursday evenings from 5–7:30 PM. **Lanikai Juice** (262-2383; **Kailua Shopping Center**, 600 Kailua Rd., Kailua) is a local company serving up fantastic natural juices and smoothies. **R. Field Wine Co.** (261-3358; Kailua Marketplace, 108 Hekili Rd.) carries an admirable little selection of gourmet foods and wines. **The Source Natural Foods** (262-5604; 32 Kainehe St.) is a family-run shop backed by 20 years of nutritional knowledge.

North Shore

Vegans and vegetarians hang out at **Celestial Natural Foods** (637-4540; 66-483 Kamehameha Hwy., Hale'iwa), where organic products and the wonderful little **Paradise Found Cafe** are located. The **North Shore Country Market** (Sunset Beach Elementary School, 59-360 Kamehameha Hwy., Sunset Beach) takes place every Saturday from 8–2 and features produce, crafts, and a neighborly atmosphere.

Late-Night Dining

Eating late can be an event in and of itself, or a fun afterthought following an evening at the bar. Here are a few places in town that can accommodate you well.

Waikīkī

For an odd-hour meal in Waikīkī, try **Sansei Seafood Restaurant & Sushi Bar** (931-6286; Waikīkī Beach Marriott, 2552 Kalākaua Ave., 3rd Floor.), open weekend nights until 2 AM, or the 24-hour diners **MAC 24/7** (921-5564; Hilton Waikīkī Prince Kūhiō, 2500 Kūhiō Ave.) and **Wailana Coffee Shop** (955-1764; 1860 Ala Moana Blvd.). **Eggs 'n Things** (949-0820; 1911-B Kalākaua Ave.) opens at 11 PM, perfect for late night munchies.

Greater Honolulu

For high-end dining in the wee hours, head to **The Bistro** (943-6500; 1750 Kalākaua Ave., 3rd Floor., Ala Moana) just outside of Waikīkī for its late night tasting menu, served until 1 AM Tuesday through Sunday. Also just outside of Waikīkī are **Mr. Ojisan** (735-4455; Kilohana Square, 1018 Kapahulu Ave., Kapahulu), serving up dishes like ginger pork until 1 AM Friday and Saturday; and **Shokudo** (941-3701; 1585 Kapi'olani Blvd., Ala Moana), which serves Japanese-and Korean-inspired dishes until 1 AM Sunday through Thursday, and 2 AM Friday and Saturday.

"Old-Timer" Fish Markets

Known for standing the test of time and, in the case of the Fish Auction, being the vortex of the seafood world, these are fun places to poke through just for the experience.

O'ahu Market is tiny by today's standards, but it's been a cornerstone of Chinatown for more than one hundred years.

Greater Honolulu

The United Fishing Agency's Fish Auction (536-2148) is *the* seafood auction. Get to Pier 38 as early as dawn to enjoy it. Wear tennis shoes and expect to mostly see fishermen, shop owners, and chefs—not tourists. Chinatown's landmark little **O'ahu Market** (corner of King and Kekaulike Sts., Chinatown) has been bustling for more than one hundred years; and although it isn't as colorful as it once was, it still has unusual stalls that sell pig snouts, jellyfish, and reef fish. Follow the trail of daily shoppers as they wind through neighboring market nooks at **Kekaulike Plaza** and **Maunakea Marketplace** to glimpse jackfruit, lychee, rambutan, bitter melon, and lotus root.

The 58-year-old **Ward Farmers' Market** (Ward Centre, 1020 Auahi St., Kaka'ako) mainly houses the members-only, Asiatic Marukai Market Place, but a few other interesting fish and Hawaiian food markets still fill the large space.

Wine Shops and Wine Bars

Nothing adds a touch of style to your meal or your day than a glass of good wine. Below are several wine bars, plus a couple of O'ahu's several exceptional wine stores. All the wine bars serve good food too, so you can stay all evening.

Waikīkī

Tucked in a cute cottage just off Kūhiō Avenue, **Pane e Vino** (923-8466; 408 Lewers St., 2nd Floor.) is primarily a wine bar, although they serve Italian food as well. Dark wood and cool music make it perfect for a night under the radar.

Greater Honolulu

Du Vin (545-1115; 1115 Bethel St., Downtown) is one of the city's newest wine bars, with an atmospheric French bistro interior and light French fare. To purchase a great bottle of wine from the experts, visit **Fujioka's Wine Times** (739-9463; Market City Shopping Center, 2919 Kapi'olani Blvd., Kaimukī), only a short drive from Waikīkī. **Formaggio Wine Bar** (739-7719) is right next door—and it serves hip Italian and Mediterranean dishes in addition to wine. **Vino** (524-8466; Restaurant Row, 500 Ala Moana Blvd., Kaka'ako) is co-owned by master sommelier Chuck Furuya and has been named one of the country's 50 most amazing wine experiences by *Food & Wine* magazine. They also offer a menu of light dishes.

Windward O'ahu

Formaggio Grill's (263-2633; 305 Hahani St., Kailua) newest location serves 40 wines by the glass along with a delicious full menu. **R. Field Wine Co.** (261-3358; Kailua Marketplace, 108 Hekili Rd., Kailua) is a little shop chock full of wines, plus cheeses and other gourmet fare. When in the Turtle Bay Resort area, head to **Tamura's** (232-2332; 54-316 Hau'ula Kai Shopping Center, Kamehameha Hwy., Hau'ula) for a wide selection of good wines for purchase.

The 1976 maiden voyage of the Hōkūle'a (here returning from Tahiti in 1992) proved to the world that Hawaiians could have traveled the open ocean using traditional navigation systems. The voyage sparked a monumental surge in ethnic pride.

6

HAWAIIANS TODAY

People of the 'Āina

Although less than 1 percent of Native Hawaiians are full-blooded, 240,000 Hawai'i residents claim part-Hawaiian ancestry—and most live right here on O'ahu. According to the *2006 Native Hawaiian Data Book*, another 160,000 Native Hawaiians live on the Mainland, with more than 60,000 in California alone.

But who are Native Hawaiians? We've added this chapter to the book in the belief that you do indeed care who Native Hawaiians are—who they *really* are—historically as a people and in contemporary times. Here you'll find brief sketches of traditional and modern

Farming precious taro, or kalo, remains a part of present-day life.

Hawaiian practices and issues, as well as background on and directions to several heritage sites. Since we're neither cultural experts nor Native Hawaiians ourselves, we turned to mostly Native Hawaiian-produced materials as sources and humbly hope that the below information below enriches your visit to Hawai'i, inspires you to make conscientious decisions about how you visit Hawai'i, and encourages you to learn even more about Hawai'i. For those who are interested in further reading we recommend numerous excellent books in Chapter 9.

The Value of Land

Ua mau kea ea o ka 'āina i ka pono—"the life of the land is perpetuated in righteousness." These were King Kamehameha III's words upon the restoration of the Kingdom of Hawai'i, after a brief takeover in the name of Britain in 1843. It is safe to say that when he spoke of *'āina*, or "the land," he meant something of much greater significance than the return of "property." The Hawaiian people considered themselves children of the land, and the concept of *malama 'āina*, or caring for the land, was ingrained in their spirit. In traditional Hawaiian culture, nature was not something that could be owned—it belonged to the gods alone.

Each island was divided into *moku,* or districts, and within each *moku* were a series of triangular-shaped *ahupua'a*—or land divisions—extending from mountain crestlines to deep valleys to beyond the reef. The *ahupua'a* system united various ecosystems into a complete, sustainable unit of resources that all shared. The king and chiefs were stewards of the land, and the commoners, who were free to move from region to region at will, worked the land. Hawaiians felt the presence of life and spirit in stones, water, trees, and other natural elements, as well as kinship with them, heightening the people's sense of belonging to the land and environment, rather than the reverse.

These beliefs and systems sat poorly with the increasing number of foreigners arriving in the kingdom, who began pressuring the Hawaiian government for the right to own the land. Despite a petition signed by thousands of Hawaiians, King Kamehameha III eventually followed the advice of several strong-willed non-Hawaiian men and in 1848, the landmark Great Mahele—or great division—of the land as private property began.

Although Hawaiians were permitted to claim the plots of land they lived on, many never pursued claims to own what they believed should not be owned; others filed claims, but because they could not support themselves, severed from the *ahupua'a* system thousands left the land to eek out a living in town. Foreigners and naturalized Hawaiian citizens, however, who fully understood the opportunity presented, wasted not a moment in obtaining as much land as possible. A mere four years after the process of distribution began, no less than 16 members of the Congregational Mission held an average of 500 acres of prime lands each—many of which are still owned by their descendants today, such as the once sacred region of Kualoa.

Nearly 30 years after the overthrow of the monarchy, Prince Kūhiō established the Hawaiian Homes Act to restore 200,000 acres of land for homesteading and cultural revival to Hawaiians of any blood relation. Non-Hawaiians, concerned over losing acreage to Hawaiians, pressured Kūhiō to require applicants to possess at least 50 percent Hawaiian heritage, which they felt few would eventually be able to meet. Despite its noble intentions the program has been abysmally managed, with only 7,200 leases awarded in 85 years; and many people died long before their names were ever called. As of 2004, the waiting list held more than 20,000 names. In the last couple of years, however, the department has shown strong commitment to achieving its goals and claims that it will serve every qualified beneficiary by 2008.

Accustomed to the breadth of resources provided by the ahupua'a system, Hawaiians struggled to survive on limited lands after the Great Mahele. Photo courtesy Hawai'i State Archives.

Fabrics of Society

Other cornerstones that governed traditional Hawaiian society and permeated the culture were living a *pono* life, family roles, religious practice, and the *kapu* (or taboo) system.

Personal life centered on *pono*—both a state of being and code of behavior that can be likened to grace, balance, justness, and righteousness. To steal, carry a grudge, act impatiently, envy, lie, slander, think badly of others, physically abuse, waste food, or act slothfully were *hewa,* or not *pono.* The concept of *pono* seems to be experiencing a revival in modern Hawai'i, although the word is perhaps overused as a politically correct catch phrase, especially in the visitor industry.

Family life—participating in and responsibilities to one's *'ohana*—was a fundamental aspect of identity and joy, and children were treasured. Family ties extended beyond the nuclear unit and blood kinship, and also reached both backward and forward in time to ancestors and descendents. Contemporary Hawaiian families have a higher poverty rate and increased risk of health problems than other Island ethnicities. Less than half of the population graduates from high school, and only 10 percent graduate from college. These situations put great strain on family life, and Hawai'i's astronomical cost of living has heightened the crisis. Of approximately 4,000 homeless citizens on Leeward O'ahu, including seven hundred children, it is estimated that 60 to 70 percent are Native Hawaiian. At the time of writing, nearly eleven thousand Hawaiian names are on the waiting list for Hawaiian homestead lands on O'ahu alone. And because of the 50 percent blood quantum requirement, many more no longer qualify for land.

Hawaiian society was polytheistic as well as animistic. Ancient Hawaiian religion focused on four main gods that originated in Central Polynesia: Kāne, Kū, Lono, and Kanaloa, each of which had numerous incarnations that worshippers appealed to—for example, timber craftsmen honored eight different forms of Kū. In addition to these four gods, or *akua,* infinite other deities existed who were honored with shrines, sacrifices, and rituals. Although most of today's Hawaiians have embraced Christianity, traces of older beliefs still linger. Most overt is respect for the volcanic fire goddess, Pele, who is said to now live within the bubbling Kilauea caldera on the Island of Hawai'i—and is sometimes seen walking among the people, accompanied by a white dog.

The *kapu* system appears to have arrived with Tahitian settlers. Essentially a set of laws governing all aspects of public and private life, the *kapu* system separated villagers into castes governed by *ali'i,* who bore powerful genealogies and intermarried to retain pure bloodlines and *mana,* or sacred power. Below the *ali'i* was the *kahuna* class, comprised of highly regarded craftspeople, professionals, and priests. The largest caste, however, was the *maka'āinana,* or the commoner class. Beneath them was a small group of outcasts and slaves called *kauwā,* or *kauā.*

The list of *kapu* was endless: it was *kapu* for women to eat pork, coconuts, or bananas, or to eat with men; certain beaches were *kapu,* so that only the *ali'i* could surf the best waves; and should a commoner's shadow fall upon the house of a sacred *ali'i, kapu* dictated how he or she was to die as punishment. A way to avoid punishment for breaking *kapu* was to successfully escape to a *pu'uhonua,* or official walled sanctuary, where safety and pardon were granted. After 40 years of exposure to Western life and the death of King Kamehameha I, the *kapu* system was broken by the *ali'i* themselves, and it faded away quickly in the face of Christianity.

Modern Hawai'i has been an American state since 1959, with two senators and two representatives serving in Washington and a total of four counties (the City and County of Honolulu is the largest, extending across the island of O'ahu and most of the Northwestern Hawaiian Islands). A semi-autonomous and controversial government body, the Office of Hawaiian Affairs (OHA) was created in 1978, instilled with the mission of "righting" all types of injustices to, and creating opportunities for, the Hawaiian community; residents disagree, however, on whether OHA does too much for the people (its existence has even been challenged in court), or too little.

The trustees of OHA, the local government, Hawaiian advocacy groups, activists, and other residents from every walk of life have been in dialogue for years regarding new political structures that could restore Native Hawaiians' rights as self-determining people, in a manner that will satisfy everyone. Possible solutions range from "nation-within-a-nation" status to complete independence from the United States—an idea particularly fueled by the U.S. government's official apology to Hawai'i in 1993 for its role in what it deemed an illegal takeover of a sovereign nation one hundred years earlier. One of OHA's tasks is to encourage ethnic Hawaiians from all over the world to register with Kau Inoa, enabling them to eventually participate in the reshaping of Hawaiian governance.

One proposed political solution that has garnered heavy media attention in Hawai'i and on the Mainland is Senator Daniel Akaka's Native Hawaiian Government Reorganization Act. Reintroduced in 2007 after it failed to win over Washington in previous sessions, the bill has yet again received vehement opposition from certain members of Congress. Hawai'i residents themselves are divided on their support of the bill—although some surveys indicate that most are in favor of it—with concerns ranging from "reverse racism" to disappointment in its willingness to compromise.

To hear community leaders discuss a broad range of subjects impacting Native Hawaiians today, tune into KKNE AM 940's 7–9 AM daily morning radiobroadcast, "Nā Oiwi Olino" (People Seeking Wisdom), launched by OHA in 2006. OHA's Web site (www.oha.org) features extensive information and news updates. The Public Broadcasting System and other local cable channels also frequently run quality programming covering Hawai'i's complex political and social issues. Another excellent introduction to Hawaiian culture is the documentary *The Hawaiians: Reflecting Spirit,* by Edgy Lee (2006).

An Excerpt from Senator Akaka's Speech to the Senate, January 17, 2007

Mr. President, I rise today . . . to introduce the Native Hawaiian Government Reorganization Act of 2007. This bill, which is of great importance to the people of Hawai'i, establishes a process to extend the federal policy of self-governance and self-determination to Hawai'i's indigenous people . . . .

Mr. President, January 17, 2007, commemorates the 114th anniversary of Hawai'i's beloved Queen Lili'uokalani being deposed. Although this event may seem like a distant memory, it is a poignant event that expedited the decline of a proud and self-governing people. The overthrow facilitated Native Hawaiians being disenfranchised from not only their culture and land, but from their way of life. Native Hawaiians had to endure the forced imprisonment of their Queen and witness the deterioration and near eradication of their culture and tradition in their own homeland at the hands of foreigners committed exclusively to propagating Western values and conventions.

While Congress has traditionally treated Native Hawaiians in a manner parallel to American Indians and Alaska Natives, the federal policy of self-governance and self-determination has not been formally extended to Native Hawaiians. The bill itself does not extend federal recognition—it authorizes the process for federal recognition.

The Native Hawaiian Government Reorganization Act of 2007 does three things: it authorizes an office in the Department of the Interior to serve as a liaison between Native Hawaiians and the United States; it forms an interagency coordinating group composed of officials from federal agencies who currently administer programs and services impacting Native Hawaiians; and it authorizes a process for the reorganization of the Native Hawaiian governing entity for the purposes of a federally recognized government-to-government relationship.

Once the Native Hawaiian governing entity is recognized, the bill establishes an inclusive, democratic negotiations process representing both Native Hawaiians and non-Native Hawaiians. Negotiations between the Native Hawaiian entity and the federal and state governments may address issues such as the transfer of lands, assets, and natural resources and jurisdiction over such lands, assets, and natural resources, as well as other longstanding issues resulting from the overthrow of the Kingdom of Hawai'i. Any transfers of governmental authority or power will require implementing legislation at the state and federal levels.

The Hawaiian Language

Languages are tremendous, fluid databanks that carry unique cultural knowledge from one generation to the next. Because Hawaiian was originally an oral language, written materials exemplifying authentic usage and meanings date back only to the early 1820s, when missionaries undertook an orthography. Use of the Hawaiian language has been in decline since the late 1800s—and in 1896 it was officially banned as the language of instruction in public schools. A 1983 survey estimated that out of more than 1 million Hawai'i residents, only 1,500 people still spoke Hawaiian at home; most of them were elderly, and many of its native speakers lived on the isolated island of Ni'ihau.

Recent estimates, however, suggest that at least 8,000 people now speak Hawaiian (as a second language) due to burgeoning educational efforts across the state and renewed interest. Since 1987, nearly 30 charter schools have emerged that not only teach Hawaiian, but also conduct all instruction in Hawaiian until students reach the 5th grade. At the University of Hawai'i's Mānoa and Hilo campuses, students can now major in or pursue graduate degrees in Hawaiian studies and the Hawaiian language, and programs are packed with participants from Hawai'i, the Mainland, and abroad. The state of Hawai'i now also recognizes both Hawaiian and English as its official languages.

Traditional Arts and Crafts

"Pre-contact" Hawaiians possessed advanced skills in many arts and crafts, including house building, outrigger canoe building, mat and basket weaving, rope making, wooden bowl carving, net making, cloth making, feather work, jewelry making, and much more. The volcanic Hawaiian Islands contained no metals, so the people used stone, human and animal bone, teeth, wood, hair, shells, and other materials to create everything they had.

One of the arts in which Hawaiians excelled over other Pacific cultures was that of creating bark cloth, called *kapa* (also *tapa*). The task of creating *kapa* fell to women, who stripped and soaked the bark from selected trees, then beat it with progressively grooved and patterned wooden implements of infinite designs. Some *kapa* were worked until they were as light and pure as lace; many were grooved as if they'd been ironed into patterns, and most were dyed or block printed in reds, browns, blacks, and various other shades and color combinations. The making of *kapa* required a great deal of time and effort, and the end products were treasured goods that served as shoulder cloaks, wrap skirts for women, and loincloths for men, as well as bedding covers.

Another craft that is astonishingly impressive, even in modern times, is that of Hawaiian feather work—especially capes, cloaks, and helmets created for the *ali'i*. We strongly recommend that you visit Bishop Museum to see original examples of these items on display. Capes and cloaks, called *'ahu'ula*—or "red garment," a symbolic color for gods and high chiefs throughout Polynesia—were made of red feathers from both the native 'i'iwi and 'apapane birds. Rare yellow feathers from the 'o'o and both yellow and black feathers from the mamo provided contrasting colors. A yellow cloak once belonging to King Kamehameha I, now in the possession of the museum, is estimated to contain no less than 450,000 feathers tied in tiny bunches to a fine mesh framework. These priceless artifacts were considered extremely valuable in traditional times as well.

Relatively few individuals today have the knowledge and skill to perpetuate traditional Hawaiian crafts, and many have modified practices in accordance with modern tastes and available resources; in some cases, arts and crafts that typify postcolonial Hawai'i, such as Hawaiian quilt work—itself a beautiful and prized skill—replace older ways. However, a growing number are relearning these arts, from canoe-building to bone carving.

Learning to paddle a traditional Hawaiian outrigger canoe is part of growing up in Hawai'i.

HULA AND MELE

Hula is probably Hawai'i's most recognizable and celebrated cultural treasure, although it has long been misunderstood and caricatured by the West. Originally connected with religious temple ceremonies, dances performed by men and women honored the gods as well as the *ali'i*, and were accompanied by offerings and prayers to the goddess of hula, Laka. During much of the 19th century, missionary disapproval of hula kept the practice underground, until King Kalākaua encouraged its revival toward the end of the century. At that time, modern styles of hula were born that incorporated tī-leaf and grass skirts, melodious music, and a lighter attitude that appealed to visitors and suited festivities.

Hula in old Hawai'i was accompanied by chanting, or *mele*—a word that in modern times has come to mean chanting and singing both, as well as song. In the past, melody and meter served only to assist chanters in recalling lengthy chants that recounted genealogies, battles, tales of love, and other histories and beliefs, which hula helped to convey in bodily form. Melodic hymnals introduced by Western missionaries profoundly shaped the future of Hawaiian music.

The Hawaiian Renaissance in the 1970s initiated a tremendous surge in interest in both traditional and modern styles of hula, as well as modern Hawaiian music—a broad category that includes everything from slack-key guitar to *hapa-haole* vintage songs to falsetto singing. Countless thousands of Hawaiian girls, boys, men, and women of every race now study hula; in Japan as well as on the Mainland, hula troupes number in the hundreds. And in 2005, Hawaiian music gained its own category at the Grammys®.

Archaeological and Sacred Sites

Hawai'i's archaeological and sacred sites include the remains of *heiau*, or places of worship, as well as fishponds, sacred stones, agricultural terraces, home foundations, petroglyphs, artifacts, gravesites, walls, and more. When visiting them, please refrain from touching anything or turning archaeological sites into picnic areas. You'd be surprised how many children are found scrambling over temple rocks or adults posing on delicate walls for photos. In addition to showing respect for cultural traditions and historic preservation, you'll also save yourself fines up to $25,000 that come with disturbing Hawaiian relics on state land.

At one time, hundreds of *heiau* dotted Hawai'i's landscape—even Waikīkī had several *luakini heiau,* at which human sacrifices took place. Once Western influence gained hold, nearly all of O'ahu's *heiau* were dismantled. The few sites that remain feature stone foundations that would have supported grass structures, such as drum houses and oracle towers, guarded by enormous *akua ki'i* (tiki gods). Although some platforms may appear to visitors as nothing more than piles of lichen-covered rocks, try to imagine what they once were and respect the power they still hold for many residents. The practices of placing tī-leaf-wrapped stones, candy, lei, and other items as offerings, or stacking stones, are neither traditional nor encouraged, as they alter the integrity of the *heiau.*

Coastal and inland fishponds (*loko 'ia*) were one of the ways in which Hawaiians supported a large population, and O'ahu had more than any other island. Several ancient fishponds are still operational, and nearly five hundred across the state are undergoing repair. Hawaiians built ponds by enclosing waterways with impossibly thick coral and rock walls, sometimes running thousands of feet long, with gates that could let fish in to feed and prevented them from escaping once they'd grown fat.

The sites listed below are some of the most well-known, easily accessible, and interesting on O'ahu.

Waikīkī

Wizard or Healing Stones (Located between Kūhiō Beach's Duke Kahanamoku statue and police station) These enormous beachfront boulders dragged from the hills are said to be the stones to which several wizards from Tahiti transferred their sacred *mana*, or spiritual power, before returning home. Although they are probably not standing in their exact original locations today, at the time they were consecrated—probably at least six hundred years ago—idols and the sacrificed body of a young chieftess were placed beneath one of them.

Greater Honolulu

Nu'uanu Pali Lookout (Located at Nu'uanu Pali State Wayside Park off I 61) Not an archaeological remain per se, the Nu'uanu Pali ("cliffs of Nu'uanu") is a historic and culturally significant site for more than its mind-blowing view of Windward O'ahu. At this approximate location in 1795, Kamehameha I backed hundreds—possibly thousands—of

Hawaiians off its 1,000-foot cliffs in the decisive battle for control of O'ahu's kingdom. During the construction of the Old Pali Road in 1897 (you'll see remnants of it to the right of the lookout), workers along the base of the cliffs found an estimated eight hundred skulls and other bones.

From Pali Highway (HI 61) headed toward Kailua, take the Nu'uanu Pali Lookout exit, just before the tunnels. From Kailua, the exit is just after the tunnels. The lookout is open daily from 4 AM until 8 PM. Prepare for possible high winds, mist, or rain.

WINDWARD O'AHU

Ulupō Heiau (Located behind the Windward YMCA, 1200 Kailua Rd., Kailua) Just outside of central Kailua is a stone *heiau* platform 140 feet by 180 feet in breadth and 30 feet in height. Built perhaps as early as 900 AD, Ulupō looks out over the former 450-acre Kawainui fishpond. Just past Castle Hospital headed toward Kailua on Kailua Road, turn left onto Ulu'oa Street and right onto Manu-Aloha Street.

He'eia Fishpond (Adjacent to He'eia State Park, 46-465 Kamehameha Hwy., Kāne'ohe) This 600-year-old pond was nearly destroyed in the 1980s to make way for a marina, and the bluff, once called "the point of shimmering light,"—where the ancient *heiau* Kalae'ula'ula had stood—was to be converted into a condo. The bluff is now a lovely park that looks south onto the enormous fishpond, which was in use until the mid-1960s, when a flood severely damaged it. Now under the jurisdiction of Kamehameha Schools, the pond is under restoration and has supported several crops of fish and seaweed.

Hawaiian fishponds still exist on O'ahu, although many are hidden from view or are unrecognizable.

NORTH SHORE

Pu'u O Mahuka Heiau (Off Pūpūkea Rd., Pūpūkea) Many find this hilltop *heiau* to be the most striking archaeological site on O'ahu, especially with its spectacular oceanview setting. Reportedly constructed by Menehune and measuring an enormous 575 feet by 170 feet, it's the largest on the island and a National Historic Landmark. History suggests that several European sailors, probably from Captain Vancouver's ship, the *Daedalus*, were sacrificed here in 1794. To get there, follow Pūpūkea Road (next to Foodland, near Waimea Bay) around the hairpin curve, take the first road off to the right, and drive until you reach the *heiau*.

Hale O Lono Heiau (At the entrance to Waimea Valley Audubon Park, 59-864 Kamehameha Hwy., across from Waimea Bay) Although the Audubon Park will be closing in early 2008, we've been told that the valley and this *heiau* will still be accessible for viewing. Pull into the park entrance and drive to the innermost parking lot area. Just behind the lot stands the excavated and restored *heiau*, complete with replica grass houses and a wooden image of the god Lono, as it would likely have appeared hundreds of years ago.

LEEWARD O'AHU

Kāne'ākī Heiau (695-8174; Ala Hele St., in Mauna Olu Estates, Mākaha) The most visited archaeological site on the Leeward Coast, this *heiau* has been restored to closely resemble its original layout, including a drum house, house of spiritual power, an offering stand, an oracle tower, and an image of the god Kū. The temple is estimated to be at least five hundred years old and was used for both agricultural and sacrificial purposes. It sits on private land and is open to the public on selected days and hours only, weather permitting, so call the above number before you trek out there. From Farrington Highway, take Mākaha Valley Road and follow it until you see a right turn for the Estates and *heiau*.

A young wild boar roots around the ruins of Pu'u O Mahuka Heiau above Waimea Bay.

When waves get this big on the North Shore, few people show up at work.

7

Recreation

Everything under the Sun

Most visitors to Hawai'i plan to spend quality time on its beautiful beaches. O'ahu has some of the best in the entire state, so we've devoted a hefty chunk of this chapter to beach sites and smarts. To round out your experience, be sure to take a hike or garden walk; you'll be amazed by the diversity of flora and fauna the island has to offer. There are endless other great activities for the adventurous or mild-mannered individual, ranging from kayaking to spa treatments to video arcades—probably enough to fill a lifetime of visits to O'ahu.

You don't have to go far for a bit of beach paradise.

The impact of burgeoning recreation industries on local fishing and coastal communities has become clearer over time. We've done our best to include as many high-quality, conscientious, local companies as possible, and we encourage you to let operators know you support authentic and respectful practices.

BEACHES

Whether you wish to drift upon shallow swells while clutching a cocktail, be wrenched into the sand by heart-pounding surf, walk along an abandoned coastline, or craft the perfect tan, your beach is calling. Slather on sunscreen with the highest SPF you can find, and be sure to reapply after swimming—a tropical latitude gives frighteningly cruel sunburns, even through a pack of clouds.

During the summer, south and east shore beaches kick up the best surf; in winter (approximately October through April), don't even think about going in the water on the North Shore or Leeward Coast when waves or red flags are up, unless you want to be dragged out of it barely breathing. Weekends are the worst times to go to the beach. For easy parking and quieter atmospheres, go weekdays instead and leave your weekends for museums and shopping.

These unsuspecting tourists looking for the ultimate photo are one rogue wave away from serious harm.

Each year about 60 people—many of them tourists—drown in Hawai'i, and many hundreds more are rescued. Even world-famous Waikīkī beaches can catch a good swimmer off guard, and rough beaches will sweep away and crush the best of them. Strong currents, undertows, and powerful waves, not to mention sharp corals and poisonous sea creatures, are just a few reasons for you to respect the unpredictable world of the Pacific Ocean.

For a safe Hawaiian beach experience, follow these simple rules: stay very far away from the shorebreak whenever surf is high; swim with a friend; stick to shallow areas with lifeguards on duty; avoid stepping on coral; stay out of the ocean when red warning flags are up; and observe what sensible-looking residents are doing in and around the water.

Every single beach in the state of Hawai'i is open to the public, even if they front private land. However, crossing private land to get to them is illegal. Be sure to use public access routes. Topless and nude sunbathing are infrequently seen on O'ahu's beaches, except in remote or well-hidden pockets; for whatever reason, Hawai'i residents never embraced the custom and in fact frown upon it overall—although that, and the occasional fine, hasn't stopped many visitors, especially on the neighbor islands. Discretion and a bit of caution are advised for those who go bare.

Hawai'i's sea turtles are federally protected animals, and it's against the law to crowd, touch, or feed them. Although you may witness some beachgoers approaching turtles in the water or on beaches, these sensitive creatures usually prefer their personal space. Should you be so lucky as to spot an endangered Hawaiian monk seal on the beach, keep your distance and report its location immediately to the **National Marine Fisheries Service** (1-888-256-9840) for the animal's safety. Although perhaps tempting, swimming out to dolphin pods can be dangerous and is not advised.

To prevent break-ins, especially in secluded areas, be sure to remove all valuables and other belongings from your vehicle.

Heyday Waikīkī beach boys, including Duke Kahanamoku's brother, at right, were the hottest kids on the block.
Photo courtesy Hawai'i State Archives.

Below are some of the best beaches on the island, organized alphabetically by region. Selected beaches have specific road addresses and telephone numbers; others do not. For further information on city-operated beach parks, contact the **Department of Parks and Recreation** (692-5585).

Waikīkī's beautiful Kūhiō Beach is perfect for young children and beginner swimmers.

WAIKĪKĪ

Waikīkī Beach may be crowded, but that's because it's a fantastic place to swim, surf, tan, and be seen. Actually, Waikīkī Beach is a string of individual beaches running the length of the district, each with its own type of sand, surf break, and personality. Most are named for a notable home, hotel, landmark, or regarded individual associated with the area.

Many of the beaches have "activity" booths from which you can rent bodyboards or sign up for surf lessons, catamaran trips, or outrigger canoe rides. During the first half of the 20th century, Waikīkī was famous for its "beach boys," a collection of young, somewhat glamorous fixtures on the beach who taught surfing, socialized, and wooed the ladies. Although the beach boy culture isn't what it once was, today's charismatic beach guys and gals know the ropes and are happy to set you up with some fun.

Box jellyfish occasionally wash in to beach areas in Waikīkī about 10 days after a full moon; if lifeguard-posted signs indicate they're present, stay out of the water.

Where you park your towel in Waikīkī says a lot about you. The wide-sand area of **Kahanamoku Beach** exudes a Hilton-provided beach umbrella atmosphere and is a bit rubbly and dry. Its water is mostly flat, shallow, swimmable, and pretty. On Sunday morning, a church service takes place on the sand.

Separated from Kahanamoku Beach by a low wall leading to a pier, **Fort DeRussy Beach** has a bit more spunk, although the beach and water conditions are similar. Resident volleyball games seem to run continuously, and the nearby military hotel Hale Koa creates a relatively heavy concentration of service personnel. A walkway that runs along both beaches is an easy way to people-watch, day or evening.

A slender strip of sand fronting the grand Moana and the Royal Hawaiian Hotel is called **Royal Hawaiian Beach** by some, and is covered with fashion conscious bodies lined up towel to towel. The water here can have a bit more of a kick, with small-wave action that encourages hundreds of first-time surfers.

Kūhiō Beach stretches all the way to the Kapahulu Groin, a cement walkway extending like a pier into the water with a shaded hut on the tip. Low seawalls run parallel to the beach and create placid, shallow bathing segments. Narrow Kūhiō Beach is a free-for-all, where you'll see local families, fresh-off-the-boat tourists, style slaves, and plenty of neighborhood kids bodyboarding and hanging out.

Queen's Surf Beach is named for a famous nearby surf site and the popular nightclub/restaurant that once stood nearby. Within this area's domain you'll find a 30-foot-high movie screen for Sunset on the Beach events, a busy food concession, trinket stands on weekends, a cement walkway leading over the Waikīkī Marine Life Conservation District (you might have a few good fish sightings from here), and a heavy population of gay men in Speedos®, as well as Samoan and Tongan family picnics.

Just beyond the Waikīkī Aquarium and the War Memorial Natatorium, a dilapidated saltwater swimming facility built to honor World War I's fallen men, you'll find **Kaimana's**. With a long channel through the reef perfect for distance swimming, and an ocean temperament at once relaxed but not wimpy, as well as close proximity to two exclusive private membership clubs, this little beach attracts a relatively stylish and athletic resident crowd.

GREATER HONOLULU

Honolulu is where most of the action is, so it's no surprise that its beaches are pumping. It also has some of the safest swimming on the island—even a few quiet nooks if you know where to go. Here are the best beaches Honolulu has to offer outside of Waikīkī.

Ala Moana Regional Park (1201 Ala Moana Blvd., Kaka'ako) This gargantuan beach park is a second home to many residents and is growing in popularity with visitors. The long, sandy beach features shallow waters sheltered by low reef, perfect for small children and lap swimmers; head to its eastern or western corners to avoid stepping on rubbly sand. Magic Island, the peninsula on the eastern edge of the park, offers a nice view of Waikīkī in the distance and is a great surfing and sailing observation point.

Nature preserve Hanauma Bay is actually the crescent of a volcanic crater.

The beach park lies just west of Waikīkī, beyond the Ala Wai Canal and across from Ala Moana Center.

Hanauma Bay Nature Preserve (396-4229; 100 Hanauma Bay Rd., Hawai'i Kai) One of O'ahu's most incredible ocean experiences is Hanauma Bay—actually a seawater inundated volcanic crater. This old fishing ground is now a protected marine life conservation district, meaning that feeding or otherwise disturbing its four-hundred-plus species of marine life is strictly prohibited, as is walking on its delicate coral reefs. Hanauma is also the first public beach in the nation to ban smoking.

Don't let these rules, the nominal nonresident fee, lines of people, or mandatory viewing of a brief educational video discourage you from visiting—they're for the protection and management of an astounding natural site that has been far overtaxed in every way for many years. In the 1980s, as many as ten thousand people tromped through its waters each day; the park has now shaved it down to about three thousand per day. Remember, this is a nature preserve, not a beer-and-volleyball picnic destination—please treat it with the utmost care and respect.

Hanauma's turquoise waters are shallow and very safe inside the reef and rougher outside it, where the very occasional ray or shark might also roam. In the visitor center you'll find tons of information on the creatures of the bay and a history of the crater itself. Even if you choose not to descend to the beach, the view from above is a very worthwhile stop and requires only a $1 parking charge. At times, schools of fish can even be seen from the cliffs.

Do not sign up with a company touting trips to Hanauma Bay. Instead, take TheBus or drive yourself and rent a snorkel, mask, fins, and even a locker down on the beach. Get up early and go—the crater fills with soft morning light, plus the parking lot jams up and closes quickly, and the beach can become very hot by noon. If the steep road down to the beach is daunting, a wheelchair-accessible tram can shuttle you back and forth for a small fee. The park is open from 6 AM to about sunset and closes on Tuesdays for a rest. On Thursday evenings the theater above the beach is open for educational films and lectures.

To get to Hanauma Bay from Waikīkī, travel east on Kalaniana'ole Highway past the community of Hawai'i Kai; at the crest of the hill, you'll see the entrance on the right.

Kahala Beach (Kahala Ave., Kahala) We suggest you enter this beach through **Wai'alae Beach Park**. Although the beach fronting the park is rubbly and the water brackish, head in either direction and you'll find a bit of paradise. To the east, a pretty little beach fronting the exclusive Kahala Hotel & Resort is good for very shallow swimming and light snorkeling, although chaises are reserved for guests. To the west lie multi-million-dollar mansions and pockets in the reef perfect for dips. During high tide, sections of the beach virtually disappear. Strong winds can be a problem. Note: Neighborhood residents covet this enclave away from Waikīkī and value its peace and privacy. Please keep your beach visit low key.

Hidden right-of-ways exist along Kahala Avenue, but the easiest plan is to park at **Wai'alae Beach Park** (go early to find a spot). From Waikīkī, head west over Diamond Head Road—it changes names to Kahala Avenue past the crater. The park will be on your right-hand side just past the only stop sign and before the golf course.

Sandy Beach Park (8899 Kalaniana'ole Hwy., Hawai'i Kai) Inaccessible until 1931 when a coastal road was built, this local favorite is what Californian dudes in the 1980s would have called "totally gnarly." Sandy's is one of the best bodyboarding sites in the state—and the second most dangerous. The crushing waves at this beach are powerful, and have been known to break necks and backs. Needless to say, stay out of the water and simply enjoy the heavy atmosphere of salt spray, competition bikinis, and partying.

From Waikīkī, take Kalaniana'ole Highway east past the community of Hawai'i Kai. Follow the coastal road until it descends to the beachfront.

Windward O'ahu

This beautiful stretch of coastline is a quintessential tropical paradise and most of its beaches are generally safe for swimming. The weather tends to be stormier, however, even when it's sunny in town, and extensive reef systems can make finding a sandy swimming patch more challenging. Also, watch out for the Portuguese man-o-war—a passive, stinging creature with a tiny, cobalt-blue bubble followed by a blue tentacle several feet long. They sometimes float in the water or wash onshore fully alive. As with bee stings, most people unlucky enough to have bumped into or stepped on one grin and bear the irritation until it passes; rinsing the welt with salt water may help, as well as applying meat tenderizer or soothing heat or cold. There's the small chance of bumping into a clump of stinging *limu*, or seaweed—also painful, but usually bearable.

Hukilau Beach Park (Kamehameha Hwy., Lā'ie) Often virtually empty on weekdays and Sundays, this golden-sand beach is an inspiring setting for a thoughtful walk and, on most days, safe for a dip. There are no lifeguards on duty, so study the water's mood and layout before jumping in. There are no toilet facilities. Located in a predominantly Mormon town, community members gathered here for decades to join in traditional fishing net hauls, or hukilau. If you've ever heard the popular "The Hukilau Song," this is where the ditty was born.

To get there, take the H-1 westbound to Like Like Highway (HI 63) and follow signs to Lā'ie. Travel north until you're nearly a mile past the Polynesian Cultural Center. The narrow beach access is across the street from the elementary school. Park on a side street.

Kailua Beach Park (233-7300; 526 Kawailoa Rd., Kailua) Kailua Beach is "a little bit country and a little bit rock and roll," and is the star performer of the relatively affluent and bustling beach community of Kailua. With numerous highbrow "best beach" recognition awards under its belt over the last 10-plus years, the beach quickly drew fans from around

Pack a picnic for the soft sands of Kailua Beach.

the world, stirring into existence countless unofficial lodgings within close proximity to its shore. But, unlike fragile Lanikai Beach, Kailua Beach offers more than 2 miles of sand and a lively atmosphere that meets the need for some "R and R", while also satiating the desire for a little spice.

In addition to brilliant water, good swimming, and playful shorebreaks, it's the center of O'ahu's famed windsurfing culture. Kailua Beach is also a takeoff point for kayaking journeys to the Mokulua Islands. The offshore seabird sanctuary Popoi'a Island (also known as Flat Island) was once graced with a fishing shrine, which was washed away in the tsunami of 1946. This beach can be moderately crowded with residents and visitors, but it's still a gem.

To get there from Waikīkī, take the H-1 westbound to Pali Highway (HI 61), following it over the mountains and on to Kailua. Stick to the same road straight through town until it ends at a T-intersection with S. Kalāheo. Turn right and travel about a mile until you reach the park.

Kualoa Regional Park (237-8525; 49-479 Kamehameha Hwy., Ka'a'awa) Coral-strewn bits of beach, a reef-bound shoreline, and frequent strong winds make this beach best for dipping only your toes—but the setting is hard to beat. On the National Register of Historic Places, this is a historically significant Hawaiian heritage site that still earns reverence from many residents. The view toward the mountains of Kāne'ohe is breathtaking, as are the sacred ridges behind the park and the triangular Mokoli'i Island (also known as Chinaman's Hat) offshore. We do not recommend wading out to Mokoli'i Island.

The park has a strong tradition of hosting traditional cultural activities and local family camping—beachgoers take note that the deeper you go into the park, the more you'll need to wear your "very low-key, respectful visitor" hat. From the farthest point in, you can wade in calm seas all the way to the so-called "Secret Island," which is actually a small beach bordering the ancient Hawaiian fishpond of Mokoli'i, a protected archaeological site. If Kualoa Ranch's tour boat hasn't pulled ashore yet, you may just have a spirit-lifting experience.

From Waikīkī, take the H-1 westbound to Like Like Highway (HI 63) and follow signs to Kahalu'u/Lā'ie. As the road becomes coastal, you'll see Mokoli'i Island in the distance. The park is adjacent to the island, and the entrance is at a sharp curve near a cow pasture.

Lanikai Beach (Mokulua Dr., Lanikai) Lanikai Beach has earned top accolades from *Condé Nast* magazine, "Dr. Beach," and the Travel Channel for good reason. Powder-soft sands ease into gentle turquoise bathwater, where a turtle lolls above the reef. Coconut trees arch carelessly in the breeze, and from one of the many multi-million-dollar homes behind you, a parrot squawks. Offshore, two peaked islets stand guard.

Sadly, Lanikai is no longer what it was, even a few years ago. This formerly hidden gem has lost some of its glory in the gold rush and, a much more permanent fate, is actually eroding away in many spots as it fights against seawalls constructed by homeowners. Note that there are no public facilities.

To get there from Waikīkī, take the H-1 westbound to Pali Highway (HI 61), following it over the mountains and on to Kailua. Stick to the same road straight through town until it ends at a T-intersection with S. Kalāheo. Turn right and travel about a mile until you pass Kailua Beach Park. Turn left at the intersection and follow the coastal road around the bend. The road becomes one way and loops back around. Park near any public right-of-way along the loopback and pray for sand.

Makapu'u Beach Park (41-095 Kalaniana'ole Hwy., Waimānalo) This gorgeous beach has more rescues per year than any other on O'ahu and is a poor choice for families with children. Deceptively mellow, it lacks a protective reef to lessen the strength of waves and the backwash quickly drags waders into its depths. Red warning flags seem to always be up at Makapu'u—and lifeguards will quickly get on their bullhorns to remind you of that so they don't have to save you five minutes later. Enjoy the waves from far up on the beach only, and don't miss the stunning views from the road above.

From Waikīkī, take Kalaniana'ole Highway past the Hawai'i Kai Golf Course. The beach will be on your right after you round the bend ahead.

The sandy strip at Makapu'u Beach can at times be completely awash in waves.

Mālaekahana State Recreation Area (293-1736; 56-335 Kamehameha Hwy., Kahuku) An enormous region with a mile-long windswept beach, campgrounds, fancy vacation homes, an ironwood forest, and offshore seabird sanctuary, Mālaekahana reminds you that you've left town far behind. There are two entrances—one in the town of Lā'ie, the other in Kahuku.

True for all windward beaches except fun-loving Kailua and chic Lanikai, the atmosphere is mellow and very real, rather than "bikini contest" or "jet ski." This beach is great for families and is perfect for daylong picnics. Although daylight-hour visits are permitted on Mokū'auia (Goat Island), getting there without damaging coral heads or struggling with the tides can be tricky (only cross in very low tide). The coastline can sometimes experience strong, longshore currents that have swept people en route to the island away into deeper waters. As always, and especially since the beach has no lifeguards, use caution and common sense. If you visit Mokū'auia, stay on marked paths and leave all birds and nests as you found them.

Traditionally Mālaekahana was a sanctuary of supernatural power for the Hawaiian people, serving as a *pu'uhonua* (place of refuge) where commoners were allowed to escape punishment for broken laws or find shelter in dangerous times. The area would have featured a temple and perhaps simple residences.

From Waikīkī, take the H-1 westbound to Like Like Highway (HI 63) and follow signs to Kahalu'u/Lā'ie. Once you've traveled through Lā'ie, look for Mālaekahana signage. Pass the first entrance and look for a white sign marking the second entrance, near telephone pole 35. If you reach the town of Kahuku, you've missed it.

Waimānalo Bay State Recreation Area (41-1055 Kalaniana'ole Hwy., Waimānalo) A drowsy landscape with an endless powdery white sand beach, whispering ironwood trees, and rumbling waves greets you at Waimānalo Beach. A favorite of windward families and rookie bodyboarders, expect a mellow, very local-style day at the beach rather than racy action. Although it can become relatively busy on weekends, weekday mornings often see only a handful of beachcombers. Located in a tight-knit, Hawaiian-oriented community, this is a true Island beach.

From Waikīkī, follow Kalaniana'ole Highway past the Hawai'i Kai Golf Course to the windward town of Waimānalo and watch for park signage across from the polo field.

On weekdays, Waimānalo Beach can be a peaceful retreat from the scene.

North Shore

Second in fame only to Waikīkī Beach, the North Shore and its string of famous surf spots have become part of cultural lore. On some winter days you won't want to swim here, unless you enjoy bone-crushing waves some two stories high crashing down onto your head, or being the center of search-and-rescue parties. In summer, beaches such as at Waimea Bay reduce to kitten-soft swells and are generally safe. Many of the North Shore's lifeguards earn near godlike status among residents for their bravery and knowledge of the ocean.

When the waves are hot (and sometimes even when they're not), traffic can back up along the coast's only thoroughfare literally for miles, and beachside parking is a nightmare. If you have a specific beach destination in mind and the paper says it's a really big surf day, consider taking TheBus instead of driving. See Chapter 2 for driving directions to the North Shore.

'Ehukai Beach (59-360 Kamehameha Hwy., Sunset Beach) Home of the legendary and hazardous "Banzai Pipeline" surf site, all roads seem to converge at 'Ehukai's shoreline when the waves are prime. The Japanese word *banzai* means "ten thousand years"—but its reputation as the World War II war cry "to the death," especially in suicide missions, is how the word is used around here. Needless to say, skip swimming and just savor the exciting experience of this renowned beach area.

Signs no longer mark the park. Look for a small parking lot filled with cars several miles past Turtle Bay Resort if you're driving west, or several miles past Foodland if you're driving east. Sunset Beach Elementary School is across the street.

Laniākea Beach Park (Kamehameha Hwy., Hale'iwa) While not the best spot for swimming due to a rocky reef shelf, Laniākea has become a popular beach for turtle watching. These mellow creatures are federally protected and must be left undisturbed, so please enjoy them from a reasonable distance. About a mile before Hale'iwa heading west, look for cars parked on both sides of Kamehameha Highway and a sandy strip near Pōhaku Loa Way. A horse pasture is across the street. Residents are at their wits' end over the traffic backup at this spot, so try to keep the flow.

Pūpūkea Beach Park (638-7213; 59-727 Kamehameha Hwy., Pūpūkea) Less of a beach than a long, rocky strand with sandy pockets called Sharks Cove and Three Tables, Pūpūkea is a visually exciting spot full of tasty (and crowded) summer snorkeling nooks within a marine life conservation district. In winter, its little pools can still be safe for swimming—but if waves are crashing on the rocks around you, it would be wise to steer clear. The park sits across from Foodland.

Mokulēi'a Beach Park (68-901 Farrington Hwy., Mokulēi'a) Beyond the strip of the North Shore's star beaches you'll find Mokulēi'a, an unpretentiously well-off country community built around the polo grounds. Along the beach, a light potpourri of visitors, illegal campers, New Ageists, homeless beachcombers, and local families each find their niche in the sand. The area can get some strong gusts and hefty waves, but is a relaxing getaway from the bustle. On Farrington Highway (HI 930), pass Camp Mokulēi'a and look for the park entrance.

Sunset Beach Park (Kamehameha Hwy., Sunset Beach) One of the most famous beaches in the world, Sunset also hosts the hottest segment of the Triple Crown, surfing's créme de la créme mega-event, and it sees many a rescue. In any season, it's also a simply beautiful setting for admiring waves, watching the sunset, deepening your tan, and picknicking. Be forewarned that this is "hot stuff" country; although tour busses dump dozens of dazed visitors in sweater vests onto the sands every hour, most local folks are bronzed and in their skimpiest beach attire.

Sunset beach isn't marked; look for a strip of sand and cars parked on the beachside of the highway about a mile past Sunset Beach Elementary School, heading east. You'll also see a white lifeguard tower and a small parking lot and public restroom across from the beach.

Waimea Bay Beach Park (Kamehameha Hwy., near Pūpūkea) This is the granddaddy of the North Shore beaches in every way. The smooth, sweeping bay is backed by a lush valley and it features lustrous golden sand and deep-aquamarine waters with a gargantuan sea

Waimea Bay's winter swells are world class.

rock lurking amid the backwash. The bay is part of a marine life conservation district, and the valley contains several significant archaeological remnants, including two Hawaiian *heiau* (sacred religious sites). Many of the valley's residents left the area after a flood swept through in 1894.

In summer, Waimea is a sleeping giant where families gather, tourists paddle about with snorkels, and the athletic and daring hike up the Jump Rock to do just that into the groaning swells. But when the northern storms stir the ocean in the winter season, this world-class bay can occasionally turn into a yawning portal for mammoth waves up to 50 feet high. When it surges above 20 feet and stabilizes, the chance increases that the Eddie Aikau Big Wave Invitational will kick into action. The contest has been held only a handful of times since its inception in 1986, and was most recently won by Kaua'i surfing star Bruce Irons, who successfully rode waves exceeding 40 feet.

From Hale'iwa, continue about 4 miles until you see the enormous bay before you. From the windward side you'll see the bay ahead just after passing Foodland. The entrance is at the apex of the sharp curve.

LEEWARD O'AHU

Sweeping, wide valleys and a drier climate typifies the leeward side, also called the Leeward or Wai'anae Coast. You'll be amazed to find mostly empty stretches of beach that look more like California than Hawaii, and a desolate, almost mysterious, atmosphere.

A region with a history of high unemployment and little desire to attract tourists—or residents from elsewhere on the island, for that matter—means that "things are as they are," and you'll see a growing population of homeless families camped along the beaches. As you might imagine, candy-apple red convertibles can cut a burning swath through its ramshackle towns and may incite resentment in some. Visit with the utmost respect for the space and circumstances of the local folks. See Chapter 2 for general driving directions to the Leeward Coast.

Keawa'ula Beach (At the end of Farrington Hwy. in Ka'ena Point State Park) Near the end of the road heading north is a long, sandy beach called Keawa'ula, or Yokohama's. Remote and virtually unpopulated, and with a vista onto pristine sea, sweeping green valleys, and rocky shores, it's a beautiful spot. There are no lifeguards and swimming can be treacherous, so use extra caution. Solo female travelers should exercise caution on this isolated stretch. Skip the string bikini—this is a beach for contemplation, not fashion.

Kō 'Olina Lagoons (679-0079; Ali'inui St., Kapolei) On the shore of the 'Ewa Plain at the gateway to the leeward side of the island, you'll find Kō 'Olina Resort & Marina, a mega-resort that's still in the process of expanding. Part of the initial development plan included blasting four lagoons out of a prehistoric reef and importing tons of powdery, white sand; the result is four superb, albeit environmentally questionable and manmade, swimming beachlets open to the general public. This is hands-down the best place in the area, and perhaps the island, to bring very young children to swim—plus, you'll have easy access to restrooms and resort cafés. Arrive very early, especially on weekends, when one of the four tiny parking lots provided for the public might still have a space available. Snorkeling along the rock piles can be good and is very safe.

Take the Kō 'Olina exit from the H-1 freeway. At the security gate let them know you're headed to the lagoons, then follow the signage to the lagoon of your choice.

Mākaha Beach Park (84-369 Farrington Hwy., Mākaha) While not as well known in the general community, Mākaha Beach is famous in the international surfing community as the site of several major surfing competitions. In winter, rip tides and powerful waves make swimming generally hazardous. On summer weekends, the beach attracts many local residents and a smattering of visitors, evidenced by the appearance of a few bright beach umbrellas. It's also the landing point for trans-Pacific cables. Headed northbound, the white sand beach appears just before a lowrise hotel, shortly after Makaha Valley Road.

Pōka'ī Bay Beach Park (85-037 Wai'anae Valley Rd., Wai'anae) Got young *keiki*? On the leeward side, one of the best water spots for kids to play is at sheltered and shallow Pōka'ī Bay, which is lined with a sandy beach. The beach is popular with local families and exudes a great deal of rural community charm. Stick to its shallow water areas.

From Farrington Highway northbound, turn left onto Wai'anae Valley Road to reach the parking area.

Many of the leeward side's beaches have a desolate feel.

Bike and Moped Cruising

O'ahu's narrow, curving, fast-paced roads and lack of good bike lanes make it less-than-ideal for bike transportation; however, some fantastic opportunities exist for recreational biking. Waikīkī, Kailua, and the North Shore are good for beach cruising, and the North Shore has some good mountain trails; TheBus system features bike racks on the front of every bus, so you can haul your bike where you like.

Contact the **Hawai'i Bicycling League** (735-5756; www.hbl.org) if you need more information, bike route maps, or to find out about their weekend rides, or the **Honolulu**

City and County Bike Coordinator (768-8335; www.co.honolulu.hi.us/dts/bikepage.htm) for information on trails or state biking laws. For guided bicycle adventures in exotic settings around the island, call **Bike Hawai'i** (734-4214; 877-682-7433; www.bikehawaii.com), run by local boy John Alford, who is also authored several good books on mountain biking in the Islands.

Mopeds aren't the best way to get between two points on O'ahu, but they can be fun for short hauls or an afternoon ride. Doubling up on a moped under 50ccs is against the law; helmets are not required.

Waikīkī

Big Kahuna Motorcycle Tours & Rentals (924-2736; 1-888-451-5544; www.bigkahunarentals.com; 407 Seaside Ave.) Mopeds and bicycles are on the menu, in addition to big gun motorcycles.

Coconut Cruisers (924-1644; 1-800-536-4434; www.coconutcruisers.com; 305 Royal Hawaiian Ave.) These guys have reasonable prices on mopeds, trek mountain bikes, beach cruisers, and road bikes.

Windward O'ahu

The Bike Shop (261-1553; www.bikeshophawaii.com; 270 Ku'ulei Rd., Kailua) This well-respected shop rents mountain bikes by the day or the week, including helmets, locks, and repair kits. A car rack is available for an extra fee.

North Shore

Barnfield's Raging Isle Surf & Cycle (637-7707; www.ragingisle.com; North Shore Marketplace, 66-250 Kamehameha Hwy., Hale'iwa) Big wave surfer Bill Barnfield is also passionate about mountain biking. Check out his North Shore shop for bicycle rentals, information on rides, trails, and even personal bike tours.

Camping

Camping in Hawai'i is very popular among extended local families, some of whom, until restrictions in recent years, would spend virtually entire summers living under makeshift tarps at windward beach parks. Most camping on O'ahu is the polar opposite of a yuppie sleepover—island campers often wake early to go spear fishing for breakfast, pit bull companions run loose around the grounds, outsiders are viewed with wary eyes, and more than likely someone's smoking *pakalōlō* somewhere.

So although you can find numerous official campgrounds on the island, we've listed the only most beautiful, safe, and welcoming sites below. If you're up to the experience and willing to go through permit hoops, it could very well turn out to be the most wonderful aspect of your visit.

Note that county and state parks are open for camping from 8 AM on Friday until 8 AM on Wednesday only. Most campgrounds operate year-round.

If you have plans to camp at a state park other than the Kahuku section of Mālaekahana described below, you'll need to obtain a free permit and pay user fees; applications are accepted no more than 30 days before you camp. Contact the **Department of**

Land and Natural Resources/Division of State Parks (587-0300; www.hawaii.gov/dlnr/dsp/fees.htm) for more information.

Ho'omaluhia and Kualoa, recommended below, are county parks and have different regulations. Campers must apply for a free permit *in person* up to two Fridays prior to camping at the **Department of Parks and Recreation** (523-4525; www.honolulu.gov/parks/permits.htm; 650 S. King St., Honolulu) or at Satellite City Hall (there's one at Ala Moana Center, open Monday through Saturday).

WINDWARD O'AHU

Ho'omaluhia Botanical Garden (233-7323; 45-680 Luluku Rd., Kāne'ohe) Pressed against sheer mountain cliffs a mile from the shoreline, you'll awaken to forest birds in this peaceful and gorgeous inland county park. Bring everything you need, including mosquito repellent, as you won't be able to leave the park at night to forage for food. Camping is permitted from 9 AM Friday until 4 PM Monday only. Read more about Ho'omaluhia in the "Parks and Gardens" section of this chapter.

Kualoa Regional Park, Campsite "B" (49-479 Kamehameha Hwy., Ka'a'awa) A more inspiring setting than this county park would be hard to find. These once-sacred grounds are bordered by a peaceful bay and backed by dramatic mountains, and an offshore islet completes the idyllic picture. Tent camping is permitted from 8 AM on Friday until 8 AM on Wednesday only. Read more about Kualoa in the "Beaches" section of this chapter.

Mālaekahana State Recreation Area (293-1736; www.malaekahana.net; P.O. Box 305, Lā'ie, HI 96762) The best tent camping is in the Kahuku section of this enormous, beautiful, and safe beachfront park that was once a sacred refuge for Hawaiians. Although it is a state park, campground management is currently under the nonprofit Friends of Mālaekahana, and normal restrictions don't apply. You can apply up to one year in advance for one of its 43 tent sites, and camping is allowed for up to 7 days of every 30. Ancient thatched cabins and family huts are also available, but they're nearly impossible to get and may soon be torn down. Read more about Mālaekahana in the "Beaches" section of this chapter.

NORTH SHORE

Camp Mokulēi'a (637-6241; www.campmokuleia.org; 68-729 Farrington Hwy., Mokulēi'a) Privately operated by the Episcopal Church, this beachfront campground is safe and in high-demand. It offers cabins and other accommodations as well as tent camping. Reservations are required far in advance.

FISHING

The Kona Coast on the island of Hawai'i is renowned worldwide for its marlin fishing and big-name competitions. However, fishing on O'ahu is also great and there are plenty of deep trenches or coastal regions to explore. Note that the time of year will dictate which fish you're more likely to catch, and you might not be permitted to keep what you conquer.

You don't need a permit in Hawai'i for basic rod-and-reel ocean fishing or to spend the day fishing from a licensed vessel. You can also let the locals take you wade or boat fishing for smaller game fish.

ISLANDWIDE

Shoreline Adventures (428-4680; www.bonefish808.com) Oliver Owens offers customized, personal, non-touristy visitor experiences built around "catch and release" fly and light tackle fishing (under 30 pounds) and environmental and cultural awareness. He'll take you all over the island for the best bonefish catches.

GREATER HONOLULU

Inter-Island Sportfishing (1-877-806-3474; 591-8888; www.fish-hawaii.com) These folks have been operating in Hawai'i since 1950 and have several boats to choose from, as well as either private or shared charters. Trips leave from Kewalo Basin, between Waikīkī and downtown.

NORTH SHORE

Ku'uloa Kai Charters (637-5783; 66-195 Ka'amo'oloa Rd., Waialua) Get up early and explore the deep waters off the North Shore aboard this big game crew's 31-foot Bertram Sport Fisher.

GOLFING

Golfing isn't new to Hawai'i—it's been played here since the late 1890s. After statehood in 1959 the sport boomed, and there are now more than 80 courses throughout the state. In the 1980s, the Japanese in particular discovered Hawai'i's perfect golfing climate, and not only did they arrive in droves to play, but they opened their own courses and clubs.

Below are some of the best public courses O'ahu has to offer. Most are outside of Honolulu, since by the time they were built, town was all booked up. This means, however, you'll get to savor a bit of the country life while you play.

You can buy tickets to several big-name golf tournaments that take place on the island each year. The PGA's Sony Open is the most famous and has been around for 40 years; it's held at the prestigious (and private) Wai'alae Country Club every January. Several other big events take place at Turtle Bay Resort on the North Shore: the PGA's Turtle Bay Championship in January; the LPGA's SBS Open in February; and the PGA Classic in March.

From Michelle Wie to Vijay Singh, top pros still turn out for the annual Sony Open.

GREATER HONOLULU

Ala Wai Golf Course (733-7387; www.co.honolulu.hi.us/des/golf/alawai.htm; 404 Kapahulu Ave., Kapahulu) This city-run, 18-hole, par-72 golf course completed in 1931 is reputedly the busiest in the entire world, with more than 500 rounds per day. Consider yourself lucky to get a tee time. The course borders Waikīkī and is the oldest on the island—hence the crowds. Green fees are $42.

Hawai'i Kai Golf Course (395-2358; www.hawaiikaigolf.com; 8902 Kalaniana'ole Hwy., Honolulu) The popular Hawai'i Kai Golf Course features a par-72, 123-slope championship course designed by William Bell that opened in 1973, and a par-54 executive course with no slope designed by Robert Trent Jones Sr., which opened in 1962. The distant ocean views and lack of urban disruption make it a spectacular setting. Wear a hat—it's hot and dry. The driving range is popular with visitors and residents. Green fees range from $29 to $100, depending on which day you play and whether or not you need a cart.

WINDWARD O'AHU

Golf Club (247-7088; www.koolaugolfclub.com; 45-550 Ki'ona'ole Rd., Kāne'ohe) Designed by Dick Nugent and built in 1992, this 18-hole, par-72 course is considered one of the most challenging courses in the nation, with a slope from the tournament tees at 75/152. Wedged against sheer cliffs and surrounded by lush, tropical foliage, it's a visual delight as well. *Golf Digest* magazine voted it the "number one golf course on O'ahu." Green fees are $135 in the mornings and $85 after 12 PM. Be sure to ask for directions—it can be hard to find the road to the course.

Luana Hills Country Club (262-2139; www.luanahills.com; 770 Auloa Rd., Kailua) Located at a semi-private country club, this 18-hole, par-72 course opened in 1994 and was designed by golf architect Pete Dye. It sits in ridiculously beautiful surroundings and is a challenge to play. This is a target course, hemmed in by rainforest with a slope of 130 and total yardage of 5,522. Green fees are $125 until 1 PM; after 1 PM you can play as many holes as you can (up to 18) before 5:30 and pay only $85.

Olomana Golf Links (259-7926; www.olomanagolflinks.com; 41-1801 Kalaniana'ole Hwy., Waimānalo) Opened in 1967, this 18-hole, par 72, 126-slope golf course designed by Bob Baldock features two distinctly different nines and gorgeous views of the Mountains. Green fees start at $80, including a cart.

Pali Golf Course (266-7612; www.co.honolulu.hi.us/des/golf/pali.htm; 45-050 Kamehameha Hwy., Kāne'ohe) This is a beautiful, challenging, and busy 18-hole, par-72 municipal course nestled at the foothills of the Ko'olau Mountains, with a slope of 127. Green fees are $42.

NORTH SHORE

Kahuku Golf Course (293-5842; www.co.honolulu.hi.us/des/golf/kahuku.htm; 56-501 Kamehameha Hwy., Kahuku) Local favorite Kahuku Golf Course is a 9-hole, 35-par course and a great value for the money, despite its windiness. You'll get 2,699 yards of fun and easy walking, plus a view of the ocean. Green fees are only $10.

Turtle Bay Resort (293-8574; www.turtlebayresort.com; 57-091 Kamehameha Hwy., Kahuku) With two championship 18-hole courses—the Arnold Palmer and George Fazio—set against a coastal, 880-acre landscape, Turtle Bay offers excellent places to play golf. The popular Palmer course is the home of yearly PGA and LPGA tournaments and a challenging play, with a slope of 143 and par of 72. Green fees for the Palmer course are

$145 for guests of the resort and $185 for visitors; for the Fazio course, fees are $115 for guests and $160 for visitors.

CENTRAL O'AHU

Hawai'i Prince Golf Club (956-1111; www.princeresortshawaii.com; 91-1200 Fort Weaver Rd., 'Ewa) Designed by Arnold Palmer and Ed Seay and built in 1992, this 27-hole course occupies 270 acres, much of which is studded by lakes. The three nines offer a variety of other exciting challenges and are beautifully located. Green fees are $80 to $90 for guests of the Hawai'i Prince Hotel and $140 for visitors.

Kō 'Olina Golf Club (676-5300; www.koolinagolf.com; 92-1220 Ali'inui Dr., Kapolei) This challenging, 18-hole championship course has hosted the Senior PGA and was cited by *Golf Digest* as one of the United State's "top 75 resort courses." It also features an excellent golf shop. Designed by Ted Robinson, the course measures 6,867 yards with a slope of 135 and par of 72. Food and beverages can be ordered from the 9th and 18th holes. Green fees are $145 for guests, $170 for visitors.

Mākaha Resort Golf Club (695-7111; www.makaharesort.net; 84-626 Mākaha Valley Rd., Wai'anae) A William Bell-designed course that suits its beautiful valley setting, this 18-hole, par-71, 122-slope championship course offers 7,077 yards of play. It's been rated by readers of *Golfweek* as one of Hawai'i's top 10 courses, and Honolulu residents have named it O'ahu's best course. Look out for an occasional peacock on the fairways. Green fees are $60 to $70.

GUIDED ADVENTURE, NATURE, AND CULTURE TOURS

For those who feel that adventures can only be had through independent travel, this may not be for you. However, one of the plusses of a guided excursion is that you'll visit multiple destinations safely and easily all in one day, plus learn some history and enriching facts along the way. Some companies will even take you to spots you wouldn't otherwise find on your own. There are about a billion operators on O'ahu, but very few that keep it low key, environmentally and culturally conscientious, and real. Here are several of the very best. They aren't listed by region, since they pick you up wherever you're located and take you all over the entire island.

ISLANDWIDE

Annette's Adventures (235-5431; www.annettesadventures.com) Annette Kaohelauili'i has spent more than 20 years understanding, interpreting, and protecting Hawai'i's cultural and natural resources. She founded the Hawai'i Ecotourism Association and leads trips for the Sierra Club. Annette creates discriminating, custom ecotours for visitors and specializes in birding experiences.

Bike Hawai'i/'Ohana Adventure Tours (1-877-682-7433; 734-4214; www.bikehawaii.com) O'ahu boy John Alford has written several great books on mountain biking in Hawai'i and has earned a good reputation in the community for his conscientious approach to trail exploration. He and his team lead biking tours, as well as several other low-impact nature adventures, across the island. If you want to do biking off-road, you'll be in the hands of an expert. Bike Hawai'i is recognized by the Hawai'i Ecotourism Association.

Fire Truck Hawai'i (590-2100; www.firetruckhawaii.com) You won't be spending an entire day traveling to remote waterfalls with these guys, but it's such a cute and original activity we had to include it. They'll take you through Waikīkī, the Diamond Head area, or downtown Honolulu in an authentic, open-air, 1936 fire engine for a narrated tour. The best part is that your narrators are professional fire fighters, so you'll get a unique perspective on the city. Tours of other areas, such as lush Tantalus, are also in the works. During the holiday season, hop the truck downtown for a "Honolulu City Lights" tour.

Hina Adventures (1-888-933-4462; 499-9753; www.hinaadventures.com) Meet fourth-generation O'ahu resident and Brown University graduate Ena, who has hiked all over the world and worked as a historical tour guide in Italy; and Uluwehi, a Native Hawaiian who's worked with Kamehameha Schools and the Polynesian Voyaging Society, and is pursuing a master's degree in Hawaiian studies. Their unique cultural trips range from night sky gazing to visiting sacred sites to exploring Hawaiian plants and gardens, and are accompanied by rich cultural narratives.

Mauka Makai Excursions (1-866-896-0596; 255-2206; www.hawaiianecotours.net) Owned and operated by local O'ahu boy Kealoha Aki, Mauka Makai takes up to 10 people at a time to archaeological and natural attractions, where you'll learn historic, geological, and cultural information that brings them alive. They also offer unusual shoreline activities by request, such as evening torch fishing. Knowledgeable and dedicated to providing accurate historical and cultural information, Mauka Makai has won several awards for their contribution to preserving Hawai'i's culture.

O'ahu Nature Tours (924-2473; www.oahunaturetours.com) This company takes groups of up to 14 at a time in their vans for fairly standard bird watching trips, hikes, and scenic sightseeing islandwide. Many of their guides were born and raised on O'ahu and have degrees in biology and other natural sciences, although some are fresh off the boat and have sketchy cultural knowledge. They also participate in various projects that help restore natural habitats and are recognized by the Hawai'i Ecotourism Association.

Hang Gliding, Paragliding, and Ultralight Flying

For many people, hang gliding is the ultimate activity. There is only one safe place to hang glide on O'ahu: the 1,200-foot Makapu'u cliffs, which jut above the ruggedly beautiful windward coastline—a truly unforgettable view.

Paragliding, a lesser-known but equally exciting activity, essentially involves parachuting from a high-altitude location and then maneuvering the equipment so you scuttle along in the air. Ultralights are lightweight, small-engine powered flying machines, and you can choose how long you stay up in the air and exactly where you'll go.

Windward O'ahu

Gravity Hawai'i (220-6302; www.gravityhawaii.com) This outfit offers tandem paragliding with a United States Hang Gliding and Paragliding Association instructor and lessons toward your pilot license. Jumps take place at the Makapu'u cliffs in Waimānalo.

Kailua Blue (381-4296; www.kailuablue.com) Phil Godwin has been hang gliding for 30 years, 15 of those years as a professional. He'll take you with him off the Makapu'u cliffs for a half-hour of magic. He can also run you up in an ultralight aquaglider for an incredible view of gorgeous and mellow Kāne'ohe Bay.

NORTH SHORE

Paradise Air (497-6033; www.paradiseairhawaii.com) Denise and Tom Sanders have two awesome ultralight trikes that they run from Dillingham Airfield in Mokulēʻia. You'll learn how to operate them and go up tandem above the North Shore for as long as you and the weather conditions allow.

HELICOPTER, AIRPLANE, AND GLIDER RIDES

On the neighbor islands, helicopter tours of otherwise inaccessible volcano eruptions, coastlines, and valleys are a big business. On Oʻahu, a flight into the sky is a still great way to grasp the island's layout, topography, and tremendous beauty—and it can be a lot of fun.

If you've never flown by helicopter before, expect a surprisingly smooth ride. Most offer views of waterfalls, Pearl Harbor, coastlines, and other key sights islandwide. Unless otherwise indicated, they take off from the Honolulu Airport area—be sure to ask for directions to their operations.

Gliders (also known as sailplanes) are towed up and then uncoupled for an engine-free ride. Hawaiʻi is one of the world's best locations for gliding and soaring and views can extend for up to 40 miles. All glider planes on Oʻahu leave from Dillingham Airfield in Mokulēʻa on the North Shore.

Note that engine-propelled air tours can be controversial, especially on neighbor islands, where formerly silent, remote spots have become swarmed with aircraft like a pack of bees around a honeypot. While Oʻahu doesn't suffer as severely from this problem, be sure to let your pilot know you support keeping a polite distance from neighborhoods (especially in rural areas), quiet beaches, and mountain valleys and trails. When you are the one trying to have a spiritual experience on one of those mountain trails or beaches you'll be glad it's quiet!

Most operators offer tours of many different regions of the island. Those listed below as "North Shore" operators fly over that region only.

ISLANDWIDE

All Island Aviation (839-1499; 1-888-773-0303; www.allislandaviation.com; 96 Nākolo Pl., Airport) These folks don't exactly provide islandwide service—they provide an interisland experience from the air. Sign up to view the magnificent coastlines of three or six Hawaiian islands via their seven-seat plane—prices are reasonable for the amount of territory you'll cover. Trips last between two and four hours, and custom tours can be coordinated.

Genesis Aviation (840-1111; www.genesisaviation.com; 120 Kapalulu Pl., Suite 211, Airport) A locally owned company with a high level of personal attention, Genesis can fly with its doors removed so passenger's have better viewing. Choose from three trips that cover island sights such as waterfalls, Pearl Harbor, pineapple fields, and the beautiful rural coastlines. Its four-seater helicopters also serve a major local television station for daily news reports.

Island Seaplane Service (836-6273; www.islandseaplane.com; 85 Lagoon Dr., Airport) Years of flying experience and an excellent safety record make this company a great choice for a seaplane trip. The owner, Pat Magie, was named National Seaplane Pilot of the Year in 2000 and has flown planes in television shows, commercials, and films. Take off from the waters of Honolulu Bay for an air tour of major island sights.

Makani Kai Helicopters (1-877-255-8532; 834-5813; www.makanikai.com; 110 Kapalulu Pl., Airport) This locally owned tour operator features six-seat helicopters and several Oʻahu tours to choose from, including over Hanauma Bay, waterfalls, and the

North Shore. Flight times range from 15 minutes to an hour. They can also arrange customized interisland trips and wedding packages.

Paradise Helicopters (293-2570; www.paradisecopters.com, Turtle Bay Resort, 57-091 Kamehameha Hwy., Kahuku) These guys are located out on the North Shore, which allows you to choose a short flight and still see lots of countryside. Their four-seat helicopter cruises waterfalls and valleys along the Windward Coast as well as the North Shore, town, and the central plains. They can take the doors off for better viewing, and headsets enable you to communicate easily with the pilot and other passengers.

Stearman Bi-Plane Rides (637-4461; www.peacock.com/biplane; Dillingham Airfield, Hanger B6, Mokulēʻiʻa) Be an original—suit up in a leather helmet and goggles for a North Shore or Pearl Harbor air tour in a fully restored, open cockpit bi-plane dating from 1941. If your stomach's strong, you can do full rolls and more. All pilots are also licensed commercial airline pilots.

North Shore

Original Glider Rides (677-3404; honolulusoaring.com; Dillingham Airfield, Gate 2, Mokulēʻiʻa) This 35-year-old operation can take you up in a glider, give you lessons, and rent you equipment if you are already licensed. Tours cruise the Waiʻanae Range and North Shore and can be as mellow or as loopy and crazy as you like.

Soar Hawaiʻi Sailplanes (637-3147; www.soarhawaii.com) In business for 25 years, these folks own six gliders and can take you for a ride or even provide lessons. Sights include Waimea Bay and Mt. Kaʻala, Oʻahu's highest peak. Or, perhaps you'd like an aerobatic experience; the pilot will tailor maneuvers to whatever you can handle.

Hiking

Oʻahu has amazing hikes along mountain crestlines, into deep valleys, up volcanic craters, and more, for all different levels of experience and capabilities. Because Honolulu is so urban, it's easy to forget that most of the island is in fact rural or remote mountain terrain in virtually pristine conditions. Much of it is also off limits, however—enormous tracts of forested land belong to the state and federal government for watersheds, conservation, military training, and other purposes, and some areas are so steep they're nearly inaccessible.

It's our duty to encourage you to ignore any secret "Indiana Jones" bushwhacking fantasies. The Hawaiian Islands abound with real-life wilderness and unique environmental elements not to be trifled with, plus there are privacy laws in place. While stumbling upon a closely guarded marijuana field might be unlikely, it is very likely that your "offroad romp" will piss people off, land you on treacherous older trails, place you in the crosshairs of wild boar hunters, or get you desperately lost. You would be surprised how many visitors have had these things happen to them—the most unfortunate returning home in Hawaiian-print body bags.

Leptospirosis has been introduced into Hawaiʻi's freshwater streams, so swim at your own risk. Also, below waterfall areas in particular, watch out for falling rocks. Centipedes hide in nest-like piles of moist leaves or under rocks, so be careful if you overturn either. Hawaiʻi does not have poison oak or ivy, but does have oleander and other imported Mainland plants that can be toxic. Although year-round hiking is possible, if you hit the mountains after heavy rains, prepare for slippery mud and the possibility of flash flooding from stream areas. Happily, we don't have Lyme disease or rabies.

Never hike alone. Always let someone know where you're going and when you'll return, stick to marked trails, and begin your hike early enough to make it back long before sunset—twilight is brief in the tropics and night falls as fast as a stage curtain. Sunscreen, covered shoes, and mosquito repellent are important—and of course, leave nature as you found it, and always clean your shoes before and after a hike to prevent the spread of invasive species. Leave nothing in your vehicle while you hike, or it may be gone when you return.

Now that we've properly terrified you regarding the potential risks, prepare for the incredible wonders ahead. Bamboo thickets, giant ferns, the cries of hidden forest birds, trickling waterfalls, sensual aromas of wild ginger and guava, sweeping views, and crashing walls of waves are just some of what you might encounter, depending on the trail you choose. If you'll be hiking within the popular **Makiki Forest Recreation Area**, especially with children, first stop by the **Hawai'i Nature Center** (955-0100; www.hawaiinaturecenter.org; 2131 Makiki Heights Dr., Makiki) for a fun and educational introduction to Hawai'i's environment and good advice about the trails. They also conduct hikes. The Center is located just inside the entrance to the park.

The **Harold L. Lyon Arboretum** (988-0456; 3860 Mānoa Rd., Mānoa) has a network of wonderful, easy-to-moderate mountain trails for guided or independent hikes/walks, as do most of the other botanical gardens, such as **Ho'omaluhia Botanical Garden** (233-7323; 45-680 Luluku Rd., Kāne'ohe). **Turtle Bay Resort** (293-6000; www.turtlebayresort.com; 57-091 Kamehameha Hwy., Kahuku) on the North Shore has 12 miles of flat, oceanfront trails open to the public, and they can provide you with a map.

Another great idea is to look through calendar listings in the papers for upcoming hikes—the **Sierra Club** (538-6616), **Nature Conservancy** (537-4508), **Hawaiian Trail & Mountain Club** (551-0227), and other similar organizations always have activities planned—sometimes even on restricted land for which they have obtained permits. These trips are highly recommended. For hardcore hikers, the **Department of Land and Natural Resources** (587-0166; www.state.hi.us/dlnr/IdxCampHike.htm) has excellent maps, Web links, and other information, plus pick up Stuart Ball's well-regarded book, *The Hiker's Guide to O'ahu* (2000).

Below are some of the safest, most accessible, and most unique hikes on the island, ranging from easy to moderate in difficulty; these are all family-style trips with few of the dangers cited above. Except for Ka'ena Point, you can reach all trailheads by public bus and a bit of walking; call **TheBus** (848-5555) for guidance.

O'ahu's mountains are some of the most beautiful anywhere. This spot has been featured in many movies, such as Jurassic Park.

GREATER HONOLULU

Diamond Head Crater (Off Diamond Head Rd., across from 18th Ave.) This "hike" is a fairly urban experience, but memorable and worth it nonetheless—you'll be rewarded with 360-degree crater summit views of Honolulu perfect for photos. The trail was established by the American military in 1908 to provide access to its observation stations along the crater rim.

Begin inside of the crater itself (there's an entrance road on the northeast side of the crater), where you'll be charged a small usage fee. Expect a moderately steep climb via mostly paved sidewalks and many stairs; the distance one-way is less than a mile, and it takes most people under an hour to reach the top, where you'll pop out at a wide platform with protective railings.

We've seen Japanese tourists manage this walk in high heels, so don't bother with fancy hiking gear. Get up at the crack of dawn and bring water; as one of the island's most popular trips, it's nose-to-buttocks by 9 AM and the crater holds in a dry heat that will scuttle you come noon. The park is open 6 AM to 6 PM daily, and restrooms are available at the trailhead.

Mānoa Cliffs Circuit (Makiki Valley) The Makiki Forest Recreation Area is a labyrinth of mostly well-maintained trails that have grown in popularity with visitors and residents recently for its easy access, lush mountain beauty, and views. The Mānoa Cliffs Trail is 6 miles of moderate challenges that include narrow stream gulches, rocks, mud, and occasional proximity to urban noise. It also offers wonderful valley and waterfall views and intoxicating foliage.

The trailhead begins in the park just off of the beginning of Makiki Heights Drive, in the foothills behind Waikīkī. Visit the Hawai'i Nature Center first for a map and instructions on the lengthy trail path.

Mānoa Falls (In the back of Mānoa Valley) This is a relatively easy and short hike extremely popular with local and visiting families. Not only is it right in town, but you'll also get an exciting taste of the thick tropical jungle, bamboo forest, and—if it has rained recently—a narrow, 100-foot waterfall to reward you at the trail's end. Wear shoes so you don't slip on the often-muddy trail, and look out for any teensy black "worms" on the path—these are actually the so-called "Hawaiian blind snake", an established and very harmless import that sadly gets smushed underfoot way too often. And dowse yourself in mosquito repellent!

Take Mānoa Road in Mānoa Valley (behind Waikīkī) all the way into the back of the valley, continuing past the suburbs and onto a curving, lush segment that runs for several hundred feet to a parking lot. Note: Vehicle break-ins are common here! Leave nothing in your car. Continue down the road via foot through the chain-link fence to the trailhead. The low-slope hike to the falls takes about an hour and is less than a mile. Keep back from the falls to avoid injury from falling rocks.

A secondary, more advanced trail (Aihualama Trail) about 50 feet before the falls (near yet another fence) can add a bit of spice to your journey—it continues on and branches out forever, but unless you have a map, we suggest you only walk a short way down the main path before returning to the Mānoa Falls trailhead.

The Mānoa Falls trailhead begins in a towering jungle complete with a babbling stream.

WINDWARD O'AHU

Makapu'u Point (Off Kalaniana'ole Hwy. between Hawai'i Kai and Makapu'u Beach) This hike is easy if you're in shape and moderate if you're a couch potato. Just over a mile walk each way with modest sloping up to about 600 feet, this trail leads you to the still-operating 1909 Makapu'u Lighthouse and to fantastic, sweeping ocean views. In the winter months of November through April you might spot whales cruising the deep waters.

This trip has become popular enough to warrant the recent creation of a parking lot off the highway, which you will see to your right just as you round the bend past the Hawai'i Kai Golf Course when traveling east from Waikīkī, and just past Sea Life Park and Makapu'u Beach when traveling south from Kailua. This is a coastal, bone dry, black volcanic rock outcropping walk that can be very hot, and even windy—so wear plenty of sunscreen and a hat, and definitely bring lots of water. No restrooms are available and the gate is open daylight hours only.

North Shore

Ka'ena Point State Park (End of Farrington Hwy.) Hawaiians believed that Ka'ena Point was where souls jumped into the endless night after leaving their bodies; you'll feel the power of this remote area when you enter it.

This fascinating lowland dune preserve is the only coastal area of the island that is impassable by car. A sugar railroad once wrapped around the point and connected to the leeward side, but the tracks were washed away long ago. You'll find a remote, rocky, wild atmosphere; enormous waves in winter (possibly up to 50 feet); Laysan Albatross nests; wave-carved arches; a few fishermen; plenty of native naupaka shrubbery; and an old lighthouse at the point. You might also see brown-and-red-footed booby birds, turtles, and even whales in the winter. Remember, this is a nature preserve, so leave everything absolutely undisturbed.

All of its beaches can be dangerous for swimming. The area can be very hot and dry, as well as windy—water, sunscreen, and snug hats are musts. In full, this is a 10-mile, moderate hike that, one way, takes at least four hours. We suggest you go only as far as the lighthouse and then turn back. Ka'ena is also a decent spot for a mountain bike adventure.

Drive down Farrington Highway (HI 930) through Mokulē'ia and park at the end of the paved road. Leave nothing in your vehicle. From there, keep to the dirt road along the coast for the entire route (even when it turns stubbly) for the highest level of safety.

Central O'ahu

'Aiea Loop Trail (Keaiwa Heiau State Recreation Area, 'Aiea Heights Dr., 'Aiea) This easy-to-moderate, unique route includes an ancient Hawaiian healing temple, Keaiwa Heiau, and a distant view onto plane wreckage dating from 1943. Its well-marked and worn 4.5-mile loop path is mostly forested, shady, and level, although it can be windy and muddy at times. For the easiest trek, enter through the upper trailhead and exit through the lower, by the campground.

From Waikīkī, take the H-1 westbound to the H-201, labeled Fort Shafter/'Aiea. From that freeway, take the Stadium/'Aiea exit, staying straight onto Moanalua Road and turning right onto 'Aiea Heights Drive. Follow the road to the end.

Horseback Riding

Bummer news: It's against the law to ride horses on the beach in Hawai'i. However, the places that offer horseback riding on O'ahu walk you through picturesque settings—including alongside the ocean. All use Western saddles for the safety of guest riders. Try the folks listed below.

WINDWARD O'AHU

Kualoa Ranch Hawai'i (237-7321; www.kualoaranch.com; 49-560 Kamehameha Hwy., Ka'a'awa) Horseback riding is one of this long-standing ranch's specialties, and its most low-key activity. One- and two-hour trail rides head through mountainous pasturelands used in movies, such as *Jurassic Park*. They also offer rides for young children and therapeutic rides for the disabled.

NORTH SHORE

Gunstock Ranch (341-3995; www.gunstockranch.com) This new ranch can take you across its wide pastureland for a moonlight ride, on an advanced trail ride (trotting and cantering permitted), sunset ride, scenic day ride, or four-hour lunch ride, plus they conduct assisted horse or pony walks for young children. The ranch is closed to the public on Sundays.

Happy Trails Hawai'i (638-7433; www.happytrailshawaii.com; 59-231 Pūpūkea Rd., Pūpūkea) This friendly local company offers low-cost rides on the pastureland above the North Shore and accepts up to 10 riders at a time for 90-minute or 2-hour trail trips.

Hawai'i Polo Oceanfront Trail Rides (220-5153; 65-411 Farrington Hwy., Mokulēi'a) Prices here are higher—but what you get is really great. Conducted by Mokulēi'a's renowned polo organization, you'll ride premium thoroughbred and quarter horse polo ponies along its oceanfront, 100-acre spread. Group rides include a maximum of six people for 90-minute day and sunset rides, plus they offer a special "sweetheart" ride just for two.

Turtle Bay Resort (293-6000; www.turtlebayresort.com; 57-091 Kamehameha Hwy., Kahuku) This full service resort offers several fun riding opportunities, including a 45-minute trail ride along the shoreline and into an interesting forest, private lessons, rides that permit a faster pace, one-hour sunset rides, and wagon rides. Guides will also take small children on pony walks.

KAYAKING AND CANOEING

Even in the excitement of riding a wave, kayaking and outrigger canoeing can be a calming, spiritual encounter. Today's kayaks are stable, relatively lightweight, and manageable for anyone with moderate upper-body strength and a touch of determination. O'ahu doesn't have any significant rivers to comb, so you'll be cruising the ocean in a one- or two-seater.

Turtle Bay Resort is one of several good locations for horseback riding.

Hawaiian canoeing isn't just a sport—it's a way of life that dates back thousands of years. The only canoe form historically used in Hawai'i is the outrigger canoe, which features a balancing arm connected to the boat by two beams, keeping it upright even against strong waves. Knowing how to paddle an outrigger canoe well is a quick way to earn respect in the Islands, and many kids and adults are members of paddling teams. In Waikīkī, the **Outrigger Waikīkī** (926-9889, 2335 Kalākaua Ave., on the beach in front of the hotel) offers outrigger canoe rides most of the day, as does **Hawaiian Oceans Waikīkī** (306-4586; look for their Kūhiō Beach stand near the Duke Kahanamoku statue).

GREATER HONOLULU

Go Bananas Kayaks (737-9514; www.gobananaskayaks.com; 799 Kapahulu Ave., Kapahulu) You can rent a single, double, or triple person kayak from this company located right up the street from Waikīkī. Rates are reasonable and rental periods run from a day to a week. Choose from touring kayaks to surf kayaks—as the largest dealer in the state, they carry more than 30 different types. Everything is included in the rental price—racks for your car, paddles, life jackets, and more; drag them where you will.

WINDWARD O'AHU

Mokulua Kayak Guides (206-8508; www.mokuluaguides.com) This organization takes you on kayaking trips to the gorgeous offshore Mokulua Islands and other exotic sites for exploration and snorkeling. Yes, there are several other companies in Kailua that will take you to the "Mokes" by kayak too, and they may cost a wee bit less; but Mokulua Kayak Guides is by far the best. Local boy and professional geographer Scott Burch takes all the right steps to ensure that the journey is safe, educational, environmentally sensitive, inspiring, and memorable—instead of a frat fiesta. Equipment is first class and groups are never larger than eight people at a time.

PARASAILING

This activity is where skydiving and water skiing meet. You'll head out on the water via sports boat and be strapped to a parachute that, when the boat speeds up, lifts you as far as 600 feet high into the air for awesome views.

For a ride off Waikīkī, contact either **Diamond Head Parasail** (597-8646) or **Hawaiian Parasail** (591-1280), both at 1085 Ala Moana Boulevard in Kaka'ako. Each can pick you up at your hotel and take you out from nearby Kewalo Basin. You can either touch down in the water or on land. Rides last between five and ten minutes.

PARKS AND GARDENS

O'ahu is filled with wonderful parks and gardens of all types, ranging from dog parks to mysterious, deep-valley preserves. Do yourself a favor and visit at least one during your stay—after all, you came to see the Islands in all their green, floral glory.

WAIKĪKĪ

Kapi'olani Park (In east Waikīkī between Monsarrat Ave. and Diamond Head Rd., along Kalākaua Ave.) This is Honolulu's oldest city park and one of the island's most significant. Established in 1877 through the good will of King Kalākaua, both residents and visitors treasure this gem. Located on beachfront property in east Waikīkī in the shadow of Diamond Head, it features tennis courts, sports fields, a bandstand, the Honolulu Zoo, Waikīkī Aquarium, and Waikīkī Shell concert arena. It also hosts major festivals and events like the Honolulu Marathon, as well as most every Frisbee® game or birthday party in town.

GREATER HONOLULU

Ala Moana Regional Park (592-2288; 1201 Ala Moana Blvd., Ala Moana) This enormous and popular city park is a grassy respite with tennis courts, food concessions, event pavilions, and a yacht harbor, plus a beautiful, shallow beach running its entire length. Ala Moana Park is in the heart of the action where you will see island life in full color; it is a no-brainer for a recreational day with friends and family. The park is officially open between the hours of 5 AM and 10 PM.

The Contemporary Museum Gardens (526-1322; 2411 Makiki Heights Dr., Tantalus) The artistically designed, 3.5-acre, 75-year-old botanical gardens at this modern art museum are a peaceful, hilly retreat with glimpses of the city below. Selective, natural works of art from the museum's collection dot the landscape. Both the museum and gardens are open Tuesday through Saturday 10–4 and Sunday 12–4, and its café serves a wonderful lunch. There is a museum admission fee to visit the gardens.

Foster Botanical Garden (522-7066; 50 North Vineyard Blvd., Downtown) An oasis since 1853, the 13.5-acre Foster Garden is a wonder of exotically lush plants and trees and is on the National Register of Historic Places. Special collections include its Orchid Gardens, Prehistoric Glen, Exceptional Trees, and Palm Collection. The exotic Kuan Yin Temple, on its grounds since 1880, is dedicated to the Chinese goddess of mercy. In the summer, its twilight concerts and activities are charming. The garden is open daily from 9–4, and guided tours are available at 1. There is a fee to enter the garden.

Harold L. Lyon Arboretum (988-0456; 3860 Mānoa Rd., Mānoa) Enough cannot be said about this exquisitely beautiful and quiet Mānoa Valley garden, established in 1918 as a forest restoration project and now a research facility of the University of Hawai'i. Nearly 200 acres of trees and plants—many of gargantuan proportions—live in this rich, wilderness-like setting, and a myriad of forest birds peek from its many nooks and crannies. Tours, demonstrations, workshops, lectures, and other programs are available. Wear mosquito repellent and dress for nature trails. Visiting is permitted Monday through Friday 9–4, except on holidays. Donations are appreciated.

WINDWARD O'AHU

He'eia State Park (247-3156; 46-465 Kamehameha Hwy., Kāne'ohe) An 18.5-acre coastal park with incredible views of Kāne'ohe Bay and an ancient Hawaiian fishpond, this is a beautiful place for contemplation and mellow picnicking. Its peaceful point, where a Hawaiian temple once stood, was targeted in the 1980s to be converted into a condo—and the six hundred-year-old fishpond to the south, a yacht marina. The community managed to save it, but with lease negotiations approaching, this culturally significant site is still threatened with takeovers. Its handful of dedicated keepers conducts hands-on educational programs for children and also rents a small banquet facility for gatherings, including weddings. The park is open 8–4 daily.

Weekday mornings at Ala Moana Park are perfect for a peaceful swim or beach jog.

Ho'omaluhia Botanical Garden (233-7323; 45-680 Luluku Rd., Kāne'ohe) Built by the U.S. Army for flood protection, this is one of O'ahu's most beautiful gardens. Sheer cliffs are the backdrop for all kinds of birds, lush foliage, and a quiet reservoir. Collections include many endangered and rare plants from Malaysia, the Philippines, Hawai'i, Polynesia, Africa, Melanesia, Sri Lanka, India, and the tropical Americas. On weekdays, Ho'omaluhia can be virtually uninhabited. The park offers guided walks on selected days, plus campgrounds, fishing, a small visitor center, and an art gallery. It's open daily 9–4, except for major holidays.

Senator Fong's Plantation & Gardens (239-6775; 47-285 Pūlama Rd., Kāne'ohe) A 55-year-old, 700-acre, family owned tropical garden founded by former U.S. senator Hiram Fong, this landscape once belonged to King Lunalilo and has changed little over hundreds of years. Its lovely valley setting includes both lush foliage and moderately arid landscapes. The park is open most days from 10–2 for shop browsing and cultural crafts. The gardens can be seen only through guided, 1-mile walking tours offered at 10:30 and 1. A fee is charged.

North Shore

Waimea Valley Audubon Center (638-9199; 59-864 Kamehameha Hwy., near Pūpūkea) We hope that you can visit this wonderful park in historic Waimea Valley during your visit. Over the years, this once-sacred valley fell into the hands of various developers, who erected a series of themed and "adventure" parks; wealthy private homes and a tourist camp were next on the agenda. In 2002, the City and County of Honolulu acquired selected parcels through condemnation and leased them to the National Audubon Society. Backed by public demand, in 2006 the city and other organizations banded together to purchase the entire 1,875-acre valley from a New York developer for its preservation forever.

The valley now again features many native and culturally significant plants and its numerous archaeological sites have been restored. Except during periods of minimal rain, a wide waterfall in the back of the valley creates a good swimming hole (be aware that leptospirosis has been introduced in Hawai'i and can be contracted from freshwater streams).

As of early 2008, the Audubon will no longer be involved with maintaining the valley, but we've been assured by the Office of Hawaiian Affairs that the area will somehow remain open to the public—although the park's name and infrastructure will surely change.

Sailing and Catamaran Excursions

Many of the island's activities, such as snorkeling, automatically involve cruising along via boat. But you can also choose to cruise just for the heck of it—and in Waikīkī, you can do it surprisingly cheaply. Along Waikīkī Beach you will see at least four catamarans pulled up onto the sand, loading passengers for a thrilling party ride (usually the cocktails are flowing too). You can also book a more formal and traditional boat trip. Below are some good options.

Islandwide

Royal Hawaiian Catamaran (593-9993; royalhawaiiancatamaran.com) For a higher end experience, book a shared or private charter on this lovely, 52-foot, custom-designed yacht. Rent her for the day, the week, or the month and direct her wherever you please.

Waikīkī

Angles' Gay Catamaran Cruise (926-9766; www.angleswaikiki.com) Geared toward gay men and women, this clothing-optional catamaran fun-cruise and swim takes place every

Sunday afternoon and features an open bar. Call in advance, as it books quickly.

Gay Hawai'i Cruise (923-0669) The famed Hula's Bar and Lei Stand also offers a 90-minute Saturday cruise for gay men and women off of Waikīkī and Diamond Head, with unlimited tropical cocktails and a great price. The 45-foot boat is fast and furious. Book early.

Maita'i Catamaran (926-5665; www.leahi.com) Pick from snorkeling to trade wind to moonlight sails aboard a 44-footer. Find Maita'i parked on the sand between the Halekulani and Sheraton Waikīkī.

Na Hoku II Catamaran (926-7700; www.nahokuii.com) This perky, 45-foot catamaran takes a 90-minute cruise along Waikīkī and past Diamond Head five times per day, right up through sunset. Pick up a ride in front of the Moana Surfrider hotel.

Go for a sail off Waikīkī with one of the many catamarans pulled up on the beach.

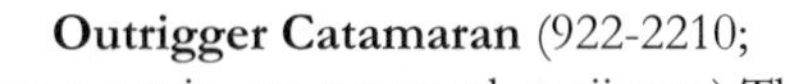

Outrigger Catamaran (922-2210; www.outriggercatamaranhawaii.com) This is the fastest of the Waikīkī Beach bunch. You can book a snorkel sail, or hit the water for their 90-minute "speed sail" or sunset sail, just for the thrill. Catch it in front of the Outrigger Reef Hotel.

The Sailing Club Hawai'i (222-9768; 1-800-908-5250; www.thesailingclubhawaii.com) These luxury sailing yachts are yours for everything from interisland travel to weddings to three-hour cruises.

Some of the Best Things in Life Are Free....

Here are 12 creative, family-oriented ideas for fun in or near Waikīkī—and most don't even cost a dime. Be sure to call ahead or check Web sites for exact schedules, directions, and details.

Catch a Movie on the Sand (923-1094) The popular Sunset on the Beach features full-sized double features right on Waikīkī Beach, across from the zoo.

Celebrate Fridays With Fireworks Waikīkī's Hilton Hawaiian Village (949-4321) launches TGIF fireworks Fridays after nightfall. Grab ice cream from Lappert's (near the Hilton's lobby) for the beachfront show.

Count the Fish The Pacific Beach Hotel (923-4511) in Waikīkī features a gargantuan visitor aquarium teeming with tropical fish and rays.

Cruise the Art Scene Join thousands of the happily artsy and artless in the First Friday downtown gallery walk (521-2903) every first Friday evening of the month.

Enjoy a Hula Show This free, city-sponsored hula event (843-8002) happens every evening at 6:30 at Kūhiō Beach's Hula Mound.

Greet the Dolphins The Kahala Hotel & Resort's (739-8888) small lagoon houses several playful bottlenose dolphins—and you don't have to be a hotel guest to visit them.

Hear Hawai'i's First Band The beloved, 172-year-old Royal Hawaiian Band (922-5331) performs Sundays at Waikiki's Kapi'olani Park and Fridays at downtown's 'Iolani Palace.

Experience a Tea Ceremony The Urasenke Foundation (923-3059) welcomes adults and well-behaved children to join in an authentic Japanese tea ceremony Wednesdays and Fridays (a small donation and advance notice are required).

Learn the Legislative Process The Hawai'i State Legislature (Senate 586-6720; House 586-6400) runs from early January to early March, and visitors are welcome to observe all proceedings.

Pet Adoptable Kitties The Hawaiian Humane Society's Cat House (946-2187) features free-range felines in a screened house that need extra love while they await new owners.

See Stars . . . Or the rings of Saturn or craters of the moon when the Hawaiian Astronomical Society (www.hawastsoc.org) busts out the "big gun" telescopes at their Kahala Star Party once a month.

Visit the Fish Auction The United Fishing Agency's (536-2148) seafood auction is the real deal and is all business. Get to Pier 38 by dawn for the best action (closed Sundays).

Wave at Friends Back Home Stand in front of the Duke Kahanamoku statue on Waikīkī Beach to show friends and family via Web cam that you're still alive and kickin'. They can see you at www.honolulu.gov/multimed/waikiki.asp.

SKYDIVING

For those of you who accept the risks associated with skydiving and want to take the plunge anyway, you will be rewarded with stellar island views in good weather, and a memorable experience. Both outfits below can pick you up and return you to Waikīkī and photograph or videotape your descent, and both require tandem jumping unless you have a skydiving license. Dillingham Airfield on the North Shore is the only authorized jumping site on the island.

Skydive Hawai'i (637-9700; www.hawaiiskydiving.com; 68-760 Farrington Hwy., Mokulēi'a) Hawai'i's oldest skydiving company features expert instructors licensed by the United States Parachute Association (USPA) and conducts jumps over the North Shore from its Cessna Caravan.

Pacific Skydiving Center (637-7472; www.pacific-skydiving.com; 68-760 Farrington Hwy., Mokulēi'a) This company runs the fastest-climbing plane of the two operators and also employs licensed, USPA expert instructors.

SNORKELING, SCUBA DIVING, AND GLASS-BOTTOM BOAT AND SUBMARINE TRIPS

With more than five hundred different kinds of fish in Hawai'i's waters—plus turtles, rays, sea urchins, dolphins, whales, seals, sea cucumbers, anemones, hermit crabs, eels, lobsters, snails, octopus, sea stars, and corals, there is plenty to see under the waves. And, plenty of ways to see them—even without getting your feet wet. Don't miss the opportunity to witness the beauty of this hidden world.

Only 2 percent of the world's oceans contain coral reefs, which house a diversity of life second only to tropical rainforests. Coral reefs are not rocks—they are made from the calcareous skeletons of thousands of tiny, stinging critters called polyps. Extremely fragile, they require certain conditions to thrive; it is important that while in the water you avoid touching live coral or kicking up sand nearby. Human activity has destroyed more than 35 million acres of reef to date world-wide.

For those who wish to snorkel, don't feel obligated to sign up for a packaged tour—you can buy or rent basic equipment and enjoy hours of exploration and fun on your own. If you can splurge on a set of swim fins also, you'll really be set. Above all, be sure to pick a well-fitting mask. **Snorkel Bob's** (735-7944; www.snorkelbob.com; 702 Kapahulu Ave., Kapahulu) is a well-known supplier near Waikīkī. In Waikīkī, check out the **Waikīkī Diving Center**, listed below under operators. In Kailua, visit **Aaron's Dive Shop**—see below for contact information. On the North Shore, call **Surf-N-Sea** (637-9887; www.surfnsea.com; 62-595 Kamehameha Hwy., Hale'iwa) for rentals and sales. **Hale Nalu** (696-5897; www.halenalu.com; 85-876 Farrington Hwy., Wai'anae) rents snorkel equipment on the Leeward Coast. Bookstores and sundry shops carry numerous marine life identification guides.

The following are some of the best snorkeling spots on O'ahu and are places you can easily access as an independent traveler. See the "Beaches" section of this chapter for an overview of the locales. Remember to give turtles plenty of space and to not feed the fish, however tempting it may be. Never snorkel alone. And be sure to pick up a cheapo underwater camera from an ABC Store or elsewhere for great souvenir photos of your experience.

In Waikīkī, the marine conservation area at **Queen's Surf Beach** yields a few critters, including Hawai'i's famous state fish, the humuhumunukunukuapua'a. In greater Honolulu, **Kahala Beach** has decent snorkeling spots, although the water can be cloudy. The renowned **Hanauma Bay**, despite its crowds, is absolutely stupendous—a must-visit. Passable equipment can be rented on-site, although it may not fit like a glove. Windward O'ahu's **Lanikai Beach** often offers decent snorkeling in clear water. On the North Shore, **Kuilima Cove** at Turtle Bay Resort, as well as **Sharks Cove** and Three Tables at **Pūpūkea Beach Park**, are excellent, conditions permitting. On summer days when the water is calm, the western end of **Waimea Bay** is also good—but swim here with extra caution and look out for swells and rocks. On the Leeward Coast, head to the mild-mannered and very kid-safe **Kō 'Olina Lagoons**.

For scuba divers, O'ahu abounds in amazing dive sites. If you are certified, you can go deep down to explore marine life hovering around sunken ships and WWII aircraft wrecks. Beginners can opt for tour dives in shallow or moderately deep waters and still see plenty of fish. Several companies also offer full certification courses that you can complete in a week's time.

Below are selected reliable operations that offer ways to get up close and personal with Hawai'i's exciting underwater environment. No tours are permitted onto Kāne'ohe Bay on Sundays. Keep in mind that trips run only when weather conditions permit and, of course, that viewing wildlife is an unpredictable endeavor.

ISLANDWIDE

Aaron's Dive Shop (262-2333; www.hawaii-scuba.com; 307 Hahani St., Kailua) This 35-year-old company is well known for leading snorkeling and other tour operations islandwide, but their specialty is scuba diving; owner Jack can cite an impressive list of celebrities who have relied on his team for safe dives. They also sell equipment.

Surf-N-Sea (637-9887; www.surfnsea.com; 62-595 Kamehameha Hwy., Hale'iwa) All things surf-n-sea-related happen at this 40-year-old North Shore fixture, from equipment rentals and sales to snorkel and scuba diving trips either to Leeward O'ahu or on the North Shore, as conditions permit.

Waikīkī Diving Center (922-2121; www.waikikidiving.com; 424 Nāhua St., Waikīkī) This 25-year-old company offers intimate, interesting dives around the island; a warm, well trained team; and competitive prices for trips and equipment. It is owned by two cheery brothers who live and breathe the sport.

Waikīkī

Atlantis Adventures O'ahu (1-800-548-6262; www.atlantisadventures.com; 1600 Kapi'olani Blvd.) If you have the cash to burn and want a unique, albeit touristy, underwater experience that doesn't muss the hair, try a submarine off Waikīkī. You will likely see numerous critters as it putters along 100 feet below the surface.

Windward O'ahu

All Hawai'i Cruises/Captain Bob's Sailing Adventures (942-5077; 1860 Ala Moana Blvd., Suite 414, Waikīkī) After being transported to the windward side from Waikīkī, you'll sail via catamaran into the achingly gorgeous and mellow Kāne'ohe Bay for light snorkeling, volleyball, and a burger barbecue. The festive young folks manning the boat jump right in the water with you. This trip is more about fun than serious undersea exploration.

Kāne'ohe Bay Cruises (292-8470; He'eia Boat Harbor, Kamehameha Hwy., Kāne'ohe) For 40 years, this simple, low-key, and incredibly affordable glass-bottom boat experience on spectacular Kāne'ohe Bay has provided those who stumbled across it with a glimpse of reef life from above. You'll need to get yourself to Windward O'ahu and the pier.

North Shore

Deep Ecology (1-800-578-3992; 637-7946; www.deepecologyhawaii.com; 66-456 Kamehameha Hwy., Hale'iwa) This environmentally responsible company offers a unique, small-scale snorkeling opportunity: a night trip with lights and wetsuits. They also have seasonal dive trips, all on the North Shore.

North Shore Catamaran Charters (351-9371; www.sailingcat.com) In the summer months, sail on a spacious catamaran along the beautiful North Shore to super snorkeling at Waimea Bay. Trips leave from from Hale'iwa Harbor.

Leeward O'ahu

Wild Side Specialty Tours (306-7273; www.sailhawaii.com; 87-1286 Farrington Hwy., Wai'anae) An excellent yacht, intimate atmosphere, expert team, stunning snorkeling location, and exceptional attentiveness to environmental concerns make this organization a winner. Snorkel-specific trips take place during the summer along the Leeward Coast. They also offer whale and dolphin trips as well as stargazing journeys.

Spas and Salons

Hawai'i is fast becoming an elegant resort spa destination and features some unique treatments that aficionados will appreciate. Try a traditional Hawaiian lomilomi massage, which involves long, rhythmic strokes that release tension and free energy.

Waikīkī

Abhasa Waikīkī Spa (922-8200; www.abhasa.com; Royal Hawaiian Hotel, 2259 Kalākaua Ave.) This 10,000-square-foot spa offers eight outdoor treatment cabanas, Hawaiian sea salt scrubs, reflexology, deluxe men's facials, wraps, and more.

Mandara Spa (945-7721; www.mandaraspa.com; Hilton Hawaiian Village, 2005 Kalia Rd., Kalia Tower, 4th Floor.) Stone therapy, a private whirlpool and sun terrace, massage by two therapists at once, and tandem massages culminating in playful chocolate body application are just some of your options.

Na Ho'ola Spa (237-6330; www.hyattregency.com; Hyatt Regency, 2424 Kalākaua Ave.) Choose from a lomilomi facial, skin brightening, seaweed wrap, macadamia nut body scrub, shiatsu massage, or just about any other luxurious body treatment you can imagine.

Paul Brown's Spa Olakino (924-2121; www.paulbrownhawaii.com; Waikīkī Marriott, 2552 Kalakaua Ave.) Island salon star Paul Brown has recently opened a spa in Waikīkī offering full-service hair and nail care, body wraps, eye-lift treatments, massages, facials and more.

SpaHalekulani (931-5322; www.halekulani.com; Halekulani, 2199 Kalia Rd.) Reflexology, Thai massage, massage for pregnant women, body scrubs and wraps, facials, nail care, waxing, and even child manicures are available here.

Waikīkī Plantation Spa (926-2880; 1-866-926-2880; www.waikikiplantationspa.com; Outrigger Waikīkī, 2335 Kalākaua Ave.) Brand new as of 2006, the Waikīkī Plantation spa is earning great reviews for its services, which include firming marine body masks, pre- and post-natal massages, solar manicures, and more.

Greater Honolulu

Aveda Lifestyle Salon & Spa (947-6141; Ala Moana Center, 1450 Ala Moana Blvd., Ala Moana) The best thing to do after a day of shopping is to get a massage and be pampered with delicious organic products—without even leaving the mall.

Spa Suites (739-8938; www.kahalaresort.com; Kahala Hotel & Resort, 5000 Kahala Ave.) Each 550-square-foot private spa suite is pure luxury. Services include Hawaiian scalp massages, firming and lifting facials, "golfer's tonic" massages, and volcanic mud envelopments.

Windward O'ahu

Paul Brown Kailua (230-2000; 25 Maluniu Ave., Kailua) Paul Brown's suburban salon offers everything from microdermabrasion, hair relaxation, waxing, and facials to massages.

North Shore

Spa Luana (447-6868; www.turtlebayresort.com; Turtle Bay Resort, 57-091 Kamehameha Hwy., Kahuku) Pregnancy massages, mud wraps, child manicures, makeup application, and waxing are just the beginning of the sevices offered here.

Leeward O'ahu

'Ihilani Spa (626-4446; www.ihilani.com, JW Marriott 'Ihilani Resort & Spa, 92-1001 'Ōlani St., Kapolei) This incredible, multi-award-winning, 35,000-square-foot facility includes men's and women's Roman-style pools, anti-stress facials, Hawaiian tī leaf wraps, medicinal massages, and endless other selections.

Surfing and Bodyboarding

Hawaiians have been surfing for centuries and are credited with inventing the sport, which by 1900 had nearly died out in the wake of Westernization. Then along came Waikīkī beach boy and Olympic medalist Duke Paoa Kahinu Mokoe Hulikohola Kahanamoku—"The Duke"—who helped popularize surfing worldwide and gave it the touch of glamour it retains today.

O'ahu is the ultimate destination for surfing, as well as the unofficial headquarters of the surfing world. On the North Shore in winter, many of the sport's biggest stars can be spotted on the waves or grabbing a bite at unobtrusive lunch wagons. More than 1,700 named surf areas exist across the state, with many of the most famous right on O'ahu. Some recall landmarks, such as "Publics" in Waikīkī, named for the public baths that once stood onshore; others, such as "Himalayas" and "Slaughterhouse" on the North Shore characterize area wave height or behavior.

A recent surge in surfing's popularity has meant that every visitor to Hawai'i now wants to learn to surf. In response, surf schools have sprouted up on every corner, lesson prices have skyrocketed, large student groups have replaced private tutoring, and already-crowded surf spots have become virtually unmanageable. Even before the spike, local surfers felt edged out of prized territories by tourist surfers and wannabes—so before you hit the beach with your board, check in at the surf shops, beach boy stands, or lifeguard shacks regarding the vibe of your destination.

Waikīkī Beach is still one of the easiest places to learn and the most tolerant to visitors. Try the surf spots in front of the Moana Surfrider hotel and Kūhiō Beach. Beach boys and girls working at equipment booths right on the sand can also take you out into the waves. Try **Star Beach Boys** (Kūhiō Beach).

For an exhaustive lineup of Hawaiian Island surfing notes and surf condition updates, check out the **Surf News Network** (596-7873; www.surfnewsnetwork.com).

Bodyboarding is a fun way to spend an afternoon and has a much shorter learning curve than surfing. Most boards are extremely buoyant, measure about 40 inches long, and should have a tether that goes around your ankle so you don't lose your board in the surf. With a pair of fins, you can kick fast enough to catch the lip of a wave and propel forward for a fantastic ride. You can get some great beginning and intermediate level breaks right in Waikīkī or at Waimānalo Bay State Recreation Area, on the windward side.

Surfboards and bodyboards can be rented by the hour up and down Waikīkī Beach from Star Beach Boys and others at a premium per hour, and around Waikīkī for much less. But if you plan to really do any surfing, you are better off renting by the day or week; you can even get a surf rack along with the board. Try **Blue Planet Surf Shop** (922-5444; 813 Kapahulu Ave., near Waikīkī). **Hawai'i Surfboard Rentals** (672-5055; www.hawaii surfboardrentals.com) charges a bit more and has a two-day minimum, but they'll deliver boards directly to you (with an optional car rack) and they offer quality equipment. On the windward side, drop by **Kimo's Surf Hut** (262-1644; 151 Hekili St., Kailua). On the North Shore, visit **Surf-N-Sea** (637-9887; www.surfnsea.com; 62-595 Kamehameha Hwy., Hale'iwa). Out on the Wai'anae Coast, contact **Hale Nalu** (696-5897; www.halenalu.com; 85-876 Farrington Hwy., Wai'anae) for surfboard rentals. Outfits that offer surf lessons and surf camps for kids and adults are listed below.

Islandwide

Girls Who Surf (371-8917; www.girlswhosurf.com) This chick-founded surf school teaches all levels of surfing and ocean knowledge to the entire family. Transportation and equipment is included, and all instructors are lifeguard, CPR, and first aid certified, as well as licensed to teach by the state. Group and private lessons are available in Waikīkī, in the leeward area, or on the North Shore; or you can just rent surfboards from them.

Hans Hedemann Surf School (924-7778; www.hhsurf.com) Pro surfer Hans Hedemann now has seven surf school locations around the island (five in Waikīkī, one at the nearby

Kahala Hotel & Resort, and one at Turtle Bay Resort on the North Shore) from which his trained instructors lead group and individual lessons. You can also take bodyboarding lessons, sign up for a surf camp, rent a surfboard, or take private lessons with the master himself.

NORTH SHORE

Sunset Suzy (781-2692; www.sunsetsuzy.com) Learn to surf with North Shore lifeguard, *Blue Crush* surfer, and former *Baywatch* stuntperson, "Sunset Suzy." Private and group lessons are available for every experience level, as is a monthly surf camp for women and girls. Instruction takes place at the famed Sunset Beach.

CENTRAL O'AHU

Hawaiian Fire (737-3473; www.hawaiianfire.com) Members of the Honolulu Fire Department can to teach you surfing and water safety on a secluded, leeward-area beach with gentle beginner waves and no crowds to worry about. Both group and individual lessons are available, and all equipment and transportation is included.

A surfer and his son catch a late afternoon wave together in Waikīkī.

TENNIS

O'ahu has nearly two hundred public, mostly outdoor courts at which you may play, and many are lit for night games. To use the courts, simply wait your turn in person; play time is limited to 45 minutes when someone is waiting.

Space-starved Waikīkī has very few hotel tennis courts. Contact **Miles James** (551-

9438), who ranked for many years as Hawai'i's number one player; he can reserve court time for you and your friends on a private Waikīkī court at a great rate, provide rental equipment, give you lessons, or even just bat (or powerhouse!) the ball around with you.

You'll also find several other private courts open to you around the island. Below is a list of some of the island's best public and private options for visitors.

WAIKĪKĪ

Diamond Head Tennis Center (971-7150; 3908 Paki Ave.) These 10 unlit courts are run by the City and County and are open from 6 AM until sunset.

Kapi'olani Tennis Courts (971-2510; 2740 Kalākaua Ave.) Located near the Waikīkī Aquarium, these four outdoor, lit courts are very popular and available 24 hours a day.

GREATER HONOLULU

Ala Moana Park (983-3713; 1201 Ala Moana Blvd.) This is a very popular public tennis area with 10 lit, open-air playing courts open from 6 AM until 10 PM.

WINDWARD O'AHU

Kailua District Park (266-7652; 21 S. Kainalu Dr., Kailua) Kailua Park features eight public outdoor courts, all of which are lit. They are always open, but the lights are turned off at 9:30 PM.

NORTH SHORE

Turtle Bay Resort (293-8811; 57-091 Kamehameha Hwy., Kahuku) This full facility offers 10 courts, equipment, and lessons, with courts open from 8 AM to 9:30 PM. A fee is charged to play and reservations are required.

CENTRAL O'AHU

Central O'ahu Regional Park Tennis Complex & Archery Range (677-8849; 94-801 Kamehameha Hwy., Waipahu) This amazing and relatively new complex features 18 field courts, a lit clubhouse court, and a lit show court. Bring your own equipment—courts are available on a first-come, first-serve basis. Play is permitted from 7 AM until 9 PM.

LEEWARD O'AHU

JW Marriott 'Ihilani Resort and Spa (679-3197; www.ihilanitennis.com; 92-1001 'Ōlani St., Kapolei) Rent a racket from the resort and book time on one of their six quality courts. A court fee is charged and reservations are required. Play from sunrise until 7 PM.

THEMED FAMILY ATTRACTIONS

For family fun away from the beach, try the well-known O'ahu attractions listed below. We recommend the Honolulu Zoo and Waikīkī Aquarium; they are both right in Waikīkī and, although smaller than some Mainland facilities, are educational, thoughtfully presented, and entertaining.

WAIKĪKĪ

Honolulu Zoo (926-3191; www.honoluluzoo.org; 151 Kapahulu Ave.) This charming zoo has been around forever and is modernizing with the times, from its well-designed African Savanna to the new petting zoo area and expanding animal facilities. Its special programs are really cool—including stargazing, night tours and sleepovers, weeklong day camps, and summer concerts. The zoo is open daily from 9–4:30. Admision is $8 for adults and youths 13 and over, $1 for children 6–12, and free for children under 6.

Waikīkī Aquarium (923-9741; www.waquarium.org; 2777 Kalākaua Ave.) Founded in 1904, this small, education-oriented facility is part of the University of Hawai'i. Don't expect Shamu—instead, enjoy its artistically presented interior filled with more than 2,500 colorful sea critters and plenty of educational facts. Fun activities include a guided night exploration of the coral reef fronting the Aquarium and naturalist-guided hikes on the North Shore. Doors open daily from 9–4:30. Admission is $9 for adults, $4 for youths 13 to 17, $2 for children 5 to 12, and free for children under 5.

Greater Honolulu

Hawai'i Children's Discovery Center (524-5437; www.discoverycenterhawaii.org; 111 Ohe St., Kaka'ako) Got hyper young kids? Hurry over to the Hawai'i Children's Discovery Center, where they can learn—and burn some energy—in a safe, 38,000-square-foot hands-on environment. They are open Tuesday through Friday 9–1, and Saturday through Sunday 10–3. The fee is $8 for adults, $6.75 for children 2 to 17.

Windward O'ahu

Kualoa Ranch Hawai'i (237-8515; www.kualoa.com; 49-560 Kamehameha Hwy., Ka'a'awa) This long-standing, 4,000-acre ranch located on sacred Hawaiian grounds offers ATV rides, sailing trips, horseback riding, kayaking, and more. The Ranch is open daily with tours from 9:30–3; gates are open longer, however, which enables you to wander. Adult activity prices range from $19 to $89.

Polynesian Cultural Center (293-3333; 800-367-7060; www.polynesia.com; 55-370 Kamehameha Hwy., Lā'ie) Some of you will love the "PCC," and others will find it boring or kitsch. This refreshingly low-tech, Mormon-run park features eight Polynesian villages and kid-oriented, cultural learning experiences. At night, the lū'au and dance extravaganzas offer surprisingly decent food and good hula performances. Trinket kiosks and a tour-bus feel downgrade the overall experience, however, and it's pretty expensive. The park is closed Sundays. Call for hours. Adult general admission and package prices range from $40 to $205.

Sea Life Park (1-866-365-7446; www.sealifeparkhawaii.com; 41-202 Kalaniana'ole Hwy., Waimānalo) Owned and operated by a Mainland corporation, this animal entertainment facility does offer some unique interactive opportunities (for large fees), such as the Dolphin Royal Swim and Hawaiian Ray Encounter, plus a lū'au. But if sea lion shows make you cringe, stay away. Sea Life Park is open daily from 9:30–5. Adult ticket prices range from $29 to $199.

The University of Hawai'i's modest Waikīkī Aquarium is a good stop before a day at the beach.

LEEWARD O'AHU

Dole Plantation (621-8408; www.doleplantation.com; 64-1550 Kamehameha Hwy., Wahiawā) This touristy, but nevertheless somewhat interesting, opportunity to learn more about the pineapple industry features a narrated train tour, the "world's largest maze," and a large plantation garden. It's open daily from 9–5. Adult ticket prices range from $3.75 to $7.50.

Hawaiian Water Adventures Park (674-9283; www.hawaiianwaters.com; 400 Farrington Hwy., Kapolei) Popular with resident families, this water-oriented park on the "dry" side of the island includes 20 water-themed rides such as The Cliffhanger, where you free-fall six stories down two unique speed slides. The park is open daily, but hours vary—call ahead. Admission is $35.99 for adults and youths 12 and over, $25.99 for children 3 to 11, and free for children under 3.

WHALE, DOLPHIN, AND SHARK WATCHING

From November through March or April, more than five thousand humpback whales spend time in Hawaiian waters. They swim several thousand miles from Alaska, bask in the warmth of the lower latitude, and give birth before trekking all the way back with babies in tow. The 1,400-square-mile Hawaiian Islands Humpback Whale National Marine Sanctuary helps to protect these still-endangered, 45-foot-long creatures. Maui undoubtedly has some of the best whale watching in the state—but you can often spot whales off O'ahu from viewpoints such as Diamond Head, Turtle Bay, and Makapu'u, or via a whale watching boat excursion. Although the gargantuan humpbacks are local stars, Hawai'i also has sperm whales, Hawaiian pilot whales, and Hawaiian melonhead whales in its waters.

If you have fantasized about swimming with dolphins, you're not alone. Entire organizations are dedicated to the spiritual healing that this experience can reputedly bring. Hawaiians recognized their power as well, and considered dolphins a form of mighty Kanaloa, the sea god. Four species of dolphin are typically found in Hawai'i: Pacific bottlenose; rough-toothed; spotted; and spinner. None are considered threatened or endangered, but they have been changing their habits in response to encroaching human activity and are protected by federal law. If you must touch a dolphin before you leave Hawai'i, consider **Dolphin Quest** (1-800-248-3316; 739-8918; Kahala Hotel & Resort, 5000 Kahala Ave., Kahala). For a hefty fee you will get right into the hotel's lagoon and interact with its resident Atlantic bottlenoses. Even though it's not in the wild, for many it is still an incredible experience.

And now we come to sharks. There are about 40 different species of shark in Hawaiian waters, from the 8-inch pygmy shark to the 50-foot whale shark. Eight of these species can be aggressive to humans and are occasionally seen close to shore; the massive tiger shark is almost inevitably the perpetrator in Hawai'i's extremely rare attacks (out of many millions of dips taken at Hawai'i's beaches each year, only a few folks get nibbled).

Two well-meaning tour companies have been offering North Shore shark encounters. Some residents feel that because of the methods these businesses use to attract sharks for viewing, an increase in attacks closer to shore is inevitable. Impact studies and policy reviews are underway at the time of writing, and since it's better to be safe than sorry, we recommend that until the results are in you refrain from this activity.

Whale watching and dolphin watching tours are not without controversy either; several whales are hit by tour boats each year, and the negative impact of dolphin–human interaction is becoming more clear. However, enabling people to encounter these incredible creatures up close in the wild is not only educational and inspiring, but it can also contribute to greater conservation awareness and support. While this can also be said for shark encounters, whale and dolphin viewing do not have the potential to increase hazards for beachgoers.

Below are several organizations that handle marine mammal encounters with care and respect. Note that the law requires a distance of at least 100 feet from humpback whales, and 50 yards from dolphins, although animals will sometimes approach you or the boat at a closer range. And remember, spotting wildlife can never be guaranteed—try to just enjoy the boat trip and consider catching a glimpse of an animal a bonus.

Spinner dolphins join the bow of Wild Side's catamaran along the Wai'anae Coast.

WAIKĪKĪ

Star of Honolulu (983-7827; 1-800-334-6191; www.paradisecruises.com) Considering that this company is in no way a small-scale, eco-adventure outfit, they do a surprisingly good job of "keeping it real" despite serving hundreds at a time on its whale watching ship. They also provide a passable lunch, mellow music, friendly atmosphere, and low-key Hawaiiana activities while aboard. These guys don't charge a lot, and if you don't see a whale, you can return for free—but if you are looking for an intimate or spiritual experience, you may want to consider other tour companies.

NORTH SHORE

Deep Ecology (637-7946; 1-800-578-3992; 66-456 Kamehameha Hwy., Hale'iwa) Among other tours they offer, this environmentally responsible company conducts whale watching trips out of Hale'iwa Harbor. They often encounter dolphins along the way as well. In addition to leading tours, they also conduct marine animal rescues and are involved in community forums relating to both eco-tourism and conservation issues.

North Shore Catamaran Charters (351-9371; www.sailingcat.com) This small catamaran powers mostly via wind for winter whale watching and leaves from the Hale'iwa Boat Harbor. An underwater hydrophone enables riders to hear whale communications.

LEEWARD O'AHU

Wild Side Specialty Tours (306-7273; www.sailhawaii.com; Wai'anae Boat Harbor, Slip A-11, Wai'anae) If you want to get close to dolphins in the most sensitive, non-touristy, and educated manner possible, this is the right outfit. Conducted by a marine biologist, Wild Side takes a handful of people aboard their spacious, 42-foot catamaran for a four-hour sail along the coast; conditions permitting, you might even swim in the vicinity of these beautiful mammals. They also offer snorkeling and stargazing journeys.

WINDSURFING AND KITEBOARDING

O'ahu is one of the world's best windsurfing locales, with Kailua Beach, Diamond Head, and the North Shore reigning supreme. This sport is harder than it looks—but even a beginner can have a good time taking a lesson or two. Serious enthusiasts will have a great time. The relatively new sport of kiteboarding is exactly as it sounds: A large, crescent kite pulls you across the water on a board for an exhilarating rush.

Although there are several outfits from which you can rent and take lessons, the best is **Naish Hawai'i** (1-800-767-6068; 262-6068; www.naish.com; 155 Hāmākua Dr., Kailua). Robbie Naish grew up on O'ahu, and by the age of 13 had already won an amateur windsurfing world championship. He eventually turned pro and is well respected in the field as both a competitor and maker of quality boards. He opened his windsurfing school more than 20 years ago. You can either rent windsurfing equipment or take lessons in windsurfing or kiteboarding.

OTHER RECREATION

Still looking for more to do with your days and nights? Here's a potpourri to pick through; also check out newspaper calendar listings for new or one-time classes, community service opportunities, and special events.

Fitness

Return from your vacation in better health than when you arrived! If you are into jogging, Waikīkī's Kapi'olani Park is the place to go. Otherwise, check out the ideas below.

WAIKĪKĪ

If you must spin, Waikīkī has a **24-Hour Fitness** (923-9090; Pacific Beach Hotel, 2490 Kalākaua Ave.) where you can let it loose. Join resident moms in Waikīkī's Kapi'olani Park for **Stroller Strides** (371-6904; www.strollerstrides.com), a mother/baby stroller workout walk at 8:45 AM Mondays, Wednesdays, and Fridays. Meet near the Aquarium. **The Waikīkī Community Center** (923-1802; www.waikikicommunitycenter.org; 310 Paokalani Ave.) features a schedule of creative pay-as-you-go classes such as Big Band dance, gentle yoga, hula, and Okinawan karate.

Yoga Under the Palm Trees (373-8833) takes place on the grass between the Waikīkī Aquarium and Natatorium on Kalākaua Avenue 8–9 AM Mondays. **Yoga Works Hawai'i** (366-4856) meets in Kapi'olani Park across from the Natatorium on Kalākaua Avenue 5–6 PM Mondays, Wednesdays, and Fridays.

GREATER HONOLULU

A few athletic steps outside of Waikīkī is the **Central YMCA** (401 Atkinson Dr., Ala Moana), with a pool, full workout facility, and classes.

WINDWARD O'AHU

Bikram Yoga College of India (262-6886; 600 Kailua Rd., Suite 205, Kailua) will sweat the toxins out and limber you up.

NORTH SHORE

Bikram Yoga North Shore (637-5700; 67-208 Goodale Ave., Suite 2, Waialua) likewise conducts yoga in a 100-degree-plus room for maximum sweat factor.

Games

In addition to the ideas below, game-heads might check local papers for Scrabble®, chess, and backgammon club gatherings.

Waikīkī

Big Kahuna's **3D Glow Golf** (924-3030; Waikīkī Shopping Plaza, 2250 Kalākaua Ave.) is open daily 10–10 and yes, indeed, it is glow-in-the-dark miniature golf.

Greater Honolulu

Dave & Busters (589-2215; 1030 Auahi St., Kaka'ako) can satisfy any extreme video game itch you might have and is open from lunchtime until at least midnight. **Hawaiian Brian's** (946-1343; 1680 Kapi'olani Blvd., Ala Moana) is within walking distance of Waikīkī and is the best pool hall on the island. Doors stay open from 8 AM until 4 AM—and the facility is smoke-free. **Jungle Fun** (949-4905; Ala Moana Center, 1450 Ala Moana Blvd., Ala Moana) is a mostly kid-oriented video and parlor game room surrounded by a squawking pack of plush animal critters.

Sporting Events

College sports—and even high school sports—are a big deal here. At the University of Hawaii at Mānoa (UHM), the women's volleyball team is renowned and the girls are local stars. Catch a game if you can. Polo has a long history in Hawai'i, and even Prince Charles has played here. Dress is totally casual, and pre-game tailgating encouraged.

Greater Honolulu

Contact the **University of Hawai'i at Mānoa** (944-2697 tickets; 956-4481 24-hour Rainbow Sports Hotline; www.uhathletics.hawaii.edu) for information on college-level volleyball, basketball, baseball, football, and so forth.

Windward O'ahu

The **Honolulu Polo Club** (www.honolulupolo.com) plays Sundays at 2:30, June through October, at the Waimānalo polo grounds on Kalaniana'ole Highway (the entrance is across from McDonald's). Gates open at 1 PM.

North Shore

The **Hawai'i Polo Club** (637-8401; www.hawaiipolo.com) plays every Sunday at 2, May through September, out at Mokulēi'a Polo Field off Farrington Highway (HI 930). Gates open at 11, and they have food vendors as well as a bar.

Many Waikiki stores stay open until 11 at night for your shopping pleasure.

8

Shopping

Taking It to the Limit

Shopping is a sport for both O'ahu residents and visitors, and new stores seem to open (and close) nearly every day. From Waikīkī to the North Shore, you will find plenty of opportunities to get it out of your system with everything from sharktooth necklaces to Versace bags.

Because Honolulu is so spread out, we don't really have a "town square"—thank goodness all roads lead to the gargantuan Ala Moana Center, which serves as a central meeting place for the entire island. Everyone turns up at Ala Moana, from celebrities cruising Harry Winston's to local homies strumming 'ukulele and playing cards next to Longs Drugs. Once the nation's largest shopping center, by early 2008 it will be home to nearly 320 excellent stores, restaurants, and other businesses.

Royal Hawaiian Shopping Center's façade has recently transformed from parking lot chic to understated glamour.

Waikīkī shopping becomes more upscale every year, and in 2007 it made a major leap with the new Waikīkī Beach Walk complex (the largest development project in Waikīkī's history) and an $84-million upgrade to Royal Hawaiian Shopping Center. The wide variety of visitors Waikīkī attracts explains how Gucci can be on the same block with 1 2 3 Fashion, and how **International Market Place** (971-2080; 2330 Kalakaua Ave.), a 1950s "Mecca" for suspect trinkets of every size and shape, persists in popularity (we must admit that walking through it can be entertainingly surreal).

Be sure to tune in for around-town craft fair events, such as the adorable **Mission Houses Museum Holiday Craft Fair** (531-0481, Mission Houses Museum, 553 S. King St., Downtown) every late November, which has some of the most authentic and well made Hawaiiana you'll find anywhere. The 700-vendor **Aloha Stadium Swap Meet** (486-6704; Aloha Stadium, 99-500 Salt Lake Blvd., 'Aiea) held every Wednesday, Saturday, and Sunday 6–3 is another popular resident and visitor destination, although we feel that 90 percent of it is the same trinkety junk sold at International Market Place. If you go, hone in on the unusual booths selling dried octopus snacks and other true local treasures and tidbits.

This chapter could become a book if we honored every worthy store, so we are going to assume you can find your way to The Gap and focus on unique vendors whenever possible.

APPAREL

Local folks actually own other pieces of clothing besides tent mu'umu'u and shorts, although most of us do treasure our island wear. Here is a smattering of great apparel shops that cover a wide range of styles and needs. And while Honolulu can't begin to compare with the trendy boutique atmosphere of cities like San Francisco and New York, you will still find a few artsy, hip shops here and there, usually with an exotic-chic emphasis.

An Aloha Wear Primer

If you are not from Hawai'i, all aloha shirts and mu'umu'u probably look alike—but that's about as true as saying all beers or wines look and taste the same. Allow us to refine your palate and encourage you to purchase at least one quality aloha item and live the spirit.

One rule of thumb is to assume that the majority of aloha wear sold in Waikīkī, especially in cheap-looking trinket shops, is Tourist Garb. Unless making a funky, vintage-oriented fashion statement, longtime residents do not wear screaming colors, parrot patterns, or anything else that may remind you of Jimmy Buffet, *Magnum P. I.*, or the state of Florida.

For men, classic aloha shirts should be of sturdy, good quality cotton, with either large or small muted, two- or multi-tone organic patterns that blur at a distance. The straight-bottom shirt can be worn untucked with shorts or pants, if the length's right, or tucked in and worn with a belt for a more formal look. Most men in Honolulu's financial district wear aloha shirts to work on a daily basis—even those who moved here recently from the Mainland. A good shirt will set you back between $45 and $90, and some of the best brands are Kahala, Ono, Tori Richard, Diamond Head, Cooke Street, and the venerable Reyn's (although each also has a "tourist" line that defies local tastes).

Mu'umu'u are a dying breed, with today's Island women preferring less conservative looks. But an elegant cotton or rayon mu'umu'u worn for special events, such as a family celebration or even Christmas dinner at the country club, especially by older women, is a well-respected statement that says, "I'm not afraid to embrace and perpetuate Hawai'i's traditions." Graceful, full-length mu'umu'u usually cost well over $150, and the ultimate look includes layering on a luxurious necklace made from Ni'ihau shells or pearls, or wearing a handmade woven hat with a *haku* lei band. The right shoes are usually muted, dressier sandals. Like aloha shirts, mu'umu'u rarely scream color or pattern—they should be soft paletted and either fan out slowly from the body like nightgowns or be fitted, with flattering, even mildly ornate, necklines and sleeves. Look for designs by Mamo Howell, Manuheali'i, and Princess Ka'iulani.

One last nugget of aloha wear information: Unless you are performing in a Hawaiian music trio or Japanese punk rock band, skip buying the his-and-hers sets.

Aloha Wear

Waikīkī

Hilo Hattie (Royal Hawaiian Shopping Center, 2201 Kalākaua Ave.) No disrespect, but Hilo Hattie isn't the greatest place to buy authentic aloha wear, despite its fame. Designs have improved lately and this new location (opening in 2008) will be enormous—potentially housing a funky gem or two. However, the company has long been known to provide a touristy experience from start to finish, and their fabric is generally a poly blend.

Reyn's (923-0331; Sheraton Waikīkī, 2255 Kalākaua Ave.) Although we have noticed that this Reyn's location offers a few shirts that would not sell well outside of Waikīkī, overall they carry a prime selection of true aloha shirts for which they are famous.

Tori Richard (924-1811; Hyatt Regency, 2424 Kalākaua Ave.) Tori Richard is a local, 50-year-old family-run business that designs and produces high quality, unique men's and women's aloha wear and other clothing, often in silk, plus jewelry with an artsy Asiatic flair.

Greater Honolulu

Bailey's Antiques & Aloha Shirts (734-7628; 517 Kapahulu Ave., Kapahulu) Aged and musty stuff overflows here, but it's well known to those wanting used and vintage aloha shirts at a few bucks on up. They have more than fifteen thousand to choose from.

Macy's (941-2345; Ala Moana Center, 1450 Ala Moana Blvd., Ala Moana) This is the Macy's mother ship in Hawai'i—and you will find a broad collection of men's and women's aloha wear here, although the aloha shirts are better than the mu'umu'u.

Mamo Howell (591-2002; Ward Warehouse, 1050 Ala Moana Blvd., Ala Moana) Over the years former fashion model and hula dancer Mamo has become well known for her beautiful mu'umu'u designs, as well as her aloha wear for men and children.

Tori Richard is a well-known local clothing label with 50 years of history.

Reyn's (949-5929; Ala Moana Center, 1450 Ala Moana Blvd., Ala Moana) Reyn's didn't invent aloha shirts, but they might as well have. Their reverse-print styles have become the definitive word in what an aloha shirt should look and feel like. Each year they come out with a new Christmas shirt that is a must-have for many of Honolulu's executives.

Reyn's Rack (524-1885; 125 Merchant St., Downtown) Want a Reyn's shirt, but can't pay the price? Head to the Rack for an oldie but goodie.

Sears (947-0399; Ala Moana Center, 1450 Ala Moana Blvd., Ala Moana) Yes, Sears. We were surprised to discover a relatively large goldmine of decent to great aloha shirts here at good prices, including several notable brands. Their mu'umu'u are not recommended.

A typical day of aloha shirts and mu'umu'u, right in the heart of the financial district.

Windward O'ahu

Macy's (235-6612; Windward Mall, 46-056 Kamehameha Hwy., Kāne'ohe) Even on the windward side, Macy's is a good stop for aloha wear shopping, especially shirts. In addition to the location above, there is a smaller store in Kailua (537 Kailua Rd.), but their selection is surprisingly touristy, with some suspect mu'umu'u.

Manuheali'i (261-9865; 629 Kailua Rd., Kailua) Manuheali'i's original location features contemporary mu'umu'u and other aloha wear inspired by garden florals and Hawaiian quilting. These pieces meld aloha vintage and modern with their large, bold, bright, simple patterns and up-to-date cuts.

North Shore

Kohala Bay Collections (293-2728; Turtle Bay Resort, 57-091 Kamehameha Hwy., Kahuku) This shop is located in the hotel lobby and has a pretty decent selection of aloha shirts, as well as other resort wear items.

Flower Power: The Lei

Residents give lei to honor almost any special occasion, such as a birthday, graduation, or retirement—or even to welcome a keynote speaker or friend from the Mainland. Our favorite place to buy lei is in Chinatown, and the grand dame of Chinatown lei shops is the family owned **Cindy's Lei & Flower Shoppe** (536-6538; 1034 Maunakea St., Chinatown). Request to peek in the back to see their lei makers at work.

You will pay anywhere from a few dollars to more than $50 for a lei, depending on the rarity of the flower and complexity of design. Some have no fragrance, such as the basic purple dendrobium orchid lei visitors often receive at lū'au, while ginger, tuberose, pikake, and many others illuminate a room with their perfume. Many people choose based on personal preference, but selecting a lei can also be an art, as some flowers and lei types carry cultural connotations.

Treat lei with grace and respect, as you would a Christmas tree or beautiful bouquet. A lei should never dangle from your neck like a cowbell; instead, adjust it so about a third falls gently over your back. If it has a ribbon bow, rotate the lei until the bow rests about where broaches are pinned. If you are giving a lei to someone else, follow the local custom of placing it over the recipient's shoulders so it lies in the correct position and follow it with a hug and perhaps even a peck on the cheek.

Lei sellers once lined the docks, and even Honolulu's airport. Photo courtesy Hawai'i State Archives.

Artsy, Trendy, and Vintage Boutiques

Waikīkī

88 Tees (922-8832; 2168 Kalākaua Ave.) Vintage and used clothing, a hip line of tight tees, and a Japanese pop atmosphere make this hidden and very groovy spot a welcome relief from Waikīkī's straight-and-narrow. 88 Tees has three locations in Waikīkī, but the other two are signature T-shirt shops only.

Cina Cina (926-0444; Royal Hawaiian Hotel, 2259 Kalākaua Ave.) Located at the world-famous Royal Hawaiian Hotel, this lovely little shop is a serene pleasure. Unique and artistic Asiatic and European clothing, jewelry, and home décor items all reveal style, charm, and subdued trendiness.

Cinnamon Girl (922-5536, 2365 Kalākaua Ave.) Cinnamon Girl boutiques carry girlie clothing ranging from sweet to sexy, and their styles are fun and playful for any age. They also specialize in surprisingly cool matching mom–daughter sets. The shops are locally owned and the designs locally created.

Diesel (923-5510; 2160 Kalākaua Ave.) A worldwide chain of hot clothing for men and women, this definitely is hot—and perfect for Honolulu's club life, even if the styles are not exactly unique.

Noa Noa (949-8980, Hilton Hawaiian Village, 2005 Kalia Rd.) Although their upscale silken scarves, dresses, and shirts are hand-printed batik, they are not at all hippie or corny. Prints feature Polynesian tapa-cloth-style designs and have primitive art appeal.

Pineapple County (926-8245; 342 Lewers St.) Fun and frisky, your sales hostesses will be lanky Japanese nationals with intense lipstick and stacked hairdos—and clothing will range from super skinny jeans to play tops. A special rack of quality, pre-loved aloha shirts are an anomaly, but a bargain at under $10.

GREATER HONOLULU

Aloha Rag (589-1352; 1221 Kapi'olani Blvd., Kaka'ako) Totally hip and vaguely funky, little Aloha Rag attracts the young Japanese crowd that knows cool stuff when they see it. They also have a few home décor items.

Anne Namba (589-1135; 1-877-578-0001; 324 Kamani St., Kaka'ako) For those with sophisticated tastes and an appreciation for fine textiles and art, this small shop is a must-visit. Vintage kimono, obi, and silk fuse with updated Hawaiian classics for one-of-a-kind pieces, and the wedding dresses are gorgeous. Namba frequently creates the costumes for Hawai'i's operas, where both patrons and performers appear in her designs.

Betsey Johnson (949-3500; Ala Moana Center, 1450 Ala Moana Blvd., Ala Moana) Some of you will feel relieved to know this flirty girl shop is here if you need it.

Bonheur (944-8744; Ala Moana Center, 1450 Ala Moana Blvd., Ala Moana) We found the perfect mix of low-key and celebrity hip at this precious little boutique. The only store in the state to carry pieces by Australia's Alice McCall, Brazil's Maria Bonita Extra, and France's Jee Vice, you will also find one-of-a-kind, locally crafted jewelry that completes the tailored and trendy international girl.

Cupcake Boutique (597-8305; Ward Centre, 1200 Ala Moana Blvd., Kaka'ako) Hip and hot mamas with babies will enjoy this little fashion boutique that offers unique gear and clothing for both.

Cina Cina at Waikīkī's Royal Hawaiian Hotel is filled with hip and unique little treasures from Asia and Europe.

Juicy Couture (942-7700; Ala Moana Center, 1450 Ala Moana Blvd., Ala Moana) With the right touch of sass and low-key for Hawai'i, this Mainland chain caught on instantly.

MisFortune (597-1556; Ward Centre, 1200 Ala Moana Blvd., Kaka'ako) Up-to-the-minute dresses, tees, velour beach shorts, and denim fill this teeny, cool shop. The perfect work dress hangs right next to the dress that says it's time to play.

Shanghai Tang (942-9800; Ala Moana Center, 1450 Ala Moana Blvd., Ala Moana) These very upscale, Shanghai-classic-inspired designs work for every age group. Check it out—the stores are found only in Asia, New York, Paris, Zurich, London, and Honolulu.

Shasa Emporium (735-5122; Kahala Mall, 4211 Wai'alae Ave., Kahala) You will find more than 250 trendy brands to pick from here, including Fighting Eel and Citizens of Humanity.

More Local Fashion Tips

Okay, now you've got the "411" on local-style aloha wear—but why stop there? For those of you who made a mental note when *Sex and the City's* Carrie told Berger that real Manhattan women would never wear a scrunchie, these Hawai'i fashion tips are for you.

Hawai'i Don'ts	Hawai'i Do's
Tevas® or Birkenstocks®	Slippers (split-toe flip-flops)
Plastic ABC Store shell necklaces	"International" ethnic beads, modern metal designs
"Hawai'i" or "Waikīkī" T-shirts	Local event or business advertisement tees
Tie-dyed rayon dresses/fringed sarongs	Hip, cutie-pie tube dresses or solid wraps
Bright bikinis embellished with glitz	Toned-down "surfer girl" styles
Cowgirl or British explorer hats	Cool caps or finely made Panamas with feather or dried lei hatbands
Muscle tees, neon tanks, or athletic shorts	Surf Company shirts, cotton boardshorts
Fussy or heavy makeup	Bare skin or "natural glow" makeup

Windward O'ahu

ADASA (263-8500; 602 Kailua Rd., Kailua) This local boutique specializes in upscale, trendy designer clothing for women and men, plus shoes, handbags, jewelry, and lingerie, ranging from brands such as Lacoste to Buddhist Punk to Diane von Furstenberg to Theory.

Global Village (262-8183; Kailua Village Shops, 539 Kailua Rd., Kailua) Pick up hip apparel with Kailua attitude, plus beads, jewelry, and other tidbits from around the world.

Mary Z's (263-1221; Kailua Shopping Center, 572 Kailua Rd., Kailua) Find dresses, jeans, and wraps, plus jewelry and other little gifts to fill in the gaps. Styles range from modestly trendy to middle-of-the-road.

North Shore

Silver Moon Emporium (637-7710; North Shore Marketplace, 66-250 Kamehameha Hwy., Hale'iwa) Most of the North Shore revels in tourist boho, so we were relieved to find a store where Betsey Johnson was as strong a muse as Stevie Nicks. Original and stylish handbags and shoes peek out from behind rows of dresses and skirts, ensuring there is something for all types.

Swimwear

Gals, we all know that finding the right bathing suit can be daunting. In Hawai'i, the hottest bikinis and one-pieces are toned-down floral prints and solids with very few embellishments. Skip the thong and leave jewelry at home.

Guys, let surf clothing shops hook you up with the coolest boardshorts—see some shop listings below under "Surf and Other Sporting Gear." Go long on length and mellow in either floral print or solid colors. Skip the 1980s new wave patterns and avoid wearing your bathing suit with homeboy tennis shoes or sandals (pick up some slippers!). A tip for anyone with pale skin: Avoid black, navy, and red and go with less contrasting colors that warm your skin tone.

Rash guards for men, women, and children are available at most surf shops. These snug, water-friendly shirts not only protect bellies from chaffing on bodyboards, but also can keep the sun from scorching you into a coma while you swim. Local folks are snapping 'em up.

Waikīkī

Allure Swimwear (926-1174; Royal Hawaiian Shopping Center, 2201 Kalākaua Ave.) One of the best swimwear collections for teen girls and women on the island is at Allure—styles are hot and trendy, and selection is copious. Allure also has a second location in Waikīkī (949-6651; Hilton Hawaiian Village, 2005 Kalia Rd.).

Loco Boutique (922-7160; Outrigger East Hotel, 150 Ka'iulani Ave.) These "bad girl" bikinis are unique and playful, with a touch of JLo flirt and urban sass. They also have a second Waikīkī location (926-7131; Waikīkī Outrigger Malia Hotel, 358 Royal Hawaiian Ave.).

Macy's (926-5217; 2314 Kalākaua Ave.) The Waikīkī Macy's has so many bathing suits that it opened a separate boutique to house them, next to the store itself. Whether you're a moody teenage girl or a mature woman hoping for a forgiving yet modern cut, you will probably find your bikini here.

Greater Honolulu

Macy's (941-2345; Ala Moana Center, 1450 Ala Moana Blvd., Ala Moana) Pick through a mountain of great styles at their main store location.

Splash! Hawai'i (942-1010; Ala Moana Center, 1450 Ala Moana Blvd., Ala Moana) One of the hottest places on the island to purchase a bikini, enter only when your tan and physique are already paid for.

North Shore

North Shore Swimwear (637-7000; North Shore Marketplace, 66-250 Kamehameha Hwy., Hale'iwa) Tons of styles, tons of fabrics, tons of patterns—take one to go or design your own for a custom-built bikini or one-piece at a price you can afford. Let them give you the perfect fit at last!

ANTIQUES AND COLLECTIBLES

Old is new again, and Hawai'i is no exception. Although Honolulu's hardly a quaint antique-shop town, vintage collectible and antique stores are tucked into little nooks around the island, with special emphasis on Asiatic and Hawaiiana pieces. In addition to the list below, head to **Kilohana Square** (1016 Kapahulu Ave., Kapahulu) just outside of Waikīkī to dig through **Mills Gallery**, **Shangri-La Asia**, and **T-Fujii**, which all feature Asiatic arts and antiques.

The Hawai'i All-Collectors Show and **Wiki Wiki One-Day Collectibles & Hawaiiana Show** (941-9754; Blaisdell Arena, 777 Ward Ave.) take place several times per year and yield unique vintage souvenirs.

WAIKĪKĪ

Antique House (923-5101; Royal Hawaiian Hotel, 2259 Kalākaua Ave.) The family owned and operated Antique House has resided at the venerable Royal Hawaiian Hotel for 40 years, and though it's small, it carries authentic and remarkable pieces from China's Ming (1368-1644 AD) and Ching (1644-1911 AD) dynasties. These are treasures you'll cherish for a lifetime.

Rock Island Café (923-8033; King's Village, 131 Ka'iulani Ave.) This funky burger joint also serves up a bit of new and old memorabilia, such as celebrity autographs and Elvis Christmas ornaments.

GREATER HONOLULU

Antique Alley (941-8551; 1347 Kapi'olani Blvd., Ala Moana) Antique Alley is dusty, jumbled, crowded, and surreal—the way a good antiques and collectibles store should be. Chock full of stuff from old and new Hawai'i and elsewhere, poke through their estate jewelry, ivory, old prints, bottles, cameras, and more.

Garakuta-Do (589-2262; 435 Koula St., Kaka'ako) Make the effort to find this incredibly atmospheric Japanese shop behind Ward Avenue. It is the ultimate source for traditional Japanese chests, old doors, antique kimono, teapots, and obi.

Lai Fong (537-3497; 1118 Nu'uanu Ave., Downtown) This is a small, family owned shop specializing in Chinese antiques and other curios, ranging from Pan Am flight bags to jade sculptures. Lai Fong was a picture bride who arrived in Hawai'i from Canton; she opened the store approximately 70 years ago. Call first—they keep odd hours.

Robyn Buntin of Honolulu (523-5913; 1-877-728-6846; 848 S. Beretania St., Makiki) A spacious interior displays quality ivory carvings, Chinese paintings, Buddhist artwork, textiles, and more from past and present Asia and the Pacific; a specialized staff will help you discover just the right piece.

WINDWARD O'AHU

Ali'i Antiques I and II (261-1705; 21 and 9A Maluniu Ave., Kailua) Lots of stuff here for the curious. Shop I carries mountains of goods such as vintage dishware, knick-knacks, jewelry, beads, and dolls. Shop II is stacked with Hawaiiana—including furniture, paintings, poi pounders, and other collectibles.

Antiques & Treasures (263-1177; 315 Uluniu St., Kailua) This charming shop was the longtime dream of owner Mihye Seo Cortese, who emigrated from Korea. She carries a variety of smaller Asiatic, European, and Hawaiian pieces from more than a dozen vendors, and welcomes visitors to enjoy a cup of tea and "talk story."

Window shopping at Chinatown's little Lai Fong is almost as delicious as going inside.

Heritage Antiques & Gifts (261-8700; 767 Kailua Rd., Kailua) Bury yourself in endless little curios from around the world, including carvings, estate jewelry, crystal, rocking chairs, figurines, and snuff bottles.

NORTH SHORE

The Only Show in Town (293-1295; 56-901 Kamehameha Hwy., Kahuku) Located inside the old Tanaka Plantation Store near Turtle Bay Resort, this collectibles shop overflows with Japanese dolls, glass net fishing floats, license plates, and a host of other appealing nuggets, as well as plenty of atmosphere. Owner Paul is an entertaining host.

BOOKS AND MUSIC

Below we have listed the main bookstores on the island, but don't forget that great collections can also by found in every museum shop. Try **The Academy Shop** (532-8703; Honolulu Academy of Arts, 900 S. Beretania St., Makiki) for an impressive, international collection of art books; **the Museum Gift Shop** (531-0481; Mission Houses Museum, 553 S. King St., Downtown) for Hawai'i-related books; and **Shop Pacifica** (848-4158; Bishop Museum, 1525 Bernice St., Kalihi), which also specializes in Hawai'i-related materials and has its own press. See Chapter 9 for a sampling of recommended volumes.

With Tower Records recently closing its doors, O'ahu has a visible absence of sizeable

CD shops—however, most of the bookstores below have relatively strong selections of Hawaiian music.

WAIKĪKĪ

Bestsellers Books & Music (953-2378; Hilton Hawaiian Village, 2005 Kalia Rd.) This is a tiny outlet featuring some front-runner books, including Hawai'i-related, as well as a few Hawaiian CDs.

Borders Express (922-4154; Waikīkī Shopping Plaza, 2270 Kalākaua Ave.) The only large general bookstore in Waikīkī is open late and also features a small selection of Hawaiian CDs

GREATER HONOLULU

Barnes & Noble (949-7307; Ala Moana Center, 1450 Ala Moana Blvd., Ala Moana) This is the only real bookstore at Ala Moana, and it has all the features you've come to expect from the chain—including endless magazines, books, bargain tables, and a café. They have a strong Hawaiiana book and CD selection.

Bestsellers Books & Music (528-2378; 1001 Bishop St., Downtown) With a surprising range of Hawai'i-related materials often reduced to excellent prices, this small, modern shop is a good browse. They also carry Hawaiian music CDs.

Borders Books & Music (591-8995; Ward Centre, 1200 Ala Moana Blvd., Ala Moana) A 30,000-square-foot store with the requisite café and late hours, you'll have access to many Hawai'i-related books and CDs, as well as material on all other subjects.

Native Books/Nā Mea Hawai'i (596-8885; Ward Warehouse, 1050 Ala Moana Blvd., Kaka'ako) A locally owned shop that carries an excellent selection of Hawaiiana books, plus Hawaiian music CDs.

WINDWARD O'AHU

BookEnds (261-1996; 600 Kailua Rd., Kailua) For those hunkering down on the windward side of the island, especially in the Kailua area, BookEnds takes special pride in its Hawaiiana collection and has a cozy bookstore feel.

Borders Express (235-8044; Windward Mall, 46-056 Kamehameha Hwy., Kāne'ohe) This "mini" Borders still carries plenty of books, as well as a collection of CDs.

Hungry Ear Records & Tapes (262-2175; 418 Ku'ulei Rd., Kailua) This is your classic itty-bitty, rundown, ska/punk/Hawaiian/classical/reggae/hip hop CD, record, and tape shop.

Hawaiian CD Must-Haves

We won't even pretend that this list begins to recognize the numerous past and present artists who deserve your attention—however it's a start, and the suggestions below are fairly accessible. We've skipped the "Little Brown Gal" stuff in favor of music most residents enjoy today, and they are listed in alphabetical order (not order of importance). Most have won prestigious local awards—and several have been nominated for, or won, Grammys®.

Amy Hānaiali'i Gilliom: *Generation Hawai'i*
Brothers Cazimero: *Best of the Brothers Cazimero, Vol. I*
Cecilio & Kapono: *Elua*
Dennis Pavao: *All Hawai'i Stand Together*
Eddie Kamae: *Sons of Hawai'i*

Gabby Pahinui: *Best of the Gabby Band 1972-1977*
Hui 'Ohana: *Best of Hui 'Ohana II*
Israel Kamakawiwo'ole: *Facing Future*
Ledward Ka'apana: *Grandmaster Slack Key Guitar*
Makaha Sons: *Ke Alaula*
Māunalua: *Maunalua*
Na Palapalai: *Ke 'Ala Beauty*
Otomana: *Like a Seabird in the Wind*
Raiatea Helm: *Sweet & Lovely*
Slack Key Guitar Vol. 2 (compilation of artists)
Sunday Manoa: *Guava Jam*

GALLERIES

It is no surprise that many artists are attracted to the inspirational beauty of Hawai'i and eventually make O'ahu their home. Like countless scenic and heavily visited regions of the world, Hawai'i galleries now swell with watercolor paintings of abandoned coastlines, lone cabins in misty glens, leaping dolphin sculptures, and the like—especially in Waikīkī and Hale'iwa. **Wyland Galleries Hawai'i**, **Galerie Lassen**, and **Tabora Gallery**, all found along Waikīkī's main strip, specialize in these themes.

If you are looking for a good price on mostly landscape paintings, walk over to Waikīkī's **Art on the Zoo Fence** (www.zoofence.com/art.html), on the right-hand side of the Honolulu Zoo. For decades, bands of artists have set up lawn chairs every weekend and hung up their works here; some of them have made a name for themselves over time.

Another good option is to check local papers for special gallery exhibitions by the **Hawai'i Watercolor Society** (521-9799), **Honolulu Printmakers** (536-5507), and other guilds. We have seen very high quality landscapes and floral themes at the shows, and the pieces are often for sale.

Not all of Hawai'i's artists are into scenery or still life, so if you have other tastes you have got some options. You'll find portraiture, ceramics, sculpture, jewelry, and other creative and modern artifacts, as well as traditional Polynesian crafts with distinction and beauty. Downtown area galleries tend to be more progressive, but most struggle to survive.

If you enjoy poking into little establishments, snacking, and socializing, we hope you are in Honolulu on the first Friday of the month for the 5 to 9 PM **First Friday downtown gallery walk** (739-9797). Hundreds, sometimes thousands, of visitors and residents head downtown to flit like trick-or-treaters from one gallery to the next, and **The ARTS** at Marks Garage is the hub where you can pick up a gallery map. Dress up, dress down—it doesn't matter. You'll see punks and heiresses alike, all out for some simple fun and to be seen. The nearby **Hawai'i State Art Museum** also holds free Hawaiian music concerts and other events on its front lawn those nights.

WAIKĪKĪ

Jeff Chang Pottery & Fine Crafts (924-5135; Waikīkī Shopping Plaza, 2250 Kalākaua Ave.) Jeff Chang's work is well regarded, and his shops are great places to purchase his pottery, as well as handcrafted items from all over the country. A second store is located in the **Sheraton Waikīkī** (923-8382; 2255 Kalākaua Ave.). Both of his Waikīkī stores have strong glitz factors compared to his Kailua location.

Greater Honolulu

The ARTS at Marks Garage (521-2903; www.artsatmarks.com; 1159 Nu'uanu Ave., Chinatown). Marks Garage is one of Honolulu's finest and most eclectic collaborative art galleries, as well as a performance and office space for businesses and nonprofits. Shows rotate frequently; you might see a Hawai'i Watercolor Society exhibit one week and an Indonesian cultural event the next. It is also the hub for the wildly popular monthly downtown art walk event, First Friday.

A crowd of First Friday gallery hoppers hover outside The Pegge Hopper Gallery.

The Art Treasures (536-7789; 1136 Nu'uanu Ave., Chinatown) Small and artfully uncluttered, this shop carries antique and ancient, as well as modern, internationally-collected textiles, pottery, jewelry, and other pieces. Everything seems carefully handpicked, your host is warm and welcoming, and prices are often very reasonable.

Bethel Street Gallery (524-3552; 1140 Bethel St., Downtown) Striking oil paintings with an emphasis on modern figures, large ceramic works, and glass are some of the finds at this gallery. Artist owned and operated, all pieces are created by Hawai'i artists, some of them well known.

The Gallery at Ward Centre (597-8034; Ward Centre, 1200 Ala Moana Blvd., Kaka'ako) A cooperative of well-known O'ahu artists, this small gallery has fine works in paper, clay, scratchboard, oils, watercolors, collages, woodblocks, lithographs, glass, jewelry, and more. The artists themselves tend the gallery in rotating shifts.

Louis Pohl Gallery (521-1812; 1111 Nu'uanu Ave., Chinatown) Dedicated to the spirit of Hawai'i's well-known painter Louis Pohl, this gallery features paintings and fine art prints by a collection of resident artists, as well as other Hawai'i artists.

The Pegge Hopper Gallery (524-1160; 1164 Nu'uanu Ave., Chinatown) Hopper's works are well known on the Mainland, as well as in Hawai'i, and are found in both private collections and museums. Her signature paintings feature sumptuous Hawaiian women in bold graphic shapes and pastel colors. Her gallery often rotates works of other artists as well, and is a major draw during First Friday events.

Mark N. Brown Gallery (227-1710; 1170 Nu'uanu Ave., Chinatown) Local boy Mark Brown has earned a strong reputation for his vibrant, Hawai'i-themed *plein air* paintings and figures. His work hangs in many fine businesses, hotels, and galleries, and his gallery buzzes on First Fridays.

WINDWARD O'AHU

The Balcony Gallery (263-4434; 442A Uluniu St., Kailua) Founded by several well-known local artists, this small gallery plays with progressive themes and pieces from a variety of artists and media. Call before you go—hours vary.

Jeff Chang Pottery & Fine Crafts (262-4060; Kailua Village Shops, 539 Kailua Rd., Kailua) Jeff's Kailua location is a great place to purchase handcrafted items from all over the country, in addition to the artist's own striking pottery pieces.

HAWAIIANA AND OTHER GIFTS

Gift registries aside, a perfect wedding or special birthday present for someone back home may be a handcrafted koa wood bowl, Hawaiian quilt, or even Ni'ihau shell necklace—all of which are highly esteemed works of art. Below are several excellent places to find large and small treasures to fit anyone's budget.

WAIKĪKĪ

Hawaiian Quilt Collection (922-2462; Royal Hawaiian Hotel, 2259 Kalākaua Ave.) The unique styles and philosophy of Hawaiian quilting began with the introduction of the art by missionaries, and carefully crafted quilt works still carry great prestige and value. This beautiful shop also has a second Waikīkī location (926-5272; Hyatt Regency Waikīkī, 2424 Kalākaua Ave., 2nd Floor.).

Little Hawaiian Gift Shop (926-2662; Royal Hawaiian Shopping Center, 2201 Kalākaua Ave.) In business since 1968, this special nook features quality work from more than one hundred local artists and emphasizes traditional crafts, such as koa bowls, classic Hawaiian-style feather hatbands, and delicate shell necklaces.

Mana Hawai'i (923-2220; Waikīkī Beach Walk, 226 Lewers St., 2nd Floor) A must. This new shop is a cooperative of authentic cultural purveyers and contains quality products.

Martin & McArthur (923-5333; Hyatt Regency Waikīkī, 2424 Kalākaua Ave.) If you want exclusive, handcrafted native koa products such as a rocking chair, hand mirror, bowl, jewelry box, or even cribbage board, this is your store. Lustrously magnificent koa wood is highly valued, so prepare to dish out a bit of cash for the perfect gift or lifelong memento.

Nohea Gallery (923-6644; Moana Surfrider, 2365 Kalākaua Ave.) Another locally owned business known for quality Hawaiiana and other arts and crafts is Nohea Gallery. They represent more than 450 artists, most whom live and work in Hawai'i. Choose from handcrafted koa boxes, ceramic pieces, paintings, jewelry, and more.

GREATER HONOLULU

The Academy Shop (532-8703; Honolulu Academy of Arts, 900 S. Beretania St., Makiki) The Honolulu Academy of Art's elegant store features 1,500 square feet of art books, textiles, handcrafted bowls and glassware, artistic jewelry, posters, stationery, basic Hawaiiana, and much more—all great gifts for someone else, or yourself. This is a must-visit for anyone with upscale artistic leanings.

The outstandingly tasteful Academy Shop at the Honolulu Academy of Arts is well worth your while.

Artlines (941-1445; Ala Moana Center, 1450 Ala Moana Blvd., Ala Moana) Jewelry, bronze sculptures, tribal masks, and other exotic items from around the world fill this fascinating little store.

Kamaka Hawai'i (531-3165; 550 South St., Downtown) It's a touch out of your way. It's expensive. And you'll wait six weeks or more for your product. But you'll get the best 'ukulele available. Whether you are a seasoned performer or have a passion for collecting beautiful musical instruments from around the world, this 92-year-old shop can craft you a prize.

The Museum Shop (523-3447; The Contemporary Museum, 2411 Makiki Heights Dr., Tantalus) From wondrous to funkalicious, this colorful little gem at the Contemporary Museum has something for everyone.

Native Books/Nā Mea Hawai'i (596-8885; Ward Warehouse, 1050 Ala Moana Blvd., Kaka'ako) An outstanding selection of Hawai'i-related books and CDs, as well as a wide variety of higher-end, artisan-made crafts ranging from handmade sachets to extremely valuable Ni'ihau shell necklaces, makes this one of the best places to shop for an authentic

Hawaiiana gift. Also visit their pocket-sized shop in Waikīkī, **Nā Mea Hawai'i** (949-3989; Hilton Hawaiian Village, 2005 Kalia Rd.).

Red Pineapple (593-2733; Ward Centre, 1200 Ala Moana Blvd., Kaka'ako) When you've maxed out on Hawaiian gifts and want something that feels more Paris or San Francisco inspired, turn to the little Red Pineapple and find Dean & Deluca products, mega-awesome totes in the hippest colors and patterns (on Oprah's "O" List), things for baby, and more.

Shop Pacifica (848-4158; Bishop Museum, 1525 Bernice St., Kalihi) Count on this museum shop to provide quality Hawaiian crafts from Ni'ihau shell necklaces to model canoes, plus posters and an excellent selection of books.

WINDWARD O'AHU

Island Treasures (261-8131; 629 Kailua Rd., Kailua) Although Island Treasures contains a few borderline-touristy trinkets, it also features beautiful objects such as Hawaiian quilts, striking pottery, koa wood crafts, and paintings, all made by Hawai'i artists—including several that are of local renown.

Kailua Beachwalk (263-1082; Malama Bldg., 602 Kailua Rd., Kailua) Relatively cool and timeless stuff—including hippie chic dresses, candles, woven doormats, "antique" signage, knick-knacks, furniture, men's hats, and more—crowd this surprisingly large gift-oriented shop.

Nohea Island Arts (261-5888; 767 Kailua Rd., Kailua) Nohea Galleries represents about 450 local artists; their Windward O'ahu shop is tucked away at the entrance to Kailua. Glasswork, ceramics, wooden bowls, and other locally handcrafted pieces are their specialty, and items are truly gorgeous.

Under a Hula Moon (261-4252; Kailua Shopping Center, 600 Kailua Rd., Kailua) This little shop carries thoughtful islandesque items such as woven bags, dried flower wreaths, and small paintings.

NORTH SHORE

Global Creations Interiors (637-1505; 66-079 Kamehameha Hwy., Hale'iwa) This shop has a split personality: tourist-oriented, tropical bric-a-brac on one side of the room; trendy upscale Asiatic gifts on the other. On the Thai/pan-Asiatic side, choose from wall hangings, placemats, candles, nature prints, and more.

HOME FURNISHINGS

While you may not be ready to shop for a four-poster bed while you are here, you might pick up some eye-catchingly different home accent pieces. Also, most stores can arrange to ship your purchases, saving you from dragging that lamp onto the plane.

GREATER HONOLULU

Baik Designs (524-2290; Gentry Pacific Design Center, 560 North Nimitz Hwy., Suite 108B, Iwilei) The popularity of Indonesian furnishings in Hawai'i and elsewhere has increased dramatically over the last 10 years, and Baik is one of the best in Honolulu. All pieces are hand selected overseas by the owners and exhibit quality craftsmanship, as well as unique design.

Bali Aga Furniture (593-9030; 307D Kamani St., Kaka'ako) This little shop specializes in imported furniture and other décor that fuses contemporary Western with new and recycled Southeast Asian elements.

Eiselin Imports (782-5300; Restaurant Row, 500 Ala Moana Blvd., Kaka'ako) Youthful owner Allen carries a small but unique selection of home accents that he designs and then has hand made in Indonesia. Items such as his upscale table runners, teak benches, and gossamer curtains are affordable and earthy.

Indich Collection (524-7769; Gentry Pacific Design Center, 560 North Nimitz Hwy., Suite 101, Iwilei) Indich has been around for years and specializes in hand-woven Oriental carpets, as well as unique Hawaiian-style rugs designed locally and woven in Nepal, China, and India.

Mesh (593-2564; 650 Iwilei Rd., Suite 110, Iwilei) Interior designer Shari Saiki recently opened this spacious store and filled it with delicious wood furnishings with exotically hip, contemporary Pacific/Asiatic flair. Even if you can't drag a platform bed onto the plane, you'll find perfect small accent pieces.

Pacific Orient Traders (531-3774; Gentry Pacific Design Center, 560 North Nimitz Hwy., Suite 123, Iwilei) Most of this stunning shop's Chinese antique furnishings date back between one hundred and three hundred years, and each original piece is hand selected and refinished by craftspeople in China.

Select (734-6950; Hee Hing Plaza, 449 Kapahulu Ave., 2nd Floor., Kapahulu) This new shop near Waikīkī was recently opened by a couple of artists who tired of flying to New York or Tokyo for cool home décor. You'll find chic glassware, fine linens, and more.

SoHa Living (591-9777; Ward Centre, 1200 Ala Moana Blvd., Kapahulu) The young, Hawai'i-raised sisters Brooke and Shyrah hit the mark with their own artsy and hip tropical/Asiatic furniture designs and décor items, which are handmade in Indonesia. You will find classics with a twist, like a Barcelona-style chair with a frame made from stained rattan instead of metal. They also handpick complementary décor items in Southeast Asia.

North Shore

Bali Moon Hawai'i (637-6666; Hale'iwa Shopping Center, 66-145 Kamehameha Hwy., Hale'iwa) Brazilian owned Bali Moon features unique lamps, kiln-dried teak furnishings, and even recycled teak pieces, most in unusual designs and dimensions.

Kids' Stuff

Skip the "My Parents Went to Hawai'i and All I Got is…" T-shirt and bring the kids something cool and original.

Waikīkī

Natural Selection Gift Shop (923-9741; Waikīkī Aquarium, 2777 Kalākaua Ave.) Cuddly sea-oriented plush snugglies and other goodies await you at the Waikīkī Aquarium's gift shop.

Today's Little People (922-1772; Outrigger Waikīkī Hotel, 2335 Kalākaua Ave.) From handmade island-style clothing to books, games, collector's dolls, and educational toys, this locally founded shop caters to the youngest of folks.

Tropical Outpost (971-7171; Honolulu Zoo, 151 Kapahulu Ave.) This children's shop at the Honolulu Zoo is an easy choice for really cute plush critters, animal masks, educational toys, and other fun finds. They also carry plenty for grown-ups, too, from shirts to Hawaiian music CDs.

Get around animal quarantine issues with these fuzzy critters from the Honolulu Zoo's Tropical Outpost shop.

GREATER HONOLULU

Animation Magic (949-2525; Ala Moana Center, 1450 Ala Moana Blvd., Ala Moana) Browse this popular, locally owned shop filled with everything from Power Rangers to Betty Boop novelty items.

Sanrio (949-2990; Ala Moana Center, 1450 Ala Moana Blvd., Ala Moana) This is the ultimate "Hello Kitty" store. Merchandise ranges from gum to television sets, and selected items are Hawai'i themed. The characters sometimes stop in for photo ops.

Thinker Toys (946-3378; Ala Moana Center, 1450 Ala Moana Blvd., Ala Moana) Pick up educational products, puzzles, and toys here.

Up and Riding (955-7433; Ala Moana Center, 1450 Ala Moana Blvd., Ala Moana) This shop features surf clothing and apparel, from greats such as Rip Curl and Billabong, for toddlers through 16-year-olds.

WINDWARD O'AHU

Baby Showers Hawai'i (262-8934; Kailua Shopping Center, 600 Kailua Rd., Kailua)

Eensy-weensy shoe sets, simple and earthy dolls, Hawaiian-style baby quilts, clothing, and other items for tiny folks abound.

Mary's Toys (262-1332; Kailua Shopping Center, 600 Kailua Rd., Kailua) We had to restrain from buying ourselves the giant plush dinosaur—and the dollhouse, tropical mobile, and wooden puzzle—in this selective little shop owned by a former local reporter.

North Shore

The Growing Keiki (637-4544; 66-051 Kamehameha Hwy., Hale'iwa) This little boutique for tiny people carries hip clothing like Paul Frank PJs, full-body rash guards, and well made aloha shirts, along with fun little gifts.

Shopping Centers

Honolulu life revolves around several major shopping centers, which not only have some of the best stores in town, but also excellent restaurants. Below is a list of the biggies that exceed standard mall expectations.

Waikīkī

Royal Hawaiian Shopping Center (922-0588; www.shopwaikiki.com; 2201 Kalākaua Ave.) This Waikīkī mega-lineup just completed an $84-million renovation in 2007. You'll find everything from Kate Spade, Cartier, and Salvatore Ferragamo to the Royal Hawaiian Golf Shop and Auntie Bella's Lei Stand. Parking is affordable with vendor validation.

Greater Honolulu

Ala Moana Center (955-9517; www.alamoanacenter.com; 1450 Ala Moana Blvd., Ala Moana) Ala Moana claims to be the world's largest open-air shopping center. As of March 2008, when an entirely new phase of the mall opens, this 60-year-old mall will have more than 320 restaurants, shops, and other businesses. Shops range from Chanel, Jimmy Choo, Sephora, Neiman Marcus, Williams-Sonoma, and the Apple Store to local nuggets like the Crack Seed Store and the Slipper House. Parking is free and plentiful on the uppermost levels.

Ward Centers (591-8411; www.victoriaward.com; four-block area bordered by Ala Moana Blvd., Ward Ave., Queen St., and Auahi St., Kaka'ako) A myriad of complexes called Ward Centre, Ward Warehouse, Ward Entertainment Center & Ward Village, and Ward Gateway & Farmers Market, businesses tend to be favorite mid-scale restaurants, charming local boutiques, and specialty stores like Hawai'i Doggie Bakery & Gift Shop and Nohea Gallery. A few powerhouses like Pier 1 Imports, a Consolidated 16-theatreplex, and Borders also live here. In 2008, a Whole Foods Market will open. Parking is free, but competitive on weekends.

Central O'ahu

Waikele Premium Outlets (676-5656; 94-790 Lumiaina St., Waipahu) Way off the beaten path is a compound loaded with deep discounts. BCBG Max Azria, Saks Fifth Avenue's Off 5th, Barney's New York, Adidas, Puma, MaxMara, Izod, and more mean that around the holidays this place is a zoo. Parking is free.

The brand new Waikīkī Beach Walk shopping and dining complex replaced an alley long known for trinket shops and budget hotels.

SURF AND OTHER SPORTING GEAR

Want to be a surfer, or at least look like one? Surf shops sell all the gear—including a dude's next pair of boardshorts. Plus, here are a few ideas on where to pick up masks and fins, tents, and more.

Billabong (923-4491; 2424 Kalākaua Ave.) Billabong clothing is more than a fashion statement; these classic, "surf hip" pieces reflect the spirit of the Aussie Billabong's pro surfer team.

Local Motion (979-7873; 1958 Kalākaua Ave.) Local Motion is a "for real" surf shop, and boards are their true calling. However, they're also celebrated for their trendy, popular, good-looking clothing and accessories. This location isn't their flagship store, but it's the biggest. On the second floor, quench your shopping-worn soul with a late afternoon brewski at Brew Moon.

Quiksilver (2181 Kalākaua Ave.) The name Quiksilver is legendary in the surfing world. This 6,200-square-foot signature shop will open in late 2007 or early 2008 and loaded with surfboards and surfing gear, plus clothing for kids, women, and men who are surfer boys at heart. Also pick up wetsuits, skateboarding equipment, and surf DVDs.

South Seas Aquatics (922-0852; Kalākaua Business Center; 2155 Kalākaua Ave.) This small shop boasts some of the best prices on the island for quality fins, masks, wetsuits, rashguards, and scuba gear.

GREATER HONOLULU

Hawaiian Island Creations (973-6780; Ala Moana Center, 1450 Ala Moana Blvd., Ala Moana) This is Hawai'i's largest locally owned surf shop and it sells tons of hot surf clothing, as well as surfboards and accessories. Their boardshorts for guys and bikinis for girls are extra cool, and a signature tee is a great souvenir.

Sports Authority (596-0166; 333 Ward Ave., Kaka'ako) Yes, the national retailer. If you need the tent, or the fishing rod, or the bodyboard, or the kerosene lamp . . . you can find it here.

Town & Country Surf Design (973-5199; Ala Moana Center, 1450 Ala Moana Blvd., Ala Moana) Yet another of the big surf shop studs in town is Town & Country, which carries popular brands of surf clothing like Quiksilver and Hurley, as well as top boards and accessories.

WINDWARD O'AHU

Aaron's Dive Shop (262-2333; 307 Hahani St., Kailua) After 35 years in business, Aaron's is a fixture in Kailua. Their thing is dive tours, but they also sell tons of ocean-related supplies such as scuba and snorkeling gear, and spear diving equipment.

Kimo's Surf Hut (262-1644; 151 Hekili St., Kailua) Owned by noted Hawaiian activist Kimo Aluli, this is a real surf shack run by a real surfer. Buy a beautiful new or vintage board here—such as a 1956 Velzy & Jacobs—and help carry the island spirit forward.

NORTH SHORE

North Shore Boardriders Club (637-5026; North Shore Marketplace, 66-250 Kamehameha Hwy., Hale'iwa) Quiksilver, Roxy, and other cool surf clothing peep from between racks of surfboards for sale.

Patagonia (637-1245; North Shore Marketplace, 66-250 Kamehameha Hwy., Hale'iwa) Hardcore outdoor fleece jackets may actually come in handy should you be planning to visit high volcanic altitudes on the Big Island or Maui. They also sell epoxy surfboards and other clothing.

Surf-N-Sea (637-7873; 62-595 Kamehameha Hwy., Hale'iwa) A North Shore surf shop deluxe with more than 40 years behind it, browse through stacks of surfboards, racks of surf clothing, and more.

Tropical Rush (637-8886; 62-620 Kamehameha Hwy., Hale'iwa) A mini-compound of shacks—one filled with skateboards, another with surfboards, and another with this-and-that—you can get a new or used board by some of today's hottest makers, plus surf clothing.

Surf-N-Sea is a North Shore landmark shop for boards and other water supplies.

9

INFORMATION

Facts Great and Small

Sometimes, we just need a few facts—even on vacation. Below you'll find the following information to keep you clued in and ready for just about anything.

Banks 257
Books about Hawai'i 258
Child Care 261
Climate Overview & Weather Reports 261
Emergency Services Contacts 262
Groceries, Sundries, & Prescriptions 263
Handicapped Services 264
Holidays 264
Hospitals & Medical Treatment Centers 265
Language Glossary 266
Magazines, Newspapers, Radio & Television 267
Marriage in Hawai'i 268
Religious Services 269
Road Service 269
Time Zones & Phones 270
Volunteering 270

BANKS

Hawai'i features numerous state, national, and international banking institutions with endless locations. If you have a bank debit card, you'll find hundreds of bank machines you can use throughout the state, plus most businesses will honor your debit card as well. If you need to enter a bank, below are several major staffed locations around the island, as well as a list of the systems their bank machines accept.

American Savings Bank (1-800-272-2566) Linked to Cirrus, Plus, and Star systems; selected machines may accept additional systems.

923-1102; 321 Seaside Ave., Waikīkī
973-4864; Ala Moana Center, 1450 Ala Moana Blvd., Ala Moana
523-6844; 1001 Bishop St., Downtown (main branch)

395-2308; 7192 Kalaniana'ole Hwy, Hawai'i Kai
262-8102; 200-C Hāmākua Dr., Kailua
637-5042; 66-197 Kamehameha Hwy., Hale'iwa
674-2288; 890 Kamōkila Blvd., Kapolei

Bank of Hawai'i (1-888-643-3888) Linked to American Express, Armed Forces Financial Network, Cirrus, Discover, Maestro, MasterCard, Novus, Plus, Quest, Star, and Visa.
543-6900; 2228 Kalākaua Ave., Waikīkī
942-6111; Ala Moana Center, 1450 Ala Moana Blvd, Ala Moana
538-4171; 111 S. King St., Downtown (main branch)
397-4010; 7192 Kalaniana'ole Hwy., Hawai'i Kai
266-4600; 636 Kailua Rd., Kailua
637-6235; 66-165 Kamehameha Hwy., Hale'iwa
693-1637; 590 Farrington Hwy., Kapolei Shopping Center, Kapolei

Central Pacific Bank (1-800-342-8422) Linked to American Express, Cirrus, Discover, Maestro, MasterCard, Plus, Quest, Star, and Visa.
971-3277; 105 Uluniu Ave., Waikīkī
971-4720; Waikīkī Shopping Plaza, 2250 Kalākaua Ave., Waikīkī
266-4765; 419 Ku'ulei Rd., Kailua
397-2626; 6600 Kalaniana'ole Hwy., Hawai'i Kai
544-0510; 220 S. King St., Downtown (main branch)
622-1626; Wahiawā Town Center, 935 California Ave., Wahiawā
674-3700; 680 Kamōkila Blvd., Kapolei

First Hawaiian Bank (1-888-844-4444) Linked to American Express, Cirrus, Discover, MasterCard, Plus, Quest, Star, and Visa.
943-4670; 2181 Kalākaua Ave., Waikīkī
525-6340; 999 Bishop St., Downtown (main branch)
373-8821; 7110 Kalaniana'ole Hwy., Hawai'i Kai
261-3371; 705 Kailua Rd., Kailua
637-5034; 66-135 Kamehameha Hwy., Hale'iwa
625-1182; 730 California Ave., Wahiawā
674-0013; 590 Farrington Hwy., Kapolei Shopping Center, Kapolei

Books About Hawai'i

There are literally hundreds of books out there that relate to Hawai'i, and many of them are fantastic. You can find incredibly specific topics, such as books on the history of a particular Honolulu district, or broad novels with local characters. Here are just a few to get you started.

Archaeology

James, Van. *Ancient Sites of O'ahu.* Bishop Museum Press, 1992.

Kirch, Patrick Vinton. *Feathered Gods and Fishhooks: An Introduction to Hawaiian Archaeology and Prehistory.* University of Hawai'i Press, 1985.

Sterling, Elspeth P., and Catherine C. Summer. *Sites of O'ahu.* Bishop Museum Press, 1993.

Autobiographies, Biographies, and Personal Accounts

Allen, Helena G. *The Betrayal of Lili'uokalani: Last Queen of Hawai'i 1838-1917.* Mutual Publishing, 1982.

Bird, Isabella Lucy. *Six Months in Hawai'i.* Mutual Publishing, 1998.
Ellis, William. *Journal of William Ellis: A Narrative of an 1823 Tour through Hawai'i or Owhyhee.* Mutual Publishing, 2004.
Lili'uokalani. *Hawai'i's Story by Hawai'i's Queen.* Mutual Publishing, 1991.
London, Jack. *Stories of Hawai'i.* Mutual Publishing, 1984.
Stevenson, Robert Louis. Day, A. Grove, ed. *Travels in Hawai'i.* University of Hawai'i Press, 1973.
Twain, Mark. Day, A. Grove, ed. *Mark Twain in Hawai'i: Roughing It in the Sandwich Islands.* Mutual Publishing, 1995.

Children's Books

Coste, Marion. *Kōlea: The Story of the Pacific Golden Plover.* University of Hawai'i Press, 1998.
Crowe, Ellie and Don Robinson. *Kamehameha, the Boy Who Became a Warrior King.* Island Heritage Publishing, 2003.
Hayashi, Leslie Ann. *Fables from the Deep.* Mutual Publishing, 2002.
Knudsen, Eric and Guy Buffet. *Spooky Stuffs.* Island Heritage Publishing, 2003.
Stender, Joshua Kaiponohea. *Nā Makana a Nā I'a/The Fish and Their Gifts.* Kamehameha Schools Press, 2004.
Tabrah, Ruth. Whatley, Kirsten, ed. *Momotaro: Peach Boy.* Island Heritage Publishing, 1995.

Cultural and Historical Explorations

Chambers, John H. *Hawai'i, On-The-Road Histories Series.* Interlink Publishing Group, 2006.
Ching, Carrie. *Things Hawai'i: A Celebration of the History, Landmarks, Flavors, Trends, and Traditions That Make Hawai'i Special.* Mutual Publishing, 2004.
Daws, Gavan. *Honolulu: The First Century.* Mutual Publishing, 2006.
Daws, Gavan. *Shoal of Time: A History of the Hawaiian Islands.* University of Hawai'i Press, 1974.
Day, A. Grove. *Hawai'i and Its People.* Mutual Publishing, 2005.
Dorrance, William H. *O'ahu's Hidden History.* Mutual Publishing, 1999.
Dudley, Michael K. and Keoni K. Agard. *A Hawaiian Nation: Man, Gods, and Nature.* Nā Kāne O Ka Malo Press, 1993.
Halualani, Rona Tamiko. *In the Name of Hawaiians: Native Identities & Cultural Politics.* University of Minnesota Press, 2002.
Hartwell, Jay C. *Nā Mamo: Hawaiian People Today.* 'Ai Pōhaku Press, 1996.
Kanahele, George H.S. *Waikīkī 100 BC to 1900 AD: An Untold Story.* University of Hawai'i Press, 1996.
Kanahele, George H.S. *Kū Kanaka, Stand Tall: A Search for Hawaiian Values.* University of Hawai'i Press, 1993.
Malo, David. *Hawaiian Antiquities: Mo'olelo Hawai'i.* Bishop Museum Press, 1997.
McGregor, Davianna Pomaika'i. *Nā Kua'āina: Living Hawaiian Culture.* University of Hawai'i Press, 2007.
Nordyke, Eleanor C. *The Peopling of Hawai'i.* University of Hawai'i Press, 1989.
Prange, Gordon W. *At Dawn We Slept: The Untold Story of Pearl Harbor.* Penguin, 2001.

Folklore

Beckwith, Martha Warren. *Hawaiian Mythology.* University of Hawai'i Press, 1970.
Kalākaua, David. Grant, Glen, ed. *The Legends and Myths of Hawai'i.* Mutual Publishing, 1990.
Kawaharada, Dennis, ed. *Ancient O'ahu: Stories from Fornander and Thrum.* Kalamaku Press, 2001.
Westervelt, William D. *Legends of Old Honolulu.* Mutual Publishing, 2003.

Food and Cooking

Hee, Jean Watanabe. *Hawai'i's Best Local Dishes.* Mutual Publishing, 2002.

Laudan, Rachel. *The Food of Paradise: Exploring Hawai'i's Culinary Heritage.* University of Hawai'i Press, 1996.

Wong, Alan and John Harrisson. *Alan Wong's New Wave Luau.* Ten Speed Press, 2003.

Hawaiian and "Pidgin" Language

Pukui, Mary Kawena. *'Ōlelo No'eau: Hawaiian Proverbs and Poetical Sayings.* Bishop Museum Press, 1997.

Pukui, Mary Kawena and Samuel H. Elbert. *Hawaiian Dictionary.* University of Hawai'i Press, 1986.

Pukui, Mary Kawena and Samuel H. Elbert. *Hawaiian Grammar.* University of Hawai'i Press, 1979.

Pukui, Mary Kawena, Samuel H. Elbert, and Esther T. Mo'okini. *Place Names of Hawai'i.* University of Hawai'i Press, 1974.

Sakoda, Kent, and Jeff Siegel. *Pidgin Grammar: An Introduction to the Creole Language of Hawai'i.* Bess Press, 2003.

Simonson, Douglas, Pat Sasaki, and Ken Sakata. *Pidgin to da Max, 25th Anniversary Edition.* Bess Press, 2005.

Tonouchi, Lee A. *Da Kine Dictionary.* Bess Press, 2005.

Wight, Kahikahealani. *Learn Hawaiian at Home.* Bess Press, 2005. Includes CD.

Literature

Harstad, James. R and Cheryl A. *Island Fire: An Anthology of Literature from Hawai'i.* University of Hawai'i Press, 2002.

Cataluna, Lee. *Folks You Meet in Longs and Other Stories.* Bamboo Ridge Press, 2005.

Chock, Eric, et al. *Growing Up Local: Anthology of Poetry & Prose from Hawai'i.* University of Hawai'i Press, 1998.

Yamanaka, Lois-Ann. *Saturday Night at the Pāhala Theatre.* Bamboo Ridge Press, 1993.

Modern Architecture, Design, and Fashion

Sandler, Robert. Haines, Frank, ed. *Architecture in Hawai'i.* Mutual Publishing, 2008.

McGrath, Mary, Kaui Philpotts, and David Duncan Livingston. *Hawai'i, a Sense of Place.* Mutual Publishing, 2005.

Brown, DeSoto and Linda Arthur. *The Art of the Aloha Shirt.* Island Heritage Publishing, 2003.

Nature and Natural History

Culliney, John L. *Islands in a Far Sea: The Fate of Nature in Hawai'i.* University of Hawai'i Press, 2005.

Hoover, John P. *Hawai'i's Fishes: A Guide for Snorkelers, Divers, and Aquarists.* Mutual Publishing, 2005.

Howarth, Francis G. *Hawaiian Insects and Their Kin.* University of Hawai'i Press, 1992.

Liittschwager, David and Susan Middleton. *Archipelago: Portraits of Life in the World's Most Remote Island Sanctuary.* National Geographic, 2005.

Pratt, Douglas H. *Enjoying Birds and Other Wildlife in Hawai'i.* Mutual Publishing, 2002.

Wood, Paul. *Flowers and Plants of Hawai'i.* Island Heritage Publishing, 2006.

Recreation

Ambrose, Greg. *Surfer's Guide to Hawai'i.* Bess Press, 2006.
Ball Jr., Stuart M. *The Hikers Guide to O'ahu.* University of Hawai'i Press, 2000.

Traditional Arts

Allen, Tricia. *Tattoo Traditions of Hawai'i.* Mutual Publishing, 2006.
Buck, Sir Peter. *Arts and Crafts of Hawai'i (The Complete Collection).* Bishop Museum Press, 2003.
Finney, Ben. *Sailing in the Wake of the Ancestors: Reviving Polynesian Voyaging.* Bishop Museum Press, 2003.
Ide, Laurie Shimizu. *Hawaiian Lei Making Step-by-Step Guide.* Mutual Publishing, 2006.

Child Care

There are several options for parents who need child care during a visit to O'ahu. If you are staying in a higher-end hotel, begin by inquiring whether they have babysitter options in-house—some do. Or, contact the reputable agencies below for child care service. Both are available to assist you wherever you are on the island.

Aloha Nannies (394-5434; www.alohanannies.com) In business since 1998, Aloha Nannies offers visitors full babysitting care at your hotel—or can take the kids to the park, beach, or wherever you like. Nannies have all had reference checks and have childcare experience, CPR/First Aid certification, TB clearance, and a clean criminal record and health history.

Sitters Unlimited of Hawai'i (674-8440; www.sittershawaii.com) This organization has served O'ahu for more than 20 years and offers clients carefully chosen sitters with CPR/First Aid certification, experience, references, TB clearance, and criminal/child abuse background clearance. They can provide day, evening, or even overnight care. There is a four-hour minimum.

Climate Overview & Weather Reports

The Hawaiian Islands sit across the Tropic of Cancer and are officially in the northern tropics. Clouds are a way of life here, and they usually come and go all day long. If the sky looks bad when you peek out the window, wait an hour and see if it doesn't change entirely—often it will. The overall average day's weather on O'ahu could be described as warm to hot, with temperatures between 74 and 88 degrees Fahrenheit, moderate humidity, partly sunny skies with several mountain-area rain showers (and maybe a rainbow, or even a double rainbow), and gentle to somewhat strong northeasterly trade winds. Not too shabby!

Summer temperatures islandwide usually hover in the mid- to high-80s during the day and dip into the 70s at night; strong rain is infrequent and breezes increase, cooling the heat. During the winter, day temperatures fluctuate between the 70s and low 80s, and at night it can sometimes drop into the 60s. Although brief rain showers are common across the island year round, extremely heavy rains and thunderstorms do occasionally occur, especially in winter months. Hurricanes are rare. Once in a while, the dreaded "Kona winds" blow from the south, bringing excessive mugginess often followed by a cleansing rain.

Most O'ahu days see pockets of clouds, which help keep temperatures comfortable.

O'ahu is made up of many microclimates that are most easily characterized by region. The Honolulu area typically has sunny skies, cooling trade winds, and modest rainfalls, while Windward O'ahu is known for blustery, overcast weather many days of the year and excessive rain. The North Shore is relatively dry, with a high percentage of sunny days, and Leeward O'ahu hits some of the island's hottest temperatures and often lacks refreshing trade winds.

Ocean temperatures along the coasts are consistently in the mid- to high-70s year round. Currents around the island are very complex, and the tide reaches two highs and two lows of different heights each day. Weather reports usually announce only the highest and lowest points and when to expect them; the information can help you decide when to go tidepooling, beachcombing, and so forth. Significant tsunamis rarely occur in Hawai'i, but sirens are positioned across the state for emergency notification.

Here are several of the millions of ways you can check the weather across the island:

National Weather Service Forecast for Hawai'i: www.prh.noaa.gov/hnl
NWS O'ahu Weather Forecast: 973-4380
NWS Hawai'i Marine Forecast: 973-4382
NWS O'ahu Surf Forecast: 973-4383
Surf News Network: 596-7873

Emergency Services Contacts

Like on the Mainland, dialing 911 will mobilize any emergency assistance unit, including the police, fire department, or ambulance. It also serves as a non-emergency dispatch.

In the face of more complicated situations ranging from criminal victimization to a death in the family, you can also contact the **Visitor Aloha Society of Hawai'i** (926-8274; www.visitoralohasocietyofhawaii.org; Waikīkī Shopping Plaza, 2250 Kalākaua Ave., Suite 403-3). They can help you figure out where to turn (after emergency care has been rendered) and help you through the process.

GROCERIES, SUNDRIES, & PRESCRIPTIONS

When you need fixin's to cook dinner at your vacation rental or that box of midnight cookies, where do you turn? See below for area supermarkets, as well as sundry stores with pharmacies. Most of the sundry and grocery stores open between 6 and 8 AM. Note that several operate 24 hours a day. In addition to these listings, Waikīkī has several 24-hour 7-Eleven stores and about a trillion late-night ABC Stores, both of which offer snacks, aspirin, trinkets, and so forth.

WAIKĪKĪ

Food Pantry (923-9831, 2370 Kūhiō Ave.) Waikīkī's only real supermarket is open until 1 AM daily. A second and smaller location (947-3763; Hobron Ln.) on the far western end of Waikīkī closes at 11:30 PM.

Kūhiō Pharmacy (923-4466; 2250 Kalākaua Ave.) This small, centrally located shop focuses on prescriptions, which they fill until 4:30 PM daily.

GREATER HONOLULU

Foodland (949-5044; Ala Moana Center, 1450 Ala Moana Blvd., Ala Moana) This 60-year-old local supermarket chain's convenient shopping center location is open until 10 PM every day except Sunday, when they close at 8 PM.

Longs Drugs (Store 941-4433; Pharmacy 949-4010; Ala Moana Center, 1450 Ala Moana Blvd., Ala Moana) This sundry store serves as an island crossroads and is open until 10 PM Monday through Saturday, and 8 PM Sunday. Their pharmacy is open Monday through Saturday until 10 PM, and 7 PM Sunday.

Longs Drugs (Store 536-7302; Pharmacy 536-5542; 1330 Pali Hwy., Downtown) This enormous sundry store and pharmacy are both open 24 hours a day.

Safeway (592-6499; 1121 S. Beretania St., Makiki) Same stuff as on the Mainland, but it's conveniently open 24 hours a day.

Whole Foods Market (Kahala Mall, 4211 Wai'alae Ave., Kahala; Ward Village, 1170 Auahi St., Kaka'ako) This Mainland chain, well known for top-of-the-line and organic products, will be opening sometime in 2008.

WINDWARD O'AHU

Longs Drugs (Store 261-8537; Pharmacy 261-9794; 609 Kailua Rd., Kailua) This sundry store is open until midnight daily; the pharmacy stays open until 10 PM weekdays, 9 PM Saturdays, and 7 PM Sundays.

Tamura's (232-2332; 54-316 Hau'ula Kai Shopping Center, Kamehameha Hwy., Hau'ula) This century-old local supermarket chain is the biggest shop on the northern Windward Coast. Note that they also carry wine and beer—the only other real supermarket in the area, located in nearby Lā'ie, does not sell alcohol and is closed Sundays. Tamura's closes at 8 PM daily.

Times Super Market (Store 266-4004; Pharmacy 266-2702; 590 Kailua Rd., Kailua) This large, local, 75-year-old supermarket stays open until 10 PM daily and also has a pharmacy, which is open until 8 PM weekdays and 5 PM on weekends.

North Shore

Foodland (638-8081; 59-720 Kamehameha Hwy., Pūpūkea) Although just a supermarket, it's also a North Shore landmark. They're open until 11 PM every day.

Mālama Market (637-4520; 66-190 Kamehameha Hwy., Hale'iwa) Mālama is small enough to feel like a country store, yet big enough to supply all of your groceries. They're open until 9 PM daily.

Central O'ahu

Longs Drugs (Store 623-6466; Pharmacy 623-6636; Mililani Marketplace, 94-780A Mehe'ula Pkwy., Mililani) The sundry store stays open until 9 PM weekdays and 7 PM weekends; the pharmacy closes at 9 PM on weekdays, 7 PM Saturday, and 5 PM Sunday.

Star Markets (564-7166; Mililani Marketplace, 95-1249 Mehe'ula Pkwy., Mililani) 75-year-old local supermarket retailer Star Markets keeps this location open until 2 AM every day.

Leeward O'ahu

Longs Drugs (Store 674-0069; Pharmacy 674-0269; Kapolei Shopping Center, 91-590 Farrington Hwy., Kapolei) The sundry store closes at midnight daily; the pharmacy closes as 10 PM weekdays, 9 PM Saturday, and 7 PM Sunday.

Safeway (674-0070; Kapolei Shopping Center, 91-590 Farrington Hwy., Kapolei) This Mainland-based supermarket serves a huge leeward population 24 hours a day.

Tamura's Superette (696-3321; 86-032 Farrington Hwy., Wai'anae) Renting a condo in Mākaha? Here's the best place to shop. The supermarket's open until 8:30 PM weekdays and 8 PM weekends.

Handicapped Services

A great resource for disabled services information is the **Hawai'i State Department of Health's Disability and Communication Access Board** (586-8121; www.hawaii.gov/health/dcab/travel; 919 Ala Moana Blvd., Room 101, Kaka'ako). Be sure to check it out in advance for a comprehensive PDF file you can print out, or at least give them a call when you arrive.

All major car rental companies these days can provide vehicles equipped for disabled drivers if you request one in advance. Remember to bring your parking placard with you and identification to prove it's yours. For more information on getting around town, please see Chapter 2.

Holidays

Hawai'i observes American national holidays, as well as several unique state holidays. While most banks remain open on state holidays, expect to find selected businesses, government agencies, and schools closed on either the holiday itself or the closest working day to it.

January 1	New Year's Day
Third Monday in January	Martin Luther King Jr. Day

Third Monday in February	Presidents' Day
March 26	Prince Kūhiō Day
Late March/April	Good Friday-Easter
Last Monday in May	Memorial Day
June 11	Kamehameha Day
July 4	Independence Day
Third Friday in August	Statehood Day (Admissions Day)
First Monday in September	Labor Day
Second Monday in October	Discoverers' Day
November 11	Veterans' Day
Fourth Thursday in November	Thanksgiving Day
December 25	Christmas Day

Hospitals & Medical Treatment Centers

O'ahu has numerous hospitals and care centers. You'll find several options for non-urgent care in the following paragraphs, and a list of major area hospitals listed below.

Kaiser Permanente operates several non-urgent care clinics on O'ahu that are open primarily during regular business hours. If you are a Kaiser member, call their 24-hour switchboard (432-0000) and let them know what area you're staying in so they can direct you to the nearest day clinic. You can also call the **Kaiser 24-Hour Advice Nurse** (432-7700) when offices have closed.

Kahuku Hospital is the only 24-hour-care hospital serving the North Shore and northern Windward O'ahu. At the time of writing it was facing possible closure; if it does close and you need to visit a hospital, prepare to drive between 20 and 45 minutes (depending on where you're staying and traffic levels) to **Wahiawā General Hospital** in Central O'ahu, or **Castle Medical Center** in Kailua.

Hospitals

Greater Honolulu

Kapi'olani Medical Center for Women & Children: 983-6000; 1319 Punahou St., Punahou
Kaiser Permanente Medical Center and Clinic: 432-0000; 3288 Moanalua Rd., Moanalua
The Queen's Medical Center: 538-9011; 1301 Punchbowl St., Downtown
Straub Clinic & Hospital: 522-4000; 888 King St., Makiki

Windward O'ahu

Castle Medical Center: 263-5500; 640 'Ulukahiki St., Kailua
Kahuku Hospital: 293-9221; 56-117 Pualalea St., Kahuku

Central O'ahu

Wahiawā General Hospital: 621-8411; 128 Lehua St., Wahiawā

Medical Treatment Centers

Waikīkī

Discovery Bay Medical Clinic: 955-5553; 1778 Ala Moana Blvd., Upper Level 5
Doctors on Call: 971-6000; Sheraton Princess Ka'iulani Hotel, 120 Ka'iulani Ave.

Urgent Care Clinic of Waikīkī: 924-3399; Kalākaua Business Center; 2155 Kalākaua Ave., Suite 308

Windward O'ahu

Braun Urgent Care: 261-4411; 130 Kailua Rd., Kailua
Straub Kailua Family Health Center: 266-6511; 629 Kailua Rd., Kailua

North Shore

Hale'iwa Family Health Center: 637-5087; 66-125 Kamehameha Hwy., Hale'iwa

Leeward O'ahu

Wai'anae Coast Health Center: 696-7081; 86-260 Farrington Hwy., Wai'anae

Language Glossary

What, no can understand when Hawai'i folks talk story? No worry, brah. The list below is a mix of commonly used Hawaiian words and some popular "pidgin" words. What we call "pidgin" in Hawai'i is in fact a colorful creole language or dialect with old origins in trading and plantation life. Some people speak it heavily, some speak it lightly, and some don't speak it at all. Most longtimers in Hawai'i do have a regional inflection and pepper their speech with regional vocabulary, even if they don't actually speak pidgin. Your best bet is to listen and enjoy, not try.

This pronunciation guide approximates the way words are most frequently pronounced by residents and general meaning in everyday conversation.

'āina (EYE-nah)—land
ali'i (ah-LEE-ee)— traditional ruling class, or "important person"
aloha (ah-LOH-hah)—hello, goodbye, love, fondness
da kine (dah-KYNE)—used in context typically to refer to a person or thing
grind—verb meaning "to chow down" (the noun "grinds" means "chow")
hālau (hah-LAOO)—hula school/troupe, long house for canoes
hale (HAH-leh)—house
hana hou (HAH-nah-HOH)—do it again
hānai (hah-NYE)—adopted
haole (HOW-leh)—Causasian
hapa (HAH-pah)—half or part, as in *hapa-haole,* or "part-Caucasian"
hāpai (hah-PYE)—pregnant
howzit (HOW-zit)—how's it going
hui (HOO-ee)—club, association, group
kama'āina (kah-mah-EYE-nah)—official state resident or longtimer
kāne (KAH-neh)—man
kapu (KAH-poo)—taboo or off-limits
keiki (KAY-kee)—child or children
kōkua (koh-KOO-ah)—help
kumu (KOO-moo)—teacher, particularly of Hawaiian cultural or spiritual knowledge
kupuna (koo-POO-nah)—elder or elders
lānai (lah-NYE)—porch or veranda

lei (LAY)—flower garland
mahalo (mah-HAH-loh)—thank you
makai (mah-KYE)—toward the sea or on the sea-side of
malihini (mah-lee-HEE-nee)—"newcomer," usually from the Mainland
mauka (MAOO-kah)—toward the mountains or on the mountain-side of
mu'umu'u (moo-oo-MOO-oo)—a loose gown, traditionally floor length
'ohana (oh-HAH-nah)—family
pau (PAOO)—finished
pidgin (PIH-jin)—common term for Hawai'i's vernacular language/dialect
pono (POH-noh)—justness, righteousness, making things "right"
shaka (SHAH-kah)—a hand gesture for "things are great," "thanks," or "hey there"
slippers—flip-flops or go-aheads
talk story—"shooting the breeze," or casual sharing of personal stories
tūtū (TOO-too)—grandmother
wahine (wah-HEE-neh)—woman (sometimes pronounced va-HEE-neh)

Magazines, Newspapers, Radio, & Television

Below are the names and contact information for major local magazines and newspapers to pick up during your visit and perhaps subscribe to when you're back home. Most of the newspapers are available at newsstands; the magazines are on shelves at local bookstores and selected sundry shops, or order direct. Also, we've included a list of radio stations and television channels so you're hooked into the action while in town.

Magazines

Hana Hou! (733-3333; www.hanahou.com) This is Hawaiian Airlines' glossy, inflight magazine, and it's filled with well-written articles on life in Hawai'i and other information.

Hawai'i Business (534-7520; www.hawaiiabusiness.com) Honolulu's a small city—reading Hawai'i Business is a great way to learn who's who and how things work.

Honolulu Magazine (534-7520; www.honolulumagazine.com) This is the definitive "sophisticated" Hawai'i living magazine, with articles on everything from legendary island musicians to urban development issues.

Spirit of Aloha (524-7400; www.spiritofaloha.com) Aloha Airlines' inflight magazine is also available for purchase and contains a variety of thoughtful articles on Hawai'i.

Newspapers

Pacific Business News (955-8100; www.bizjournals.com/pacific) This little weekly paper is in every executive office waiting room and keeps readers up to date on local business activity.

The Honolulu Advertiser (525-8000; www.honoluluadvertiser.com) The Advertiser is Hawai'i's big daily, delivered hot off the presses every morning.

Honolulu Star-Bulletin (529-4747; www.starbulletin.com) This is Hawai'i's second largest daily.

The Honolulu Weekly (528-1475; www.honoluluweekly.com) This locally written and owned, heavily-read, free alternative weekly pumps out relevant, liberal, and timely pieces on everything from fashion to politics.

MidWeek (235-5881; www.midweek.com) Connected to the *Star-Bulletin* and widely read across O'ahu, this free paper comes out twice weekly and includes everything but the kitchen sink. Its synicated and locally written articles range from moderately liberal to conservative.

Radio Stations

KHPR, 88.1 FM: Hawai'i Public Radio's classical music and NPR news.
KIPO, 89.3 FM: Hawai'i Public Radio's world music, jazz, BBC news, and other programming.
KTUH, 90.3 FM: University of Hawai'i's Hawaiian, jazz, and alternative programming.
KSSK, 92.3 FM: Adult contemporary mix and talk radio.
KHNR, 97.5 FM: Talk station featuring local and national speakers.
KCCN, 100.3 FM: Island music and reggae.
KPHW, 104.3 FM: Hip hop and R&B hits.
KINE, 105.1 FM: Classic and contemporary Hawaiian music.
KPOI, 105.9 FM: Classic rock.
KGMZ, 107.9 FM: Oldies from the 50s, 60s, and 70s.
KKNE, 940 AM: Classic Hawaiian music with very few commercials.
KORL, 1180 AM: Local talk and multicultural radio.
KNDI, 1270 AM: Samoan, Tongan, Laotian, and other "ethnic" programming.
KKEA, 1420 AM: Local and national sports and talk radio.

Television Stations

In addition to nationally broadcast stations from ABC to TCM to MTV, O'ahu has several alternative local stations. Channel numbers can differ according to subscriber service. Here are a few of the most unique.
KBFD, Channel 4: Independent Korean-language programming.
KIKU, Channel 9: Mostly Japanese-language and other "ethnic" programming.
KHET, Channel 10: Hawai'i public television.
OC16, Channel 16: Very cool, local-style programming focusing on Hawai'i.
HILOC, Channel 52: Hawai'i-oriented cultural programming.
HINATV, Channel 53: Hawaiian and South Pacific programming, plus Deutsche Welle.
VIEWS, Channel 54: City council meetings and island viewpoint programming.

Marriage in Hawai'i

More than 750,000 people come to Hawai'i each year to wed or honeymoon—so trust us that elements are in place to facilitate yours. You would be wise to hire a local wedding consultant, who can guide you through the entire process and set everything up. Many of Hawai'i's hotels are also fully capable of planning and executing your wedding as well. And yes, they can coordinate a beach ceremony. Note that while at one time Hawai'i gave the legal stamp to same-sex marriages, they no longer do.

Assuming you're planning the event far in advance, you might consider ordering the book *Hawai'i Weddings Made Simple* by Keri Shepard (2003), which covers all the basics and includes local contacts for every area of need. *Hawai'i Bride & Groom Magazine* (428-1596; www.hawaiibride.com) comes out twice each year and is filled with local wedding planning facts. The new *Something Blue Magazine* (www.somethingbluemagazine.net) also comes out bi-annually and gives you the full scoop in stylishly fresh and hip style. All of the above were available through www.amazon.com at the time of writing. Also, definitely check out the **O'ahu Wedding Association** (www.oahuweddingassociation.com), an association of numerous Hawai'i wedding industry businesses with a beautiful Web site full of information and discriminating contacts.

For you rebels who are already here and have spontaneously decided to go for it with the justice of the peace, read below for instructions on getting your marriage license squared away.

Obtaining a Marriage License

Pick up a marriage license packet at the **State of Hawai'i Department of Health's Marriage License Section** (Recorded information 585-4545; Staff 586-4544; www.hawaii/gov/doh; 1250 Punchbowl St., Room 101, Downtown) and coordinate with them for an appointment no earlier than 30 days before your intended wedding date.

You must both be present at the appointment, your application must be complete, you must show proper identification, and you must fork over $60 in cash. No blood tests are necessary and there is no waiting period. Upon approval, you'll be free to marry anywhere in Hawai'i for up to 30 days, at which time the license expires.

Religious Services

Worshipping and prayer are part of many people's lives in Hawai'i, and its multicultural climate encourages a very healthy and happy mix of viewpoints. O'ahu has hundreds of churches and other houses of worship and meditation ranging from Catholic to Russian Orthodox to Buddhist to Muslim, with services offered in English, Hawaiian, Tongan, Mandarin, Tagalog, and more. Ask your hotel or lodging hosts for assistance in locating the closest facility of your choice.

In Waikīkī, there are a couple of especially interesting services open to the public. **St. Augustine By-the-Sea** (923-7024; 130 'Ōhua Ave.) holds mass Monday through Saturday and liturgy both Saturday and Sunday. The **Hilton Hawaiian Village** (949-4321; 2005 Kalia Rd.) hosts a one-hour, nondenominational Christian service at 10:30 every Sunday morning right on the beach in front of the hotel. Different churches come out to minister, and songs, as well as dance performances, sometimes take place. Beach mats are provided for seating and the atmosphere is completely casual—you can even show up in your bathing suit!

This 1919 Mormon temple in Lā'ie is an art deco masterpiece, as well as the center of life in this Windward Coast town.

Road Service

If you've experienced a car accident resulting in roadway or vehicular damage, you'll need to report it to the police by calling 911 at the time of the accident, as well as follow up with paperwork afterward. If the accident's relatively minor, move your car out of the way (if it's blocking traffic) and wait for the cops.

If your car isn't moving, the tire's flat, or you're locked out, and you're a member of the **American Automobile Association** (AAA), you can reach them for help at 1-800-222-4357. If you're not an AAA member, try calling **A Roadrunner Towing Service** (Dispatch 957-0236). In business for 12 years, these guys will get you up and running, or drag you somewhere where you can get help. Doesn't matter where you are on the island, what time it is, or what happened: they're there to help. They accept MasterCard and Visa, but it's cheaper if you pay in cash.

Time Zones & Phones

Although once you've arrived you may not care what time it is anywhere else in the world, note that you're now in Hawai'i-Aleutian Standard Time—not far enough to cross the International Dateline, but far enough to be irritating when trying to make a business call to New York or check in with grandma in Cleveland. And, since Hawai'i doesn't observe Daylight Saving Time (DST), the time difference between Hawai'i and the Mainland depends on the season.

In November, when clocks are set back on the Mainland, we become two hours behind Pacific Time, three behind Mountain Time, four behind Central Time, and five behind Eastern Time. Once you move your clocks forward for DST in March, however, we remain behind these zones by yet an extra hour. Since most of Arizona doesn't observe DST either, we're three hours behind them year-round. You can set your watch locally by calling 643-8463 for the exact time.

Hawai'i has only one area code: 808. However, things get tricky when calling another Hawaiian Island. Even though we all share the same area code, you will need to dial "1-808" before your number to get through to them. In this book we've left out area codes whenever the numbers are on O'ahu and included them if they're off-island or toll free. Of course, if you're calling O'ahu from the Mainland, you will still need to add "1-808" to reach us.

For directory assistance, the standard 411 applies.

Volunteering

One of the best ways to experience another city or culture from the inside and to feel good about the world is through a bit of volunteering—and "volunteer vacations" have become very popular.

If you'd like to investigate opportunities in Hawai'i that don't require you to pony up dollars for the experience, check out **Volunteer Hawai'i** (543-2214; www.volunteerhawaii.org). The organization is linked with the United Way, and through their Web site you can do a search on long- and short-term positions—and even search by the dates you'll be in town. If you find the perfect opportunity, but it's listed as a long-term position, submit a request anyway and let them know your schedule; they often can find a way to use your skills for even just a day or two. If you don't have access to a computer, call Judith Cantil at the number above and get set up with something great.

Mālama Hawai'i (www.malamahawaii.org) is an organization of more than 70 community and environmental groups committed to the care of Hawaii. Check out their website for exciting short- and long-term opportunities.

Another place to look is in the calendar section of papers such as *The Honolulu Weekly, MidWeek,* or the dailies, which often post one-time community environmental cleanups and other projects.

General Index

A

Aaron's Dive Shop (Windward O'ahu), 223, 255
Abhasa Waikīkī Spa, 224
Access Aloha Travel, 36
ADASA (Windward O'ahu), 241
afternoon tea, 167
Agnes' Portuguese Bake Shop (Windward O'ahu), 170
ahupua'a system of land management, 180
AIA Architectural Walking Tour, 85
'Aiea Loop Trail, 216. *See also* Central O'ahu
airlines: local, interisland flights, 32; national and international, 31
Air New Zealand, 31
airplane rides, 212
Airport-Island Shuttles, 33
Airport Waikīkī Express, 33
air travel, 31–32
Akaka, Daniel, 183
Akamai Cab Company, 39
Ala Moana. *See* greater Honolulu
Ala Moana Center (Honolulu), 253
Ala Moana Regional Park (Honolulu): beaches, 196; gardens, 219; tennis, 228
Alamo car rentals, 37
Alan Wong's Restaurant (Honolulu), 149
Ala Wai Golf Course (Honolulu), 209
Alexander & Baldwin company, 23; building, 97–98
Ali'i Antiques I and II (Windward O'ahu), 243
Ali'i Lū'au, 167
Ali'iolani Hale (Honolulu), 81, 88
All Hawai'i Cruises/Captain Bob's Sailing Adventures (Windward O'ahu), 224
All Island Aviation, 212
Allure Swimwear (Waikīkī), 242
Aloha Airlines, 31, 32
Aloha Festivals Waikīkī: Ho'olaule'a and Floral Parade, 126
Aloha Nannies, 261
Aloha Rag (Honolulu), 240
Aloha Salad (Windward O'ahu), 172
Aloha Stadium Swap Meet (Central O'ahu), 236
Aloha Tower (Honolulu), 88–89
aloha wear, 236–39
American Airlines, 31
American Automobile Association, 270
Americanization, 26–27
American Savings Bank branches, 257–58
Angles' Gay Catamaran Cruise (Waikīkī), 220–21
Angles Waikīkī, 118
animal life, 16–17
Animation Magic (Honolulu), 252
Anna Bannanas (Honolulu), 119
Anne Namba (Honolulu), 240
Annette's Adventures, 210
annexationists, annexation, 24–26
Antique Alley (Honolulu), 243
Antique House (Waikīkī), 243
Antiques & Treasures (Windward O'ahu), 243
antiques and collectibles, 243–44
Aoki's Shave Ice (North Shore), 170
apparel: aloha wear, 236–39; swimwear, 242; vintage clothing, boutiques, 239–41
Aqua Bamboo & Spa (Waikīkī), 55
Aqua Café (Waikīkī), 137
Aqua Coconut Plaza (Waikīkī), 55
Aqua Hotel Renew (Waikīkī), 56
Aqua Island Colony (Waikīkī), 57
Aqua Waikīkī Wave, 56
Arancino (Waikīkī), 137
archaeological sites, 186–88
architecture, 79–83
area code, 270
Army Community Theatre (Honolulu), 123
Artlines (Honolulu), 249
arts and crafts, traditional, 184–85
ARTS at Marks Garage, The (Honolulu), 246, 247

Art Treasures, The (Honolulu), 247
Atlantis Adventures O'ahu (Waikīkī), 224
Aveda Lifestyle Salon & Spa (Honolulu), 225
Avis car rentals, 37

B

Baby Showers Hawai'i (Windward O'ahu), 252–53
Baci Bistro (Windward O'ahu), 159
Backpacker's Vacation Inn (North Shore), 72
Baik Designs (Honolulu), 250
Bailey's Antiques & Aloha Shirts (Honolulu), 237
bakeries, sweet treats, 168–70
Balcony Gallery, The (Windward O'ahu), 248
Bali Aga Furniture (Honolulu), 250
Bali by the Sea (Waikīkī), 137–38
Bali Moon Hawai'i (North Shore), 251
Ballet Hawai'i (Honolulu), 123
Bank of Hawai'i, 258
banks, 257–58
Banyan Veranda (Waikīkī), 167
Banzai Sushi Bar (North Shore), 163–64
Barnes and Noble (Honolulu), 245
Barnfield's Raging Isle Surf & Cycle (North Shore), 206
Battleship *Missouri* Memorial (Central O'ahu), 105
Bayfest Hawai'i (Windward O'ahu), 126
"Bayonet Constitution," 24
Beach Bar (Waikīkī), 118
beaches: general information, 192–94; Honolulu, 195–97; North Shore, 201–4; Waikīkī, 195; Windward O'ahu, 197–201
Beard Papa's Cream Puffs (Waikīkī), 168
Bestsellers Books & Music: Honolulu, 245; Waikīkī), 245
Bethel Street Gallery (Honolulu), 247–48
Betsey Johnson (Honolulu), 240
bicycling, bike rentals, 205–6
Big Kahuna Motorcycle Tours & Rentals (Waikīkī), 206
Big Kahuna Rentals, 37
Bike Hawai'i/'Ohana Adventure Tours, 210
Bike Shop, The (Windward O'ahu), 206
Bikram Yoga College of India (Windward O'ahu), 232
Bikram Yoga North Shore, 232
Billabong (Waikīkī), 255
Bishop Museum (Honolulu), 79, 109; Library and Archives, 106–7
Bistro, The (Honolulu), 176
"Blue Hawai'i" Cocktail Hour, 118
Blue Planet Surf Shop (Waikīkī), 226
bodyboarding. *See* surfing and bodyboarding
Bogart's Café (Honolulu), 170
Bonheur (Honolulu), 240
book and music stores, 244–46
BookEnds (Windward O'ahu), 245
books about Hawai'i, 258–61
Boots & Kimo's Homestyle Kitchen (Windward O'ahu), 160
Borders Books & Music (Honolulu), 245
Borders Express: Waikīkī, 245; Windward O'ahu, 245
Brasserie Du Vin (Honolulu), 120
Braun Urgent Care (Windward O'ahu), 266
Breakers, The (Waikīkī), 57
Brent's Restaurant & Deli (Windward O'ahu), 160
Brew Moon Restaurant & Microbrewery (Waikīkī), 119
Broadrider's Bar & Grill (Windward O'ahu), 120
Bubbies Homemade Ice Cream & Desserts (Honolulu), 169
Budget Rent-A-Car, 37
buses, shuttles: airport transportation, 33; TheBus, 38–39, 214
Buzz's Original Steak House (Windward O'ahu), 120, 160–61
Byodo-In Temple (Windward O'ahu), 45, 103–4

C

Cabana at Waikīkī, The (Waikīkī), 57–58
Café Hale'iwa (North Shore), 163–64
Café Laufer (Honolulu), 169
cafés, on-the-go foods, 170–73, 176
California Pizza Kitchen: Waikīkī, 138; Windward O'ahu, 161
camping, 206–7
Camp Mokulēi'a (North Shore), 207
canoeing, 217–18
Canoes at the 'Ilikai (Waikīkī), 138
Capital Historical District (Honolulu), 80; buildings and sites, 91–96; walking tours, 85
Carey Hawai'i Chauffeured Services, 39
Carnival Cruise Lines, 33

car rentals, 36–37; at Honolulu airport, 33
Cassis by Chef Mavro (Honolulu), 149–50
Castle & Cooke, 23, 26
Castle Medical Center (Windward O'ahu), 265
catamaran excursions, 220–22
C. Brewer & Co., 23
Celebrity Cruises, 33
Celestial Natural Foods (North Shore), 176
Central O'ahu: cafés, on-the-go foods, 173; geographical overview, 47; golfing, 210; historic buildings and sites, 105–6; hospitals and medical services, 265; map, 50; movie houses, 84; museums and galleries, 113–14, 117; restaurants, 166; shopping centers, 253; surfing and bodyboarding, 227; tennis, 228
Central O'ahu Regional Park Tennis Complex & Archery Range, 228
Central Pacific Bank branches, 258
Central YMCA (Honolulu), 232
Cha Cha Cha Waikīkī, 138–39
Chai's Island Bistro (Honolulu), 150
Chamber Music Series (University of Hawai'i), 122
Char Hung Sut (Honolulu), 168
Charley's Taxis & Tours, 39
Cheesecake Factory, 139w
childcare services, 261
Chinatown Historic District (Honolulu): Eateries Tour, 174; historic buildings and sites, 89–90; parking, 38; walking tour, 85
Chinese immigration, 23
Cholo's Homestyle Mexican (North Shore), 173
Cina Cina (Waikīkī), 239–40
Cindy's Lei & Flower Shoppe (Honolulu), 239
cinema, movies, 83–84
Cinnamon Girl (Waikīkī), 240
Cinnamon's Restaurant (Windward O'ahu), 161
citizenship, 26
classes and lectures: University of Hawai'i, 84; Windward Community College, 85
Cleveland, Grover, 25
climate, 16, 261–62
clothing. *See* apparel
Cobalt Lounge (Waikīkī), 120
Coconut Cruisers (Waikīkī), 206
Coffee Bean & Tea Leaf, The: Waikīkī, 173; Windward O'ahu, 174
Coffee Gallery (North Shore), 174
coffee houses, tea cafés, 173–74
Cold Stone Creamery (Waikīkī), 168
Consolidated Theatres movie houses, 84
Contemporary Café, The (Honolulu), 150
Contemporary Museum, The (Honolulu), 109–10; First Hawaiian Center extension, 110; gardens, 219; Museum Shop, 249
Continental Airlines, 31
Cook, James, 19–20
cooking classes, 174
Cook's Tour of Chinatown, A, 174
coral reefs, 222–23
cost of living, 29, 182
Crack Seed Center, The (Honolulu), 168
cruise boats, 33
cuisine, 133–36, 166–67
culinary tours, 174
Culinary Walking Tour of Chinatown, 174
cultural diversity, 78–79
cultural values, native Hawaiian, 180–83
Cupcake Boutique (Honolulu), 240

D

dance, traditional, 185–86. *See also* performing arts/art houses
Dave & Busters video games (Honolulu), 233
daylight savings time, 270
Deep Ecology (North Shore), 224; whale watching trips, 231
Delta Airlines, 31
Department of Land and Natural Resources, 214
Department of Parks and Recreation, 194, 207
DFS Starbucks (Waikīkī), 173–74
Diamond Head Beach Hotel (Waikīkī), 58
Diamond Head Crater (Honolulu), 16; driving to, 41, hiking, 214–15
Diamond Head Grill (Waikīkī), 139
Diamond Head Lighthouse, 91
Diamond Head Market & Grill (Honolulu), 170
Diamond Head Parasail (Honolulu), 218
Diamond Head Tennis Center (Waikīkī), 228
Diamond Head Theatre (Honolulu), 123
Dickey, Charles, 79, 98
Diesel (Waikīkī), 240
disabled travelers: accessible transportation, 36; handicapped parking, 36; services for, 264
discounts: air fares, 31–32; TheBus, 39

Discovery Bay Medical Clinic (Waikīkī), 265
Distinguished Lecture Series (University of Hawai'i), 84
Dole, James, 26
Dole, Sanford, 25
Dole Plantation (Leeward O'ahu), 230
Dollar Rent A Car, 37
dolphin watching, 230–31
Doris Duke Theatre, The (Honolulu), 83, 123
Doubletree Alana Hotel Waikīkī, 58
Down to Earth (Honolulu, Windward O'ahu), 175
driving: advantages, 34–36; car rentals, 36–37; emergency road service, 269–70; gasoline prices, 37; Honolulu parking, 38; local rules and tips, 37–38; road and street signs, 36
drug stores and pharmacies, 263–64
Duke Kahanamoku statue (Waikīkī), 222
Duke's Canoe Club (Waikīkī), 119, 140
Du Vin (Honolulu), 177

E

E & O Trading Co. (Honolulu), 151
Easter Sunrise Service, 126
East-West Center Gallery (Honolulu), 115
economy, economic growth, 28–29
Eddie Aikau Big Wave Invitational, 204
Eggs 'n Things (Waikīkī), 140, 176
'Ehukai Beach (North Shore), 202
88 Tees (Waikīkī), 239
Eiselin Imports (Honolulu), 251
Elite Limousine Service, 39
Elvin's Bakery & Café (Windward O'ahu), 170
emergency services contacts, 262
Enterprise Rent-A-Car, 37
Euro Market Café (Waikīkī), 173
events, seasonal, 122, 126–31, 243
'Ewa Hotel (Waikīkī), 58–59

F

factoring agencies, 23
family-oriented activities, 221, 228–30, 233
farmer's markets, 175–76
fashion-tips, what to wear, 241
fast food. *See* cafés, on-the-go foods
ferries, interisland, 33–34
Fire Truck Hawai'i guided tours, 210–11
fireworks, 221
First Friday gallery walks (Honolulu), 221, 246
First Hawaiian Bank branches, 258
fishing, 207–8
fish markets/fish auctions, 176–77
fishponds, 186
fitness facilities, 232
food glossary, 135–36
Foodland: Honolulu, 263; North Shore, 264
Food Pantry (Waikīkī), 263
Formaggio Grill (Windward O'ahu), 161–62, 177
Formaggio Wine Bar (Honolulu), 120, 177
Fort DeRussy Beach (Waikīkī), 59, 195
Foster Botanical Garden (Honolulu), 219
Fujioka's Wine Times (Honolulu), 177
Fusion Waikīkī, 118–19

G

Galerie Lassen (Waikīkī), 246
galleries, arts and handcrafts, 246–48. *See also* museums
Gallery at Ward Centre, The (Honolulu), 248
Gallery 'Iolani (Windward O'ahu), 116
games, 233
Garakuta-Do (Honolulu), 243
gasoline prices, 37
gay travelers: nightlife, 118–19; sailing and catamaran excursions, 220–21
Gay Hawai'i Cruise (Waikīkī), 221
Genesis Aviation, 212
Genki Sushi (Honolulu), 171
geography: Hawai'i, 15; O'ahu, 15
geology, 14–16
Germaine's Lū'au, 167
Giovanni's Shrimp Truck (Windward O'ahu), 172
Girls Who Surf school, 226
glass-bottom boat trips, 224
glider rides, 212–13
Global Creations Interiors (North Shore), 250
Global Village (Windward O'ahu), 241
glossary of Hawaiian terms, 266–67
Go Bananas Kayaks (Honolulu), 218
Godiva Chocolatier's (Waikīkī), 168
Golf Club (Windward O'ahu), 209
golfing, 208–10
gourmet and health food stores, 175–76
Gourmet Cooking Hawai'i, 174

Gourmet Trilogy Tour for Food & Wine Lovers, 174
Grand Café & Bakery (Honolulu), 150–51
Grass Skirt Grill (North Shore), 173
Gravity Hawai'i (Windward O'ahu), 211
greater Honolulu, 128; afternoon tea, 168; aloha wear, 237–38; antiques and collectibles, 243; archaeological/sacred sites, 186–87; arts and crafts galleries, 247–48; bakeries, sweet treats, 168–69; beaches, 195–97; books and music, 245; cafés, on-the-go foods, 170–71; coffee houses, tea cafés, 174; commercial movie houses, 84; cruise boats, 33; driving and parking in, 37–38; family-oriented activities, 229; farmer's markets, general information, 10; geographical overview, 41; gourmet & health food, juice bars, 175; fishing, 208; fish markets/fish auctions, 177; fitness facilities, 232; food markets and drug stores, 263; golfing, 209; Hawaiiana and other gifts, 249–50; hiking, 214–15; home furnishings, 250–51; hospitals and medical services, 265; kayak/canoe rentals, 218; kid's stuff, 252; late-night dining, 176; libraries, 106–8; lodging, 70–71; maps, 40, 42; museums and galleries, 109–13, 115–16; nightlife, 118–21; parks and gardens, 219; performing arts/art houses, 83, 123–26; public transportation, 33, 38–39; restaurants, 148–59; seasonal and special events, 126–30; shopping centers, 253; snorkeling/scuba diving, 223; spas and salons, 225; surfing and sporting gear, 255; swimwear, 242; tennis, 228; vintage clothing, boutiques, 240–41; walking tours, 85; wine bars, wine shops, 177. *See also* Waikīkī
Green Room/Opium Den & Champagne Bar (Honolulu), 121
Grill, The (Honolulu), 170
groceries and sundries, 263–64
ground transportation from airport, 32–33
Growing Keiki, The (North Shore), 253
guided adventure, nature tours, 210–11, 218
Gunstock Ranch (North Shore), 217

H

Hale'iwa, 46. *See also* North Shore
Hale'iwa Family Health Center (North Shore), 266
Hale'iwa Joe's Seafood Grill: North Shore, 164; Windward O'ahu, 162
Hale Koa Hotel (Waikīkī), 59
Halekulani (Waikīkī), 59; House Without A Key, 118; La Mer, 143; Lewers Lounge, 120–21
Hale Nalu (Leeward Coast), 223, 226
Hale O Lono Heiau (North Shore), 188
Hale Vietnam (Honolulu), 151–52
Hall, E. O., 21–22
Hana Hou! magazine, 267
Hanauma Bay Nature Preserve (Honolulu), 16, 196–97; snorkeling/scuba diving, 223
Handi-Cabs of the Pacific, 36
handicapped services, 264
hang gliding, 211–12
Hans Hedemann Surf School, 226–27
Hapa Grill (Central O'ahu), 173
Happy Trails Hawai'i (North Shore), 217
Harbor Pub (Waikīkī), 119
Harleys® and Sportbikes Hawai'i, 37
Harold L. Lyon Arboretum (Honolulu), 214, 219
Hau Tree Lānai (Waikīkī), 140–41
Hau'ula. *See* Windward O'ahu
Hawai'i All-Collectors Show (Honolulu), 126, 243
Hawai'i Business magazine, 267
Hawai'i Chauffeur & Limo Services, 39
Hawai'i Children's Discovery Center (Honolulu), 229
Hawai'i Department of Agriculture (HDA), Animal/Plant Quarantine Station, 32
Hawai'i Department of Health's Marriage License Section, 269
Hawai'i Department of Land and Natural Resources/Division of State Parks, 207
Hawai'i Events Online website, 78
Hawai'i Food Tours, 174
Hawai'i Geographic Society Tours, 85
Hawai'i International Film Festival (Honolulu), 127
Hawai'i International Jazz Festival, 122
Hawai'i Kai Golf Course (Honolulu), 209
Hawai'i Loa, 18
Hawai'i Maritime Center, 110–11
Hawai'i Nature Center (Honolulu), 214
Hawai'i Opera Theatre (Honolulu), 124
Hawai'i Polo Club (North Shore), 233
Hawai'i Polo Oceanfront Trail Rides (North Shore), 217

Hawai'i Prince Golf Club (Central O'ahu), 210
Hawai'i Prince Hotel Waikīkī, 59–60
Hawai'i Public Radio, 78
Hawai'i State Archives (Honolulu), 108
Hawai'i State Art Museum (Honolulu), 112, 246
Hawai'i State Capitol (Honolulu), 82, 92
Hawai'i State Department of Health's Disability and Communication Access Board, 264
Hawai'i State Legislature (Honolulu), 222
Hawai'i State Library (Honolulu), 106–7
Hawai'i Superferry, 33–34
Hawai'i Super Transit, 33
Hawai'i Surfboard Rentals, 226
Hawai'i Theatre (Honolulu), 81, 92–93, 123
Hawai'i Visitors and Convention Bureau, 78
Hawai'i Watercolor Society, 246
Hawaiian Airlines, 31, 32
Hawaiian ancestry, 179
Hawaiian Astronomical Society Kahala Star Party (Honolulu), 222
Hawaiian Brian's pool hall (Honolulu), 233
Hawaiian culture and values, 180–83
Hawaiian Feast in Paradise Tour, 174
Hawaiian Fire surf school (Central O'ahu), 227
Hawaiian food, 166–67
Hawaiian Historical Society (Honolulu), 107–8
Hawaiian Homes Act, 180
Hawaiian honeycreeper, 17
Hawaiian Humane Society Cat House (Honolulu), 222
Hawaiian Island Creations (Honolulu), 255
Hawaiian Islands, 15; air travel to, 31–32; climate, 16, 261–62; the Hawaiian archipelago, 34; history, 17–29; interisland ferries, 33–34; interisland flights, 32; plant and animal life, 16–17
Hawaiian language: glossary, 266–67; spoken language, 108
Hawaiian Mission Children's Society Library (Honolulu), 108
"Hawaiian music," 122
Hawaiian Parasail (Honolulu), 218
Hawaiian Princess at Mākaha (Leeward O'ahu), 73
Hawaiian Quilt Collection (Waikīkī), 248
Hawaiian Railway Society (Leeward O'ahu), 117
"Hawaiian Renaissance," 28, 186
Hawaiian Slack Key Guitar Festival (Waikīkī), 126
Hawaiian Trail & Mountain Club, 214
Hawaiian Water Adventures Park (Leeward O'ahu), 230
Hawaiiana and other gifts, 248–50
Hawaiiana Hotel (Waikīkī), 60
Hawai'i's Plantation Village (Central O'ahu), 113–14
He'eia Fishpond (Windward O'ahu), 187
He'eia State Park (Windward O'ahu), 219
heiau (places of worship), 186
Helemano Plantation (Central O'ahu), 166
helicopter rides, 212
Heritage Antiques & Gifts (Windward O'ahu), 244
Hertz car rentals, 37
Hideaway, The (Waikīkī), 119
Hiker's Guide to O'ahu (Ball), 214
hiking, 213–16
Hilo Wattie (Waikīkī), 237
Hilton Hawaiian Village Beach Resort & Spa (Waikīkī), 60; fireworks, 221; religious services, 269
Hilton Waikīkī Prince Kūhiō, 61
Hina Adventures, 211
historic buildings and sites, 85–86. See also museums and galleries
History Makers Walking Tour of Honolulu's Greater Capital Cultural District, 85
hitchhiking, 34
Hōkū's (Honolulu), 152
Hole-In-The-Wall Tour, 174
holidays, 264–65
Holland America, 33
Holokai Grill (Waikīkī), 141
home furnishings, 250–51
Hong Kong Harbour View Seafood Restaurant (Honolulu), 152–53
Honolulu area. *See* greater Honolulu
Honolulu Academy of Arts, 108, 113; Academy Shop, 249; museum store, 244
Honolulu Advertiser, The, 267
Honolulu Box Office, 123
Honolulu Café, 171
Honolulu City Lights, 128
Honolulu Coffee Company: Honolulu, 174; Waikīkī, 173
Honolulu Festival & Parade, 128
Honolulu Hale (City Hall), 81, 93–94

Honolulu International Airport (HNL): airlines serving, 31–32; ground transportation, 32–33
Honolulu Magazine, 267
Honolulu Marathon, 128
Honolulu Police Department Law Enforcement Museum, 115
Honolulu Polo Club (Windward O'ahu), 233
Honolulu Printmakers, 246
Honolulu Star-Bulletin, 267
Honolulu Symphony, 124
Honolulu Theatre for Youth, 124
Honolulu Weekly, The, 267
Honolulu Zoo (Waikīkī), 228–29
ho'okipa (sense of place), 83
Ho'omaluhia Botanical Garden (Windward O'ahu), 214, 220; camping, 207
horseback riding, 216–17
hospitals, 265–66
House Without A Key (Waikīkī), 118, 141
Hukilau Beach Park (Windward O'ahu), 197–98
hula, 185
Hula Grill Waikīkī, 142
Hula's Bar & Lei Stand (Waikīkī), 119
Hungry Ear Records & Tapes, 245
Hyatt Regency Waikīkī Resort & Spa, 61
Hy's Steak House (Waikīkī), 142

I

'Ilikai Hotel (Waikīkī), 61–62
'Ilima Hotel (Waikīkī), 62
Imin Center-Jefferson Hall (University of Hawai'i), 123
India Café (Honolulu), 153
Indich Collection (Honolulu), 251
Indigo Eurasian Cuisine (Honolulu), 153
Inter-Island Sportfishing (Honolulu), 208
International Market Place (Waikīkī), 236
'Iolani Palace State Monument (Honolulu), 81, 94–95
Iona Contemporary Dance Theatre (Honolulu), 124–25
Island Air, 32
Island Seaplane Service, 212
Island Snow (Windward O'ahu), 170
Island Treasures (Windward O'ahu), 250

J

Jamba Juice sites, 175
Jameson's by the Sea (North Shore), 164–65
Japan Airlines, 31
Japanese Cultural Center of Hawai'i (Honolulu), 115
Japanese immigration, 23
Jeff Chang Pottery & Fine Crafts: Waikīkī, 246–47; Windward O'ahu, 248
John Young Museum of Art (Honolulu), 115–16
Judiciary History Center (Honolulu), 88, 116
juice bars, 175–76
Juicy Couture (Honolulu), 241
Jungle Fun video games (Honolulu), 233
JW Marriott 'Ihilani Resort and Spa (Leeward O'ahu), 73–74, 225, 228

K

Ka'a'awa. *See* Windward O'ahu
Ka'ahumanu, 22
Ka'apuawa-okamehameha, David and Myrtle, 79
Ka'ena Point State Park (Leeward, O'ahu), 50, 204, 216
Kahala. *See* greater Honolulu
Kahala Beach (Honolulu), 197; snorkeling/scuba diving, 223
Kahala Hotel & Resort, The (Honolulu), 71; dolphin watching, 221
Kahanamoku Beach (Waikīkī), 195
Kaho'olawe, 18, 34
Kahuku. *See* North Shore
Kahuku Golf Course (North Shore), 209
Kahuku Hospital (Windward O'ahu), 265
Kailua. *See also* Windward O'ahu: map, 46
Kailua Beach Park (Windward O'ahu), 198–99
Kailua Beachwalk (Windward O'ahu), 250
Kailua Blue (Windward O'ahu), 211
Kailua District Park (Windward O'ahu), 228
Kailua Farmers' Market, 175
Kaimana's beach (Waikīkī), 195
Kaimukī. *See* greater Honolulu
Kainoa's Sports Bar (North Shore), 120
Kaiser 24-Hour Advice Nurse, 265
Kaiser Permanente Medical Center and Clinic (Honolulu), 265
Kaka'ako. *See* greater Honolulu
Kaka'ako Kitchen (Honolulu), 171

Kalakaua, David ("Merry Monarch"), 22, 24
Kalanimoku "Lot G", 38
Kalapawai Café & Deli (Windward O'ahu), 172
Kalapawai Market (Windward O'ahu), 172
Kalihi. *See* greater Honolulu
kalo plant, 167
Kamaka Hawai'i (Honolulu), 249
Kamehameha I, 186–87; reign, 20; statue of, 88
Kamehameha II, 21; royal descendants, 22
Kamehameha III, 22, 23
Kamehameha V, 112
Kamehameha V Post Office (Honolulu), 96–97
Kāne'ākī Heiau (Leeward O'ahu), 188
Kāne'ohe, 45. *See also* Windward O'ahu
Kāne'ohe Bay Cruises (Windward O'ahu), 224
Kapahulu. *See* greater Honolulu
Kapi'olani Medical Center for Women & Children (Honolulu), 265
Kapi'olani Park (Waikīkī), 122, 218, 222. *See also* seasonal and special events
Kapi'olani Tennis Courts (Waikīkī), 228
Kapolei. *See* Leeward O'ahu
kapu (taboo) system, 18, 21, 182
Kapuāiwa, Lot, 22
Kaua'i, 15, 16; Cook's arrival at, 19; Menehune on, 18
Ka'ū Desert (Hawai'i), 16
Kauikeaouli (Kamehameha III), 22
Kawaiaha'o Cemetery (Honolulu), 95–96
Kawaiaha'o Church (Honolulu), 80, 95–96
kayaking, 217–18
Keaiwa Heiau State Recreation Area (Central O'ahu), 216
Keawa'ula Beach (Leeward O'ahu), 204
Kē Iki Bungalows (North Shore), 72
Kekaulike Plaza and Maunakea Marketplace (Honolulu), 177
Kennedy Theatre (Honolulu), 125
Keo's in Waikīkī, 142–43
kid's stuff, 251–53
Kilohana Square (Waikīkī), 243
Kimo's Surf Hut (Windward O'ahu), 226, 255
King Kalākaua Building (post office), 81
King Kamehameha Floral Parade, 128
King Kamehameha Hula Competition (Honolulu), 128
King Kamehameha Statue (Honolulu), 88
kiteboarding, 232
Kiwani Ramen (Waikīkī), 170
Koa Pancake House (Windward O'ahu), 162
Kohala Bay Collections (North Shore), 238
Kōkua Market (Honolulu), 175
Kona Brewing Co. & Brew Pub, The (Honolulu), 119
Kona Coast, fishing, 207
Kona winds, 16
Ko'olau Range, 16, 42, 47
Kō 'Olina Golf Club (Central O'ahu), 210
Kō 'Olina Lagoons (Leeward O'ahu), 204; snorkeling/scuba diving, 223
Korean Festival, 128–29
Korean immigration, 23
Kua 'Āina: Honolulu, 171; North Shore, 173
Kualoa Ranch Hawai'i (Windward O'ahu), 217, 229
Kualoa Regional Park (Windward O'ahu), 199; Campsite "B", 207
Kuan Yin Temple (Honolulu), 89
Kūhiō, Jonah, 26, 180
Kūhiō Beach (Waikīkī), 195; Hula Mound, 221
Kūhiō Pharmacy (Waikīkī), 263
Kuilima Cove snorkeling/diving site (North Shore), 223
Kumu Kahua Theatre (Honolulu), 125
Ku'uloa Kai Charters (North Shore), 208

L

L & L Barbecue (Central O'ahu), 173
Lā'ie. *See* Windward O'ahu
Lā'ie Cinemas (Windward O'ahu), 84
Lai Fong (Honolulu), 243
La Marina Sailing Club (Honolulu), 118
La Mer (Waikīkī), 143
land redistribution, 23, 28
language, Hawaiian: glossary, 266–67; spoken language, 108
language, Hawaiian. *See* Hawaiian language
Laniākea Beach Park (North Shore), 202
Lanikai Beach (Windward O'ahu), 199; snorkeling/scuba diving, 223. *See also* Windward O'ahu
Lanikai Juice (Windward O'ahu), 175
Lappert's Gourmet Ice Creams and Coffees (Waikīkī), 168

Laysan Island, 34
Le Bistro (Honolulu), 154
Leeward O'ahu: archaeological/sacred sites, 188; beaches, 204–5; coffee houses, tea cafés, 174; commercial movie houses, 84; family-oriented activities, 230; food markets and drug stores, 264; geographical overview, 49, 51; lodging, 73–75; map, 51; medical services, 266, museums and galleries, 117, restaurants, 166; snorkeling/scuba diving, 223, 224; spas and salons, 225; surfing and bodyboarding, 226; tennis, 228; whale watching trips, 231
lei, 239
Lei Day Celebration, 128
Lei Lei's (North Shore), 165
Le Jardin (Waikīkī), 170
Leonard's Bakery (Honolulu), 169
lesbian travelers: nightlife, 118–19; sailing and catamaran excursions, 220–21
Lewers Lounge (Waikīkī), 120–21
libraries, 106–8
Liholiho, Alexander (Kamehameha IV), 22
Lili'uokalani, 22, 24–25
limousines. *See* sedans and limousines
Little Hawaiian Gift Shop (Waikīkī), 248
Little Village Noodle House (Honolulu), 154
"local culture," 108
Local Motion (Waikīkī), 255
Local Motion Surf into Summer (Honolulu), 128
Loco Boutique (Waikīkī), 242
lodging: general information, 51; Leeward O'ahu, 73–75 North Shore, 72–73; price codes, 55; Waikīkī, 55–70
Lō'ihi Seamount (Hawai'i), 15
Longs Drugs: Central O'ahu, 264; Honolulu, 263; Leeward O'ahu, 264; Windward O'ahu, 263–64
Louis Pohl Gallery (Honolulu), 248
Louis Vuitton Hawai'i International Film Festival, 83
lounges and clubs, 120–21
Luana Hills Country Club (Windward O'ahu), 209
Lū'au, 167
Lucy's Grill & Bar (Windward O'ahu), 162–63
Lunalilo, William, 22, 24
Lunalilo Mausoleum (Honolulu), 95–96
Luxury Rentals, 37

M

MAC 24/7 (Waikīkī), 143–44, 176
Macy's: Honolulu, 237, 242; Waikīkī, 242; Windward O'ahu), 238
magazines, 267
MaHaLo Hawai'i Deep Sea Water Showroom (Waikīkī), 174
Mai Tai Bar: Honolulu, 119; Waikīkī, 118
Maita'i Catamaran (Waikīkī), 221
Mākaha. *See* Leeward O'ahu
Mākaha Beach Park (Leeward O'ahu), 204–5
Mākaha Resort Golf Club (Central O'ahu), 210
Makai Garage, 38
Makani Kai Helicopters, 212–13
Makapu'u Beach Park (Windward O'ahu), 199–200
Makapu'u Point (Windward O'ahu), 215–16
Makiki. *See* greater Honolulu
Makiki Forest Recreation Area (Honolulu), 213–14
Makiki Valley, hiking, 215
Mālaekahana State Recreation Area (Windward O'ahu), 200–201; camping, 207
Mālama Hawai'i, 270
Mālama Market (North Shore), 264
Mamo Howell (Honolulu), 237
Mana Hawai'i (Waikīkī), 248
Mandara Spa (Waikīkī), 225
Mānoa, Mānoa Valley, 81. *See also* greater Honolulu
Mānoa Cliffs Circuit hiking (Honolulu), 215
Mānoa Falls (Honolulu), 215
Mānoa Valley Theatre, 125
Manuheali'i (Windward O'ahu), 238
maps: Central O'ahu, 50; downtown Honolulu, 40; Kailua, 46; metropolitan Honolulu, 42; North Shore, O'ahu, 48; O'ahu, 35; Waikīkī beach detail, 43; Windward O'ahu, 44
Marie's Health Foods/Organic Café (Waikīkī), 175
Mariposa (Honolulu), 154–55
Mark N. Brown Galley (Honolulu), 248
Maro Reef, 34
Marquesas Islands, migrations from, 18
marriage licenses, 269
Marriott's Kō 'Olina Beach Club (Leeward O'ahu), 75
Martin & McArthur (Waikīkī), 248–49
Mary's Toys (Windward O'ahu), 253
Mary Z's (Windward O'ahu), 241

Matsumoto Shave Ice (North Shore), 170
Mauka Makai Excursions, 211
Mauna Kea (Hawai'i), 15
McKinley, Henry, 26
medical services, 265–66
Mediterraneo (Honolulu), 155
mele (traditional chanting), 185–86
Memorial Day Celebrations (Punchbowl-Tantalus), 128–29
Menehune, 18
Men's Moloka'i to O'ahu Canoe Race (Waikīkī), 129
Merchant Street Historic District (Honolulu), 96–98
Mesh (Honolulu), 251
Messiah at Central Union Church (Honolulu), 129
Michel's (Waikīkī), 144
Midway, 34
MidWeek newspaper, 267–68
Mililani. *See* Central O'ahu
Mills Gallery (Waikīkī), 243
MisFortune (Honolulu), 241
missionaries, 21, 185–86
Mission Houses Museum (Honolulu), 80, 98–99; Holiday Craft Fair, 129, 236; Museum Gift Shop, 244
Missouri Memorial (Central O'ahu), 105
Miyako Japanese Restaurant (Waikīkī), 144–45
Moanalua. *See* greater Honolulu
Moana Surfrider (Waikīkī), 62, 86–87; Beach Bar, 118
Mō'ili'ili. *See* greater Honolulu
Mokulēi'a Beach Park (North Shore), 202
Mokulele Airlines, 32
Mokulua Kayak Guides (Windward O'ahu), 218
Mokumanamana, 18, 34
Mondo Gelato (Waikīkī), 168
mopeds, moped rentals, 205–6
Morning Brew (Windward O'ahu), 174
motorcycle rentals, 37
Mount Wai'ale'ale (Kaua'i), 16
Movie Museum, 83
Mr. Ojisan (Honolulu), 176
Murphy's Bar & Grill (Honolulu), 119
museums and galleries: central O'ahu, 113–14; Greater Honolulu, 108–13
music, Hawaiian, recommended CDs, 245–46
music, live. *See* performing arts/art houses
music, traditional, 185–86

N

Na Hoku II Catamaran (Waikīkī), 221
Na Ho'ola Spa (Waikīkī), 225
Naish Hawai'i (Windward O'ahu), 232
Nānākuli. *See* Leeward O'ahu
National Car Rental, 37
National Memorial Cemetery of the Pacific (Honolulu), 99–100
National Weather Service Forecasts, 262
Native Books/ Nā Mea Hawai'i (Honolulu), 245, 249–50
Native Hawaiian Government Reorganization Act, 183
Native Hawaiians, 179–83; cultural values, 180–83; language, 184; traditional arts and crafts, 184–85
Natural Selection Gift Shop (Waikīkī), 251
Nature Conservancy events, 214
nature tours, 210–11
Nāwao (wild people), 18
Neal S. Blaisdell Center, 122
Neiman Marcus (Honolulu), 168
Nene Goose Bakery (Windward O'ahu), 170
New Otani Kaimana Beach Hotel (Waikīkī), 63
newspapers, 267–68
NFL professional football (Central O'ahu), 129
nightlife: general information, 117–18; greater Honolulu, 118–21; North Shore, 120; Waikīkī, 118–21; Windward O'ahu, 120
Nihoa, 18, 34
Ni'ihau, 18, 34
Noa Noa (Waikīkī), 240
Nohea Gallery (Waikīkī), 249
Nohea Island Arts (Windward O'ahu), 250
North Shore: aloha wear, 238; antiques and collectibles, 244; archaeological/sacred sites, 188; bakeries, sweet treats, 170; beaches, 201–4; bicycling, bike rentals, 206; cafés, on-the-go foods, 173; camping, 207; coffee houses, tea cafés, 174; farmer's markets, gourmet & health food, juice bars, 176; fishing, 208; fitness facilities, 232; food markets and drug stores, 264; geographical overview, 45–47; golfing, 209–10;

hang gliding, paragliding, ultralight flying, 212; Hawaiiana and other gifts, 250, 251; helicopter, airplane, glider rides, 213; hiking, 214, 216; horseback riding, 217; kid's stuff, 253; lodging, 72–73; map, 48; medical services, 266; museums and galleries, 117; nightlife, 120; parks and gardens, 220; polo, 233; restaurants, 163–66; seasonal and special events, 130; snorkeling/scuba diving, 223, 224; spas and salons, 225; surfing and bodyboarding, 226–27; surfing and sporting gear, 255–56; swimwear, 242; tennis, 228; vintage clothing, boutiques, 242; whale watching trips, 231
North Shore Boardriders Club (North Shore), 255
North Shore Catamaran Charters, 224; whale watching trips, 231
North Shore Country Market, 176
North Shore Surf and Cultural Museum, 117
North Shore Swimwear, 242
Northwest/KLM Airlines, 31
Norwegian Cruise Line, 33
Nu'uanu. *See* greater Honolulu
Nu'uanu Pali Lookout (Honolulu), 186–87

O

O'ahu Airport Shuttle, 33
O'ahu Market (Honolulu), 89
O'ahu Nature Tours, 211
O'ahu Wedding Association, 269
OceanFest (Waikīkī), 129
Office of Hawaiian Affairs (OHA), 182
'Ohana Waikīkī Beachcomber (Waikīkī), 63
Okinawan Festival (Waikīkī), 129
Ola (North Shore), 165–66
Olive Tree Café (Honolulu), 171
Olomana Golf Links (Windward O'ahu), 209
Only Show in Town, The (North Shore), 244
Ono Hawaiian Foods (Honolulu), 170
Ono Loa Hawaiian Foods (Windward O'ahu), 172
Orchids (Waikīkī), 145
Original Glider Rides (North Shore), 213
Ossipoff, Vladimir, 79
Our Lady of Peace Cathedral (Honolulu), 100
outdoor markets, 236
Outreach College (University of Hawai'i), 84
Outrigger Catamaran (Waikīkī), 221
Outrigger Luana Waikīkī, 63–64
Outrigger Reef on the Beach (Waikīkī), 64
Outrigger Waikīkī on the Beach, 64

P

Pacific Aviation Museum (Central O'ahu), 114
Pacific Beach Hotel (Waikīkī): aquarium, 221; fitness facilities, 232
Pacific Business News, 267
Pacific Handcrafters Christmas Fair (Honolulu), 129
Pacific Orient Traders (Honolulu), 251
Pacific Place Tea Garden, The (Honolulu), 174
Pacific Skydiving Center (North Shore), 222
Pacific Wings, 32
Padovani's Chocolates (Honolulu), 168
palapala (written word), impact of, 21
Pali Golf Course (Windward O'ahu), 209
Paliku Theatre (Windward O'ahu), 126
Pane e Vino (Waikīkī), 120, 177
Pan Pacific Hula Festival Matsuri Parade (Waikīkī), 130
Panya Bistro & Bar (Honolulu), 155
Papahānaumokuākea Marine National Monument, 34
Paprika (Windward O'ahu), 172
Paradise Air (North Shore), 212
Paradise Found Café (North Shore), 173, 176
Paradise Helicopters, 213
Paradise Rent-a-Car, 37
paragliding, 211
parking in Honolulu, 38
parks and gardens, 218–20
Park Shore Waikīkī, 65
Patagonia (North Shore), 255
Patisserie, The (Honolulu), 169
Patisserie La Palme D'Or, The (Honolulu), 168
Paul Brown Kailua (Windward O'ahu), 225
Paul Brown's Spa Olakino (Waikīkī), 225
Pavilion Café, The (Honolulu), 155
Pearl City. *See* Central O'ahu
Pearl Harbor (Central O'ahu), 105; handing over to U.S., 24; 1941 bombing of, 27
Pearl Ultralounge (Honolulu), 121
Pegge Hopper Gallery, The (Honolulu), 248
performing arts/art houses: general information, 122–23; greater Honolulu, 83, 112, 222;

Windward O'ahu, 126
pets, traveling with, quarantine requirements, 32
Phuket Thai (Honolulu), 156
Pineapple Country (Waikīkī), 240
pineapple industry, 26
Pineapple Room by Alan Wong, The (Honolulu), 156–57
Pipeline Cafe & Sports Bar (Honolulu), 119
plantations, 22–23
plant life, 16–17
Pleasant Holidays, 31
Plumeria Beach House (Honolulu), 157
Pōka'i Bay Beach Park (Leeward O'ahu), 205
polo, 233
Polynesian Cultural Center (Windward O'ahu), 167, 229
Polynesian migrations, 17–18
Polynesian place names, 18
Preis, Alfred, 79
prescriptions, 263–64
Prince Hot Hula Festival (Honolulu), 130
Princess Cruises, 33
Punahou. *See* greater Honolulu
Punalu'u. *See* Windward O'ahu
Punchbowl Crater, 16
Pūpūkea. *See* North Shore
Pūpūkea Beach Park (North Shore), 202; snorkeling/scuba diving, 223
Pu'u O Mahuka Heiau (North Shore), 188

Q

Qantas Airways, 31
Queen Emma Summer Palace (Nu'uanu), 100–101
Queen Kapi'olani Hotel (Waikīkī), 65
Queen's Medical Center, The (Honolulu), 265
Queen's Surf Beach (Waikīkī), 195; snorkeling/scuba diving, 223
Queen's Surf/Waikīkī Grand Hotel, 65–66
Quiksilver (Waikīkī), 255
Quiksilver Big Wave Invitational in Memory of Eddie Aikau (North Shore), 130

R

radio stations, 268
Rainbow Drive-In (Honolulu), 170
Ramen Nakamura (Waikīkī), 170
Ramsay Museum (Honolulu), 116
Red Pineapple (Honolulu), 249–50
religious beliefs, traditional, 21, 182
religious services, 269
ResortQuest at the Executive Centre Hotel (Greater Honolulu), 70–71
ResortQuest at the Waikīkī Banyan, 66
ResortQuest Waikīkī Beach Hotel, 66–67
ResortQuest Waikīkī Beach Tower, 67
ResortQuest Waikīkī Circle Hotel, 67
ResortQuest Waikīkī Joy, 67–68
restaurants: Central O'ahu, 166; food glossary, 135–36; general information, 133–35; greater Honolulu, 148–59; late-night dining, 176; North Shore, 163–66; Waikīkī, 137–48; Windward O'ahu, 159–63
Reyn's (Waikīkī), 237
Reyn's/Reyn's Rack (Honolulu), 238
R. Field Wine Co. (Honolulu, Windward O'ahu), 175, 177
rip currents, 16
Roadrunner Towing Service, 270
road service, 269–70
Robyn Buntin of Honolulu, 243
rock clubs, 119–20. See also nightlife
Rock Island Café (Waikīkī), 243
Romy's (Windward O'ahu), 172–73
Royal Caribbean International, 33
Royal Hawaiian Band performances, 122, 222
Royal Hawaiian Beach (Waikīkī), 195
Royal Hawaiian Catamaran, 220
Royal Hawaiian Hotel (Waikīkī), 68, 81; history, 87; Lū'au at, 167; Mai Tai Bar, 118
Royal Hawaiian Shopping Center (Waikīkī), 253
Royal Saloon (Honolulu), 97
Roy's Restaurant: Leeward O'ahu, 166; Waikīkī, 145
rRed Elephant (Honolulu), 174
Ruffage Natural Foods (Waikīkī), 175

S

sacred sites, 186–88
Safeway: Honolulu, 263; Leeward O'ahu, 264
sailing, 220–22
Sailing Club Hawai'i, The (Waikīkī), 221
Saint-Germain Bakery (Waikīkī), 168
Sam Choy's Diamond Head (Honolulu), 157
sandalwood trade, 22

Sandy Beach Park (Honolulu), 197
Sanrio (Honolulu), 252
Sansei Seafood Restaurant & Sushi Bar (Waikīkī), 145–46, 176
Schrader's Windward Country Inn (Windward O'ahu), 71–72
scuba diving, diving equipment, 222–24
Sea Life Park (Windward O'ahu), 229
Sears (Honolulu), 238
seasonal and special events, 122, 126–31, 243
sedans and limousines, 39
Select (Honolulu), 251
Senator Fong's Plantation & Gardens (Windward O'ahu), 220
Shack, The (Honolulu), 171
Shanghai Bistro (Waikīkī), 146
Shanghai Tang (Honolulu), 241
Shangri La (Honolulu), 101–2
Shangri-La Asia (Waikīkī), 243
Sharks Cover snorkeling, dive site (North Shore), 223
shark watching, 230–31
Shasa Emporium (Honolulu), 241
Sheraton Waikīkī Beach Resort (Waikīkī), 68; Cobalt Lounge, 120; Jeff Chang Pottery & Fine Crafts, 247
Shirokiya (Honolulu), 168
Shiso-Zen (Windward O'ahu), 163
Shop Pacifica (Honolulu), 244, 249–50
shopping: antiques and collectibles, 243–44; apparel, 236–42; books and music, 244–46; galleries, arts and handcrafts, 246–48; Hawaiiana and other gifts, 248–50; home furnishings, 250–51; kid's stuff, 251–53; shopping centers, 253–54; surf and sporting gear, 255–56
shopping centers, 253–54
Shoreline Adventures fishing charters, 208
Shung Chong Yuein (Honolulu), 168–69
Sierra Club events, 214
Signature Theatres Dole Cannery (Greater Honolulu), 84
Signature Theatres Windward Stadium (Windward O'ahu), 84
Silver Moon Emporium (North Shore), 242
Sitters Unlimited of Hawai'i, 261
Skydive Hawai'i (North Shore), 222
skydiving, 222
Snorkel Bob's (Honolulu), 222–23
snorkeling, snorkeling equipment, 222–24
Soar Hawai'i Sailplanes (North Shore), 213
SoHa Living (Honolulu), 251
Sony Open in Hawai'i (Honolulu), 130
Soul de Cuba (Honolulu), 157–58
Source Natural Foods, The (Windward O'ahu), 175
South Seas Aquatics, 255
SpaHalekulani (Waikīkī), 225
Spa Luana (North Shore), 225
Spanish-American War, 26
spas and salons, 224–25
Spa Suites (Honolulu), 225
species extinction, 17
Spirit of Aloha magazine, 267
Splash! Hawai'i (Honolulu), 242
sporting events, 233
Sports Authority (Honolulu), 255
St. Andrew's Cathedral (Honolulu), 81, 102
Star Beach Boys (Waikīkī), 226
Starbucks: Leeward O'ahu, 174; Windward O'ahu, 174
Star Markets (Central O'ahu), 264
Star of Honolulu whale watching trips (Waikīkī), 231
statehood, 28, 182
St. Augustine By-the-Sea (Waikīkī), 269
Stearman Bi-Plane Rides, 213
Straub Clinic & Hospital (Honolulu), 265
Straub Kailua Family Health Center (Windward O'ahu), 266
Stroller Strides (Waikīkī), 232
submarine trips, 224
sugar industry, 22–23, 24
summer season, 16
Sunset Beach. *See* North Shore
Sunset Beach Park (North Shore), 202
Sunset on the Beach movies (Waikīkī), 83, 221
Sunset Suzy surf school (North Shore), 227
SunTrips charters, 31
surf and sporting gear, 255–56
surfing and bodyboarding: general information, 225–26; lessons, 226–27; North Shore, 203–4; rentals, 226
Surf News Network, 226, 262

Surf-N-Sea (North Shore), 223, 226, 256
swimwear, 242

T

Tabora Gallery (Waikīkī), 246
Tahiti, migrations from, 18
Tamura's (Windward O'ahu), 177, 263
Tamura's Superette (Leeward O'ahu), 264
Tanaka of Tokyo Central (Waikīkī), 147
Tanaka of Tokyo East (Waikīkī), 147–48
Tanaka of Tokyo West (Waikīkī), 147–48
Tantalus. *See* greater Honolulu
taxis: O'ahu, 39; to Waikīkī, 31; wheelchair-accessible, 36
tea, afternoon, 167. *See also* coffee houses, tea cafés
tea ceremony, 222
Teddy's Bigger Burgers (Waikīkī), 170
Teddy's Burgers (Windward O'ahu), 172
Ted's Bakery (North Shore), 170
telephones, 270
television stations, 268
temperatures, average, 16
Tennent Art Foundation Gallery (Honolulu), 116
tennis, 227–28
Teuscher (Waikīkī), 168
T-Fujii (Waikīkī), 243
theater. *See* performing arts/art houses
TheBus, 38–39, 214
Theo. H. Davis & Co., 23
Thinker Toys (Honolulu), 252
3-D Glow Golf (Waikīkī), 233
Thrifty Car Rental, 37
Ticketmaster, 122
Tiki's Grill & Bar (Waikīkī), 147–48
Times Super Market (Windward O'ahu), 264
time zones, 270
Todai (Waikīkī), 148
Today's Little People (Waikīkī), 251
Tori Richard (Waikīkī), 237
tours, guided: adventure/nature tours, island-wide, 210–11; culinary tours, 174; greater Honolulu, 85
Town (Honolulu), 158
Town & Country Surf Design (Honolulu), 255
toys. *See* kid's stuff
transportation, public: accessible transportation, 36; greater Honolulu, 33; TheBus, 38–39, 214
Traphagen, Oliver, 79
Tropical Outpost (Waikīkī), 251
Tropical Rush (North Shore), 256
Tropic Lightning Museum, 117
Turtle Bay Condos (North Shore), 73
Turtle Bay Resort (North Shore), 72–73, 209–10, 214; horseback riding, 217; snorkeling/scuba diving, 223; tennis, 228
12th Avenue Grill (Honolulu), 137–48
21 Degrees North (North Shore), 163
24-hour Fitness (Waikīkī), 232

U

'Ukelele Festival (Waikīkī), 130
ultralight flying, 211
Ulupō Heiau (Windward O'ahu), 187
'Umeke Market and Deli (Honolulu), 175
Under a Hula Moon (Windward O'ahu), 250
United Airlines, 31
United Fishing Agency's Fish Auction (Honolulu), 177, 222
University of Hawai'i at Mānoa (UHM) (Honolulu): Art Gallery, 116; Chamber Music Series, 122; classes and lectures, 84; Hamilton Library, 108; Imin Center-Jefferson Hall, 123; John Young Museum of Art, 115–16; sporting events, 233
Up and Riding (Honolulu), 252
Urasenke Foundation tea ceremonies, 222
Urgent Care Clinic of Waikīkī, 266
US Army Museum of Hawai'i (Waikīkī), 115
USS *Arizona* Memorial (Central O'ahu), 106
USS *Bowfin* Submarine Museum & Park (Central O'ahu), 106

V

Vans Triple Crown of Surfing (North Shore), 130
Veranda, The (Honolulu), 121
Vim 'N Vigor (Honolulu), 175
Vino (Honolulu), 177
Vino Italian Tapas & Wine Bar (Honolulu), 120
vintage clothing, boutiques, 239–42
VIP Rentals, 37
VIP Transportation, 33
Visitor Aloha Society of Hawai'i, 263

visitor information, 78
volcanic eruptions, 15
Volunteer Hawai'i, 270
volunteer opportunities, 270–71

W

Wahiawā. *See* Central O'ahu
Wahiawā General Hospital (Central O'ahu), 265
Waiāhole. *See* Windward O'ahu
Wai'alae Beach Park (Honolulu), 197
Waialua. *See* North Shore
Wai'anae Coast, 49, 226. *See also* Leeward O'ahu
Wai'anae Coast Health Center (Leeward O'ahu), 266
Wai'anae Range, 16, 47, 213
Waikele Premium Outlets (Central O'ahu), 253
Waikīkī: afternoon tea, 167; aloha wear, 237; Americanization, 26–27, 28; antiques and collectibles, 243; archaeological/sacred sites, 186; arts and crafts galleries, 246–47; bakeries, sweet treats, 168; beaches, 195; bicycling, bike rentals, 206; books and music, 245; cafés, on-the-go foods, 170; climate, 16; coffee houses, tea cafés, 173–74; Diamond Head Crater, 16; family-oriented activities, 228–29; farmer's markets, gourmet & health food, juice bars, 175; fitness facilities, 232; food markets and drug stores, 263; general information, 10–11; Hawaiiana and other gifts, 248–49; historic buildings and sites, 86–89; kid's stuff, 251; late-night dining, 176; lodging, 55–70; medical services, 265–66; museums and galleries, 115; nightlife, 118–21; parking, 38; parks and gardens, 218; religious services, 269; restaurants, 137–48; sailing and catamaran excursions, 220–21; seasonal and special events, 126, 128–31; shopping centers, 253; snorkeling/scuba diving, 223; spas and salons, 224–25; submarine trips, 224; surfing and sporting gear, 255; swimwear, 242; tennis, 228; vintage clothing, boutiques, 239–40; whale watching trips, 231; wine bars, wine shops, 177
Waikīkī Aquarium, 229
Waikīkī Beach, 195
Waikīkī Beach Marriott Resort & Spa, 69
Waikīkī Beachside Hostel, 69–70
Waikīkī Community Center, The, 232
Waikīkī Diving Center, 223, 224
Waikīkī Farmers' Market, 175
Waikīkī Nei, 121
Waikīkī Parc Hotel, 70
Waikīkī Plantation Spa, 225
Waikīkī Shell, 122
Waikīkī Trolley, 39
Wailana Coffee House (Waikīkī), 148, 176
Waimānalo. *See* Windward O'ahu
Waimānalo Bay State Recreation Area (Windward O'ahu), 201
Waimea Bay Beach Park (North Shore), 203
Waimea Bay snorkeling/dive site (North Shore), 223
Waimea Valley Audubon Center (North Shore), 220
Waiola Bakery & Shave Ice (Honolulu), 169
Wai'oli Tea Room (Honolulu), 158, 168
Waipahu. *See* Central O'ahu
walking tours, 85, 174
Wallace Theatres Restaurant Row (Greater Honolulu), 84
Ward Centers (Honolulu), 253
Ward Farmers' Market (Honolulu), 177
Washington Place (Honolulu), 102–3
waves, cautions, 16
weather information, 262
weddings, planning aids, 268–69
whale watching, 230–31
whaling industry, 22
wheelchair-accessible transportation, 36
Whole Foods Market (Honolulu), 175, 263
W Honolulu Diamond Head (Waikīkī), 68–69
Wiki Wiki One-Day Collectibles & Hawaiiana Show (Honolulu), 243
Wild Side Specialty Tours (Leeward O'ahu), 224; whale watching trips, 231
Willows, The (Honolulu), 159
windsurfing, 232
Windward Community College's Office of Continuing Education, 85
Windward O'ahu: aloha wear, 238; antiques and collectibles, 243–44; archaeological/sacred sites, 187; arts and crafts galleries, 248; bakeries, sweet treats, 169–70; beaches, 197–201; bicycling, bike rentals, 206; books

and music, 245; cafés, on-the-go foods, 172–73; camping, 207; coffee houses, tea cafés, 174; commercial movie houses, 84; family-oriented activities, 229; farmer's markets, gourmet & health food, juice bars, 175; fitness facilities, 232; food markets and drug stores, 263; geographical overview, 42–45; glass-bottom boat trips, 224; golfing, 209; hang gliding, paragliding, ultralight flying, 211; Hawaiiana and other gifts, 250; hiking, 215–16; historic buildings and sites, 103–4; horseback riding, 217; hospitals and medical services, 265–66; kayaking and canoeing, 218; kid's stuff, 252–53; lodging, 71–72; map, 44; museums and galleries, 116; nightlife, 120; parks and gardens, 219–20; performing arts/art houses, 126; polo, 233; restaurants, 159–63; seasonal and special events, 126; snorkeling/scuba diving, 223, 224; spas and salons, 225; surfing and bodyboarding, 226; surfing and sporting gear, 255; tennis, 228; vintage clothing, boutiques, 241; windsurfing, kiteboarding, 232; wine bars, wine shops, 177

wine bars, wine shops, 120, 177. *See also* nightlife

winter season, 16

Wizard or Healing Stones (Waikīkī), 186

Wolfgang Puck Express (Waikīkī), 170

Wonder Lounge (Waikīkī), 121

Wood, Hart, 79, 98

World Invitational Hula Festival (Waikīkī), 131

World War II, 27–28, 34

Wyland Galleries Hawai'i (Waikīkī), 246

Wyland Waikīkī, The, 70

Y

Yanagi Sushi (Honolulu), 159

YMCA building, 81

yoga, 232

Yoga Under the Palm Trees (Waikīkī), 232

Yoga Works Hawai'i (Waikīkī), 232

YWCA of O'ahu, Laniākea, 103

Lodging by Price Code

Inexpensive	Up to $100
Moderate	$100–200
Expensive	$200–300
Very Expensive	More than $300

GREATER HONOLULU

Expensive

ResortQuest at the Executive Centre Hotel, 70

Very Expensive

The Kahala Hotel & Resort, 71

LEEWARD O'AHU

Moderate

Hawaiian Princess at Mākaha, 73

Very Expensive

JW Marriott 'Ihilani Resort & Spa at Kō 'Olina, 73
Marriott's Kō 'Olina Beach Club, 75

NORTH SHORE

Inexpensive–Moderate

Backpacker's Vacation Inn, 72

Moderate–Expensive

Kē Iki Bungalows, 72
Turtle Bay Condos, 73

Expensive–Very Expensive

Turtle Bay Resort, 72–73

WAIKĪKĪ

Inexpensive

Waikīkī Beachside Hostel, 69

Inexpensive–Moderate

Hale Koa Hotel, 59

Moderate

Aqua Bamboo & Spa, 55
Aqua Coconut Plaza, 55
Aqua Island Colony, 57
Aqua Waikīkī Wave, 56
The Breakers, 57
The Cabana at Waikīkī, 57
Diamond Head Beach Hotel, 58
'Ewa Hotel, 58–59
Hawaiiana Hotel, 60
'Ilima Hotel, 62
Outrigger Luana Waikīkī, 63
Park Shore Waikīkī, 65
Queen Kapi'olani Hotel, 65
Queen's Surf/Waikīkī Grand Hotel, 65

Moderate–Expensive

Doubletree Alana Hotel Waikīkī, 58
'Ilikai Hotel, 61
New Otani Kaimana Beach Hotel, 63
'Ohana Waikīkī Beachcomber, 63
Outrigger Reef on the Beach, 64
ResortQuest at the Waikīkī Banyan, 66
ResortQuest Waikīkī Circle Hotel, 67
ResortQuest Waikīkī Joy, 67

Expensive

Hawai'i Prince Hotel Waikīkī, 59
Outrigger Waikīkī on the Beach, 64
Waikīkī Parc Hotel, 70
Honolulu Diamond Head, 68
The Wyland Waikīkī, 70

Expensive–Very Expensive

Aqua Hotel Renew, 56
Hilton Hawaiian Village Beach Resort & Spa, 60
Hilton Waikīkī Prince Kūhiō, 61
Hyatt Regency Waikīkī Resort & Spa, 61
ResortQuest Waikīkī Beach Hotel, 66

Sheraton Waikīkī Beach Resort, 68
Waikīkī Beach Marriott Resort & Spa, 69

Very Expensive
Halekulani, 59
Moana Surfrider, 62
ResortQuest Waikīkī Beach Tower, 67
Royal Hawaiian Hotel, 68

WINDWARD O'AHU
Moderate
Schrader's Windward Country Inn, 71–72

Dining by Price Code

Inexpensive	Up to $15
Moderate	$15–30
Expensive	$30–65
Very Expensive	$65 or more

CENTRAL O'AHU

Inexpensive

Helemano Plantation, 166

GREATER HONOLULU

Inexpensive–Moderate

Hong Kong Harbour View Seafood Restaurant, 152
India Café, 153
Little Village Noodle House, 154
Panya Bistro & Bar, 155
The Pavilion Café, The, 155
Phuket Thai, 156
Soul de Cuba, 157
Wai'oli Tea Room, 158

Moderate

The Contemporary Café, 150
Grand Café & Bakery, 150
Hale Vietnam, 151
Mediterraneo, 155
Town, 158
12th Avenue Grill, 148
The Willows, 159

Moderate–Expensive

E & O Trading Co., 151
Indigo Eurasian Cuisine, 153
The Pineapple Room by Alan Wong, 156
Yanagi Sushi, 159

Expensive

Alan Wong's Restaurant, 149
Cassis by Chef Mavro, 149
Chai's Island Bistro, 150
Hoku's, 152
Le Bistro, 154
Mariposa, 154
Plumeria Beach House, 157
Sam Choy's Diamond Head, 157

LEEWARD O'AHU

Expensive

Roy's Restaurant, 166

NORTH SHORE

Inexpensive–Moderate

Café Hale'iwa, 164

Moderate

Banzai Sushi Bar, 163
Hale'iwa Joe's Seafood Grill, 164

Moderate–Expensive

Lei Lei's, 165

Expensive

Jameson's by the Sea, 164
Ola, 165
21 Degrees North, 163

WAIKĪKĪ

Inexpensive

Eggs 'n Things, 140
Wailana Coffee House, 148

Inexpensive–Moderate

Ca Cha Cha Waikīkī, 138

Moderate

Aqua Café, 137
Arancino, 137
California Pizza Kitchen, 138

Cheesecake Factory, 139
Holokai Grill, 141
Hula Grill Waikīkī, 142
Keo's in Waikīkī, 142
MAC 24/7, 143
Todai, 148

Moderate–Expensive
Canoes at the 'Ilikai, 138
Duke's Canoe Club, 140
House Without A Key, 141
Miyako Japanese Restaurant, 144
Sansei Seafood Restaurant & Sushi Bar, 145
Shanghai Bistro, 146
Singha Thai Cuisine, 146
Tanaka of Tokyo Central, 147
Tiki's Grill & Bar, 147

Expensive
Hau Tree Lānai, 140
Hy's Steak House, 142
Orchids, 145
Roy's Restaurant, 145

Expensive–Very Expensive
Bali by the Sea, 137
Diamond Head Grill, 139
Michel's, 144

Very Expensive
La Mer, 143

WINDWARD O'AHU

Inexpensive
Boots & Kimo's Homestyle Kitchen, 160
Koa Pancake House, 162

Inexpensive–Moderate
Brent's Restaurant & Deli, 160
Cinnamon's Restaurant, 161

Moderate
Baci Bistro, 159
California Pizza Kitchen, 161
Shiso-Zen, 163

Moderate–Expensive
Buzz's Original Steak House, 160
Formaggio Grill, 161
Hale'iwa Joe's Seafood Grill, 162

Expensive
Lucy's Grill & Bar, 162

Dining by Cuisine

CENTRAL O'AHU

American/Chinese

Helemano Plantation, 166

GREATER HONOLULU

American/Regional American

The Contemporary Café, 150

Grand Café & Bakery, 150

The Pavilion Café, 155

Plumeria Beach House, 157

Town, 158

12th Avenue Grill, 148

Wai'oli Tea Room, 158

The Willows, 159

Asian Fusion/Eurasian

E & O Trading Co., 151

Indigo Eurasian Cuisine, 153

Panya Bistro & Bar, 155

Chinese

Hong Kong Harbour View Seafood Restaurant, 152

Little Village Noodle House, 154

Cuban

Soul de Cuba, 157

French/Bistro

Cassis by Chef Mavro, 149

Le Bistro, 154

Hawai'i Regional

Alan Wong's Restaurant, 149

Cassis by Chef Mavro, 149

Chai's Island Bistro, 150

The Pineapple Room by Alan Wong, 156

Sam Choy's Diamond Head, 157

Indian

India Café, 153

International

Plumeria Beach House, 157

Italian

Mediterraneo, 155

Japanese

Yanagi Sushi, 159

Mediterranean

The Contemporary Café, 150

The Pavilion Café, 155

Town, 158

Pacific Rim

Chai's Island Bistro, 150

Hoku's, 152

Mariposa, 154

Thai

Phuket Thai, 156

Vietnamese

Hale Vietnam, 151

LEEWARD O'AHU

Hawaiian Fusion

Roy's Restaurant, 166

NORTH SHORE

American/Regional American

Café Hale'iwa, 164

Cheesecake Factory, 139

Eggs 'n Things, 140

Hale'iwa Joe's Seafood Grill, 164

Jameson's by the Sea, 164

Lei Lei's, 165
MAC 24/7, 143
Todai, 148

Continental
Lei Lei's, 165

French
21 Degrees North, 163

Hawai'i Regional
Ola, 165
21 Degrees North, 163

Japanese
Banzai Sushi Bar, 163

Mexican
Café Hale'iwa, 164

Pacific Rim
Hale'iwa Joe's Seafood Grill, 164

Seafood
Jameson's by the Sea, 164

WAIKĪKĪ
American/Regional American
Aqua Café, 137
California Pizza Kitchen, 138
Duke's Canoe Club, 140
House Without A Key, 141
Tiki's Grill & Bar, 147
Wailana Coffee House, 148

Asian Fusion
Shanghai Bistro, 146

Caribbean
Cha Cha Cha Waikīkī, 138

Chinese
Shanghai Bistro, 146

Continental
Bali by the Sea, 137
Hy's Steak House, 142

Eclectic
Hy's Steak House, 142

French
La Mer, 143
Michel's, 144

Hawai'i Regional/Fusion
Canoes at the 'Ilikai, 138
Hula Grill Waikīkī, 142
Keo's in Waikīkī, 142
Roy's Restaurant, 145

Italian
Arancino, 137
Diamond Head Grill, 139

Japanese/Teppanyaki Steak
Miyako Japanese Restaurant, 144
Sansei Seafood Restaurant & Sushi Bar, 145
Tanaka of Tokyo Central, 147
Todai, 148

Mexican
Cha Cha Cha Waikīkī, 138

Pacific Rim
Bali by the Sea, 137
Hau Tree Lānai, 140
Holokai Grill, 141
Orchids, 145
Sansei Seafood Restaurant & Sushi Bar, 145
Singha Thai Cuisine, 146
Tiki's Grill & Bar, 147

Seafood
Orchids, 145
Sansei Seafood Restaurant & Sushi Bar, 145
Tanaka of Tokyo Central, 147

Thai
Keo's in Waikīkī, 142
Singha Thai Cuisine, 146–47

WINDWARD O'AHU
American/Regional American
Boots & Kimo's Homestyle Kitchen, 160

Brent's Restaurant & Deli, 160
Buzz's Original Steak House, 160
California Pizza Kitchen, 161Cinnamon's Restaurant, 161
Hale'iwa Joe's Seafood Grill, 162
Koa Pancake House, 162

Eclectic
California Pizza Kitchen, 161

Italian
Baci Bistro, 159

Mediterranean
Formaggio Grill, 161

Pacific Rim
Hale'iwa Joe's Seafood Grill, 162
Lucy's Grill & Bar, 162

Seafood
Formaggio Grill, 161

Steak
Formaggio Grill, 161